THE EXPERIENCE OF HYPNOSIS

The Experience of Hypnosis

A shorter version of *Hypnotic Susceptibility*

ERNEST R. HILGARD

Stanford University

With a chapter by

JOSEPHINE R. HILGARD, M.D.

A Harvest/HBJ Book

Harcourt Brace Jovanovich, *New York and London*

Library of Congress Catalog Card Number: 68–25372
Printed in the United States of America
  EFG

Acknowledgments (complete citations appear in the bibliographic index):

American Journal of Psychiatry
American Psychological Association
Appleton-Century-Crofts
Holt, Rinehart and Winston, Inc.
International Journal of Clinical and Experimental Hypnosis
International Universities Press
The Journal of Nervous and Mental Disease
The Journal Press
Medical Journal of Australia
The Nebraska Symposium on Motivation
Peace Publishers, Foreign Languages Publishing House, Moscow
Stanford University Press

The author also wishes to thank those authors who have given their permission to quote or reproduce materials issued by them.

Dedication

The investigations that provided the observations and data which made the writing of this book possible were done at Hawthorne House, Stanford University. This book is dedicated to the many staff members, research assistants, and students who participated in that work. Their names are given here in alphabetical order with no attempt to evaluate their separate contributions but to express appreciation to every one of them:

Arvid Ås
John M. Atthowe, Jr.
Peter M. Bentler
Roland G. Boucher
Dana Bramel
Stanley R. Clemes
Kenneth M. Colby
Michael B. Conant
Janet Melei Cuca
Margaret deRivera
J. David Gaines
Philip B. Gough
Alvin I. Haimson
Josephine R. Hilgard
Leonard S. Hommel
Charles Imm
Nancy S. Kautz
Judah Landes
Lillian W. Lauer
Evelyn M. Lee

Robert M. Liebert
Perry London
Lawrence E. Moore
Rosemarie K. Moore
Ursula S. Moore
Arlene H. Morgan
Gosaku Naruse
Martha F. Newman
John W. O'Hara
Mary R. Roberts
Norma H. Rubin
Errol D. Schubot
Bernard M. Sjoberg, Jr.
Robert S. Slotnick
Clifford O. Smith
Charles T. Tart
Suzanne H. Troffer
Takao Umemoto
Elaine H. Walster
André M. Weitzenhoffer

Introduction

The interest in hypnosis, which began to accelerate after World War II, has now become much more widespread, and hypnosis is becoming more acceptable as a part of normal science. Of the many books that appear, however, some are still of the familiar type, making exaggerated claims, and leading to skepticism by some who might otherwise find hypnosis useful in their laboratory investigations, in their medical practice, or for personal benefit. This book is offered, therefore, as a sober corrective to overpopularized accounts of hypnosis, by trying to separate fact from fiction in what we find out about the experience of hypnosis in the psychological laboratory.

The appearance of a paperbound version of an earlier clothbound book no longer requires any explanation, but some comments are doubtless needed on why this version has been shortened and why its title has been changed. The book on *Hypnotic Susceptibility,* upon which this is based, served two functions, one of which was to present the technical materials based on the research behind the construction of the Stanford Hypnotic Susceptibility Scales, the second of which was to present a contemporary viewpoint toward hypnosis as it is studied in the psychological laboratory. These two purposes were not inharmonious, but the first purpose made parts of the book little comprehensible to those uninterested in, or unprepared for, the technical discussion of the problems of psychological scaling. The rest of the book was concerned largely with the phenomena of hypnosis, what it is like to be hypnotized, interesting to layman and professional alike, and this version emphasizes those chapters and omits the more technical ones concerned with scale construction and factor analysis. One chapter on the scales provides enough material for the general reader, while the specialist can turn to the original book to satisfy his needs.

As noted in the foreword to *Hypnotic Susceptibility,* I owe debts of gratitude particularly to Andre M. Weitzenhoffer, my co-worker from 1957 through 1962, and to my wife, Josephine R. Hilgard, a co-worker throughout the investigations on which the book is largely based. Numerous other collaborators, postdoctoral fellows and graduate students, also participated in the investigations. Inadvertently, in the earlier introduction I failed to mention the help given on the original manuscript by Dr. Vincent Nowlis of the University of Rochester and by Dr. David L. Rosenhan of the Educational Testing Service. This edition permits me to correct an omission of justly deserved credit.

The work of our laboratory was supported initially by a grant from the Ford Foundation and later by grants from the Robert C. Wheeler Foundation, the San Mateo County Heart Association, the National Institute of Mental Health, Public Health Service (Grant MH-3859), and the U.S. Air Force Office of Research (Contract AF 49[638]-1436). To these foundations and agencies which supported our work, to Stanford University, and to some private donors, I wish to express my appreciation for permitting us to undertake these collaborative investigations.

ERNEST R. HILGARD

Department of Psychology
Laboratory of Hypnosis Research
Stanford University
February, 1968

Contents

Part I

The Nature of Hypnosis and Hypnotizability

Almost everyone has some knowledge of hypnosis—through theatrical demonstrations; in reference to its uses by medical doctors, dentists, and psychotherapists; from college or university classes in psychology or medicine; or even as a result of actual participation in experiments designed to unravel its mysteries. Nevertheless, knowledge about hypnosis is in another sense very elusive. We begin, then, with some characterizations of the hypnotic state, turning next to the nature of the procedures used to induce it and to some of the evidence that a person is indeed in the hypnotic state. Following that, some of the consequences of submitting to hypnosis are considered, refuting the fear that submitting to hypnosis is dangerous. Finally there is a summary of tests that have been developed to show how people eager and willing to be hypnotized differ in their hypnotizability.

CHAPTER 1

What Is Hypnosis?

Hypnoticlike states were described by the ancients, and they can be found within the ceremonies of nonliterate cultures today. Although hypnotic phenomena are well-nigh universal, modern hypnosis began through the attention attracted to it by Franz Anton Mesmer (1734–1815), a Viennese physician working in France who promulgated the doctrine that hypnotic phenomena were induced by "animal magnetism," a force he believed to be emanating from his own hands. Mesmer's theory was discredited by official scientific commissions, but his followers carried on, recognizing that the phenomena were there, regardless of the falsity of the theory. The name mesmerism still persists as a synonym for hypnotism. While there are many other persons with roles in the history of hypnosis, the man who did most to revive a scientific interest in hypnotic phenomena, after animal magnetism had been disproved, and the one to whom the name hypnosis is due, was the Englishman James Braid (1795–1860). Although his theories underwent changes during his lifetime, he gradually came to appreciate the role of suggestion.

Interest in hypnosis revived gradually in France, and the respectability of hypnosis as a field of inquiry owes much to the distinguished neurologist Jean Martin Charcot (1825–93), who taught at the Salpêtrière in Paris and there influenced such prominent figures as Sigmund Freud (1856–1939) and Pierre Janet (1859–1947). An important controversy went on between Charcot and another medical school professor, Hippolyte Bernheim (1837–1919) of Nancy. Bernheim had become interested in hypnosis through a simple country

3

doctor, A. A. Liébeault (1823–1904), who was very successful in the use of hypnotic therapy and saw the results as due to suggestion. The controversy between the Salpêtrière and the Nancy schools, as they came to be called, placed Charcot's interpretation of hypnosis as pathological and connected with hysteria against the Liébeault-Bernheim theory that the effect was strictly psychological, due to suggestion. According to the Nancy school, a neurotic personality was not required in order for hypnosis to be successful, and this is the position that eventually triumphed. The debate raised the level of discussion of hypnosis to that of differences in scientific interpretation and lifted it out of the fringe association with mysticism and charlatanism. It seemed altogether natural for William James (1842–1910) to devote a chapter to hypnosis in his *Principles of Psychology* (1890).

The therapeutic use of hypnosis was temporarily encouraged by the successes of Breuer and Freud (1895), but hypnosis received one of its periodic setbacks when Freud presently rejected it in favor of his method of psychoanalysis. After a period of relative quiescence, new interest was aroused by the researches of a well-known experimental psychologist, Clark L. Hull (1884–1952), although his book summarizing this work, *Hypnosis and Suggestibility* (1933), did not produce a marked acceleration of research interest in the field, possibly because Hull himself abandoned it. It took World War II, with successful psychotherapeutic use of hypnosis in treating psychogenic war casualties, its use in dentistry, and, after the war, in obstetrics, to call attention again to its possibilities. Presently both the British Medical Association (in 1955) and the American Medical Association (in 1958) issued statements supporting the teaching of hypnosis in medical schools and urging its cautious use in medical practice. The Society for Clinical and Experimental Hypnosis was established in 1949, the American Society of Clinical Hypnosis in 1957; both publish journals and both have established international affiliations (Marcuse, 1964). The American Psychological Association in 1960 gave official recognition to a certifying board known as the American Board of Examiners in Psychological Hypnosis, and those meeting its qualifications are listed in the official directories of the American Psychological Association. Two classes are recognized: experimental hypnosis and clinical hypnosis. Thus there emerges a recognition of hypnosis as an experimental and clinical field, which attests to its current vitality.

Despite this long history, it is hard to specify just what hypnosis is. Many psychological states are difficult to define without pointing to familiar examples of them. Hypnosis aside, it is not easy to be precise about an alert state, a drowsy state, a sober state, an intoxicated state, an elated state, or a depressed state. Each of these descriptive expressions has meaning when it refers to very clear or typical examples of the state, or in contrast to its opposite; hence the terms, while imprecise, are not meaningless, even though the exact boundaries are hard to state. Our language is not good for specifying states of awareness, because these are not stable enough to permit exact labeling; hence we have a rich but somewhat loose vocabulary. The behavioristic era in psychology was not helpful because in the effort to be precise it was easier to ignore than to specify states of awareness; our vocabulary is therefore very largely a prescientific one. If in describing hypnosis we use such words as *induction, trance, suggestion, command, dissociation,* it is because their more exact scientific equivalents have not been forthcoming, or at least have not won wide acceptance. This calls for a little tolerance of vocabulary, for it very often turns out that the ostensive definitions (that is, those pointing to examples of the overt behavior and to the subjective reports of the hypnotized person) have in fact a high level of social agreement. In that case it does not really matter whether we speak of the hypnotic "state" or the hypnotic "trance," for the ostensive definition will not lead us to assume that all "trance" states (for example, in hypnosis, in religious ecstasy, or under LSD) are alike, any more than that all "unconscious states" (in sleep, under drugs, and after a blow on the head) are alike. By being clear about the conditions under which events occur we may use somewhat imprecise labels and yet communicate clearly. The failure of communication comes not so much through poor vocabulary as through not knowing very clearly the requisite circumstances or the concomitant phenomena; in areas in which we are still ignorant or uncertain about the facts, a better vocabulary will not save us from ambiguity.

CHARACTERISTICS OF THE HYPNOTIC STATE

The hypnotic state or trance recognized today is essentially that which came to be described in the nineteenth-century heyday of hypnosis. Some of its characteristics, as shown by subjects who illustrate a high degree of susceptibility to hypnosis, follow.

1. Subsidence of the planning function. The hypnotized subject loses initiative and lacks the desire to make and carry out plans on his own. In an older vocabulary, he lacks the desire to will action. This was well illustrated by an informal experiment reported by Gill and Brenman (1959, p. 36) in which they asked a subject how he knew he was hypnotized. If he said he was relaxed, they alerted him (still under hypnosis); if he said his arm was numb, they restored its feeling, thus removing one by one the symptoms that he said meant to him that he was hypnotized. He finally said: "I know I am in hypnosis because I *know* I will do what you tell me." If a subject is told to circulate around a room, trying to fool the people there into believing he is not hypnotized, he does this successfully for a while, but eventually seeks a comfortable chair in a remote place, closes his eyes, and resumes his inert planlessness.

It should be noted that there is always a relative, rather than an absolute, change in state under hypnosis. Thus the hypnotic subject has the *ability* to initiate action, to deliver a speech, and so on; what is important is that he has little desire to do so. In repeating an observation similar to that of Gill and Brenman's, I asked a young woman subject who was practicing appearing awake while hypnotized to examine some interesting objects in a box on a table at the far end of the room and to comment to me upon them as she would if she were not hypnotized. She was quite reluctant to make this effort, eventually starting to do it with a final plea: "Do you *really* want me to do this? I'll do it if you say so."

The avoidance of initiative is illustrated by statements from our subjects such as the following, quoted from our verbatim records:

"Once I was going to swallow, but decided it wasn't worth the effort. At one point I was trying to decide if my legs were crossed, but I couldn't tell, and didn't quite have the initiative to move to find out. . . ."

Another:

"I panic in an 'open-end' situation where I am not given *specific* directions. I like very *definite suggestions* from the hypnotist. . . ."

Thus the planning function, while not entirely lost, is turned over very largely to the hypnotist, willingly and comfortably, with some annoyance shown when the subject is asked to take responsibility for what he is to do.

2. Redistribution of attention. To state that attention is redistributed is a loose way of saying, first, that attention is selective, that we do not attend equally to all aspects of the environment, and, second, that under hypnosis selective attention and selective inattention go beyond the usual range. It does not follow that hypnosis is characterized by an unusual concentration of attention; it may be, in fact, that attention under hypnosis is generally diffuse, and that the attentive functions under the control of the hypnotist are residual ones. If the subject is paying very little attention to the environment, his focus on what the hypnotist tells him may appear heightened in contrast to his lack of interest in his surroundings. Attention to the hypnotist may be as much selectivity as he can exercise; the appearance of heightened selectivity may be illusory.

The familiar comment that hypnosis represents an ability to concentrate attention, based on the capacity to be selectively attentive in ordinary waking life,[1] has been reasserted by Barber (1960) and Leuba (1960), but the experimental evidence gives only moderate support to this plausible belief. Amadeo and Shagass (1963) found hypnotic subjects less able to attend to a mental arithmetic task than the subjects in the waking state, and their study of eye movements corroborated the performance measures by showing an increase in diffuse activity under hypnosis. The poor learning results of the hypnotized subjects in experiments such as those of Schulman and London (1963a) may very well rest on this inability to sustain attention to a task. Roberts (1964), using a number of attention tests deriving from Süllwold (1954), found essentially no correlations with hypnotic susceptibility. Although Das (1964) found some correlations with a measure of vigilance (what he called for was a response to every third consecutive odd number in a series of random numbers read slowly and monotonously), the correlations were negative, showing that the more sustained his attention the *less* hypnotizable the subject. Thus the possibility that attention is sluggish during hypnosis must be considered seriously.

Selective inattention within hypnosis is shown in a number of ways. For example, the subject may hear only the voice of the hypnotist and neither hear nor respond to other voices; he may see an ace of

---

[1] If "waking state" is used as a contrast with "hypnotic state" it must be understood that this means simply a nonhypnotized state; it need not imply that hypnosis is a sleep state.

spades as a blank white card but still perceive the ace of clubs. When having a positive hallucination of the presence of an object not actually there, he may blank out the objects in the room that would interfere with that hallucination.

This kind of selective inattention is puzzling to describe, for some sort of registration of what is there in the environment is required before it can be ignored, if such discriminations as those between two black aces have to be carried out. William James in his excellent chapter on hypnosis described the experiment of having a subject blind to one stroke on a blackboard or piece of paper:

> . . . Make a stroke on paper or blackboard, and tell the subject it is not there, and he will see nothing but the clean paper or the board. Next, he not looking, surround the original stroke with other strokes exactly like it, and ask him what he sees. He will point out one by one all the new strokes and omit the original one every time, no matter how numerous the new strokes may be, or in what order they are arranged. . . .
>
> Obviously, then, he is not blind to the *kind* of stroke in the least. He is blind only to one particular stroke of that kind in a particular position on the board or paper—that is, to a particular complex object; and paradoxical as it may seem to say so, he must distinguish it with great accuracy from others like it, in order to remain blind to it when the others are brought near. He "apperceives" it, as a preliminary to not seeing it at all! [James, 1890, II, 607–08]

Whether or not a perceptual distortion of this kind should be included within attention is a question for systematic theorizing; in a practical sense the selectivity of perception is illustrated, and such selectivity is an attentionlike phenomenon.

3. Availability of visual memories from the past, and heightened ability for fantasy-production. Experiments and demonstrations of hypnosis commonly make use of age-regression, in which the subject is asked to return to a scene experienced in the past. He may then experience a vivid recall of what transpired at the time, although he remains an external observer of these events; the recall appears to be facilitated by the availability of visual images. If the regression suggestions are more successful, the subject may feel that he is actually living again in the past, once again a child playing with his dog, or whatever the scene may be. How real the age-regression is and how many the processes involved have remained matters of controversy.

The memories are not all veridical, and the hypnotist can in fact suggest the reality of memories for events that did not happen. Thus memories under hypnosis, like memories outside hypnosis, may be productive as well as reproductive. In any case, the arousal of visual memories and the play of visual imagination appear to be more vivid than in the usual waking state.

Fantasy production can take various forms. Among them are dreams within hypnosis, which are in some instances very much like night dreams, and hallucinations, which may incorporate memories or recombine experiences in novel or bizarre ways. Just as memories of the past can be so vivid as to be experienced as reliving, so fantasies in the present can be so real as to have hallucinatory quality.

4. Reduction in reality testing and a tolerance for persistent reality distortion. The amount of reality testing that goes on in ordinary life is overlooked because it is so familiar, but once it is called to attention it is easy to notice how frequently people check their orientation by squirming, scratching, looking around, noting the time, adjusting clothing. The "stimulus-hunger" that Piaget and others have noted is in part this need for a contact that maintains the location and boundaries of the body in its relation to the environment of things and other people. This reality testing is reduced in the hypnotized person, partly as a result of the manipulations by the hypnotist, with his emphasis on relaxation and detachment. Reduction of reality testing leads to the acceptance of reality distortions.

Reality distortions of all kinds, including acceptance of falsified memories, changes in one's own personality, modification of the rate at which time seems to pass, doubling of persons in the room, absence of heads or feet of people observed to be walking around the room, inappropriate naming, presence of hallucinated animals that talk, and all manner of other unrealistic distortions can be accepted without criticism within the hypnotic state. This fact has led Orne (1959) to speak of *trance logic,* denoting this peculiar acceptance of what would normally be found incompatible. Again, this does not mean that *all* critical or logical abilities are suspended, but a certain uncritical literalness is often found. Shor (1959, 1962c) has included tolerance of reality distortion as one of his dimensions of hypnotic depth.

5. Increased suggestibility. The suggestibility theory of hypnosis is so widely accepted that hypnosis and suggestibility come to be equated by some writers on hypnosis. Both Hull (1933) and Weitzenhoffer (1953) see the relationship between hypnosis and suggestibility to be so intimate that they link the terms in the titles of their books. This characteristic of the hypnotized subject has been placed somewhat late in the list because it is but one of the features of hypnosis, arising at least in part as a consequence of the foregoing changes in the state of the person. It is often convenient to study hypnosis in terms of alterations in suggestibility, regardless of how these changes come about.

6. Role behavior. The suggestions that a subject in hypnosis will accept are not limited to specific acts or perceptions; he will, indeed, adopt a suggested role and carry on complex activities corresponding to that role. Perhaps there is something of the actor in each of us; in any case, the hypnotized subject will throw himself into a role, particularly if it is a congenial one, and act as if he were deeply involved in it. This characteristic of hypnosis is so impressive that it has led to one of the current theories of hypnosis, the role-enactment theory of Sarbin (Sarbin, 1950, 1956; Sarbin and Andersen, 1967).

7. Amnesia for what transpired within the hypnotic state. Ever since its discovery by the Marquis de Puységur in 1784, posthypnotic amnesia has been found to be one of the most dependable concomitants of hypnosis; it has been used ever since as the mark of what is called the highly susceptible or "somnambulistic" subject. It is not an essential aspect of hypnosis; even a subject capable of spontaneous posthypnotic amnesia can be told that he will recall what went on in the trance and will then recall it. Yet it is a very common phenomenon, and it can be furthered through suggestion.

These seven points suffice to indicate the sort of thing that hypnosis is; as we go on to discuss many of the specific things that hypnotized subjects can do, the picture of what hypnosis is will gradually increase in its richness and meaning, even though hypnosis resists precise definition.

HOW THE SUBJECT PERCEIVES THE HYPNOTIC STATE

In order not to associate hypnosis entirely with responsiveness to suggestions, but to consider it in its aspects as an altered state of awareness, subjects in our studies were asked to tell us what it was like to be hypnotized. The Stanford Hypnotic Scales will be described later on, but at this point it suffices to characterize them as tests that sample a variety of suggested performances under hypnosis, including motor items such as arm movements or rigidity, and more cognitive items such as dreams, age-regression, hallucinations, amnesia, and so on. The subject who conforms to more of the suggestions after hypnotic induction than before ("passes" more of the items) is judged to be more susceptible to hypnosis than one who does not respond. In the most detailed forms of these scales, the Stanford Profile Scales of Hypnotic Susceptibility, the subject has had an opportunity to experience a very wide selection of tests based on the conventional lore regarding what a hypnotized subject can do. At the end of each of two sessions with these profile scales, the subject was asked to tell about aspects of the hypnotic state that were not directly suggested to him, in other words, that arose as spontaneous accompaniments of the general situation in which he found himself. The replies from the first of these two sessions, before the subject had had a chance to think over and hence in retrospect edit his comments, are summarized in Table 1. For this purpose the subjects have been classified into high, medium, low, and nonsusceptible subjects, based on their responsiveness to the hypnotist's suggestions within hypnosis. The more exact bases for classification are given in the footnote to the table, but they are not essential for an understanding of the table.

It is well known that there is some fluctuation in the depth of hypnosis in the midst of an experimental session (for example, Brenman, Gill, and Knight, 1952). Thus it is appropriate to ask the subject if he knows when he is hypnotized. Even among the subjects who responded well, only some two-thirds felt confident that they could tell when they were in the hypnotic state. It is not surprising that the percentage decreased with decreased susceptibility, for some probably never experienced the state at all.

The general passivity of the subject, reflected in disinclination to speak, or to move, or even to think, is again reflected most strongly in the highly susceptible and decreases with decreasing susceptibility; the relaxation instructions have produced a disinclination to move in half the insusceptible subjects as well. Related to this passivity, so far as initiating action is concerned, is its obverse: a feeling of compulsion to do the hypnotist's bidding. This is by no means universal. Many highly susceptible subjects do not feel coerced by the hypno-

TABLE 1. SUBJECTIVE REPORTS BY SUBJECTS VARYING IN MEASURED
SUSCEPTIBILITY BASED ON AN INQUIRY FOLLOWING ATTEMPTED HYPNOSIS

	Affirmative replies to inquiry			
Inquiry	High ($N = 48$)	Medium ($N = 49$)	Low ($N = 45$)	Nonsus- ceptible ($N = 17$)
	percent	*percent*	*percent*	*percent*
Were you able to tell when you were hypnotized?	65	60	47	31
Disinclination to speak?	89	79	68	31
Disinclination to move?	87	77	64	50
Disinclination to think?	55	48	32	12
Feeling of compulsion?	48	52	20	6
Changes in size or appearance of parts of your body?	46	40	26	0
Feeling of floating?	43	42	25	12
Feeling of blacking out?	28	19	7	6
Feeling of dizziness?	19	31	14	0
Feeling of spinning?	7	17	0	6
One or more of prior four feelings?	60	60	39	25
Any similarity to sleep?	80	77	68	50

SOURCE: Previously unpublished data, based on replies to the final inquiry,
Stanford Profile Scales of Hypnotic Susceptibility, Forms I or II (whichever
came first). The high subjects scored 14 or more out of a possible 27 points, the
middle subjects 8 to 13, and the low subjects 0 to 7. The low subjects all had
scored at least 4 points on the Stanford Hypnotic Susceptibility Scale, Form A,
so that they were somewhat responsive to hypnotic suggestions of the motor type;
the most insusceptible subjects came from a group ordinarily not tested on the
profile scales, with scores of 0 to 3 on Form A. For form of inquiry, see Hilgard,
Lauer, and Morgan (1963), pp. 49, 64.

tist's suggestions; they feel, somehow, that they want to do what he
suggests. As one of them put it: "I didn't feel that I had to, but I
felt I might as well do it." Thus only about half the high and medium
susceptibles report this feeling of compulsion; the percentage reporting
drops off rapidly as susceptibility decreases.

Finally, the loss of ties to reality, changes in body image, feelings
of floating, blacking out, dizziness, and spinning, are reported by an

appreciable number; the exact form of the reported experience varies from subject to subject, but nearly half the highly susceptible subjects report some distortion in size or appearance of the body, and three-fifths report at least one of the "feelings" (of floating, blacking out, dizziness, or spinning). The medium subjects report these experiences about as frequently as the high ones; such reports fall off rapidly among the low and insusceptible ones.

The similarity to sleep is undoubtedly related in part to the nature of the induction procedures; four-fifths of the highly susceptible subjects recognize some similarity, and even half of the insusceptible subjects do. Even so, the subject differentiates hypnosis from sleep: "My body felt a little as if it were asleep, but my mind remained unusually alert."

Although a tabular summary cannot reveal the richness of the statements made by the subjects, these assertions give verbal support for some of the inferences made from the subjects' objective responses. In order to give a little further impression of the vividness of some of the remarks, here are a few quotations from the comments made by subjects following a "yes" answer to some of the questions in our inquiry:

"Hypnosis is just *one thing* going on, like a thread . . . focusing on a single thread of one's existence. . . ."

"My thoughts were an echo of what you were saying. . . ."

"I was very much aware of the split in my consciousness. One part of me was analytic and listening to you. The other part was feeling the things that the analytic part decided I would have."

"My head sunk into my body like a black sponge."

"Your voice came in my ear and *filled* my head."

"When I felt deepest, I was down in the bottom of a dark hole. I turned over and over on the way down. Now and then I would float up toward the top of the hole. . . ."

"It felt like my eyes were turned around and I could see inside myself . . . as though my eyes and head were not part of my body but suspended on the ceiling. I was completely unaware of any other part of my body."

"I felt as though I were 'inside' myself; none of my body was touching anything. . . ."

"My eyes were unfocused, even when closed. . . ."

"I felt I was being squeezed in a closed place—like a tube perhaps—but it wasn't unpleasant."

Thus hypnosis represents to many subjects a somewhat unusual state of awareness, with many contents not summarized under "hypersuggestibility."

SKEPTICISM REGARDING THE HYPNOTIC STATE

Most investigators can accept the foregoing account of hypnosis as essentially descriptive of what they find, though they might emphasize one or more of the features. The reality of the state is of the same order as the reality of emotions or dreams; subject to some disagreements (as indeed we find in discussions of emotions and dreams), this reality is not something to rule out or to deny. Most investigators of hypnosis find the phenomena fascinating and elusive but no less tangible than other topical fields within psychology. If in what follows some skeptical views are emphasized, these must be seen against the experience of numerous investigators and practitioners who are entirely satisfied with accepting hypnotic phenomena at their face value.

Several investigators of hypnotic phenomena have wittingly or unwittingly led readers to doubt the reality of hypnosis. This comes about in part because hypnosis lends itself readily to extreme statements, and those who claim too much for hypnosis are its scientific enemies as much as those who claim too little. Science grows upon skepticism; every scientist tries to disprove his own pet theories, happy as he may be to find them stand up under his attacks. Sutcliffe, himself an able hypnotist and investigator of scientific hypnosis, has made a point of distinguishing between the "credulous" and "skeptical" views of hypnotic phenomena; in favoring the "skeptical" position he has appeared to debunk hypnosis to such an extent that little is left of such favorite hypnotic phenomena as hypnotic anesthesias, hallucinations, and delusions (Sutcliffe, 1960, 1961). He himself has not been discouraged from continuing to study hypnosis as a promising field of investigation, and he supports the work of graduate students at the University of Sydney, where both his laboratory and that of Hammer are active. Still the impression that his articles create is that those who believe in hypnotic phenomena are tenderminded in James's sense, while those who disbelieve are toughminded. Hence what he has done and what he has actually concluded call for some comments.

In the first place, the credulous view, as proposed by Sutcliffe, is stated in such an extreme form that it is essentially a "straw man," in that it is a position held by scarcely any scientific workers in hypnosis. Thus it requires that responses in hypnosis have the same physiological correlates as responses to actual physical stimuli. Scarcely anyone expects this to be the case; even Erickson, whom he cites as the chief proponent of the credulous view (for example, Erickson, 1937, 1938, 1944), describes the similarity between actual and suggested experiences according to the subject's experiences and verbal responses, not according to the physiological correlates. Surely nobody expects the chemistry of the retina to be the same in halluci-nated vision as in actual stimulation by light. Let us begin then by denying the extreme credulous position, and see what the alternatives are for the skeptical position. Sutcliffe (1961) lists two possibilities: simulation and delusion. In simulation the subject misrepresents his true experience in order to please (or to fool) the hypnotist. In delusion, the subject "in some sense does not know that the real state of affairs is otherwise than suggested" (p. 190). Sutcliffe recog-nizes that this view has some affinities with the credulous view, but he associates it with the skeptical view because of his concern with sensory content as revealed by behavioral (physiological) measures. Thus it might be possible to detect some physiological differences between the hypnotic experience and the veridical experience, even though the subject were "deluded" into thinking them alike. Most of Sutcliffe's experiments show this alternative to be correct; he does not accuse his hypnotic subjects of simulation and can show that their behavior differs from that of simulators; he does show, however, that there are some differences between reaction to suggestions within hypnosis and to actual physical stimuli (or to their absence). Hence his skeptical position is not more skeptical than that of most experi-menters in the field, and it does not deny that something important is happening within hypnosis.

To be more specific, let us examine the results from his three experiments on anesthesia, hallucination, and delusion. Consider first anesthesia to shock. He found that the galvanic skin response (GSR) as an indicator of pain was not altered by hypnotic anesthesia, al-though the subjects reported no pain and made no flinching move-ments. Because the GSR persisted, he denied the absence of "painful sensory content." In this he went a little too far: what he obviously could deny was the blocking of input from stimulation; he had no way of assuring the persistence of "painful sensory content," which is as well defined by subjective report, according to which it was lacking. The only way that one knows that the GSR is an indicator of pain is its correlation with other indications of pain, such as verbal reports; if this correlation is now destroyed, so much the worse for the GSR as an indicator of pain. Sutcliffe concludes: "The puzzle remains that hypnotically anaesthetic subjects report in many cases that they feel no pain. Future research might well be directed to resolving this discrepancy between the evidence of bodily reaction and the reported subjective experience" (1961, p. 77). It may be noted also that this is different from the possibility noted in his earlier paper (Sutcliffe, 1960, p. 76) that surgical patients who undergo surgery under hypnosis may be insensitive to pain in the first place: his subjects were not insensitive to pain in the waking state. The experiments on hallucinations led to similar conclusions. The experiment was a fairly complex one, involving suggested deafness and delayed auditory feedback. Because there was interference by the distraction of delayed feedback in the hypnotic as well as in the waking condition, the skeptical position was supported. Still, the subjective effects were very different for the hypnotized subjects, and no question of simulation is involved: "There remains the puzzling discrepancy between the subject's reports of hallucination and the evidence of their objective performance" (Sutcliffe, 1961, p. 197). Finally, the delusional experience was one in which the subject was asked to adopt the opposite sex role. While Sutcliffe reported this experiment as somewhat ambiguous on the credulous-skeptical issue, he made the significant statement that "the qualitative data support the view that in a number of cases hypnotized subjects were deluded about their sex" (Sutcliffe, 1961, p. 199).

Thus Sutcliffe's "skeptical" conclusions, while yielding important data about some of the correlates of hypnotic performance, leave the essential characteristics of what happens in the experience of the hypnotic subject about what they have been all along.

Another leading investigator of hypnosis, Orne, has also tended to mislead the hasty reader into doubts about the reality of hypnosis, although this is by no means his intention. On the skeptical side he has pointed out that subjects tend to respond to what he calls the *demand characteristics* of the hypnotic situation, so that much that passes for hypnosis is a normal response to what is expected, and might occur equally well outside hypnosis. Thus he asks students in a class to take off their shoes, to exchange coats, to hand him a wristwatch, and in other ways to do odd things, merely because he is the instructor and students acquiesce to his requests; he points out that if these things were done within hypnosis everyone would be impressed by the kinds of things you can make the hypnotized person do. His demonstration shows that nonhypnotized people do these things, too, when the social situation calls for them. Furthermore, when he gave a hypnotic demonstration with an indication that certain kinds of behavior (a hand contraction) was the normal consequence of trance, and then hypnotized volunteers not previously hypnotized, they showed this nontypical behavior in line with their expectations (Orne, 1959, 1962b). It appears, therefore, that the "typical" behavior in hypnosis may be just what the subject believes "typical" of hypnosis. In studying the possibility of getting student subjects to do "dangerous" things within hypnosis, he found he could equally well get nonhypnotized subjects to do "dangerous" things, such as picking a coin out of a glass of fuming nitric acid (a task that, while it looks frightening, is not actually harmful).

A favorite control device of Orne's is to use simulating subjects, that is, subjects who are unhypnotizable and hence unhypnotized, but who are instructed to mislead a hypnotist into thinking they are becoming hypnotized. They are often successful in thus fooling even an experienced hypnotist; this gives the hasty reader the impression, further, that this must be something happening fairly commonly when subjects appear to be hypnotized. Actually this interpretation is quite unfair to Orne, who does not intend this at all. He is aware of this possibility, as every scientific student of hypnosis must be. His experience, however, is the same as that of the rest of us; most subjects, if they are hypnotizable, give many evidences that they are not simulating, such as their disappointment at some of the things that they are unable to do while hypnotized, even though they understand the demands fully, and could readily simulate, were they so inclined. Correspondingly, those not hypnotizable seldom simulate, and they, too, are often disappointed and ask to have further trials in the hope that they may actually experience hypnotic effects.

An important further point is that his trained simulators, who know the demands of the situation well enough to meet them in a form to fool a hypnotist, *do not thereby become hypnotized.* Sham hypnotic behavior, although it may fool an audience, does not fool the subject. This is hard to state in fully convincing form because of the remote possibility of fraud-within-fraud, yet in practice there are countless signs of good faith on the part of participants in experi-

ments, with an awareness of the difference between being hypnotized
and not being hypnotized. Austin, Perry, Sutcliffe, and Yeomans
(1963) have shown that highly hypnotizable subjects can be trained
to simulate hypnosis without becoming "entranced," although some
of them find it difficult; this team includes the same skeptical Sutcliffe,
who definitely accepts the hypnotic trance.

Orne has another useful concept, which attests to his acceptance
of the reality of hypnosis. This is his concept of trance logic (see
p. 9), which expresses a difference between the trance and waking.
He finds, for example, that the following demonstration is instructive. Ask a hypnotized subject to attend to a person, Mr. X, just
introduced to him, sitting on his right. After they exchange a few
remarks, have the subject close his eyes. Tell him that the person has
moved to the chair on the other side of him (though he remains where
he was); have the subject open his eyes and continue the conversation
with Mr. X, now on his left. If he is capable of hallucinations with
his eyes open, he will not find this difficult.

Now have him look back toward the chair on his right, and ask:
"Whom do you see sitting in the chair on your right?" He will answer
without hesitation, and without bewilderment, "Mr. X." Trance logic
permits this doubling of a person without any disturbance. Ask now:
"How do you account for two Mr. X's?" and he will try to solve the
problem posed. "One must be an hallucination." "Perhaps you do it
with mirrors." "All right," you say, "one is indeed Mr. X, and one
an hallucination of Mr. X. Can you tell me which is the true Mr. X?"
Several things may happen at this point. The subject may have no
difficulty at all, for the hallucinated Mr. X may be diaphanous, and
the subject may be able to see the chair through him. This does not
trouble him, but it makes it easy to distinguish between his hallucination and the true Mr. X. He may have genuine difficulty, and may
seek consensual validation, only to become more confused: if he
touches them, both are warm; if he asks them questions one at a
time, each answers with the voice of Mr. X. If the hallucination is
veridical, it will be supported by all sensory avenues. But the reserve
of realistic logic has not been lost under the sway of trance logic, and
many subjects find ways of solving the problem. A good solution
takes the form that the hallucination belongs to the hypnotized subject, and hence will be obedient to him. Hence by wishing the hallucinated Mr. X to distinguish himself by raising his arm or by leaving
the room, the Mr. X who obeys the hypnotized subject is the hallu-

cination. The first of these solutions (arm raising) has been reported for one of his subjects by Orne; the second (leaving the room) occurred with one of my subjects in a repetition of the demonstration. It is important to note that the subject, even while having hallucinations, is capable of this ordered thinking. Repeat this same experiment with a naive simulator and very different results will be found.[2] He will not produce a diaphanous hallucination, because this is hardly to be expected; having accepted a "veridical" hallucination, he will not accept the doubling and will tend to deny that the "true" Mr. X is in the chair to his right after he has hallucinated him on his left. Of 30 simulators, Orne found only two willing to act as if two images of the same person were simultaneously present (Orne, 1959). This is the kind of argument that Orne used for the reality of hypnosis; if hasty readers infer that because he emphasizes demand characteristics and uses simulators he does not believe in hypnosis, they have simply not read carefully enough.

The situation with respect to Sarbin, who has proposed and defended a role-enactment theory of hypnosis (Sarbin, 1950, 1956; Sarbin and Andersen, 1967) is similar, though a little more difficult to harmonize with conventional views of hypnosis. He, too, believes that role-expectations (that is, responses to demand characteristics) influence what subjects do within hypnosis, and his extreme behaviorism makes him find any references to a "state" or "trance" unacceptable. Yet he is clear that hypnotic role-enactment is *not* sham behavior; and he goes to some pains to discuss the meaning of involvement in a role, the extreme illustration being psychic suicides or voodoo deaths (on the supposition that they do indeed occur). Hence the difference between someone who is hypnotizable and someone who is not is a matter of the degree to which they can lose themselves in the roles that the hypnotist suggests; it is *not* just a matter of voluntary cooperation with the hypnotist. Thus individual differences in susceptibility are a reality, and the scale that has served as the background for most of the present hypnotic scales is one on which Sarbin collaborated (Friedlander and Sarbin, 1938). The main point of disagreement between Sarbin and the conventional interpretation of hypnosis does not have to do with the established state

---

[2] A troublesome problem in using simulators as controls is to decide how much training to give the simulator. Had he witnessed such a demonstration as that just described, he could simulate it very well; the point is that the naive subject will yield this behavior, if he becomes hypnotized, while the naive simulator will not.

of hypnosis (though he would object to its characterization as a state), but rather to the role of induction in bringing about the behavior manifested within hypnosis. This we shall discuss in the next chapter.

Another active worker in hypnosis, Barber, takes a point of view similar to that of Sarbin, in that the role of induction is minimized, and the trance state is also minimized. What is left, then, is an *ability* to yield hypnoticlike phenomena, which some people possess and other people do not possess. He believes that the major phenomena of hypnosis can be demonstrated, with individual differences in the ability to produce them, but that the phenomena do not require an induction procedure or a special sort of state (except, in some instances, it is necessary to control motivation or to arouse imagination). Of the authors mentioned, Barber is the only one who is inclined to write the word "hypnosis" in quotation marks as though he doubts that it stands for something distinct (for example, Barber, 1963). But even he is fascinated by the phenomena and succeeds in producing most of them, so that his quarrels are at a level of methodology and theory and do not cast doubt on the reality of the phenomena associated with hypnosis, as this reality is understood by other scientific workers within the field.[3]

Although there is much to be learned from the "skeptical" views here described, upon examination it turns out that hypnosis has not been "debunked" or discredited. Some genuine issues exist, but the questions raised are of the same order as asking whether reinforcement is necessary for learning, or whether stereoscopic vision is inherited or acquired. Because of some uncertainty about the evidence, contemporary workers have areas of disagreement; these turn out to be no more serious in hypnosis than in other areas of psychological investigation, and no issue of the legitimacy of hypnosis as a field of scientific inquiry is involved.

CONCLUSIONS REGARDING THE HYPNOTIC STATE

The testimony of investigators and subjects over 150 years leaves little doubt about the distinctiveness of the phenomena associated

---

[3] There are some semantic and theoretical problems raised by the word "reality," but it would be a digression here to go into them. One might say that a diaphanous hallucination is not as real as an hallucination confused with the actual object hallucinated; from my point of view it is different, but equally real.

with the hypnotic state, despite the difficulty of defining hypnosis and of specifying exactly how it differs from other states.

The seven characteristics selected for discussion (subsidence of planning function, redistribution of attention, availability of memories and heightened ability for fantasy production, reduction of reality testing and tolerance for reality distortion, increased suggestibility, role behavior, and posthypnotic amnesia) delineate the state sufficiently to invite its further examination as a field of potentially important psychological inquiry.

The subject's own reports of passivity, compulsion to follow the hypnotist, changes in size or appearance of parts of his body, feelings of floating, blacking out, dizziness, spinning give some indications of how the subject knows something unusual has happened to him; these statements justify Orne's observation: "Any subject who has experienced deep trance will unhesitatingly describe this state as basically different from his normal one. He may be unable to explicate this difference, but he will invariably be quite definite and certain about its presence" (Orne, 1959, p. 297).

Although there are many areas of uncertainty and disagreement, as shown by controversies over credulous and skeptical views, demand characteristics, simulation, role enactment, and the similarities between waking and hypnotic responses to suggestion, the result of criticism is to alert the investigator to problems, not to shake his belief in the distinctiveness of hypnotic phenomena or in the significance of hypnosis as an area in which research is needed and where a rich yield can be expected.

CHAPTER 2

The Role of Hypnotic Induction

When a person wishes to become hypnotized, he ordinarily asks an experienced hypnotist to hypnotize him. The things that the hypnotist has him do, and the things that the hypnotist says and does, constitute the procedures known as *hypnotic induction*. While the term *induction* may have had its origin in the outmoded interpretation of hypnosis as a magnetic phenomenon, another use of the word *induction* in English—as in induction into office—fits the hypnotic situation appropriately. Many techniques of induction are available to the hypnotist. He may have the subject stare fixedly at some small target object while he suggests that the subject's eyes will close, employ the hand levitation method in which the subject's hand begins to rise slowly in waking suggestion (the state gradually being entered as the hand reaches the face), or make use of whirling disks, metronomes, pendulums, and many other such devices (Weitzenhoffer, 1957). The methods have in common a withdrawal from usual environmental relationships through relaxation, contemplation of sleep, free play of imagination, or concentration upon a small target or some part of the body and upon the hypnotist's voice. Various metaphors are used, but no one of them appears to be essential. It is not necessary, for example, for the subject to close his eyes or to believe that he is entering a sleeplike state, although most usually he is asked to close his eyes, and the metaphor of sleep is used because it is familiar and indicates the desired relaxation and passivity.

In order to induce hypnosis, the hypnotist uses the kind of instructions known as *suggestions;* once the hypnotic state is established he continues to give suggestions, to which the subject is presumably now more responsive than he would be in the waking state. There is lack of clarity about the role of suggestions because the subject must respond to suggestions in order to become hypnotized; it is not surprising to discover a correlation between responsiveness to suggestions in the waking state and in the hypnotic state. Still there is some usefulness in distinguishing between induction and the established state because induction is transitional and something important ought to be happening during this transition.

There is another source of confusion that arises because of the possibility of trance deepening. Once a person has entered the hypnotic state, induction is not necessarily over; if induction procedures are continued, he may become more deeply involved in hypnosis, so that we may speak not only of initial induction but of techniques for trance deepening that are essentially continuations of induction. In the case of trance deepening, induction procedures are again transitional, but now between "levels" of hypnosis rather than between the waking state and hypnosis. It is no wonder that in an era when hypnosis has been largely in the hands of practitioners rather than of laboratory investigators there are many areas of ambiguity centering around the roles of induction and of trance deepening.

The study of hypnotic induction is plagued by another difficulty, one created by the well-established fact that with practice the hypnotic state can be established very quickly, at a signal such as a code word or the snap of a finger.[1] It is thus necessary, in studying what happens in induction, to seek inexperienced subjects, and to study them during their first experience of hypnosis.

INDUCTION AS A TRANSITION TO THE HYPNOTIC STATE

In attempting to describe what happens within the transition from the waking state to the hypnotic state in the first induction of hypnosis, we face a most difficult problem because we must ask the subject

---

[1] A study by Krueger (1931) showed a curve of decreasing time for the eyes to close in repeated inductions that looked very much like a learning curve. This led Hull (1933) to consider hypnosis to be a habit phenomenon, but he failed to distinguish between learning to enter hypnosis more promptly and learning to enter at all. Krueger used only subjects who closed their eyes in initial induction, and thus his evidence does not bear upon the problem of learning to be hypnotized in the first place.

cate what is going on when the reference points for such
tion are obscure and the states of awareness ill-defined.
em is similar to that of describing the onset of sleep, in
casionally hypnagogic imagery can be caught, or dreams
captu against a waking background, but the oscillations are rapid
and the phenomena difficult to put into words. It is not surprising that
some of the better descriptions have been provided by psychoanalysts,
who are accustomed to dealing with phenomena on the edge of awareness. Their descriptions are intermingled with inference as to what
is going on, but to make some inferences is the only way in which
to make the material at all coherent and understandable. Two psycho-
analytically oriented teams of investigators have grappled with the
problems created by induction as a transition between waking and the
established hypnotic state: Kubie and Margolin (1944) and Gill and
Brenman (1959).

Kubie and Margolin (1944) point out that, in the initial induction,
through *immobilization* (sitting quietly, often fixating the eyes) and
through *monotony* (the simple repetitive and rhythmical words of the
hypnotist) a kind of "partial sleep" is produced, in which most channels of communication with the outside world are cut off, and only
the voice of the hypnotist continues to enter. This reduction in sensorimotor channels blurs the ego-boundaries of the subject, so that there
is a psychological fusion between subject and hypnotist; as this
stage is reached the hypnotist's words are confused with the subject's
own thoughts. The subject's apparent suggestibility arises out of this
confusion.[2] These restrictions also permit hypnagogic revery, in which
vivid sensory memories and images are released. In general alertness
is diminished; the hypnotist allays anxieties and fears as well as reducing direct sensory input. Sensory warning signals are thus supressed.
It is conjectured that the hypnotic state can be viewed as a regressive
one, approaching the sensorimotor state of the infant in the first weeks
of life.

Following these steps of induction, something happens as the shift
occurs to the final phase of the hypnotic state. To quote:

> The shift to the fully developed final phase of the hypnotic state
> involves:
> a. A partial re-expansion of ego boundaries.

[2] A similar point is made by Miller, Galanter, and Pribram (1960). A subject who listens to himself talk presently listens to the hypnotist's voice instead. "The subject gives up his inner speech to the hypnotist" (p. 105).

b. An incorporation of a fragmentary image of the hypnotist within the expanded boundaries of the subject's ego.

In this final phase the compliance of the subject to the hypnotist's commands is again more apparent than real, in that the incorporated image of the hypnotist which echoes the hypnotist's voice has for the time being become a part of the subject's temporary ego.

It is obvious that the final phase in the hypnotic process, which occurs with the full development of the hypnotic state, parallels precisely that phase in the development of the infant's ego in which its boundaries gradually expand, with the retention of parental images as unconscious incorporated components of the developing ego of the infant. The incorporated image of the hypnotist plays the same role in the hypnotic subject as does the incorporated and unconscious image of the parental figure in the child or adult. Hypnosis thus is seen to be an experimental reproduction of a natural developmental process [Kubie and Margolin, 1944, p. 620].

Gill and Brenman (1959) also emphasize the difference psychologically between entering the trance and the established trance itself. In agreement with Kubie and Margolin they find two components in the induction, either of which may serve as an entering gate into the hypnotic state. One of these is sensory withdrawal and monotony, and the other is a regressive transference based on a relationship to the hypnotist as in some sense a parent-substitute.

In describing what the hypnotist does, Gill and Brenman point out that he (1) impoverishes the inflow of sensory stimuli to the subject by limiting the subject's bodily activity, (2) attempts to alter the quality of bodily awareness of the subject, (3) suggests a kind of dissociation, by focusing his attention on a movement itself, so that movements that normally take place voluntarily may take place involuntarily, and, finally, (4) breaks into the normal adjustment of the subject's human relationships by taking over control of the subject through creating an atmosphere of quasi-magic (rational or irrational in its justification). The hypnotist has essentially a two-pronged strategy: that of sensory deprivation and that of developing a "special" kind of human relationship.

What the subject does, in turn, is to experience changes in his body image, in equilibrium, in affect, in the availability of the motor system and, finally, in his relationship to the hypnotist. We may note how these descriptions square with our quantitative findings reported in Chapter 1 (Table 1, p. 12).

Some of the reported distortions by our subjects are quite bizarre:

"I had the feeling I was completely reclined in the chair, then my body contorted, long and short. Then I fell out of the chair into open space. There was no building, or room, just space. . . ."

"My body began to swell up, until it broke off in great chunks, and there was nothing left but my mind."

"As you counted, the numbers came out on a mental screen like a Twentieth Century Fox movie."

"I had an odd sensation as though I was immense in size—maybe three or four miles high—sitting on earth—each movement covering a great distance—as if I had some new conception of distance and size."

The interpretation that Gill and Brenman give of such changes is in terms of ego processes and transference. The induction initiates a regression (in the psychoanalytic sense) leading to a special type of established regressed state that is what we know as the hypnotic state. Regression in psychoanalysis does not mean a literal age-regression as studied in hypnosis; it means rather a primitive state in which impulse is dominant over rationality and in which transference can be defined as archaic because it reflects earlier relationships to parental figures. The hypnotist brings about a regression in which normal ego-functioning is temporarily disrupted; a new substructure within the ego is said to characterize the established hypnotic state, corresponding to the type of reversible regression known as regression in the service of the ego (Kris, 1952). The overall ego-structure remains intact.

Gill and Brenman's transference interpretation of hypnosis is integrated with their regressed-ego interpretation by assuming that the hypnotic transference depends upon "the constellation of strivings within the [ego] subsystem," while another kind of transference, that of the therapist–patient relationship, belongs rather to the overall ego (1959, p. 199). While this is quite conjectural and difficult to pin down, at least it is a recognition by these authors that we are dealing with a complex problem not to be solved by easy formulas.

The main point of these discussions, for our present purposes, is that they indicate that in induction something happens that is distinguishable from the final hypnotic state. The purpose of the induction is to facilitate the establishment of the hypnotic state.

BEHAVIOR DURING THE COURSE OF INDUCTION

If induction is a disruptive and regressive process, there ought to be some manifestations of regressed behavior during induction. We have already referred to some of the changes that take place—for example, distortions of body image—that can perhaps be thought of as regressive. Gill and Brenman cite a number of other behaviors, such as appearance (and disappearance) of hysterical symptoms, depersonalization, dizziness. It is asserted that in a nonpatient population "emotional outbursts, though not universal, were extremely common" (Gill and Brenman, 1959, p. 20). Our own experience has not shown such outbursts to be at all common; for example, in some 1000 inductions, not more than 4 or 5 cases could be classified as such. The following three cases are illustrative.

Case 1. Mark, a college student who began to sob audibly and to shed tears when experiencing hypnotic induction for the first time. Aroused from hypnosis, Mark could not account for this unusual outburst and went on for further hypnosis without event.

Case 2. Another student, Howard, who reported being disturbed during hypnosis by the hallucination of a blackish cylindrical form, swirling, rotating on its axis . . . tumbling, rolling as though being rolled on a wave. The subject's later associations made it quite clear that this was a symbolic representation of a hypodermic syringe that had been used at age thirteen to relieve pain while a leg fracture was being set. Hence this was a redintegrative experience (Hilgard, Hilgard, and Newman, 1961, p. 468).

Case 3. Dick, also one of our student subjects, who had a kind of panic reaction during induction. Upon the suggestion that his eyes would close, he closed them tightly, became markedly tense, and began to shed tears. He sighed, moaned, sobbed, clenched his fists tightly, and set his jaw. When roused he immediately calmed down, and the session was carried through with his willing cooperation, though he failed to re-enter hypnosis. This reaction also proved to be redintegrative of early punishment situations in which he was "cornered" by his parents and beaten (Hilgard, Hilgard, and Newman, 1961, p. 472).

Disturbances are not limited to the induction phase; while we have found relatively few cases of disturbance in either induction or the established state, they are equally frequent in both states, the trouble within the trance state usually coming as a result of specific suggestions, such as the suggestion to regress to a particular age, or to dream; some such cases are reported in the next chapter.

The somewhat primitive and regressive quality of the untoward experiences within induction is evident, but their infrequency in our sample, compared with the reported frequency in the Gill and Brenman sample, remains unexplained. Whether it has to do with the nature of the sample selected, the fact that Gill and Brenman were known to be psychotherapists, or something about their induction procedures cannot be judged from the evidence available. In any case, the fact that a few subjects have these extreme reactions and that a substantial proportion have mild experiences of changes in body size or proportions, or some kind of disorienting experience of spinning, floating, and the like, is enough to call attention to the special problems of induction.

INCREASE OF SUGGESTIBILITY FOLLOWING INDUCTION

It has long been accepted that the hypnotic induction increases the subject's responsiveness to suggestion, although not much actual experimental evidence was available until recently.

Some of the early experiments were done in Hull's laboratory. He and his collaborators tested postural sway, lateral arm movement, and eyelid closure, within and outside hypnosis, and found an increased responsiveness within hypnosis. As Hull put it:

> Accordingly, one of the most widely held views concerning hypnosis is confirmed, though the amount of hypersuggestibility thus revealed, while considerable, is probably far less than the classical hypnotists would have supposed had the question ever occurred to them [Hull, 1933, p. 298].[3]

Individual differences persisted as between the waking and hypnotic states; correlations between responsiveness under the two conditions fell between .67 and .99 for the various small samples tested.

The next significant study was done in the Stanford laboratory by Weitzenhoffer and Sjoberg (1961). Using a 17-point scale which they devised, they found a significant increase in hypnotic perform-

---

[3] From *Hypnosis and Suggestibility: An Experimental Approach* by Clark L. Hull. Copyright, 1933, D. Appleton-Century Company, Inc. Reprinted by permission of Appleton-Century-Crofts.

ance following induction, as compared with responsiveness to the same items in the waking state. Waking performance again correlated with hypnotic performance, the rank-order coefficient being .54 for

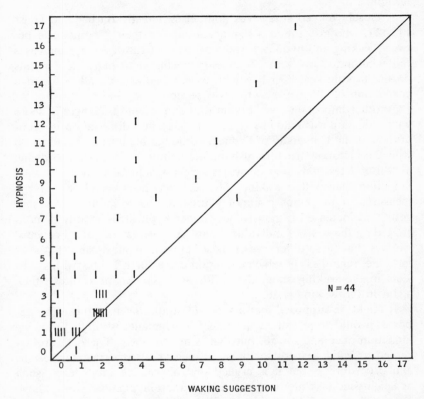

FIGURE 1. INCREASE IN SCORES ON 17-POINT SUGGESTIBILITY SCALE BE-TWEEN WAKING TEST AND HYPNOTIC INDUCTION. All scores above the diagonal have increased following induction. Plotted from the data of Weitzenhoffer and Sjoberg, 1961.

the total sample. Their results are presented in graphic form in Figure 1.

Because the axes of Figure 1 are symmetrical, cases that fall above the diagonal are more responsive under hypnosis than within waking suggestion. It is evident by inspection that a large fraction of the cases show this enhancement of suggestibility through induction. It is noteworthy that a few subjects (3 of 44) were able to achieve very high suggestibility scores (10 to 12) in the waking state, a fact known for a long time but here demonstrated in clear quantitative fashion.

A closely related study was done elsewhere by Barber and Glass (1962), who also found a significant gain on their 8-point scale between waking and hypnosis. Some 50 percent showed score increases following induction, with 27 percent showing gains of 1.5 to 3 points on the 8-point scale. In line with earlier findings, they too found a correlation of .85 between the two sessions.

Another important contribution to the problem of changes in score with induction was made by Evans (1963a) in a dissertation in preparation at the University of Sydney. Although his purposes had to do with the factorial structure of hypnotic ability, he preferred to define as a useful test only that on which scores would be higher following induction than within waking. The fact that he was able to salvage measures of the kinds commonly used in susceptibility scales suggests that increased responsiveness under hypnosis is readily demonstrated on the basis of individual items. An interesting point in Evans' work is that these differences persist between hypnosis and the waking state, regardless of which condition comes first. He tested his subjects in the waking state, then with an induction procedure,[4] then again in the waking state.

It might be supposed that a series of studies such as those just reported would have settled the issue of hypersuggestibility following induction once and for all, but that is not the case. The data are accepted as valid (except for minor criticisms of experimental designs and procedures), but it is argued that alternative procedures, such as heightened task motivation or imagination instructions, would have increased suggestibility without trance induction. Hence, while our conclusions from these experiments is that the traditionally expected hypersuggestibility through induction is in fact found, we have to submit this conclusion to critical review.

[4] His induction procedure was an indirect one in which the usual suggestions of relaxation, imagination, and the like were made, but without reference to hypnosis. Apparently a large fraction of his subjects did not know that they were being hypnotized at all.

HYPERSUGGESTIBILITY WITHOUT PRIOR INDUCTION OF HYPNOSIS

Because the trance state itself depends upon responsiveness to suggestion, once the Bernheim-Liébeault suggestion theory of hypnosis gained the ascendancy, the induced trance state came to be minimized. William James noted this at the time:

> The radical defenders of the suggestion-theory are thus led to deny the very existence of the hypnotic state, in the sense of a peculiar trance-like condition which deprives the patient of spontaneity and makes him passive to suggestion from without. The trance itself is only one of the suggestions, and many subjects in fact can be made to exhibit the other hypnotic phenomena without the preliminary induction of this one [James, 1890, II, p. 598 f.].

This position, which James reported but did not accept, has received contemporary support from those who find the prior induction unnecessary for the eliciting of the behaviors commonly associated with hypnosis. Therefore this issue has to be faced, both empirically and theoretically. James was convinced that the position was wrong. He put it this way:

> *The suggestion-theory may therefore be approved as correct, provided we grant the trance-state as its prerequisite.* The three states of Charcot, the strange reflexes of Heidenhain, and all other bodily phenomena which have been called direct consequences of the trance-state itself, are not such. They are products of suggestion, the trance-state having no particular outward symptoms of its own; but without the trance-state there, those particular suggestions could never have been successfully made [James, 1890, II, p. 601].

The issue is therefore an old one, but today we do not turn to authorities for our answers, we look to the evidence from experiments.

Weitzenhoffer, Gough, and Landes (1959), in an experiment from our laboratory concerned with the influence of visual fixation unaccompanied by suggestions, used one condition in which subjects expected hypnosis, the other in which no expectation of hypnosis was involved. Although treated just alike in other respects, the group expecting hypnosis became hypnotized by the eye-fixation technique, while the other did not; the amount of hypnosis demonstrated was the same as that following a more usual induction procedure. Thus the formal induction was not necessary if eye fixation *plus expectation* were present.

Barber and his associates have undertaken a large number of studies dealing with this problem. Among their results are:

1. A placebo, which the subject believed to have hypnotic powers, succeeded in producing responses equivalent to those following a standard induction (Glass and Barber, 1961).

2. Task motivation instructions yielded an increase in suggestibility equal to hypnotic induction (in which task motivation was both explicit and implicit) (Barber and Calverley, 1962, 1963a).

3. Waking-imagined analgesia served to produce tolerance for pain equal to that engendered by hypnosis, including equal responsiveness on the concomitant physiological measures (Barber and Hahn, 1962).

These results appear devastating to the usual conception of hypnosis. In fact, this is the experimenters' interpretation:

> If these experimental findings are confirmed in replicative studies, the concepts of "trance" and "hypnosis" may no longer be useful in conceptualizing the factors involved in "hypersuggestibility" and performance of so-called "hypnotic behaviors"; response to "direct suggestions" or "commands" and performance of behaviors traditionally associated with the word "hypnosis" may be more parsimoniously conceptualized under the more general psychological concept of task motivation [Barber and Calverley, 1962, p. 388].

These studies have been useful in pointing out that suggestibility within hypnosis is indeed correlated with susceptibility outside hypnosis and that various techniques can be used to enhance suggestibility. It is worth knowing that some subjects make very superior performances on suggestibility tests without having undergone hypnotic induction. This much all must accept.

The question remains: Has the evidence really demonstrated that hypnotic induction does nothing and that there is no such thing as the hypnotic state? The answer is that the evidence, when carefully examined, and when supplemented by other evidence, does *not* in fact lead to these conclusions. But this will take a bit of explaining.

First let us consider some problems of experimental design. What may be an appropriate design for one study may not be an appropriate design for another, for the design must fit the problem being investigated, the magnitude of the effects under study, and so on. Hypnotic susceptibility happens to be a measure in which there are very wide individual differences, and even a tendency to bimodality in the distributions that are found (Hilgard and others, 1961). In that case selecting two groups for treatment on a random basis requires fairly large groups before significant mean differences will be detected. In view of the costliness and inconvenience of large random groups in time, effort, and availability of subjects, there are two alternatives to the testing of large random groups. The first is to stratify subjects on the basis of their known (measured) hypnotic susceptibilities and then to assign them randomly to experimental and control groups. Although this looks fine in the abstract (and is often to be recommended) it eliminates the possibility of beginning with naive subjects, and any contrast between waking and hypnotic conditions will be detected by the experienced subject who serves within this design. The second alternative is to use subjects as their own controls. While this has some disadvantages also, in view of the subtle demand characteristics of hypnotic experiments, it is in the end the most economical and instructive method, despite the arguments against its use. It permits the use of naive subjects in the initial conditions, thus sharing that advantage with the random assignment method, but it also permits some later equation according to individual differences in hypnotic susceptibility under standard conditions. It is thus not correct to assume that some canonical method is the most appropriate for all experiments, and the experimenter, using entirely acceptable methods, may in fact through their use bias the results in favor of (or against!) his own predilections.

When subjects do not serve as their own controls in studies of suggestibility with and without induction, no advantage is taken of the very high correlation between waking and hypnotic suggestion in determining gains from one condition to the other. In view of the wide dispersion of scores it is not surprising that treatment differences are seldom found under these circumstances. There is the substantive fact that many people are not hypnotizable, so that a contrast between a hypnotic treatment and a nonhypnotic treatment is not to be expected for them according to anybody's theory; randomly selected groups will contain a large fraction (perhaps half) falling in this relatively insusceptible category. At the other end of the scale are those subjects known to yield the hypnotic phenomena without induction; for them treatment differences will also be ineffective. One comes out then with a design that can scarcely be sensitive to any small treatment effects due to hypnotic induction. It is true that if the effects were very large they might show up, but there are effects *known to be small* ever since Hull's experiments, and to these the design is not sensitive. If subjects are not chosen at random but are selected on some basis of hypnotic performance, then care also has to be exercised to prevent bias. The subjects in the analgesia experiments of Barber and Hahn (1962) were selected as those who scored high in *waking suggestibility,* so that any differences between their waking responsiveness and hypnotic responsiveness would be attenuated. There is thus much to be said for using subjects as their own controls despite precautions that must be taken (Barber, 1967).

The above considerations lead to fairly straightforward observations with respect to studies on the effects of hypnotic induction compared with other prior conditions on subsequent responsiveness to suggestions:

1. If subjects are used as their own controls, it can be shown that hypnotic induction does indeed increase responsiveness to suggestions (Hull, 1933; Weitzenhoffer and Sjoberg, 1961; Barber and Glass, 1962).

2. If subjects are not used as their own controls but are assigned at random to different groups, the effects of treatment differences are so attenuated that differences between responsiveness to suggestions following hypnotic induction, imagination instructions, or task-motivating instructions may not, and often will not, prove to be statistically significant, particularly if the groups are of only moderate size (Barber and Calverley, 1962, 1963a).

There would be little point in stressing these methodological matters, except that sometimes a shift leads to ambiguity in interpreting modified findings. In the shift from the Barber and Glass (1962) experiments to the Barber and Calverley (1962, 1963a) experiments, the differences between the two series of experiments tend to be attributed to the use of motivating instructions in the Barber and Calverley series, while in fact the change in design to one in which subjects are not used as their own controls is equally important. Even so, the Barber and Calverley results are not unequivocal. In the 1962 study, Experiment 1, suggestibility following hypnosis averaged higher (numerically) than five other conditions antedating the suggestion test and was significantly higher than four of these. The only condition that approached it was a task-motivation suggestion that invited low standards for acquiescent responses through instructions such as: "Everyone passed these tests when they tried. . . . Yet when these people [who felt that imagining a movie so vividly that they felt as if they were actually looking at the picture was awkward or silly] later realized that it wasn't hard to imagine, they were able to visualize the movie and they felt as if the imagined movie was as vivid and as real as an actual movie . . . if you try to imagine to the best of your ability, you can easily imagine and do the interesting things I tell you and you will be helping this experiment and not wasting any time" (Barber and Calverley, 1962, p. 366). Because these instructions, and none of the others, equaled hypnotic induction (despite hypotheses that they would) there is the possibility that the actual wording of universal conformity had something to do with the results.

In the later experiments (Barber and Calverley, 1963a) task-motivating instructions were used in interaction with hypnotic induction. Although task-motivating instructions alone equaled hypnotic induction with task motivation it must be pointed out that the task-motivating instructions used in connection with induction were verbally quite unlike those used alone. There were no statements within induction about universal compliance. The strongest statement within induction was as follows: ". . . if you pay close attention to what I say, and follow what I tell you, you can easily fall into a hypnotic sleep and experience the interesting things I will tell you to experience. In this case you will be helping this experiment and not wasting any time" (p. 109). This is quite different from saying that everyone passed the tests, or that all finally saw the movie as vividly as if they were actually looking at the picture. The matter of motivation is a most subtle one, and we shall return to a discussion of it in Chapter 5. We felt, however, after reviewing the studies of Barber and Glass and of Barber and Calverley that we would get some further clarification by doing a study of our own on the effects of induction, in which we would test at once the effects of random assignment to treatment groups *and* the use of the subject as his own control.

NEW EVIDENCE BEARING ON THE EFFECTS OF INDUCTION

The best way to clear up the contradictions between the several experiments showing increased suggestibility under hypnosis and the other series of experiments, chiefly by Barber and Calverley, showing no significant differences between a motivated waking state and hypnosis, seemed to be to design an experiment of our own, in which we could have internal evidence to answer some of the questions that the group statistics might not bring to light. The staff of our laboratory turned to such an experiment in the fall of 1963, and the results are being reported in detail elsewhere (Hilgard and Tart, 1966). Some of the main findings will be given here, along with some of the qualitative material.

Actually two experiments were performed. While the second was a little tighter in its controls than the first, the results were essentially similar, and the controls in the first were fully equal to those of the experiments that the study was designed to replicate. Hence the results of the two experiments will be presented in order.

Experiment 1. The effect on suggestibility of waking instructions, imagination instructions, and hypnotic induction. The instructions in this experiment were modeled very closely upon those of Barber and Glass (1962). Each subject was assigned to one of three treatment conditions on the first day of the experiment, the groups being designated *Waking, Imagination,* and *Hypnotic Induction.*

For the Waking instructions, the following statement was made to the subject prior to his receiving the test suggestions:

> Today you will be given tests of responsiveness to waking suggestion. You will not be hypnotized. We want to be sure that you do not become hypnotized; if you slip into a hypnotic state inadvertently, as indicated by your state report, we will bring you back to your normal state. It is still possible to respond well to hypnotic-like suggestions in the wide-awake normal state.

For the *Imagination* instructions, the following statement was read to the subject:

> Today you will be given tests of imagination under normal conditions. You will not be hypnotized. The better you can imagine, the more you'll respond; try as hard as you can to concentrate and to imagine that the things I tell you are true.

For the *Hypnotic Induction* condition the standard induction of Form C of the Stanford Hypnotic Susceptibility Scale was followed (Weitzenhoffer and Hilgard, 1962). This induction involves eye fixation and eye closure, along with test suggestions of relaxation and sleep, and it requires some 10 minutes. It will be noted that the waking and imagination instructions were much briefer than these induction procedures. The same test suggestions used in waking and imagination followed this induction. They consisted of 10 of the usual 12 items of Form C. Thus the first day of the experiment follows the random assignment procedure of Barber and Calverley (1962) and permits a replication of their findings. In view of our criticisms of such a design, we did not anticipate significant differences between the scores on this first day. Our experiment differed from their standard design by including a second day for all subjects, in which all received the hypnotic induction prior to the test suggestions of an alternate form of the shortened Form C. We would, of course, not expect differences on this day either, because subjects were assigned at random. In view of the high correlation anticipated between Day 1 and Day 2, we did hypothesize, however, that this design would be more sensitive to small differences than the first and *that the change from a nonhypnotic condition to a hypnotic one would result in a significant increase in scores, beyond the change brought about by the repetition of two days of hypnosis.*

The major results are shown in Table 2. Although the means of the first day are in ascending order by conditions, they do not differ significantly, as we anticipated, and were we to stop with these data we would agree with the typical Barber and Calverley conclusions that hypnotic induction adds nothing significant to suggestibility. According to our original conjectures there would be no significant differences on the second day either, and this proved to be the case. *There were significant gains between the two days,* however, for both the waking and imagination groups, and no gain (a trivial loss instead) for the group experiencing hypnosis on both days, a result that Barber and Glass (1962) had also found.

The reason that it is possible to detect the effects of induction in this design, and not in the random assignment one alone, is that this design takes into account the correlations between waking and hypnosis scores. In this experiment these were: for waking–hypnosis, $r = .65$; for imagination–hypnosis, $r = .66$; for hypnosis–hypnosis, $r = .87$.

TABLE 2. RESPONSES TO SUGGESTIONS IN WAKING CONDITION, IMAGINATION CONDITION, AND FOLLOWING HYPNOTIC INDUCTION (EXPERIMENT 1) (HILGARD AND TART, 1966)

| | Scores on suggestion tests (Max. = 10) | | Difference: change from first to second |
	First session	Second session	
Group 1 (N = 20)	*Waking condition*	*Hypnotic induction*	
	Mean 2.88	Mean 4.90	Mean +2.02
	SD 2.78	SD 2.41	
Group 2 (N = 20)	*Imagination condition*	*Hypnotic induction*	
	Mean 3.70	Mean 5.70	Mean +2.00
	SD 3.15	SD 2.79	
Group 3 (N = 20)	*Hypnotic induction*	*Hypnotic induction*	
	Mean 4.90	Mean 4.55	Mean −0.35
	SD 2.50	SD 2.53	

Results of analysis of variance: Groups not significantly different on either day but change scores significant overall (p = .001), and treatment interaction significant (p = .01).

Two-day correlations:
  Group 1, waking–hypnosis (N = 20)   = .65
  Group 2, imagination–hypnosis (N = 20) = .66
  Group 3, hypnosis–hypnosis (N = 20)   = .87

The experiment just described is generally satisfactory from two points of view: (1) by using their design, it replicates the findings of Barber and Calverley (1963a), thus validating the desired similarity between the experiments,[5] and (2) by adding the possibility of studying change scores from a nonhypnotic condition to a hypnotic one, we succeeded in showing that the designs of Barber and Calverley (1962, 1963a) are not sensitive to the small but significant changes that may indeed occur. As a consequence we are led to a conclusion opposite to theirs, namely, to the conclusion that hypnotic

[5] Although our task motivating instructions were not as strong as theirs, we found no significant differences by treatment on Day 1, so that the differences in instruction do not affect the argument from the data.

induction increases suggestibility in a statistically significant manner over these other conditions.

There is a flaw in our experiment, however, that is also in the experiments replicated, in that the instructions were given verbally by a hypnotist who conceivably might unwittingly have biased the results. The seven of us who participated in the experiment were of course aware of this danger. We sought to surmount it by reading all instructions verbatim and by changing experimenters from one day to the next, the experimenter lacking knowledge of his subject's performance on the prior day. A control experiment showed, however, that the experimenter's voice was demonstrably different after he had spent 10 minutes in inducing hypnosis than after he had merely read off very short waking or imagination instructions (Troffer and Tart, 1964). While this may not have made any difference,[6] we designed a second experiment with tighter controls.

Experiment 2. The effect on suggestibility of imagination with and without expectation of hypnosis, and of hypnotic induction. Although the main new control in this experiment was the use of taped suggestions throughout, to avoid any hypnotist effect, it seemed wasteful merely to repeat the earlier experiment, so several other changes were made. Most of these would tend to reduce the differences between waking suggestion and hypnotic induction; we were quite prepared to have the results of Experiment 1 "wash out," for we had no stake in the outcome and merely wanted to know what was the case. We used three different instruction conditions, in various combinations. These included, first, an imagination condition without expectation of hypnosis, second, an imagination condition in which the expectation was aroused that this would lead to a hypnotic state, and, third, the usual standard hypnotic induction. The uninstructed waking condition of Experiment 1 was dropped, and the imagination condition was subdivided, as indicated. Furthermore, the time allowed the subject "to exercise his imagination" was equal to the time spent in hypnotic induction, so that if relaxed immobility for 10 minutes or so is important, it was equally there for the "waking" conditions as for the "hypnotic" ones.

The exact wording of the instructions for those who were in the

---

[6] Barber and Calverley (1964b) have shown that a single hypnotist may adopt either a "forceful" or a "lackadaisical" tone and produce significantly different results in hypnosis.

Imagination Without Expectation of Hypnosis condition was as follows:

> Today you will be given tests of imagination while you are relaxed. It has generally been found, however, that exercising your imagination strongly in these experimental tasks will allow you to experience the things I say quite vividly, even though you have not been hypnotized. The better you imagine, the more you'll respond. Try as hard as you can to concentrate and to imagine that the things I tell you are true.

In addition, the subjects were told whether or not they would receive a formal hypnotic induction on the second day.

The corresponding wording for those in the condition calling for *Imagination with Expectation of Hypnosis* was:

> Today you will be given tests of imagination while you are relaxed. It has generally been found that exercising your imagination strongly in these experimental tasks produces a hypnotic state, even though we don't go through the formalities of inducing hypnosis. The better you imagine, the more you'll respond. Try as hard as you can to concentrate and to imagine that the things I tell you are true.

These subjects were also told whether or not they would receive a formal hypnotic induction on the second day.

The groups receiving a formal hypnotic induction were told:

> Today you will be hypnotized and given a number of hypnotic tests. It has generally been found that exercising your imagination strongly during the hypnotic induction and throughout the whole experiment today will help induce and maintain a hypnotic state. The better you imagine, the more you'll respond. Try as hard as you can to concentrate and to imagine that the things I tell you are true.

These instructions were followed by the standard induction of Form C of the Stanford Hypnotic Susceptibility Scale.

Thus for each of the three conditions there was a group in which a second day repeated that condition, and the criticisms of having the subject serve as his own control were met: in the one case he knew he would have a change of condition on the next day, in the other case he knew he would not. If there were any preparatory adjustments in view of these expectations, they should show up in the group comparisons.

Rather than spell out in detail how the experiment was conducted, suffice it to say that all instructions were on tape, both the instructions defining the conditions of the experiment and the test suggestions. One tape (prepared by me) was used on the first day to give the test suggestions in all conditions, another tape (which I also prepared) on the second day in all conditions. The "live" experimenter who was present simply escorted the subject into the room, explained why tapes were being used, and remained taking notes during the period, and, of course, keeping score. He had a few tasks, such as placing bottles of odorous substances under the subject's nose, or presenting some boxes on a small table, but these were nonverbal, and were practiced to be uniform under all conditions.

That the alternate forms of shortened Form C were very much alike in their effect on the two days is shown in Table 3, in which

TABLE 3. EFFECT OF PRACTICE ON RESPONSES TO SUGGESTIONS UNDER TWO IMAGINATION CONDITIONS AND FOLLOWING HYPNOTIC INDUCTION, REPEATED ON TWO DAYS (EXPERIMENT 2) (HILGARD AND TART, 1966)

	Scores on suggestion tests (Max. = 10)		Difference: change from first to second
	First session	Second session	
Group 1' (N = 15)	*Imagination—no expectation of hypnosis*	*Imagination—no expectation of hypnosis*	
	Mean 2.37	Mean 2.33	Mean −.04
	SD 1.99	*SD* 1.71	
Group 2' (N = 15)	*Imagination—expectation of hypnosis*	*Imagination—expectation of hypnosis*	
	Mean 2.73	Mean 3.23	Mean +.50
	SD 1.99	*SD* 1.81	
Group 3' (N = 15)	*Hypnotic induction*	*Hypnotic induction*	
	Mean 3.83	Mean 3.77	Mean −.06
	SD 2.91	*SD* 2.80	

Results of analysis of variance: Groups do not differ significantly on either day, nor do the two days differ significantly, and the interaction is also negligible.

Two-day correlations:
IE vs. IE (*N* = 15)   = .40
INE vs. INE (*N* = 15) = .65
Hyp. vs. Hyp. (*N* = 15) = .98

subjects responded under the same condition on each of the two days. The groups are too small to expect any significant differences between treatment means, although the means fall in the expected order, with the imagination–no expectation of hypnosis lowest and hypnosis highest. The reliability of the measures is attested by the similarities over the two days, both in means and in the two-day correlations.

A comparison most similar to that of Experiment 1, Table 2, is given in Table 4. Here the changes in which we are interested are from the first session to the second session of those who move from a waking condition to a hypnotic one. In agreement with Experiment 1, there is a tendency for an increase in scores when the move is in

TABLE 4. RESPONSES TO SUGGESTIONS IN TWO IMAGINATION CONDITIONS AND FOLLOWING HYPNOTIC INDUCTION (EXPERIMENT 2) (HILGARD AND TART, 1966)

	Scores on suggestion tests (Max. = 10)		Difference: change from first to second
	First session	Second session	
Group 1 (N = 15)	*Imagination—no expectation of hypnosis*	*Hypnotic induction*	
	Mean 2.80	Mean 3.70	Mean + .90
	SD 2.57	SD 3.08	
Group 2 (N = 15)	*Imagination—expectation of hypnosis*	*Hypnotic induction*	
	Mean 4.00	Mean 5.13	Mean +1.13
	SD 2.11	SD 2.42	
Group 3 (N = 15)	*Hypnotic induction*	*Hypnotic induction*	
	Mean 3.83	Mean 3.77	Mean − .06
	SD 2.91	SD 2.80	

Results of analysis of variance: Groups not significantly different on either day, but the day effect is significant ($p = .001$) and the treatment interaction (group $\times$ day) approaches significance ($.10 > p > .05$).

Two-day correlations:
  INE vs. H ($N = 15$)   = .86
  IE vs. H ($N = 15$)   = .72
  Hyp. vs. Hyp. ($N = 15$) = .98

this direction, although the differences are not quite as significant as they are in Experiment 1. The reduced significance may be due to the absence of an uninstructed waking group, to the longer time devoted to free play of imagination in the second experiment, and to the smaller group size quite as much as to the use of tapes.

In the comparisons thus far the direction has always been from waking to hypnosis. In the experiment proper we included one group that moved in the other direction, from hypnosis to imagination without expectation of hypnosis. After the experiment was all over, we invited back those subjects who had served in one condition only (the subjects whose scores make up Table 3), and those who had imagination only were then tested following hypnotic induction, and those who had hypnosis only were tested on imagination without expectation of hypnosis. This did not violate our good faith in telling some subjects that they were in a control group; many of them had asked when the experiment was over if they might not return to experience hypnosis. In Table 5 these supplementary results are included to show that there is a kind of "metering" of responses by instructions whether the condition comes first or second.

Thus when hypnosis follows imagination, scores tend to rise; when imagination follows hypnosis, scores tend to fall. It should be noted that the imagination scores of the groups with the third session were obtained without any expectation of eventual hypnosis. If those expecting later hypnosis "hold back," then there should have been no "holding back" here. The fact that responses change coherently when instructions change indicates that there is some reality to the setting that the instructions create.

Our second experiment, like our first, shows that there is indeed an effect to be attributed to hypnotic induction *beyond the effect of motivating instructions including exercise of imagination and expectation of hypnosis.* The effects are indeed small, and this fact is important; that they exist at all means that, *for some subjects at least,* the induction procedures may be very important.

Reports from the subjects. Using a subject as his own control has other advantages beyond those that come from the statistics of change scores, for subjects who do and do not change their responses between sessions can often throw light on what is actually happening.

A feature of the experiments that I have not described (included in both Experiment 1 and Experiment 2) was a "state report" in

TABLE 5. EFFECT ON SUGGESTIBILITY OF ORDER OF SESSIONS, IMAGINATION, AND HYPNOTIC INDUCTION (HILGARD AND TART, 1966)

	Scores on suggestion tests (Max. = 10)		Difference: change between two sessions
	First session	Second session	
Group 1 (N = 15)	Imagination—no expectation of hypnosis	Hypnotic induction	
	Mean 2.80	Mean 3.70	Mean +0.90
	SD 2.57	SD 3.08	
			t = 3.15
Group 4 (N = 15)	Hypnotic induction	Imagination—no expectation of hypnosis	df = 28 p < .01
	Mean 5.03	Mean 3.53	
	SD 2.52	SD 2.38	Mean −1.50
	Second session	Third session	
Group 5 (N = 8)	Imagination—no expectation of hypnosis	Hypnotic induction	
	Mean 2.75	Mean 4.00	Mean +1.25
	SD 0.60	SD 1.73	
			t = 2.74
Group 6 (N = 6)	Hypnotic induction	Imagination—no expectation of hypnosis	df = 12 p < .02
	Mean 5.00	Mean 2.42	
	SD 3.26	SD 1.71	Mean −2.58
Combined groups (N = 23)	Imagination—no expectation of hypnosis	Hypnotic induction	
	Mean 2.78	Mean 3.80	Mean +1.02
	SD 2.08	SD 2.65	
			t = 4.21
Combined groups (N = 21)	Hypnotic induction	Imagination—no expectation of hypnosis	df = 42 p < .001
	Mean 5.02	Mean 3.21	
	SD 2.67	SD 2.23	Mean −1.81

which from time to time the subject was asked to characterize his state of awareness, 0 being normal and wide awake, 1 quite relaxed and perhaps borderline, 2 lightly hypnotized, and 3 more deeply hypnotized. Because depth of hypnosis often fluctuates within a session these reports were called for periodically throughout the session, typically before and after each test suggestion. This is a short and somewhat crude scale, but it has served usefully as a supplement to the performance scores. Within hypnosis we have found consistently high correlations between such "state" reports and the objective hypnotic susceptibility scores, of the order of $r = .68$ or $.75$ (Table 6). Within

TABLE 6. CORRELATION BETWEEN STATE REPORTS AND OBJECTIVE SCORES, ALL CONDITIONS, BOTH DAYS (HILGARD AND TART, 1966)

Subject group	State report correlation with scores
Experiment 1	
Waking ($N = 40$)	.22
Imagination ($N = 20$)	.67
Hypnosis ($N = 80$)	.68
Experiment 2	
Imagination–no expectation of hypnosis ($N = 45$)	.65
Imagination–expectation of hypnosis ($N = 30$)	−.01
Hypnosis ($N = 60$)	.75

the waking and imagination states the situation is far less clear, the correlations occasionally being substantial but sometimes being low or negligible. Thus a subject who responds well to suggestions in one of the waking or imagination conditions may spontaneously enter hypnosis or he may not. Equal correlations also need not signify comparable regression lines; even though imagination and hypnotic conditions result in similar correlations between state reports and suggestibility scores, this does not mean that highly responsive imagination subjects give as high state reports as highly responsive hypnotized subjects. This is well illustrated by the results from Experiment 1 plotted in Figure 2.

Note that the correlations for the imagination group and for the hypnotic induction group are essentially alike (.67 and .68), but the regression lines have a quite different slope when plotted in raw score form. The waking group of course has the lowest slope, but it also has the lowest average level. What these lines mean is that subjects who yield very high suggestion scores under these conditions

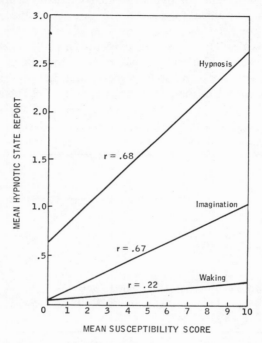

FIGURE 2. RELATIONSHIP BETWEEN SUBJECTIVE REPORTS OF TRANCE STATE AND OVERT SUGGESTIBILITY SCORES UNDER WAKING AND IMAGINATION INSTRUCTIONS AND FOLLOWING HYPNOTIC INDUCTION. Regression lines are plotted between the "state" reports and the scores on modified Form C. Subjects who respond very well to the suggestions of Form C in the waking conditions do not feel themselves to be as much "entranced" as those who have had a prior hypnotic induction (Hilgard and Tart, 1966).

feel themselves in the hypnotic state according to the instructional condition preceding the tests of suggestion, in the order from high to low of hypnotic induction, imagination, and waking conditions. Although there tends to be a relationship between responsiveness to suggestion and the subjectively reported state, the relationship differs very much under the three conditions and hence provides evidence against defining hypnosis according to hypersuggestibility alone.

There are evidently wide individual differences not only in responses to suggestion under various instructions, but also in the state reports following such instructions. If this were not the case, the unstable correlations of Table 6 would not have been found for the waking and imagination conditions. Such individual differences are sometimes better illuminated by individual reports than by statistical indices. Here are three cases that show the kinds of things subjects tell us.

Case 4. Nancy, with low responsiveness to suggestions in waking, high in hypnosis. Nancy, who received a score of 3.5 of a possible 10 when suggestions followed instruction for imagination without expectation of hypnosis, and 9 of 10 following hypnotic induction, reported in part as follows:

> In imagination it didn't feel anything like a trance. I agreed with the person on the recorder, I was going along and cooperating, but it was more under my own power. . . .

By contrast, when she described hypnosis she said there was:

> . . . a barrier to control over myself. I could not get started to thinking on my own, I didn't take time to agree. Two or three times I became aware of myself, that is, wondering if I was hypnotized. It's this feeling of not being aware that was the difference between hypnosis and imagination. It was concentrating on a voice, not aware of the rest of the room. The voice was all there, was very close, very agreeable, kind, and I liked to go along.

Her "state" reports were 0 (fully awake and alert) throughout imagination and averaged 1.5 (light trance) within hypnosis.

Case 5. Dennis, highly responsive to suggestions both within imagination and hypnosis; no subjective difference on two days. This boy obtained a susceptibility score of 9.5 on the imagination day, followed by a score of 8 on the 10-point scale on the hypnosis day. His state reports indicated that he was in a borderline trance on the imagination day (rising gradually from 0 to 1 through 2, averaging 1.0), and somewhat more consistently in a trance state on the hypnosis day (average 2.0). Yet his own summary was that there was no real subjective difference between the two days.

> I thought imagination was a trick to relax me, so I relaxed . . . when he asked me to imagine, I just imagined, and then I had a response . . . I was aware I was responding . . . I don't perceive a difference between the two days.

It appears that for this subject, capable of a high level of response to suggestions while in a moderate hypnotic state, it is possible to produce this state through his own imaginative efforts, accompanied by relaxation.

Case 6. Charles, highly responsive to suggestions within both imagination and hypnosis; great subjective differences between the days. Charles, who scored near the maximum in suggestibility on the two days (10 of 10 on the imagination day and 9.5 of 10 on the hypnosis day), still felt entirely different on the two days. On the imagination day his state reports began low and remained borderline (1) through many items but gradually rose to reports of trance (2 and 3) late in the series of suggestions, falling to 1 again before the end of the session. He felt he was being hypnotized on the imagination day. "I felt that I wanted to respond. It was automatic to some extent, I wanted to in an automatic way . . ." The hypnotist noted some signs of trance, such as a "trance stare," psychomotor retardation, waxy flexibility.

Yet for Charles the actual induction was a much deeper and more involved experience. He gave the maximum state response of 3 throughout, and reported that it wasn't high enough for him. The effects of the induction were profound:

> I felt lethargic, my eyes going out of focus and wanting to close. My hands felt real light, sitting on thighs as though they were feathers . . . I felt I was sinking deeper into the chair . . . I felt like I wanted to relax more and more. I wished noises outside would stop so that I could concentrate more and more on the tack . . . Distractions were hateful . . . My knees seemed to get real big . . . heavy from knees down to feet. Momentarily I got real dizzy, ready to spin and pass out; mind started to spin, as though dragged under completely . . . unaware . . .

In comparing the two days he commented further:

> What they said on the two days was the same—the same routine, but the second day [hypnotic induction] my responses were more automatic. I didn't have to *wish* to do these things so much or *want* to do them . . . I just did them . . . I felt floating . . . very close to sleep . . . I didn't reflect at all on state reports before I reported . . .

These three cases represent but a few variants, but they help point out again that there is no uniform relationship between hypnotic state and response to suggestions. This does not invalidate the use of responsiveness to suggestions as an indicator of hypnotic state under some circumstances, but the relationship is by no means one-to-one, and the circumstances have to be specified before the inference can be made from responsiveness to state.

CONCLUSIONS REGARDING THE EFFECTS OF INDUCTION

Hypnotic induction furnishes the conditions for transition to the hypnotic state, which is characterized *only in part* by heightened suggestibility. The increase in suggestibility, while of moderate average amount, can be detected by appropriate experiments, from which it becomes evident that for some subjects the increase is very great indeed.

Case material supports the interpretation that regressive manifestations commonly appear in induction, but puzzling problems remain as to just what happens in induction and after the hypnotic state becomes established.

CHAPTER 3

The Aftereffects of Hypnosis

Because of the historical affiliations with the mysterious and the uncanny that hypnosis has, many people are uneasy about submitting to it. The fears take various forms: fear that submitting to the hypnotist will weaken the person's "will" and make him generally weak and submissive; fear that through repeated hypnosis he may fall into a trance spontaneously and be rendered helpless; fear that his unconscious wishes may be revealed, and that these will prove unacceptable or embarrassing to him; fear that he will act in a silly or stupid manner; and so on. When hypnosis is combined with psychotherapy there is the further fear (one shared by some psychiatrists) that symptomatic treatment may remove defenses and produce more serious (even psychotic) trouble. We wish here to examine some of the aftereffects of hypnosis in order to allay the fears of those who might otherwise offer themselves as subjects or who might wish to enter upon hypnosis as a field of scientific research were it not for some lingering uneasiness about the hazards involved. Most of what will be reported in this chapter came as a result of follow-up interviews with 220 nonpatient university students (114 males and 106 females), over two years, each of whom had at least two sessions of attempted hypnotic induction (Hilgard, Hilgard, and Newman, 1961).[1]

---

[1] Much of the substance of this chapter and the reported cases are taken from the earlier report (Hilgard, Hilgard, and Newman, 1961), and I wish to express my appreciation to my collaborators and to the editors and publishers of the *Journal of Nervous and Mental Disease* for permission to reproduce extensive sections of that report.

REPUTED HARMFUL EFFECTS

The fear of "weakening of the will" is probably the layman's greatest fear of hypnosis, while the dangers to mental health through ill-advised hypnotherapy are of most concern to professional workers. With respect to the former, the evidence is only that, with practice, a person tends to become more quickly hypnotizable, but there is no evidence that he is unable to continue to resist hypnosis if he wishes to. Some subjects do in fact tire of hypnosis, even though they earlier enjoyed it; if they do not wish to be hypnotized, they easily avoid making engagements for further hypnosis, or even become insusceptible when they do report for hypnosis. Thus repeated hypnosis does not make a person become "addicted" to hypnosis or make him fall unusually under the sway of the hypnotist. Of course there may develop a master–disciple relationship, or a "transference" similar to that which develops in other forms of continued psychotherapy; in such cases, however, we have to distinguish what belongs to the hypnosis and what belongs to the repeated social relationship between two people. There is nothing generally "weakening" as a result of hypnosis. The other question—of undesirable mental health effects through hypnosis or through attempted hypnotic treatment of symptoms—requires more discussion.

Before turning to our own data we wish to review some of the earlier findings concerning the unintended consequences of hypnosis. Possible dangers in the use of hypnosis, particularly when practiced by amateurs and by stage hypnotists, have been noted for a long time. For example, Schultz (1922), on the basis of a questionnaire study, uncovered 100 cases of health-damaging consequences of hypnosis, including such aftereffects as headaches, tremor, and more severe neurotic and psychotic symptoms.

Most of the reports more recently published have addressed themselves to the undesirable consequences, commonly called adverse "sequelae," of hypnotic therapy. Brenman and Gill (1947), reviewing pertinent studies, including that of Schultz, believed the dangers of hypnotherapy to have been exaggerated. They concluded:

> It would appear that in general the actual dangers of employing hypnosis are slight when the fundamentals of responsible interpersonal relationships are observed by the hypnotherapist; but there is a con-

traindication when the patient is on the verge of a psychosis [1947, p. 90].

Their later experience indicated marked success in symptom alleviation through direct suggestion:

> Our experience with this technique since our last summing up of its applications was largely restricted to soldiers complaining of circumscribed symptoms of recent origin. . . . Thus our records contain many examples of short periods of treatment of men in a veterans hospital (10 to 15 hours) where by direct suggestion various psychosomatic symptoms have disappeared [Gill and Brenman, 1959, p. 340].

They mention no undesirable sequelae. Unfortunately, no systematic studies or case reports on this material are available.

Those who have emphasized some disastrous consequences of hypnotherapy have usually cited cases of severely ill patients, often with symptoms of varied kind and of long duration, commonly (but by no means always) treated by incompetent therapists. The large number of successful cases without reported sequelae, and a few striking cases of damaging consequences, indicate that the present impressionistic summaries need to be supplemented by more precise definition of the total group of patients studied and the nature of the aftereffects that occur.

Some cases reported over the last few years are listed in Table 7; details about these cases are insufficient to show more than that some patients treated for their symptoms by hypnosis developed much more severe symptoms at a later time, whatever the ultimate course of their illnesses. Most of the cases had a fairly long history of illness, and the complaint that brought them to hypnosis was but one among many; this complaint was usually a form of psychosomatic symptom, and the most commonly reported severe symptoms that developed later were those of psychotic states. The presumption is that many of these patients would have revealed psychotic tendencies had careful histories been taken; symptom removal in patients on the verge of psychosis can deprive such patients of a major area of defense, and is ill-advised.

It may be noted that similar unfortunate results are reported for nonhypnotic therapies directed toward symptom removal. Thus Penman (1954) showed that new and occasionally severe symptoms can result when *tic douloureux* is treated by alcoholic injections in the ganglia to relieve the pain; Saul and Bernstein (1941) reported that

TABLE 7. REPORTED ADVERSE SEQUELAE TO SYMPTOM REMOVAL THROUGH HYPNOSIS (HILGARD, HILGARD, AND NEWMAN, 1961)

Subject	Original symptom relieved	Most severe later symptom [a]	Reported by
Female (38 years)	Neurodermatitis	Acute schizophrenia	Joseph et al. (1949)
Female (49 years)	Choreiform spasms and jerking movements	Many substituted symptoms, including nausea and vomiting	Seitz (1951)
Female (39 years)	Bulimia (weight. 325 lbs.)	Depressed and suicidal when most symptom-free	Seitz (1953)
Male (41 years)	Parkinsonian tremor following attempt to strangle boss	Murderous impulses when most symptom-free	Seitz (1953)
Male	Phantom-limb pain	Schizo-affective psychosis	Rosen (1953, 1960)
Male	Severe leg pain	Depressive reaction	Rosen (1959)
Male	Abdominal pain	Judged to be suicidal risk	Rosen (1959)
Male (41 years)	Fear of flying	Personality decompensation	Meldman (1960)
Female (30+ years)	Compulsive smoking	Overeating replaced by alcoholism	Rosen (1960)
Male	Back pain following laminectomy	Committed suicide a week later	Rosen (1960)
Female	Generalized pruritus	Sexual desire for and homicidal rage against lover who deserted her	Rosen (1960)
Adolescent male	Spasmodic torticollis	Overt homosexuality	Rosen (1960) Rosen and Bartemeier (1961)
Female	Obese; hypnotized for weight loss and delivery	Paranoid about physician who delivered her under uneventful hypnosis	Rosen and Bartemeier (1961)
Male	Numbness in one arm	Schizophrenic psychosis	Rosen and Bartemeier (1961)
Female (45 years)	Continuing back symptoms after injury	Paranoid psychosis	Teitel (1961)

[a] The most severe later symptom is not necessarily the final symptom; occasionally there was complete recovery, in other cases a return to the original symptom relieved the more serious pathology; for others, final outcome unreported.

chronic weeping was converted to urticaria by threatened hospital commitment, without hypnosis; Menninger (1948) described a patient in whom a successful gastrectomy for peptic ulcer was followed by suicide because the painful symptom could no longer mask a depressive tendency.

When therapy is involved along with hypnosis, the dynamics of the therapy are superimposed on the dynamics of the hypnosis, and there is no way short of further investigations to determine what to assign to the therapy and what to assign to the hypnosis. Careful studies are needed in which entire samples of subjects or patients are studied with the necessary controls to determine and to understand the effects that are attributable to hypnosis itself.

SEQUELAE WITHIN A NONPATIENT SAMPLE OF STUDENTS

The student sample studied at our laboratory consisted of a run-of-the-mill selection from students enrolled in the introductory psychology course at Stanford University. They served in the hypnotic experiments as part of the course requirement that called for participation in experimentation of various kinds for a given number of hours; while the subjects were not required to participate in hypnotic experiments and thus "volunteered," they did so under a kind of social pressure that produced a sample quite different from that produced by those who seek out hypnotic experiences for their novelty or who come for hypnotherapy.

This study departs from the hypnotherapy group of cases (Table 7) in two major ways. First, the experiments did not involve therapy. What belongs to hypnosis is therefore separated from what belongs to treatment of symptoms. Second, enduring posthypnotic suggestions were not made to the subject, as is usually the case in symptom removal. When sequelae do occur, therefore, they are not appearing in combination with (or as a consequence of) suggested posthypnotic phenomena.

All subjects had follow-up interviews within a day or two of the hypnotic induction; in addition, we invited all subjects to report back if there were aftereffects that they noticed later. When sequelae were reported, subjects were seen again in brief psychotherapy (usually nonhypnotic). Examples of comments by those whom we have classed as having disturbing sequelae include: "I was 'in a fog' for one hour." "Things were hazy and vague for four hours." Another subject continued to be drowsy, felt ill the night after the first induction, and returned the next day in a state of acute anxiety over continuing the experiments.

The cases who reported any aftereffects attributed to the hypnotic induction or the hypnotic experience are summarized in Table 8. The

TABLE 8. SEQUELAE TO HYPNOTIC INDUCTION AMONG 220 UNIVERSITY STUDENTS (HILGARD, HILGARD, AND NEWMAN, 1961)

Cases grouped according to susceptibility to hypnosis	Number of cases	Mean hypnotic score (SHSS, Forms A, B) (Max. = 12)	Disturbance intense for several hours or long continued	Transient headache after session	Dream attributed to experience[a]
More susceptible	7	10.0	3	2	3
Less susceptible	10	4.7	2	5	4
Total	17	6.9	5	7	7
Percent of sample ($N = 220$)	7.7		2.3	3.2	3.2

[a]No suggestions pertaining to dreams occurred in the hypnotic session.

17 cases located among the 220 represent 7.7 percent of the total; of these only five (2.3 percent of the total) had sequelae that were intense for a few hours, at most for several weeks; none persisted. No reaction was of psychotic intensity. The results in this student population support the view that although a routine experience of hypnosis is generally harmless, the experimenter (or therapist) should be alert for possible aftereffects. It should be noted again that our experiments did *not* involve treatment (hence no symptom removal), and no posthypnotic suggestions were given that were not removed before the subject left the hypnotic session. Thus, precautions were taken against sequelae, and yet some occurred.

It is of interest that the frequency of sequelae is similar for the more susceptible subjects and for the less susceptible ones. One interpretation is that the sequelae are produced by the maneuvers within induction, although for the more susceptible subjects other factors may be at work. In other words, the interaction with the hypnotist as an authority figure is one thing; the consequence of having hypnotic experiences is perhaps another.

On the whole, the mildness of the aftereffects of experimental hypnosis is encouraging. Further work with a total of over 1000 students has led to no disturbing effects that could not be readily handled. The conclusion is that such experimentation is not unduly hazardous; at the same time hypnosis should be carried on only by professionally competent people who are sensitive to the occasional untoward reaction and who are prepared to deal with such individual cases as may arise. The general harmlessness of hypnosis does not mean that it is something that should be treated lightly; it is an interpersonal relationship that involves intrusion into privacy and responsibility upon the part of the hypnotist to handle the relationship wisely and maturely.

DIFFICULTIES IN AROUSAL FROM HYPNOSIS AND THE PROLONGATION OF HYPNOTIC EFFECTS

There is often the expressed fear that one might enter the hypnotic state and be unable to come out of it. There is, of course, a transition from the hypnotic state to the waking state that has its own problems; dehypnotizing deserves consideration along with induction. The difficulties tend to be exaggerated in our folklore, but occasional problems arise, and the experienced hypnotist is prepared to handle them. We have had almost no difficulties whatever, except, as to be noted presently, some tendency for a prolongation of aspects of the experience after the trance has appeared to be terminated. It is reassuring to know that the problems of dehypnotizing have been faced and techniques are readily available to the hypnotist for handling difficult cases. These have been well delineated by Williams (1953) and by Weitzenhoffer (1957, pp. 224–29). The simplest method is to ask the subject who does not wake up why he does not, and he usually will tell why. Sometimes he tells through automatic writing. Usually a subject left to himself will spontaneously become dehypnotized in a short time.

Sometimes the subject, though partially aroused, does not seem fully in the normal state; in that case, rehypnotizing him and giving appropriate suggestions for full alertness will meet the problem. One of our subjects emerged from hypnosis with an inability to talk, but this symptom was easily removed by again hypnotizing him and by assuring him that he would be able to talk when aroused from the state.

This prolongation of the hypnosis, after the session is presumably ended, is one of the more important aftereffects of hypnosis. Two cases are illustrative:

Case 7. Margaret, whose later hallucinations reinstated the hypnosis suggestions. The fact that a suggestion has been given under hypnosis, responded to (or not responded to), and then removed prior to the termination of the hypnosis does not guarantee that there is no residue from this suggestion. Margaret was disturbed the night following hypnosis by the buzzing of a fly that she knew to be hallucinatory and by hearing someone call her name when no one was near. At the termination of the hypnosis her memory for all experiences had been reviewed; she had known that the fly hallucination was one of the tests, and that in another she had been supposed to hear someone calling her name. During the hypnotic session she had reacted to the fly and passed this test, but when she was interviewed the next day she had apparently repressed this experience, for she insisted she had not reacted at all to the fly. Near the end of the hypnotic session she had heard a voice calling her name when the hypnotist was counting for her to wake up: "It seemed silly to answer, so I didn't." Margaret had a need to please others and to fulfill their wishes. Her reaction to unfinished business: "I have a guilt feeling if I haven't done something I was supposed to do. . . . Something must happen if it's supposed to happen." At the same time she was very reality-oriented, and the hallucinatory items threw her into conflict: she reacted to the fly, but repressed the memory of having reacted so irrationally; she reacted reluctantly to hallucinating her name as being called and failed this test in the eyes of the hypnotist. Thus her conflict was over unfinished business, not over being able to fulfill the wishes of the hypnotist as to items that were ego-alien because of their degree of unreality. At one point, in describing her relations to teachers, she said, "At school, if a teacher told me to do something, I had to go home and do it." Is that essentially what she did that night in response to the commands of the hypnotist? Perseveration may occur in the midst of such compulsiveness. After this interview the subject was hypnotized again, this time by a senior staff member, and was told that she had fully completed the job, to her satisfaction and to ours. When seen later she had had no return of symptoms.

Case 8. *Barbara, who found herself growing smaller as she left hypnosis.* Barbara participated in the pretest of another scale that included an age-regression item. She failed to respond to the suggestion to regress within the hypnotic state but, returning home after the hypnotic session, she suddenly imagined that her body was shrinking in size. In an interview the next day she described it in the following terms: "I had an actual physical sensation of shrinking. It seemed odd that the objects around me stayed constant. The change in my size was so real that I thought the objects should change too." She had shrunk to about half her actual size, and she *felt* that somehow the angles of the roof and other objects around her should be viewed through the eyes of a small person; instead she was still looking at the objects around her from the angle of one who was tall. She found this shrinkage and incongruity an upsetting experience, tried to turn it off, and discovered that she could. Then she decided it had been so interesting she wondered if she could turn it on again. Trying, she immediately became half size. She alternated a few times. At the very end she became dizzy and felt some loss of equilibrium. The whole experience lasted about three minutes.

What thoughts preceded this episode? When she was asked this, she replied that, just before this experience occurred, she had been thinking of the hypnotist's question as she finished writing her name. She had been asked to write as though she were back in the second grade: "He asked me if I had become any smaller. I hadn't then, but maybe I did it later."

In this subject there was a conflict between being very responsible and being a carefree child again. At home, as the protected child of much older parents, she had been asked to do very little and much had been done for her. Good grades at school in a small community had come easily. At college, adjustment had been more difficult, and winning friends and making good grades took more effort. She was trying to make that effort and to be responsible. At the same time the wish to regress—that is, to return to the easier life of childhood—was a strong one. The defenses against such regression had been built up as she realized the necessity for being on her own.

In the overall regression demanded by hypnosis, Barbara responded in only moderate degree, scoring at the 50th centile for the test as a whole. We believe that the specific demand for age-regression touched her intense wish in a way she was unable to resist. Hence in her subsequent unconscious response to the hypnotist's asking her if she felt smaller, she relived briefly her wish to be a little girl again.

Barbara's experience represents both perseverative and redintegrative processes. The perseverative question (Do you feel smaller?) recurred because it had touched on a deep facet of the personality; what was redintegrated was not a specific experience but a way of life (being a child again).

The cases of drowsiness often reported after hypnosis may also indicate a prolongation of hypnosis. Thus in one case a young woman subject, who had participated in a public demonstration of hypnosis without showing much responsiveness, hallucinated the voice of the hypnotist in a troublesome manner as she drove her car home and slept on a davenport at home for three hours, missing her dinner.

These are unusual cases, yet the fact that they may occur alerts the hypnotist to care in assuring himself that his subject is wide awake and alert before leaving the hypnotic session.

THE SPONTANEOUS REINSTATEMENT OF EARLY TRAUMATIC EXPERIENCES

The hypnotic situation is apparently one in which memories or habits belonging to an earlier period of life are readily activated; this feature makes possible hypermnesia and age-regression, but it also may reactivate unpleasant or traumatic experiences that have undergone some sort of inhibition or repression.

We were led into one line of investigation by the report of one of our subjects, interviewed early in the course of our aftereffects study, who indicated that his headache experienced in attempted hypnotic induction reminded him of a headache he had had under chemical anesthesia as a child. This led us to inquire specifically about reactions to chemical anesthesia, as in the tonsillectomies so common within our population. Information was eventually available from 125 of our subjects, whose memories of an operation under chemical anesthesia were clear enough to be scorable. We rated their reactions on a five-point scale, and only those rated 5 (at the top of the scale) were considered to have had a discordant reaction to the anesthetic. By an unusual or discordant reaction we mean struggling, requiring an excessive amount of anesthetic, extremely disturbing headaches and nausea after coming out of the anesthetic. The extreme cases turned out to include 26 of the 125 subjects. The relationship to sequelae following hypnotic induction is indicated in Table 9. Of

TABLE 9. SEQUELAE TO HYPNOTIC INDUCTION AS RELATED TO CHILDHOOD EXPERIENCE WITH CHEMICAL ANESTHESIA (HILGARD, HILGARD, AND NEWMAN, 1961)

Discordant reaction to chemical anesthesia	Sequelae to hypnosis		Total cases
	None	Some	
High	16	10	26
Low or none	94	5	99
Total	110	15	125

$\chi^2 = 30.4; p > .001.$

the 26 cases reporting extreme reactions to chemical anesthesia as a child, ten (38 percent) reported some sequelae to hypnotic induction; of the 99 cases reporting more usual reactions to anesthesia as a child, five (5 percent) reported sequelae to hypnotic induction. Or, stated the other way around, 10 of 15, or two-thirds of those with hypnotic sequelae for whom the information on anesthesia was available, had had unusual reactions to anesthesia as children. By contrast, of the others with no sequelae, only one in seven had had discordant reactions to earlier anesthesia. This relationship, which is statistically significant, appears to deserve further study. It means to us, in terms of a theory of hypnosis, that the similarities between the psychological situation in hypnotic induction and the psychological situation in being anesthetized for surgery as a child bring the two experiences into communication, and reinstate the trauma of the first experience in the midst of attempted hypnotic induction.

Two cases illustrate this relationship between anesthesia and sequelae to hypnotic induction: [2]

Case 9. Joe, with three headaches in his life. The relationship between the sequelae and earlier anesthetic experiences first came to our attention in an interview with Joe two days after his hypnotic

[2] Another case (Case 2) has already been cited in Chapter 2, p. 27. More details on that case have been reported in Hilgard, Hilgard, and Newman, 1961, p. 468 f.

sessions. Joe reported: "I have had only three headaches in my life. Two of these followed operations, and the other followed the last time I was hypnotized." The first operation, at the age of six, was a tooth extraction for which he was given gas; the second, at the age of nine, was a tonsillectomy under ether. He reported that while on the operating table he could "still hear them counting at 50," and they gave him "three times as much ether as they had planned to." As he put it, "I wasn't struggling; I just wanted to watch." It is not surprising to learn that Joe was not a very susceptible hypnotic subject. He scored at the 28th centile on both days of attempted hypnosis, passing three of the 12 tests on each of the days, only those tests commonly passed on the basis of waking suggestion. After the first day of attempted hypnosis he felt groggy for 15 minutes. After the second day he (1) had a severe headache that, although it lasted only 45 minutes, was sharply penetrating between the temples, "like a needle stuck between them"; (2) felt extremely disorganized for three hours, and (3) was amnesic most of the day: "If someone asked my name, I'd have to stop and figure. . . . I couldn't even remember what was wrong with my car which was being repaired." These symptoms are interesting in terms of the last hypnotic instructions, one suggesting that he would be amnesic for his own name, and another suggesting that he be amnesic for the preceding tests. Joe passed neither of these tests at the time (that is, his memory was excellent).

In the course of the interview Joe was asked whether he could think of any reason why, after being so little hypnotized, he had such an extensive after-reaction. He was thoughtful: "I usually am in control. I wanted very much to be hypnotized enough that when there was no one forcing me I slipped into it. I have a notorious history: if anyone forces me, I *won't,* or I do the opposite. I would have liked to do the hypnotizing myself, with no one forcing me into it. . . . In childhood, I could produce a similar state in myself by concentrating. . . . I was an only child; we made many moves so that I often didn't have friends to play with. When I was alone, I'd experiment—I could think so hard that the noises outside would sound distant. I called it self-hypnosis. I also experimented with how I felt under drugs."

We see in this unusually lucid statement intense, conflicting motivation: a strong desire to experience hypnosis and an antipathy to force from outside authority. Joe later amplified his statements about his doing nothing, or doing the opposite when his parents told him to do something; even if he knew quite well that the opposite way was very bad for him, he would go ahead.

Let us turn now to a brief description of Joe's reactions to anesthesia. With the gas at age six he experienced disorganization, people spinning around, coming closer or going further away; afterward he had a headache for 24 hours. As already mentioned, he required three times the usual amount of ether for the tonsillectomy at age nine, and the severity of his subsequent symptoms may be related to this excessive dosage: "I felt really bad for two days. I felt the aftereffects of the anesthetic for three days more—upset stomach, headache, and couldn't see well." The year before hypnosis he had another anesthetic experience, this time with Pentothal Sodium in connection with oral surgery; after this he had no headache but slept for 24 hours.

When asked if he could think of reasons why his reaction to anesthesia and hypnosis might be similar, Joe replied that it was ". . . not wanting to lose control, my love of freedom." We suggest that this statement focuses the present conflict over the anesthesia. Is there also an element of redintegration? Does the submissiveness demanded by hypnosis remind him of the submissiveness demanded by the operations when he was a child? The fear and conflict, the marked reactions of headache and disorganization of those days were very likely reinstated by gross similarities between the two situations.

Joe's is essentially a struggle over induction ("to be or not to be hypnotized"), and his posthypnotic symptoms stem from this phase of the hypnotic process.

Case 10. Dorothy, with hysteroid symptoms as sequelae. Dorothy illustrates the spontaneous symptomatology which can ensue when motivation for hypnosis is high enough for it to take place in a subject who ordinarily does not relinquish control. The material suggests a relation to earlier anesthesia.

Dorothy showed marked symptoms issuing from her submission in the established state: complaints of hysteroid symptoms after hypnosis, including occasional dizziness and numbness in arms and legs when lying down.

As Dorothy participated in some of the advanced tests, the hypnotist noted that when he reached the count of 15, she reacted with nervousness. Afterward, in the interview, she showed confusion as to the counting that had actually been done. Asked later about operations, Dorothy replied that at age six she had had a tonsillectomy with ether as the anesthetic. When she was told that she should try to reach a count of 20 she tried very hard but "got to 15 or 16, went off and remembered nothing." This experience has recurred to her many times since, how she *tried* to reach 20 and got only as far as 15 or 16. She has been told that while under the anesthetic she kicked and reacted so violently she had to be held down. Her preparation for the tonsillectomy as a child involved no mention of the approaching anesthesia: she had waved goodbye gaily to her parents—then the advent of the ether took her completely by surprise.

One of the advanced tests was hand anesthesia. She said that, in hypnosis, "anesthetizing my hand was the most vivid of all the experiences." As the hypnotist was testing her hand with pins, she had the thought that anesthesia could "spread to my arm, other hand and arm, all over." Do we see here a generalization potential typical of ether anesthesia and not of what should have been circumscribed hand anesthesia? Dorothy, who had marked verbal facility, displayed her conflict over anesthesia in still another way: she asked the interviewer how to pronounce "anesthetize," saying that though she had used the word many times she always stumbled over it.

During the hysterical attack that followed hypnosis by a week or so, and that was in some ways related to it (but with other precipitating factors also operating), Dorothy said her major symptom was the feeling that her hands, arms, legs, and mouth were becoming numb and anesthetized. We see how these symptoms carry out the thought she had had when her hand was anesthetized in hypnosis. In the fact that she added her "mouth" to the list, do we see some reflection of the earlier operation for a tonsillectomy via the mouth and the ether mask that covered it?

This subject, coming from a home where individual freedom was emphasized and where correspondingly less emphasis was placed on discipline and conformity, had a childhood more like our less susceptible subjects than our more susceptible ones. Hypnosis threw her into conflict because she had to submit to authority to have the novel experiences she was always seeking. She submitted and scored above the 90th centile. In describing herself, Dorothy spontaneously mentioned how she liked to be in control of all situations: "I *hate* giving up leadership, the control . . ." When asked why, then, she let herself submit to the control of the hypnotist, she replied, "Curiosity. Intense curiosity about hypnosis. I wanted to *know*. In a process of thorough investigation, you experience it." This trait appeared in other situations—for example, if she was curious about mountain climbing she would see to it that she climbed the mountain even if it was dangerous and meant some risk to her life. She spoke of her will to do, the "I'm going to be hypnotized" attitude with which she came to hypnosis. At the time she didn't visualize the degree of loss of control: "Later I realized I didn't like it."

Dorothy idolized and idealized her father, who was a very able, forceful person; she both identified with him and was close to him. She was not interested in boys her own age—they could not "measure up." In such a setting of Oedipal attachment, hysterical symptomatology frequently takes place. The hypnotic situation, with its emphasis on the passive role and submission to a male hypnotist, mobilized sexual desires as well as defenses against them. Conflictual feelings over sex, as well as conflictual feelings over control, are reflected in the symptoms of numbness stemming from earlier experiences, including that of anesthesia.

The symptoms closely related to hypnosis were cleared through several psychotherapeutic sessions, so that there were no lingering effects of the experience with hypnosis.

The demonstrated relationship between early anesthesia and hypnosis is valuable because the traumatic event is well located in time and is frequent enough to permit quantitative study. Any other traumatic childhood event may in some cases be stumbled upon, with idiosyncratic results for hypnosis. For example, Turner (1960) reported the case of a forty-year-old secretary who participated in an experiment on hypothermia under hypnosis. When the suggestion was made that her body was becoming cold she had a heart pain and reacted violently to it, clutching at her heart. This appeared to be an anginal attack. She recalled how, as a child, she had been caught in a blizzard and had nearly frozen to death. The hypnotic suggestion of lower body temperature had reintegrated the feelings of this early experience.

A posthypnotic suggestion may also result in symptoms that develop when the posthypnotic suggestion becomes activated. One such case, described as a miniature psychotic storm, was reported by Brickner and Kubie (1936) as the accompaniment of a simple posthypnotic suggestion that was said to produce a superego conflict.

One of our college student subjects, a sophomore woman, when asked to dream under hypnosis had essentially a nightmare, and reported that she had dreamt again a troublesome dream that had often recurred in childhood but had ceased to trouble her. She was worried now lest this revived dream might haunt her at night again. A little psychotherapeutic interviewing placed the dream in the context of the events of her childhood, when it bothered her, and she was not again troubled by it, either at night or within hypnosis, to which she frequently submitted.

One young woman subject enjoyed playing with her dog while in age-regression. When she was asked to grow up and her dog was taken away she became very disturbed, because the dog had been killed a few months after the period to which she had been regressed; taking the dog away reinstated her grief. She later refused to accept regression instructions under hypnosis.

Sometimes, as in the psychotherapy of phobias, it is desirable to uncover early traumatic experiences. In such cases the availability of early memories under hypnosis is made use of, but the use of these memories for therapeutic purposes does not belong primarily to hypnosis as such. The problem is essentially the same as how to use memories uncovered through barbiturates, as in narcosynthesis. Our concern here is with the spontaneous appearance of personal material in an experimental setting, when it is not being sought, and where preparations for handling it may be minimal. These awkward cases are infrequent, but in experimenting with human beings in a situation where personal matters may arise, those responsible must be ready for them.

CONCLUSIONS REGARDING AFTEREFFECTS OF HYPNOSIS

The very infrequent and generally mild aftereffects of hypnosis in nonpatient populations are reassuring, and on the whole experiments can be conducted in the confidence that nothing alarming is likely to take place. While this is the general conclusion, it needs a few cautionary amendments. Hypnosis for many subjects is a highly charged personal experience that may communicate with traumatic experiences of early life and bring evidences of these earlier traumas into the hypnotic situation. Therefore the responsible investigator must be aware of the human interrelationships involved, even though his experimental topic is the experimental study of learning or the physiological concomitants of hypnotic responses. If he himself lacks training in psychotherapy, someone with such training ought to be available within the research team to meet the occasional (if rare) emergency.

Without exaggerating the dangers, there appears to be justification for discouraging amateur hypnosis and the use of hypnosis for entertainment purposes. Some tranquilizers, for example, are harmless enough that physicians prescribe them widely and repeatedly; at the same time this would not justify amateur experimentation with such drugs in uncontrolled quantities. So, too, with hypnosis; while generally harmless, it is something that ought to be kept in the hands of professionally trained and responsible hypnotists.

CHAPTER 4

Who Can Be
Hypnotized?

In considering the degree to which an individual enters into hypnosis and becomes involved in the experiences and behaviors characteristic of it, a distinction is sometimes made between *susceptibility* to hypnosis and *depth* of hypnosis. The nonsusceptible person is not able to achieve any appreciable depth of hypnosis whatever; the susceptible person is capable of an experience of some depth under appropriate circumstances. The most obvious reason for distinguishing between susceptibility and depth is that the person who is susceptible (capable of hypnosis) does not go around hypnotized all of the time. Susceptibility, defined as the ability to become hypnotized, to have the experiences characteristic of the hypnotized person, and to exhibit the kinds of behavior associated with it, may thus be a stable and enduring feature of individuality—before one has ever been hypnotized at all. In this chapter we shall not be concerned with the distinction between susceptibility and depth in view of their close relationship for measurement purposes. For assessment purposes we may define susceptibility as the depth achieved under standard conditions of induction, the more susceptible becoming more hypnotized than the less susceptible when common procedures of induction are followed. The earlier workers implied that susceptibility was measured by the *greatest* depth that could be reached, but in view of possibilities of modification of this limit under special circumstances, it is preferable to remain with the depth achieved under standard conditions. The earlier scales of hypnotic ability were commonly called "depth" scales but they did not differ essentially from those that are now called "susceptibility" scales. Most of these are direct measures of hypnotic behavior, that is, some kind of estimate of the depth of involvement shown after hypnotic induction has been attempted.

SUSCEPTIBILITY TO HYPNOSIS AS AN ABILITY

Hypnotic susceptibility can be considered to be an ability in which men differ, just as they differ in intelligence or athletic skill. Differences in ability must have some persistence in time in order to be measurable, but in order for an ability to be measured it need not be invariant over time. Thus the measurement of intelligence does not require "constancy of the IQ," and athletic ability may well change with training and good coaching but still be constant enough that the invitation to join a team for a season is extended to one man and not to another. Thus, as long as hypnotic susceptibility is not completely whimsical or kaleidoscopic, it becomes an empirical question whether or not it will be modified by repeated experiences of hypnosis, or by motivational change, or by the manipulation of other conditions.

In choosing to construct ability tests, various options are open to the test constructor. If he prefers to study *aptitude* (the capacity that exists prior to direct experience with the subject matter of the test) then he turns to more general experiences that may be related to his criterion. In the case of hypnosis this might be the study of various hypnoticlike experiences in ordinary life conceivably related to hypnosis. Attempts to prepare such tests for hypnosis have been rather unsuccessful, although as we shall see later (Chapters 13 to 15), some kinds of behavior outside hypnosis have been found to have low positive correlations with later hypnotic behavior. Another option is to provide an opportunity to experience the actual performances in question (that is, performances that are themselves part of the criterion) and to use these as representative of the wider aspects of the criterial behavior. Thus in some of the tests used in industrial psychology the worker is given an opportunity to do the kinds of things (for example, operate a lathe) that he is going to be called upon to do on the job. If this work-sample shows him competent, he is taken on. This option has proved the most successful for hypnosis, because the behavior following a very brief attempted induction (say, 10 minutes) is quite predictive of the wider range of hypnotic manifestations. Even this induction may be omitted, for, as we saw in Chapter

2, many suggestibility tests given in the waking state show a high correlation with the same tests used following hypnotic induction. That is why a stage hypnotist is able to choose his subjects from among those whose fingers readily remain locked, or whose eyes remain closed upon suggestion. Because the behaviors sampled are essentially of the same kind as those being predicted, it is preferable to think of these as falling within the work-sample category, rather than as aptitude tests as described above. The further option open to a tester is the *achievement* test, which is the established ability after appropriate opportunities to learn, such as a test in a foreign language after studying it. Perhaps a test of hypnotic responsiveness after considerable experience, and following the most appropriate trance deepening techniques, would yield such a measure for hypnosis. These options are listed merely to place the present susceptibility tests where they belong. The susceptibility tests to be described (whatever their names) are simply samples of hypnotic performance under standard conditions of induction and testing; wide individual differences are observed, and those who under these conditions behave more like hypnotized persons are the ones scored as most susceptible to hypnosis.

THE STABILITY OF HYPNOTIC SUSCEPTIBILITY

Whenever a human ability is subjected to measurement the question arises as to how stable that ability is, how enduring it is through time. The historical studies of the constancy of the IQ are addressed to this problem, and we face the same kind of problem concerning the stability of the ability to enter hypnosis and to respond to tests of hypnotic susceptibility. The evidence to be presented, based on retest reliabilities, shows that under standard conditions hypnotic susceptibility is a quite dependable trait, with retest correlations commonly lying in the 80's and 90's. As in the case of the IQ, which also shows such retest reliabilities, there is a good deal of room for individual variation, and the assertion of stability is not the whole story.

It is commonly assumed that hypnotic performance depends upon at least two underlying conditions, one a kind of basic and enduring hypnotic ability and the second a more readily modifiable attitudinal component. Thus the capacity to resist hypnosis on the part of a hypnotizable person is recognized; if this is the case, subjects may presumably show varying degrees of resistance, depending upon circumstances, and underestimates of potential hypnotizability may therefore result from testing under unfavorable circumstances. There is also the other side of the coin, that is, a capacity to simulate hypnotic performances, and test results may occasionally be contaminated by scores that indicate a higher hypnotic susceptibility than is actually present. On strictly logical grounds it would seem that an attempt to measure susceptibility is very precarious indeed, and some writers are strongly of this opinion (for example, Dorcus, 1963). In practice, the situation is not so bad, with most subjects being fully cooperative, as, indeed, they usually are on interest and personality tests, which are subject to the same possibilities of falsification.

Although it is commonly believed that hypnotic susceptibility is readily modified with practice, this belief may come about because of the greater speed with which the hypnotic state can be induced with practice, so that, for example, a signal set up in advance can be used to bring on the state at once. It would be entirely possible for hypnotic susceptibility to remain unchanged while speed of entering the state was reduced; thus a person unable to have positive hallucinations might remain unable to have them.

Studies addressed to this problem have led to somewhat contradictory results, and more evidence is needed. Shor, Orne, and O'Connell (1962) report little success in modifying susceptibility; the same is true of Gill and Brenman (1959). Wiseman and Reyher (1962) have reported a technique for using dreams to deepen the hypnotic trance. Their success was attested by the number of subjects who became completely amnesic following their method; after using the method, 70 percent of 30 subjects experienced complete amnesia as contrasted with 33 percent before the method was used. They point out that the method is more successful in developing complete amnesia among those who already experienced partial amnesia than in converting a totally nonamnesic subject into an amnesic one. Blum (1963, p. 137) reports choosing three subjects, one scoring low, one medium, and one high, on the Stanford Hypnotic Susceptibility Scale, Form A. After a dozen hours of training, both medium and low subjects were reported to have scored in the high range on the Stanford Hypnotic Susceptibility Scale, Form B. This is Blum's answer to the objection to using hypnosis in personality investigations because such investigations are limited to "good" subjects: if any subject can be converted to a usable subject this objection does not hold. Were his finding generalizable, it would show the limitation in any attempt to correlate persisting personality characteristics with hypnotizability. However, the results are too sparse to serve as acceptable refutation of wider experience of stability of hypnotic performance.

One study from our laboratory has been addressed to this problem (Ås, Hilgard, and Weitzenhoffer, 1963). Selecting subjects who scored in the middle ranges of the Stanford Hypnotic Susceptibility Scale, Form A, we attempted by the use of various techniques to modify hypnotizability. Considerable freedom was exercised, some of the time being spent in psychotherapeutic attitude discussions, some in building upon the achieved successes to obtain further gains, some in a variety of induction techniques, such as fractionation methods and induction-within-induction. Despite this freedom of methods, the three experienced hypnotists involved achieved only very slight gains as revealed by before-and-after tests of susceptibility with the two forms of the Stanford Profile Scales of Hypnotic Susceptibility. The main limitation of the study is that the repeated sessions numbered only 4 to 10, and a fuller test would perhaps require many more sessions. The general conclusion was that hypnotic susceptibility, as measured by the existing scales, is at least fairly stable, and little likely to change dramatically. This conclusion is, of course, contradictory to that of Blum and, to a lesser extent, to that of Wiseman and Reyher.

A cautious interpretation of the evidence would lead to the moderate conclusion that, without special intrusion, hypnotic susceptibility is reasonably stable; with intrusions of various kinds, with repeated inductions running upward of a dozen or so, some dramatic changes may occur, including loss of susceptibility as well as increase. Hypnotic scales do not rest for their usefulness on the persistence of a dead-level of susceptibility; they are equally useful in studying such fluctuations as may occur, and in specifying the amount of change from time to time.

NINETEENTH-CENTURY STUDIES OF INDIVIDUAL DIFFERENCES [1]

Although nineteenth-century hypnotists debated the question whether or not everyone was in principle hypnotizable, they recog-

---

[1] This section borrows heavily from the monograph by Hilgard and others (1961), and acknowledgment is hereby made to my collaborators and the editor and publisher of *Psychological Monographs* for permission to use that material here.

nized that the hypnotic state was characterized by degrees, and that subjects could be classified according to the degree of hypnosis that they were able to reach.

Braid (1843) characterized the true state of hypnotic sleep according to complete spontaneous amnesia for all events occurring during the trance, but he was troubled by finding that many of his patients were helped by his procedures even though they failed to meet his criterion. Charcot (1882) and his co-workers Richer (1885) and Gilles de la Tourette (1889) specified three kinds of hypnotic state (catalepsy, lethargy, and somnambulism). These were thought of as discrete, with sharp transitions between them. It was an easy further step, however, for writers such as Pitres (1891), influenced by Charcot, to add other borderline, mixed, and incomplete states (*états frustes*). The implication is still that of a mixture of states, rather than a true continuum, but once there are enough borderline conditions there is little distinction between a mixture and a continuum.

The analogy with sleep makes the notion of degrees of hypnosis,

TABLE 10. DEPTH OF HYPNOSIS ACCORDING TO LIÉBEAULT (1889) (HILGARD, WEITZENHOFFER, LANDES, AND MOORE, 1961)

I. Light sleep
  1. *Drowsiness.* Torpor, drowsiness, heaviness of the head, difficulty in opening the eyes.
  2. *Light sleep.* Above signs plus catalepsy, but with ability to modify the position of members if challenged.
  3. *Light sleep: deeper.* Numbness, catalepsy, automatism. The subject is no longer able to interfere with rotary automatism.[a]
  4. *Light sleep: intermediate.* In addition to catalepsy and rotary automatism, the subject can no longer attend to anything else but the hypnotist and has memory only for the interchange between them.
II. Deep or somnambulistic sleep
  5. *Ordinary somnambulistic sleep.* Total amnesia on waking. Can have hallucinations during sleep. Hallucinations vanish with waking. Subject submits to the will of the hypnotist.
  6. *Profound somnambulistic sleep.* Total amnesia on waking. Hypnotic and posthypnotic hallucinations possible. Complete submission to the hypnotist.

---

[a]Catalepsy refers to waxy flexibility, in which the arms remain where they are placed. Rotary automatism refers to the persistence of rotary movement of the hand and forearm, once set into motion by the hypnotist.

expressed as degrees of depth, a plausible one. This manner of thinking seems to have been first proposed by Richet (1884). He recognized that the induced somnambulism of the Mesmerists was the same as that produced by other methods, and he rejected the animal magnetism explanation. Three degrees that he recognized were: (1) *torpor,* in which the eyes close spontaneously and can be opened with great difficulty, if at all; (2) *excitation,* with total inability to open the eyes, unresponsiveness except to the hypnotist, some "automatism" and "double-consciousness"; (3) *stupor,* with previous phenomena in greater degree, spontaneity totally lacking, subject a complete automaton, "contractures" and "catalepsies" easily produced. There is usually amnesia in the second state, more complete amnesia in the third. Here we have the beginning of a depth scale.

Not long afterward, Liébeault (1889) proposed a six-point scale, and Bernheim (1888) a nine-point scale. These are summarized in Tables 10 and 11. Liébeault felt that his scale was undimensional in the sense used much later in Guttman-type scales; that is, that an individual who showed the symptom characteristic of one of his degrees of depth would always show all of the symptoms of lesser degree. Both scales emphasize spontaneous amnesia as a character-

TABLE 11. DEPTH OF HYPNOSIS ACCORDING TO BERNHEIM (1888) (HILGARD, WEITZENHOFFER, LANDES, AND MOORE, 1961)

I. Memory retained on waking

1st degree. Torpor, drowsiness, or various suggested sensations such as warmth, numbness.

2nd degree. Inability to open the eyes if challenged to do so.

3rd degree. Catalepsy suggested by the hypnotist and bound up with the passive condition of the subject, but may be counteracted by the subject.

4th degree. Catalepsy and rotary automatism that cannot be counteracted by the subject.

5th degree. Involuntary contractures and analgesia as suggested by the hypnotist.

6th degree. Automatic obedience; subject behaves like an automaton.

II. Amnesia on waking

7th degree. Amnesia on waking. No hallucinations.

8th degree. Able to experience hallucinations during sleep.

9th degree. Able to experience hallucinations during sleep and posthypnotically.

istic of the deeper stages. This is equally true for Bernheim, despite his theoretical position that all phenomena of hypnosis are the result of suggestion. Perhaps he interpreted amnesia as a natural accompaniment of other suggestions, although it was not itself suggested.

With the appearance of such scales it became meaningful to speak of the distribution of susceptibility according to the depth of hypnosis that could be reached. Many of those who worked with hypnosis were satisfied with simpler classifications of hypnotic states. A common three-point scale distinguished between "somnolence," "light sleep" or "hypotaxy," and "deep sleep" or "somnambulism." This classification was used by Forel, Loewenfeld, Fontan, Ségard, and Ringier. Others preferred a twofold classification, whereby individuals fell in Group I if only their motor behavior was affected, and into Group II if in addition they yielded also perceptual and ideational changes. Gurney, Delboeuf, Hirschlaft, and Dessoir preferred this scheme.

These nineteenth-century scales have enough in common to make possible some relevant comparisons among the findings of the various authorities. All, for example, give a good deal of weight to spontaneous ("nonsuggested") posthypnotic amnesia as a criterion of deep hypnosis. Other stages are usually described according to classes of events, rather than according to specific tests, so that there is an element of uncertainty about borderline states. Induction procedures were not standardized, except within master–disciple groups, and there was always a certain amount of accepted folklore. For example, it was assumed by many hypnotists that hallucinations were produced by a simple posturing of the subject, without verbal suggestions of hallucination. The word "suggestion" to one hypnotist might mean a verbal command, while to another it might mean a nonverbal suggestion produced by some sort of manipulation. Thus in comparing the distributions of susceptibility as reported by these early writers, one naturally must recognize large elements of uncertainty in making quantitative comparisons.

It comes as something of a surprise to find the very large numbers of subjects for whom records were kept and reported in the latter part of the nineteenth century. In Table 12 are digested the results from two major reviews (Loewenfeld, 1901; Schmidkunz, 1894), adding some cases reported a little later by Bramwell (1903). The 14 summarized distributions in this table are based on records from 19,534 patients—a very substantial number, even with allow-

TABLE 12. DISTRIBUTION OF SUSCEPTIBILITY TO HYPNOSIS: NINETEENTH-CENTURY STUDIES (HILGARD, WEITZENHOFFER, LANDES, AND MOORE, 1961)

Investigator	Source	Date	Age range	No. of sessions	No. of cases	Distribution of Susceptibility (in percent)			
						Refractory: non-susceptible	Drowsy-light	Hypotaxy-moderate	Somnambulistic-deep
1. Peronnet	a	ante 1900			467	25	10	20	45
2. Forel	a	ante 1898			275	17	23	37	23
3. Lloyd–Tuckey	a	ante 1900			220	14	49	28	9
4. Bramwell	b	ante 1900	4–76	Mean: 23	200	11	24	26	39
5. Von Schrenck-Notzing	a	ante 1900			240	12	17	42	29
6. Mosing	c	1889–93	a few children	Mean: 20–30	594	12	42	17	29
7. Hilger	a	ante 1900			351	6	20	42	32
8. Von Schrenck-Notzing (pooling of 15 reports)	a	1892			8,705	6	29	50	15
9. Liébeault	a	1884–89	7–63		2,654	5	22	62	11
10. Von Eeden and von Renterghem	a	1887–93			1,089	5	43	41	11
11. von Renterghem	a	ante 1900			414	4	52	33	11
12. Wetterstrand	a	1890		Failures, 1 or 2 trials	3,209	3	36	48	13
13. Velander	a	ante 1900			1,000	2	32	54	12
14. Vogt	a	ante 1900			116	0	2	13	85
Total cases					$N = 19,534$				
Range of percents						0–25	2–52	13–62	9–85
Mean of percents						9	29	36	26

[a] Loewenfeld (1901) [b] Bramwell (1903) [c] Schmidkunz (1894)

ance for some duplications in the reports. There are included only those reports which permitted classification (always with a margin of uncertainty) into refractory or nonsusceptible subjects and three degrees of susceptibility: drowsy-light, hypotaxy-moderate, and somnambulism-deep. Because the conditions of each investigation differed, the means of the investigations have been reported without respect to the variation in numbers of cases, thus using each report as one case in computing the means at the bottom of Table 12.

Recognizing the great variability in these figures, a rough summary would be that about a fourth of the subjects enter into only very light states, half are moderately susceptible, and perhaps a fourth can reach a somnambulistic state under favorable circumstances, although very highly susceptible subjects are more likely to be of the order of 10 percent.

EARLY QUANTITATIVE SUSCEPTIBILITY SCALES

The twentieth-century interest in hypnotic susceptibility scales began with the publication in 1930 of a scale by M. M. White (1930). He made use of specific responses to suggestions given in hypnosis as a means of arriving at scores and thus began a practice adopted by most of the later scales. Shortly thereafter the Davis and Husband (1931) scale appeared, which, while more detailed than White's and covering a wider range of depth, assigned scores on the basis of responses to classes of suggestions rather than to specific responses. At about the same time Barry, MacKinnon, and Murray (1931) proposed a scale based on a short list of specific suggestions. They placed much weight upon the subject's ability to have some suggested posthypnotic amnesia and upon suggested inhibition of response, that is, loss of ability to control certain types of movement, such as separating interlocked fingers. Although Hull (1933) did not develop a scale of susceptibility, he often used speed of eye closure upon suggestion as a measure of susceptibility. The well-known scale of Friedlander and Sarbin (1938) combines this emphasis upon eye closure with the kinds of items used in the Barry, MacKinnon, and Murray scale. The scale developed by Eysenck and Furneaux (1945) was similar in many respects to that of Friedlander and Sarbin, while the scales of LeCron and Bordeaux (1947) and of Watkins (1949) were more nearly variations of the Davis–Husband type of scale. Of these, the scale by LeCron and Bordeaux is the longest and covers

TABLE 13. DAVIS AND HUSBAND HYPNOTIC SUSCEPTIBILITY SCORING
SYSTEM WITH NORMATIVE DATA (DAVIS AND HUSBAND, 1931)

Depth	Score	Objective symptoms	Number of cases	Percent of cases
Insusceptible	0		5	9
Hypnoidal	2	Relaxation	16	29
	3	Fluttering of lids		
	4	Closing of eyes		
	5	Complete physical relaxation		
Light trance	6	Catalepsy of eyes	10	18
	7	Limb catalepsies		
	10	Rigid catalepsy		
	11	Anesthesia (glove)		
Medium trance	13	Partial amnesia	8	15
	15	Posthypnotic anesthesia		
	17	Personality changes		
	18	Simple posthypnotic suggestions		
	20	Kinesthetic delusions; complete amnesia		
Somnambulistic trance	21	Ability to open eyes without affecting trance	16	29
	23	Bizarre posthypnotic suggestions accepted		
	25	Complete somnambulism		
	26	Positive visual hallucinations, posthypnotic		
	27	Positive auditory hallucinations, posthypnotic		
	28	Systematized posthypnotic amnesias		
	29	Negative auditory hallucinations		
	30	Negative visual hallucinations; hyperesthesias		
Total			55	100

the largest variety of hypnotic phenomena. The most widely used of these scales have been those of Davis and Husband and of Friedlander and Sarbin, and these will be considered in more detail.

The Davis–Husband Scale. The scoring system of Davis and Husband is outlined in Table 13, along with their report of the distribution

TABLE 14. FRIEDLANDER–SARBIN SCALE WITH NORMATIVE DATA (FRIEDLANDER AND SARBIN, 1938)

Item	Scoring criteria	Score
1. Final lid closure	Depends on period of instructions during which eyes close.	0–5
2. Negative suggestion tests: (eye catalepsy, arm immobilization, arm rigidity, finger lock, verbal inhibition)	Resistance time for each item totaled, maximum of 10 seconds per item. Score is multiple of 10 seconds.	0–5
3. Posthypnotic voice hallucination	No prodding needed, 5; prodding needed, 3; no hallucination, 0.	0, 3, 5
4. Amnesia	No items recalled, 5 One item recalled, 4 Two items recalled, 3 Three items recalled, 2 Four to five recalled, 1 More than five recalled, 0	0–5
	Possible scores	0–20

Obtained scores	Cases	Percent
15–19	12	11
10–14	18	17
5–9	33	30
0–4	46	42
	109	100

of susceptibility among 55 university students. Although this scale has been fairly widely used as a kind of reference standard, the lack of specificity with respect to induction techniques and quantification of response make it unsatisfactory as a psychometric research instrument.

The Friedlander–Sarbin Scale. This scale is presented in Table 14 along with their original normative data.

Katkov's Stages of Depth. Katkov's scale, which appeared in a Russian version in 1941, has more recently been made available in the English version of Platonov (1959). In this nine degrees of depth are distinguished. The theoretical formulations and general categorizations are in terms of a Pavlovian physiology, with many references to "weakening of the tone of the cerebral cortex," "inhibition of the second signal system," "irradiation of inhibition," and the like, but the actual indices of behavior have a very familiar ring, indicating that hypnosis is much the same the world over. The indices for the greatest depth of hypnosis (third stage, third degree) are reproduced in Table 15.

TABLE 15. INDICES FOR GREATEST DEPTH OF HYPNOSIS ACCORDING TO KATKOV'S SCALE (PLATONOV, 1959, p. 428)

1. Positive and negative hallucinations of all types occur with the patient's eyes open.
2. Positive and negative hallucinations are effectuated posthypnotically.
3. Effectuation of "incongruous" posthypnotic suggestions is possible.
4. Total amnesia after awakening is experienced.
5. "Transformation" of age (transition to childish state) easily effectuated.
6. When patient opens his eyes they appear dull and moist.
7. It is possible to produce hypnosis with lightning speed.

There are no norms whatever and no indication of the kinds of observations that led to the scale. One of its more interesting features is the cyclical appearance assigned to some indices, so that, for example, suggestions of arm movement are said to be readily followed in the very lightest stage, not responded to in the fourth stage, present again in the sixth and (presumably) later stages. We shall have occasion in the next chapter (Chap. 5, p. 106) to discuss the cyclical aspects of arm catalepsy as proposed by Katkov.

TABLE 16. DISTRIBUTION OF SUSCEPTIBILITY TO HYPNOSIS: SOME TWENTIETH-CENTURY STUDIES (HILGARD, WEITZENHOFFER, LANDES, AND MOORE, 1961)

Investigators	Date	Scale	Subjects	Cases	Distribution of cases (in percent)[a]			
					Refractory; Nonsusceptible	Drowsy; light	Hypotaxy; moderate	Somnambulistic; deep
Barry, MacKinnon, and Murray	1931	own	college students	73	16	37	29	18
Davis and Husband	1931	own	college students	55	9	47	15	29
Friedlander and Sarbin	1938	own	college students	57	33	50	12	5
Eysenck and Furneaux	1945	own	neurotic patients	60	37	38	17	8
Weitzenhoffer	1956	b	college students	200	23	59	15	3
Hilgard, Weitzenhoffer, and Gough	1958	b	college students	74	3	51	30	16
Total cases				519				
Range of percentages					3–37	37–59	15–30	3–29
Mean of percentages					20	47	20	13

[a] The original data have been redistributed according to the most comparable categories.
[b] Friedlander-Sarbin Scale, as modified slightly by Weitzenhoffer (1956).

The *purposes* of Katkov's scale, as summarized by Platonov, are exactly those proposed for our own scales:

> The working scheme is interesting and has practical importance, particularly since it makes it possible to determine the degree of the subject's suggestibility, the extent to which suggested sleep [2] grows deeper in the subsequent sessions, the dependence of the efficacy of psychotherapy on the depth of suggested sleep, and lastly, it permits the use of a unified scheme to determine the depth of suggested sleep in all cases [Platonov, 1959, p. 425].

In order to compare the results that were obtained following the renewed interest in measuring hypnotic susceptibility, the distributions from a few representative studies have been converted in Table 16 to a scale similar to that of Table 12. The story that is told is not very different, although the typical findings are of a higher proportion of refractory subjects and a lower proportion of somnambulistic ones than in the nineteenth-century reports.

CURRENT HYPNOTIC SUSCEPTIBILITY SCALES

Owing to some dissatisfaction with the existing scales, particularly the skewed distributions resulting from their use, the lack of alternate forms, and somewhat inadequate norms, a number of investigators have recently set about constructing scales to serve many purposes, such as those summarized above by Platonov.

The Stanford Scales. Beginning in 1957, Weitzenhoffer and I, with a group of collaborators, undertook at Stanford University an extensive revision and expansion of the Friedlander–Sarbin type of scale, resulting finally in three series of published scales.

The Stanford Hypnotic Susceptibility Scales, Forms A and B, to be referred to hereafter as SHSS, Forms A and B, were the first ones published. Their norms were based on 124 university student subjects (Weitzenhoffer and Hilgard, 1959). SHSS, A and B, were essentially an expansion and refinement of the Friedlander–Sarbin scales, with similar inductions, many of the same items, a few easier ones, and a simplified scoring basis. The two forms, essentially equivalent, permit before-and-after studies.

---

[2] *Suggested sleep* is the expression used throughout Platonov's book as a synonym for hypnosis.

A third form, the Stanford Hypnotic Susceptibility Scale, Form C (SHSS, Form C), was added next, in order to meet some new specifications (Weitzenhoffer and Hilgard, 1962). It was published with norms from 203 university student subjects. While the induction procedures as published are similar to those for Forms A and B, they are optional, and induction is not scored. The remaining twelve items are listed in an ascending order of difficulty, based on pretests,[3] and shortened forms of administration are possible. The content of the items is somewhat richer than those in SHSS, A and B, with more cognitive-type material (hallucinations, dreams, age-regression), so that SHSS, C, has some advantages as a sampling of hypnotic behavior over Forms A and B.

Finally, the Stanford Profile Scales of Hypnotic Susceptibility, Forms I and II (SPS, Forms I and II), were prepared, tested, and published with norms on 112 student subjects (Weitzenhoffer and Hilgard, 1963; Hilgard, Lauer, and Morgan, 1963). Because this was to be an advanced scale, the normative group consisted of subjects who scored 4 or more on SHSS, Form A. Although this started out to be a scale of achieved depth by contrast with a susceptibility scale, it soon became apparent that what was needed was a scale diagnostic of the differential hypnotic abilities of moderately susceptible subjects. In plan, Forms I and II are equal-difficulty scales with a wide variety of content, leading to a profile of hypnotic abilities—that is, a chart indicating what kinds of experiences and behaviors the subject yields under hypnosis and what kinds he does not yield.

Recognizing the usefulness of keeping data comparable, investigators at Harvard, who had been at work on a group scale, decided to adapt the Stanford scale to their purposes, and a scale closely related to the Stanford one (Form A) was developed for use with children at the University of Illinois. These scales will now be characterized more fully.

Harvard Group Scale of Hypnotic Susceptibility (HGS). In order to introduce the economies of group administration, Shor and Emily

---

[3] The ordering of items was aided by experience with a 17-item scale (Weitzenhoffer and Sjoberg, 1961).

TABLE 17. ITEMS IN THE HARVARD GROUP SCALE OF HYPNOTIC SUSCEPTI-
BILITY (HGS) COMPARED WITH THOSE IN THE STANFORD HYPNOTIC SUS-
CEPTIBILITY SCALE (SHSS), FORM A

Stanford Scale Form A (SHSS)	Equivalent item in Harvard Group Scale (HGS)	Scoring criterion, Harvard Group Scale (HGS)
1. Postural sway	1. head falling	head falls forward at least 2 inches
2. Eye closure	2. same	eyelids closed before told to close them deliberately
3. Hand lowering	3. same	lowered at least 6 inches before told to let hand down deliberately
4. Arm immobilization	4. same	hand not lifted more than 1 inch when told to stop trying
5. Finger lock	5. same	fingers incompletely separated when told to stop trying
6. Arm rigidity	6. same	arm bent less than 2 inches before told to stop trying
7. Moving hands together	7. same	hands not more than 6 inches apart when told to return them to resting position
8. Verbal inhibition (name)	8. communication inhibition (headshake, "No")	did not shake head before told to stop trying
9. Fly hallucination	9. same	outward acknowledgment of effect
10. Eye catalepsy	10. same	eyes remained closed
11. Posthypnotic suggestion (changes chairs)	11. posthypnotic suggestion (touches ankle)	makes at least observable partial movement to touch ankle
12. Amnesia	12. same	3 or fewer items listed in 3 minutes, before amnesia lifted

C. Orne have developed a group adaptation of the Stanford Hypnotic Susceptibility Scale, Form A, arranged for self-scoring (Shor and Orne, 1962). It is thus possible to test a whole class for hypnotic susceptibility at a single sitting; this is useful for demonstration purposes as well as in the selection of subjects for further hypnotic experimentation.

The items are very similar to those of Form A, SHSS, as shown in Table 17. Several experiments have shown the high correspondence between the group form and the individual form of the test (for example, Shor and Orne, 1963; Bentler and Hilgard, 1963; Bentler and Roberts, 1963).

In using the procedure with a large group, it is usually desirable to have not only an experienced person conducting the session but also an experienced observer free to move about the room and handle individual matters as they arise. There are seldom problems, but occasionally a subject ceases to cooperate in the midst of the session and needs to be warned not to disturb others. Someone may fall asleep and no longer attend to instructions; this is relatively unimportant unless it becomes disturbing to others during the interrogation. Some subjects are slow to throw off the effects of the hypnotic experience. It is our practice at Stanford to offer the opportunity to discuss the experience afterward, in case any sequelae should arise, though care is taken not to suggest that there will be any aftereffects. The Form A content is so innocuous that few problems are likely to arise.

The comparability between self-scoring and observer-scoring has been studied in the case of both group and individual administration. It comes as something of a surprise that a subject can, in retrospect, score himself on 12 items essentially as the observing hypnotist scores him, but this is found to be the case, even when the subject is not informed in advance that he will be expected to do this (Bentler and Hilgard, 1963). Self-scoring tends to yield scores averaging a fraction of a point higher than observer-scoring (Shor and Orne, 1963), but self-scoring and observer-scoring correlate from .83 to .89 in different comparisons. It is not unreasonable that self-scoring should be a little higher: there are often genuine self-observed effects that do not quite meet the psychometric criteria when precise times or precise measures of movement are used. Some results are summarized in Table 18.

Self-scoring is necessary when subjects are tested in large groups. Even if the scoring proved adequate the group induction might pro-

TABLE 18. SCORES ON HARVARD GROUP SCALE (HGS) COMPARED WITH SCORES BASED ON INDIVIDUAL TESTING

	Group administration			Individual administration			
	N	Mean	SD		N	Mean	SD
Three samples compared: control sample, participating first in nonhypnotic experiment; individual sample of volunteers; group sample of volunteers[a]	152	7.41	3.04	Control	54	6.63	2.96
				Volunteer	115	8.68	2.64
Subjects tested in small groups, with both observer-scoring and self-scoring (omitting amnesia)							
Observer-scored	45	6.56	2.41				
Self-scored	45	6.71	2.43				
Subjects tested individually and scored as usual; then self-scored as a test of the adequacy of self-scoring[b]				Objective scoring	34	6.44	2.54
				Self-scoring	34	6.64	2.26
Subjects tested in large groups; some returned for individual testing							
Selected volunteers	19	10.11	1.45		19	9.16	2.21
Unselected "coerced" volunteers[c]	22	6.00	3.23		22	5.73	3.58

[a]Shor and Orne, 1963, supplemented by data supplied by D. N. O'Connell.
[b]Bentler and Hilgard, 1963.
[c]Bentler and Roberts, 1963.

TABLE 19. ITEMS, THE CHILDREN'S HYPNOTIC SUSCEPTIBILITY SCALE (CHSS) (LONDON, 1962a)[a]

| | Part I | | Part II |
Item	Minimum for plus score	Item	Minimum for plus score
1. Postural sway	Loses balance and recovers without falling	13. Posthypnotic suggestion (reinduction)	Closes eyes; eyes open but glazed
2. Eye closure	Eyes close within 10 seconds of final instruction before request to close eyes	14. Visual and auditory hallucination (television)	Sees TV set, turns it on; may fail to see picture clearly
3. Hand lowering	Hand moves through arc of 30 degrees or more	15. Cold hallucination	Appropriate verbal response
4. Arm immobilization	Hand rises from 1 inch to 3 inches, or with effortful movement, up to 4 inches	16. Anesthesia	May be aware of stimulus, but unable to describe it
5. Finger lock	Incomplete separation of fingers, little effort	17. Taste hallucination	Experiences at least slight or vague taste sensations
6. Arm rigidity	Arm bends less than 2 inches, with little effort	18. Smell hallucination (perfume)	Affirms odor of perfume
7. Hands together	Hands move to within 2 inches of each other	19. Visual hallucination (rabbit)	Sees rabbit, describes it; may not pick it up

TABLE 19 (Continued)

8. Verbal inhibition (name)	Name not spoken; little effort	20. Age regression	Changes writing of name or figure drawing appropriately
9. Auditory hallucination	Appropriate movement	21. Dream	Perfunctory report, but does not appear to be composing story during the report
10. Eye catalepsy	Eyes remain closed; little effort	22. Awakening and posthypnotic suggestion	Completes significant portion of suggested sequence, seeing rabbit posthypnotically
11. Posthypnotic suggestion (standing up, stretching)	Remains seated and stretches; or, stands but does not stretch		
12. Amnesia	Three or fewer items recalled with relative ease		

[a]The items and scoring standards of Parts I and II are alike for older and younger children, but the items are worded somewhat differently in the two forms.

duce changes significantly different from individual induction. This turns out not to be the case, and group results are quite comparable to individual ones. The most stringent comparison is that between self-scores on the group test and observer-scores on a subsequent individual test; the correlation for 45 subjects turns out to be $r = .74$ (Bentler and Hilgard, 1963). In general, this means that for three-fifths of the subjects self-scores on the group form will lie within one point of later objective scores by the hypnotist in an individual session, and over 90 percent will have scores falling within three points of each other on the two occasions.

The Children's Hypnotic Susceptibility Scale (CHSS). A scale designed especially for children, classified into two age categories (ages 5–0 through 12–11 and ages 13–0 through 16–11) has been prepared by London (1962a). Part I of the scale is very comparable to Form A of the Stanford Hypnotic Susceptibility Scale; it is a 12-item scale with items chosen to parallel those of SHSS, Form A, though adaptations have been made in order to ease the use with children. Part II consists of items that were originally part of the depth scale being tested at Stanford, most of which are now found in Form C or in Forms I and II of the Stanford Profile Scales.[4] Each item is presented as a 4-point scale (0–3), convertible to a ± scale by considering scores of 2–3 to be + and of 0–1 to be −. London believes that it is important to record qualitative observations along with the quantitative ones, and provision is made on the scoring forms for doing this. Actually, then, a series of scores are available, overt and subjective scores for both shorter and longer forms, and scores combining the overt and subjective scores.[5]

The items of the Children's Hypnotic Susceptibility Scale, with the minimum responses required for an objective score of 2 (that is, +), are given in Table 19.

It is said that the first part of the test (Part I) requires about 20 minutes of actual testing time. If a child has been generally unresponsive, it may not be desirable to go on to Part II. The remaining items of Part II require about 30 minutes to administer.

[4] Some of the items are from the 17-point scale described by Weitzenhoffer and Sjoberg (1961).

[5] In combining the scores, the overt score for each item (0–3) is *multiplied* by the subjective score for that item (1–3), so that overt scores are weighted much more heavily if confirmed by the subjective score. Details will have to await the appearance of the fuller account by London (1965b).

Some normative data by age groups are given in Table 20. These are the overt behavior scores on the 12-item Part I, with a maximum of 36 points (3 per item). The scores reach their maximum at ages 9–10, but drop off little until ages 15–16, when they approach adult levels. In this sample the sexes average exactly alike.

In reporting preliminary work on the scale, London (1962b) has correlated the overt behavior and the "subjective involvement" in hypnosis that accompanies these performances. The tendency for these

TABLE 20. NORMATIVE DATA BY AGE GROUPS, CHILDREN'S HYPNOTIC SUSCEPTIBILITY SCALE (CHSS), PART I (COURTESY OF PERRY LONDON)

Score	Age groups						Totals		
	5–6	7–8	9–10	11–12	13–14	15–16	Male	Female	Total
35–36	2	1	3	1	4	6	5	12	17
33–34	0	1	9	6	4	4	17	7	24
31–32	3	8	7	8	4	2	17	15	32
29–30	2	4	5	1	7	2	10	11	21
27–28	3	5	3	4	3	2	10	10	20
25–26	3	4	2	6	2	3	8	12	20
23–24	5	3	2	4	3	1	8	10	18
21–22	2	1	1	0	2	2	4	4	8
19–20	3	2	1	2	2	4	7	7	14
17–18	5	2	1	2	3	3	8	8	16
15–16	2	4	1	1	2	2	7	5	12
13–14	3	0	1	2	0	3	4	5	9
11–12	3	2	0	0	3	2	5	5	10
9–10	2	1	0	1	1	0	4	1	5
7–8	1	1	0	1	0	1	1	3	4
5–6	0	1	2	1	0	3	4	3	7
3–4	0	0	1	0	0	0	0	1	1
1–2	1	0	0	0	0	0	1	0	1
0	0	0	1	0	0	0	0	1	1
N	40	40	40	40	40	40	120	120	240
Mean	20.7	23.7	26.4	25.4	25.5	22.9	24.1	24.1	24.1
SD	8.0	7.8	9.5	7.8	7.7	9.5	8.6	8.6	8.6

TABLE 21. ITEMS OF THE BARBER SUGGESTIBILITY SCALE (BSS) (BARBER AND GLASS, 1962)

Item	Scoring criteria
0. Chevreul pendulum	Not scored
1. Arm lowering (eyes open)	1 point for 4 inches or more
2. Arm levitation from horizontally extended position (eyes open)	1 point for response of 4 inches or more
3. Hands locked in lap (eyes open)	½ point for incomplete separation after 5 seconds of effort, or 1 point for incomplete separation after 15 seconds of effort
4. Suggestion of extreme thirst (eyes closed)	½ point for swallowing, lip moistening, etc., and ½ point for indication, during posthypnotic interview, that subject became thirsty
5. Verbal inhibition (name) (eyes closed)	½ point if name not said after 5 seconds of effort, or 1 point if name not said after 15 seconds of effort
6. Body immobility (inability to stand up) (eyes closed)	½ point if not completely standing after 5 seconds of effort, or 1 point if not completely standing after 15 seconds of effort
7. Posthypnotic response (cough to a click) (suggested while eyes closed; tested with eyes open)	1 point if coughs to click
8. Selective amnesia (to remember all tests except arm moving up) (suggested while eyes closed; tested with eyes open)	1 point if recalls all other tests but Test 2 and recalls it in response to cue words

Total possible score: 8 points

two aspects to be highly correlated attests to the validity of the objective scores. Despite some of the difficulties in working with children, the hypnotic scores are satisfactorily reliable. A retest on the CHSS, using a plus–minus scoring of all 22 items with 30 children, yielded a reliability of .92.

The Barber Suggestibility Scale (BSS). A scale that has been extensively used by Barber and his associates (for example, Barber and Glass, 1962; Barber and Calverley, 1963b) differs from those previously discussed in that it is intended to test hypnoticlike be-

TABLE 22. ADULT NORMS ON THE BARBER SUGGESTIBILITY SCALE (BSS) BASED ON EIGHT DIRECT SUGGESTIONS WITHOUT PRIOR HYPNOTIC INDUCTION (BARBER AND GLASS, 1962)[a]

Level of suggestibility	Raw score	Number of subjects		Percent of subjects		Centile equivalent	T-score
High	8	12		2.6		99	72
	7.5	8		1.7		96	68
	7	16	102	3.5	22	94	65
	6.5	17		3.7		90	63
	6	26		5.6		86	60
	5.5	23		5.0		80	58
Medium	5	24		5.2		75	56
	4.5	28		6.1		70	55
	4	39		8.4		62	53
	3.5	27	231	5.8	50	55	51
	3	44		9.5		48	49
	2.5	31		6.7		40	47
	2	38		8.2		32	45
Low	1.5	25		5.4		25	43
	1	35	129	7.6	28	19	41
	0.5	25		5.4		12	38
	0	44		9.5		5	33
Total		462		100			
Mean	3.31						
SD	2.21						

[a]All subjects tested by Joan Burke at Regis College and Boston University.

haviors *without prior induction* of hypnosis. It can, of course, be used following induction, and has been used in that way to study the effects of induction procedures. The items of Barber's scale are given in Table 21, with their scoring standards summarized.

In calling attention to normative data on this scale, it must be noted that these data were gathered *without prior attempted induction of hypnosis.* The preliminary instructions, substituting for induction, were as follows:

> These are all tests of imagination. The better you can imagine and the harder you try, the more you'll respond. Try as hard as you can to concentrate, and to imagine the things I tell you to [Barber and Glass, 1962].

Data for 462 adults are given in Table 22, and data for 724 subjects, ages 6–22 in Table 23.

TABLE 23. RESPONSES OF VARIOUS AGE GROUPS TO THE BARBER SUGGESTIBILITY SCALE (BSS) WITHOUT PRIOR INDUCTION OF HYPNOSIS (BARBER AND CALVERLEY, 1963b, P. 593)

Age	Year in school	Number of subjects	Responses to eight test suggestions	
			Mean	SD
6–7	1–2	55	4.54	1.76
8	3	79	5.36	1.92
9	4	54	5.91	1.70
10	5	51	5.76	1.94
11	6	83	4.77	2.30
12	7	87	4.61	2.23
13	8	75	4.24	2.36
14–15	9–10	59	3.56	2.70
16–17	11–12	60	3.55	2.38
18–22	13–15	121	3.53	2.28
Total		724	4.50	2.35

It is important to know that a considerable fraction of the responses to suggestion that are associated with hypnosis can be obtained from susceptible subjects who have not gone through the usual induction procedures. While the percent passing each item tends to be less than following a usual hypnotic induction, some 14–15 percent of the subjects were found by Barber and Glass to pass even the items considered to be difficult, such as verbal inhibition and selective amnesia.

CONCLUDING REMARKS ON SUSCEPTIBILITY SCALES

The general success in achieving scales that have satisfactory reliabilities and face-validity permits them to be used for a number of purposes. The most direct result of the use of the scales is the yielding of distributions of susceptibility, so that we know about how many people are hypnotizable by standard criteria. By intercorrelating the individual items and treating the data by factor analysis, additional information is given about the nature of hypnotic abilities. The scores can then be used to study various parameters of susceptibility, such as age and sex differences, hypnotist effects, and so on. Investigators of psychotherapy with the aid of hypnosis find many uses for such scales.

Part II

What the Hypnotized Person Can Do and Experience

It is widely known that people can become rigid when hypnotized, or they can become insensitive to pain, or they can see things that are not there. What is not so widely known is whether or not these experiences can be had by people who are little hypnotizable, or whether the hypnotized person can do anything and everything that the hypnotist suggests. In the six chapters that comprise this section we examine the many things that the hypnotized person can do, how they are related to his degree of hypnotizability, and how experiencing one thing under hypnosis is related to experiencing another.

Part II

What the Hypnotized Person Can Do and Experience

CHAPTER 5

Control and Loss
of Control of Muscles

Suggested eye closure, arm movements, inability to move, and stiffness of the joints are among the most familiar manifestations of suggestions responded to within hypnosis. These follow the general principles of ideomotor action, that is, the principle that thinking about a movement tends to lead to that movement. William James had this to say about ideomotor action:

> We may then lay it down for certain that *every representation of a movement awakens in some degree the actual movement which is its object; and awakens it in a maximum degree whenever it is not kept from so doing by an antagonistc representation present simultaneously to the mind* [James, 1890, II, page 526].

In this, James followed Féré (1887), who based many of his conclusions on his own experiments with hypnosis. Thus the significance of hypnotic response in relation to ideomotor action was early recognized, and modern experiments on motor phenomena within hypnosis are in historical succession to these early beginnings.

PROBLEMS OF VOLUNTARY AND INVOLUNTARY ACTION

It is implicit in the hypnotic contract between hypnotist and subject that the suggested movements are to be made involuntarily. Thus when told that he cannot bend his arm, the subject must exert "voluntary" effort to bend it, and the stiffness must be "involuntary." If he merely keeps his arm stiff and does not try to bend it, he is not behaving like a hypnotized person. Although the voluntary–involuntary distinction implied here is very complex psychologically, the susceptible subject is not bothered by it.

One way of getting at the distinction is to examine more carefully the kinds of communications that the hypnotist gives to his subject. There are three main kinds of communications given with respect to movements (although there are many subtle variations and supplementations of these). The first may be called the ordinary instruction, the second, the direct suggestion, and the third, the inhibitory suggestion.

An *ordinary instruction* is given under hypnosis just as it is in the waking state, and it leads to a deliberate (voluntary) movement if the subject is cooperating. The hypnotist requests: "Please interlock your fingers." The subject does this within hypnosis as he does in the waking state, and there is no implication that he has relinquished any control to the hypnotist. The totally nonsusceptible subject usually responds to ordinary instructions just the same as the susceptible one. This, then, is merely cooperative social behavior, of the kind we expect from people acting courteously toward each other. When the ordinary instruction is enhanced by special pleading, and the subject is urged to do his utmost, it takes on some additional qualities, and may then produce differential effects between the susceptible and the nonsusceptible; in its ordinary form, however, it elicits the ordinary social responses expected in the waking state.

A *direct suggestion* is different. The hypnotist says: "Your hand and arm are light, and they are beginning to rise from your lap." This is not an invitation to raise the arm and hand, as it would be were this an ordinary instruction. If the subject raises his arm deliberately, as he would if told to raise his arm, he violates an understanding that the rise must be "involuntary." The *arm* must do the rising; *you* must not lift it. Most adults understand this readily, so that, for the susceptible subject, the arm slowly rises, and for the insusceptible subject the arm stays resting in his lap.

The third type of communication, the *inhibitory suggestion,* is usually made in a more complex three-step fashion, the hypnotist first suggesting an involuntary effect ("Your arm is getting stiff") and then proposing an inhibition of control ("You cannot bend it"), followed by a test of the inhibition ("Go ahead and try to bend it!").

Such a series of suggestions, involving in the end loss of volu
control, is sometimes called a *challenge* test, because it ends with
challenge to try to do what the hypnotist has said you cannot do.

With adult subjects it is usually not necessary to stress the difference between voluntary and involuntary action, because this distinction (at a common-sense level of understanding) is more or less implied by the hypnotic situation. However the standardized hypnotic
scales make provision for introducing the subject to the distinction;
the SHSS, Forms A and B, for example, use a postural sway test to
"teach" about ideomotor action and what it feels like to respond to
suggestions. Occasionally a subject is unable to tell the difference between responding to an ordinary instruction and responding to a suggestion; he believes that, if cooperative, he will do what he is told.
The hypnotist usually detects fairly promptly that the subject is not
behaving like a hypnotized subject and corrects any misunderstand-
ing that the subject may have. Even so, the problem of "being cooperative" is a very puzzling one and deserves more psychological
analysis than it has been given; many hypnotic subjects, particularly
those of moderate susceptibility, have an uncertainty about how much
they "helped out" the suggested movements, and most of them have
the feeling that they need not have done what they did, although in
"letting it happen" it seemed quite involuntary. With young children
the problem is more difficult, for they may "help out" without any
feeling of guilt; care is needed to communicate to them the difference between *trying to do* what is called for and *just letting it happen* (if it does) and *just letting it not happen* (if it doesn't). In view
of the theoretical difficulties inherent in trying to distinguish between
a cooperative response to an invitation to act voluntarily and a cooperative response to a suggestion to let some movement occur (if
it does), it is surprising that the difficulties are felt so little at the
practical level of hypnotic experimentation. This does not mean that
the difficulties are absent; some of the controversies in the hypnotic
literature arise over problems of control by the hypnotist (based on
the kinds of communications he makes, and the manner in which he
makes them), and self-control by the subject (varying between resistance and simulation).

This is not the place for such a theoretical digression, but the above
discussion is enough to indicate the possible relevance of hypnosis to
the study of a more general problem of social psychology, the dyadic

ween one in authority and one under him, and for
control of movement lying at the heart of the prob-
and planfulness.

TOR RESPONSES TO WAKING SUGGESTIONS

As indicated earlier (Chap. 2) a subject has to be somewhat responsive in the waking state in order to be influenced by hypnotic induction. We may well ask: What proportions of college students respond well enough within the induction period to be likely candidates for hypnosis? Data are available from all of the Stanford scales (SHSS, Forms A, B, and C; SPS, Forms I and II). A general summary of responsiveness within induction, presumably prior to the established hypnotic state (or in transition to it) is given in Table 24.

TABLE 24. RESPONSES TO DIRECT SUGGESTION PRIOR TO HYPNOSIS OR IN THE MIDST OF ATTEMPTED HYPNOTIC INDUCTION[a]

Item	Source	N	Percent responding on initial opportunity
Postural sway	SHSS, Forms A, B	124	69
Eye closure	SHSS, Forms A, B	124	58
Hand levitation	SPS, Form I	58	33
Hand lowering	SPS, Form II	61	85

[a]Postural sway and eye closure are from the standardization sample of Forms A and B; hand levitation and hand lowering are from a special sample in which SPS was administered to an unselected population of student subjects, thus including those who score 0–3 on SHSS, Form A, normally excluded from SPS. The responses on hand levitation and hand lowering are those whose hands reached the face or lap unaided; partial responses are not counted.

Except for the hand levitation form of induction, these are all relatively easy items, the hand-lowering induction being the easiest.[1]

Postural sway. What is called for is falling backward, to be caught by the hypnotist. This test, in various forms, has been a favorite with

[1] It was found necessary in SPS, Form II, in which a hand-lowering induction is used, to introduce "slowing" instructions, in order to allow time for induction. Such "slowing" instructions are occasionally used with hand levitation as well.

experimenters for a long time (for example, Hull, 1933; Berreman and Hilgard, 1936; Eysenck and Furneaux, 1945). If the subject is unable to fall through response to suggestion, in SHSS, Forms A and B, he is invited to permit himself to fall voluntarily, to see what it feels like to "let go." The item turns out to be rather diagnostic. A subject who steps back to break his fall, as though some part of him lacks confidence that he will be caught, almost invariably turns out to be a poor subject; the extreme form of this is inability to fall at all, even though trying to cooperate voluntarily.

Scored by us merely on an all-or-nothing basis, the response is quite consistent from one day to the next, the retest reliability, expressed as a tetrachoric correlation, being $r_t = .96$ ($N = 124$).

Eye closure. Closing of the eyes upon the suggestion that they will close (although a counter-instruction has been given to look steadily at a target) is commonly taken as a sign that the subject has entered hypnosis, and in the Friedlander–Sarbin scale, the earlier the eyes close the higher the score. In some of Hull's studies, eye closure was taken as the sufficient sign of entering hypnosis. As we score it, to pass the item the eyes must close before the end of a section of the induction instructions at which time the subject is invited to close his eyes voluntarily. He has failed the item if he must be told to close his eyes at this point. The retest reliability, as thus scored, was $r_t = .78$ ($N = 124$).[2]

Before rejecting the Friedlander–Sarbin type of scoring we made a study to see what kind of score would best correlate with other criteria of hypnotic susceptibility. The results are shown in Table 25. It can be seen that those who close their eyes early tend to score somewhat higher than those who close their eyes later, but the sharp change comes between those who close their eyes late and those who do not close their eyes at all to suggestion, and have to be instructed to close them. We therefore found it simplest to score this also on an all-or-none basis, scoring a pass for those who closed their eyes "involuntarily" and a failure for those who awaited instructions to close the eyes voluntarily. It is of interest that 10 percent of those who did not close their eyes through suggestion still ended up in the upper half of the distribution of susceptibility. It is evident that eye closure as a single indicator of susceptibility is not enough.

[2] In other samples reliabilities have been higher, for example, $r_t = .92$ ($N = 59$) in Table 26.

TABLE 25. HYPNOTIC SUSCEPTIBILITY OF THOSE WHO CLOSED THEIR EYES AT VARIOUS STAGES OF INDUCTION INSTRUCTIONS

Paragraph of induction in which eyes closed	(Total $N = 123$)	Percent in upper half of susceptibility as measured by total score minus eye closure	Mean SHS score, omitting eye closure (possible, 11)
I.	—	—	—
II.	3	33	7.33
III.	13	77	8.31
IV.	21	76	7.29
V.	16	56	6.56
VI.	19	58	6.00
Did not close eyes by suggestion	51	10	2.86

Hand levitation and hand lowering. Induction by hand levitation and hand lowering are useful methods for the practicing hypnotist because the rate and nature of the movements tell him something of what is happening. They were used in the profile scales (SPS) as a means of gaining additional information and to lend some variety to the induction techniques used when a subject was brought back repeatedly to the laboratory. The correlation between successful hand levitation and successful hand lowering, as used in the separate administrations of Forms I and II by different hypnotists, turned out to be $r_t = .75$ ($N = 59$).

Interrelations of induction techniques. Some subjects respond better to one induction technique than to another. We have intercorrelated the results for a sample of subjects who had an eye-closure induction on two occasions, and arm-movement inductions on two occasions. The design is imperfect in that the eye-closure inductions were on consecutive days, and the arm-movement inductions on consecutive days some weeks later. Hence there is a possible time-interval effect attenuating the correlations between the unlike inductions. The fact that all correlations are significant and positive indicates both that the various inductions have much in common, and that whatever is being measured has some persistence over time (Table 26).

TABLE 26. INTERCORRELATIONS (r_t) OF SEVERAL METHODS OF HYPNOTIC INDUCTION ($N = 59$)

	Eye closure II	Hand levitation	Hand lowering
Eye closure I	.92	.41	.50
Eye closure II		.54	.52
Hand levitation			.75
Hand lowering			

We thus find that a substantial proportion of subjects can respond to suggestion in the waking state, and that these responses can be made use of in the transition to the established hypnotic state.

MOTOR RESPONSES TO DIRECT SUGGESTION FOLLOWING ATTEMPTED HYPNOTIC INDUCTION

Once induction was over (the susceptible subjects now presumably being hypnotized, the others relatively uninfluenced), a number of additional opportunities were given to respond to direct motor suggestions. The ones that appear in SHSS, Forms A and B, are arm lowering (right and left arms) and arm movement, the outstretched hands moving together in one form and moving apart in the other. One nonverbal test was used during the standardization experiments, a test of passive arm catalepsy in which the forearm was raised from a resting position, so that the elbow remained on the arm of the chair. After the hypnotist released his grip, the item was considered "passed" if the hand remained up, and "failed" if it fell back to the arm of the chair. Because this test is used widely by practicing hypnotists, the relevant data are presented here, although the test was not ultimately included in our scales. Table 27 presents the intercorrelations of the direct suggestion items, based on the first experience with each item.

It is evident that hand lowering and moving hands have a great deal in common, but what they have in common is not shared with passive arm catalepsy. Had arm catalepsy correlated with other items indicative of hypnotic susceptibility, it would have been retained; its

TABLE 27. PASSING FREQUENCIES, RELIABILITIES, AND INTERCORRELATIONS OF DIRECT MOTOR SUGGESTION ITEMS FOLLOWING ATTEMPTED INDUCTION ($N = 124$)

| | Percent passing[a] | Retest reliability (r_t) | Intercorrelations (r_t) | |
			Moving hands	Arm catalepsy
Arm lowering	81	.78	.72	−.29
Moving hands	70	.72		.05
Passive arm catalepsy	52	.92		

[a]First attempt only.

correlations were universally so low, or even negative, that it was dropped. This calls for some discussion, which follows a few remarks on arm movements.

Arm lowering and moving hands. It is evident from Table 27 that these are items easily passed by our criteria. They are also among the easier items in waking suggestion; this follows, in fact, from the proportion passing them, for that high a proportion of subjects is not hypnotizable by any ordinary criteria of the hypnotic state.

What the scores do not show are some of the characteristics of the movements themselves. It is characteristic of the more susceptible subject to move his hands with a slow and somewhat jerky movement. The response may be rapid or extreme; for example, the hands may move apart until the arms are stretched out on either side of the body. The less susceptible subject often shows considerable delay before the arms start to move, or a movement is arrested after a very short distance. These quantitative aspects are of course subject to study; even without study the experienced hypnotist soon detects aspects of the movement related to an established trance state.

Passive arm catalepsy. Because of the prominence given to passive arm catalepsy in a number of treatments of hypnosis (beginning at least with Charcot) we were somewhat surprised to find this measure (itself highly reliable) so unrelated to the others that we were using. We entered into correspondence with Milton H. Erickson, who uses this device very successfully in his public demonstrations of hypnosis, to determine whether or not there were some practices that we had overlooked.[3] Although we modified our procedures to correspond with his suggestions, the same result was repeated: no correlation with other measures of hypnosis, including a more varied set of tests used in our profile scales. The percentages who passed the arm catalepsy item (arm stayed up when released) are shown in Table 28, with subjects grouped according to their susceptibility

TABLE 28. PASSIVE ARM CATALEPSY IN RELATION TO HYPNOTIC SUSCEPTIBILITY

Susceptibility score (minus arm catalepsy)	Number of cases	Arm remained up, percent
SHS (Forms A or B)[a]		
8 to 11	31	51.6
5 to 7	39	48.7
0 to 4	54	55.6
Total	124	52.0
SPS (Form I)[b]		
12 to 21	6	33.3
7 to 11	20	60.0
1 to 6	10	30.0
Total	36	47.0

[a]Based on first attempt. Some subjects had Form A first, others Form B.
[b]After modification of practice in lifting arm to correspond to Erickson's recommended procedure.

scores, before and after the instructions were modified according to Erickson's comments on our earlier instructions. It is evident that no correlation could arise from the data in these tables.

Several explanations are possible of our failure to find passive arm catalepsy indicative of hypnosis. In the first place, the expectations of subject and hypnotist may in fact be responsible for Erickson's success with it. This supposes that he in some way communicates to the subject that this is to be his test of hypnosis. Another explana-

[3] Grateful acknowledgment is made to Milton Erickson for clarifying the manner in which he uses arm catalepsy.

tion is that this test is subtly related to the depth of hypnosis, and has in fact a cyclical relation to depth. This is clearly the implication of the Russian scale developed by Katkov and quoted favorably by Platonov (1959). According to this scale, the arm drops flaccidly in the third of the nine degrees of hypnosis, becomes lightly cataleptic (slow fall) in the fourth, has waxy flexibility in the fifth, shows intermittent contraction (tetany) in the sixth, and catalepsy then disappears in the three deeper stages. We have a little hint of this cyclical appearance in our results with the profile scale (SPS, in Table 28), for the cataleptic response is more prominent in the middle group than at either extreme. Our subjects are too few to make this a firm finding, however; the lack of overall correlation is all that we have established.

It may be noted at this point that the only test we have rejected because of failure to correlate with the other items is this one. Hence a criticism that a common factor in hypnosis tests is created by our accepting only tests that correlate with each other is hardly pertinent when we found only one to reject. It is possible for tests to correlate very low with each other and still correlate with a common criterion, but that is not the case here. The passive arm catalepsy response, as we measured it, stood all alone and did not belong as a test of hypnosis.

I would not care to argue that failure of the arm catalepsy test was due to its being essentially a nonverbal test, while all others used words. It is quite possible, however, that its being *imbedded* in a strongly verbal test may have puzzled the subject and hence led to ambiguous response. This ambiguity could not have been great for the individual subject, however, for the high retest reliability over two days shows that the subject did not typically vary his response in order to find out what was expected.

THE INHIBITION OF VOLUNTARY CONTROL: CHALLENGE ITEMS

We have five items in the SHSS, Forms A and B, that reflect the inhibition of voluntary control: arm rigidity, arm immobilization, eye catalepsy, verbal inhibition, and finger lock. That these form a coherent "family" of items is evident from Table 29. They are all rather difficult, reliable, and interrelated.

These items are most representative of what is measured by SHSS, Forms A and B, and it is therefore of some interest to see if there

TABLE 29. PASSING FREQUENCIES, RELIABILITIES, AND INTERCORRELA-TIONS OF CHALLENGE ITEMS ($N = 124$)

	Percent passing[a]	Retest relia-bility (r_t)	Intercorrelations (r_t)			
			Finger lock	Eye cata-lepsy	Verbal inhi-bition	Arm immobi-lization
Arm rigidity	32	.88	.88	.75	.83	.77
Finger lock	32	.86		.74	.78	.60
Eye catalepsy	30	.95			.86	.74
Verbal inhibi-tion	23	.92				.78
Arm immobili-zation	14	.73				

[a]First attempt only.

is any additional evidence to support their validity as tests of hypnotic susceptibility. One such test is the amount of change brought about by hypnotic induction over what is achieved in waking suggestion. For this purpose we turn to some evidence from the earlier reported experiments concerned primarily with the problem of changes induced by hypnotic induction (Hilgard and Tart, 1966).[4]

We have usable evidence from two of the tests of direct suggestion (hand lowering, moving hands) and from two items of the challenge type (arm rigidity, arm immobilization). Shifts in percentage passing between waking conditions and hypnotic induction conditions are shown in Table 30. In all comparisons except one there was a statistically significant rise in the percentage of subjects responding between the waking (or imagination) conditions and the hypnotic induction conditions. The conjecture that the results would be found less significant for the easy items was not borne out in general, although the one nonsignificant gain was with the easy item (moving hands) in Experiment 2. Significant increases were found throughout for the challenge items. Thus motor items (including easy ones) are found suitable for including in tests of hypnotic susceptibility, if we adopt as one of the criteria that there should be an increase in the response as a result of induction. The minor exception of the mov-

[4] These are Experiments 1 and 2 described in Chapter 2, pp. 33–48.

TABLE 30. CHANGES IN RESPONSIVENESS TO DIRECT SUGGESTION MOTOR ITEMS AND TO CHALLENGE ITEMS FROM WAKING SUGGESTION TO SUGGESTION FOLLOWING ATTEMPTED HYPNOTIC INDUCTION

	Experiment 1 (Live)			Experiment 2 (Taped)		
	Waking suggestion $(N = 60)$[a]	Hypnotic induction		Waking suggestion $(N = 52)$[b]	Hypnotic induction	
	Percentage passing	*Percentage passing*	*p* of Diff.	*Percentage passing*	*Percentage passing*	*p* of Diff.
Direct suggestion items						
Arm lowering	63	92	.001	54	87	.001
Moving hands	50	92	.001	62	65	ns
Challenge items						
Arm rigidity	31	51	.01	13	42	.001
Arm immobilization	22	38	.05	15	29	.05

[a]Both waking and imagination instructions in waking condition.
[b]All subjects for whom imagination condition preceded hypnosis, including those hypnotized on a third day, after major experiment completed.

ing hands item seems unimportant, in view of the gain shown in Experiment 1 and the gain with the arm-lowering test which was similar.

The challenge items also permitted a test of the conception that subjects who are responsive fall into two types, the active and the passive. The active should struggle to overcome the rigidity of a stiffened arm by making visible effort; the passive should find it hard to make any effort at all. This classification was proposed by White (1937), and others have from time to time found the distinction useful (for example, Willey, 1951). In the case of arm rigidity we not only scored the maintenance of the rigidity for 10 seconds as the criterion of passing the test, but also recorded the amount of effort that seemed to be made in the attempt to bend the arm. Of 24 cases in the standardization sample in which the item was "passed" and appropriate notes recorded, 19 of the 24 struggled strongly, four showed some signs of effort, and only one remained entirely passive.

This did not encourage us to continue further with this classification. Perhaps this is not an appropriate test of the passive–active distinction; had we, for example, accepted the passive arm catalepsy item as an indication of passive hypnosis, we would have had another basis for sorting. However, the lack of relationship of such catalepsy to other criteria of hypnosis gave little justification for making use of it.

The high interrelatedness among the challenge items, their relative difficulty as indicated by the proportion of subjects who pass them, their satisfactory reliabilities, and their increase with induction make them useful for susceptibility scales. Their face validity, as reflecting loss of voluntary control, makes them representative of an important domain of hypnotic behavior.

FURTHER EVIDENCE ON DEGREE OF VOLUNTARY CONTROL WITHIN HYPNOSIS

Many subjects are in conflict about their performances within hypnosis. This arises out of the curious demands made upon them to be cooperative, to let happen whatever happens (thus to respond involuntarily), but not to help or hinder. Particularly in the challenge type of items, a large fraction of the subjects have the belief that they could have broken the inhibition had they tried hard enough; somehow they did not want to try, it did not seem worth the effort, or they felt some compulsion to use antagonistic muscles and prevent the arm bending (or lifting) to occur.

In order to test the validity cf this retrospective account of what they might have done, a few subjects were called in for a special experiment concerned with resisting suggestions (Hilgard, 1963). Previous experiments along these lines by Young (1927) and by Wells (1940) had led to contradictory results; all of Young's subjects were able to resist, but Wells's subjects, with minor exceptions, were unable to resist. Each of our subjects had passed a number of direct suggestion and challenge items in a prior hypnotic session, accepting suggestions and failing to break the suggested inhibition. It was now proposed to see if they could cancel the influence of suggestions if they set themselves to do it. The method was to hypnotize them again, requesting them to permit themselves to become hypnotized as before. They knew that they were going to be given six opportunities to respond to suggestions similar to those upon which they had been tested before, but they did not know just which ones they were to be or in what order they would come. They were told to indicate in the interval between test items by means of a telegraph key concealed from the sight of the hypnotist which upcoming item would be resisted; they were to choose any two of the six. After tests with these six were completed, the rest of the scale was administered as usual.

In an experiment of this kind the detailed instructions are very important. If it is clear that the hypnotist wants them to bend their arms, they can do so, as in fact they always do in the experiment when he releases them from their inhibition. If he wants to prove that hypnosis is effective, and that they cannot really resist, then it is the old challenge experiment over again. This is troublesome, and later experiments will have to grade suggestions along some kind of continuum to see just how effective different kinds of communications are, but even within the limitations of this experiment what would happen was not predictable, so that the obtained results are instructive. The background for the experiment was explained to the subject as follows:

> This experiment is concerned with the degree of initiative and control that a subject retains within hypnosis. Although you will be hypnotized as you were before, it may be that you will be able to make some decisions affecting what you do, *even* in the midst of hypnosis. We do not know whether or not you will be able to do this; whether or not you can is what we are trying to find out.

Note that great care was taken to make clear the fact that we were trying to find answers to our questions. We did not indicate our presuppositions. There was a slight indication that it would be difficult to do these things, but the subject knew that already because he was unable to control his responses in his earlier experiences of hypnosis.

The experiment was so arranged that the instructions were given to the subject by a professional assistant (not the hypnotist) so that the hypnotist did not hear the conversation that went on. It was felt to be important that the subject be assured that the hypnotist had no stake in trying to force his compliance, hence the instructions continued:

> The purposes of the experiment require that you make some decisions without letting the hypnotist know what you are doing. Some of these will involve resisting his suggestions. The hypnotist knows that this is

part of the design of the experiment, so that you need have no qualms about it.

After a few explanations about the arrangements of keys for concealed reporting, the final detailed instructions were:

> We would like you to try to resist on *two* of the trials, going along on the rest. It does not matter which two you choose, except that we would rather not have you choose two in a row. In other words, after you have resisted once, wait at least a time or two before resisting again. Otherwise do whatever occurs to you to do within hypnosis. Do not make your plan in advance, other than to remember that you are to resist twice.

Every subject understood and followed the instructions and indicated appropriately through the concealed mechanism when he was about to resist; on that trial he made the appropriate effort. I served as hypnotist throughout; not having hypnotized any of the subjects on their earlier trials, we had built up no special relationship.

The induction procedures and the testing procedures were those of SHSS, Form B. It should be noted that the scale is quite permissive, and the temptation to strengthen the suggestions was avoided in keeping with the purposes of the experiment. The experiment was not designed to see how powerful a control a hypnotist might conceivably exert, but to determine the nature and extent of the subject's capacity to resist *in a setting in which he does not normally resist*. These subjects had all failed to resist on the items that they were here trying to resist; some believed they could resist, others not. The introduction to the first suggestion in Form B, after the subject's eyes are closed, contains the sentences: "Perhaps you will not experience everything I tell you about. That will be all right." In the context of the special instructions that the subject received before induction, this is further permission to resist.

The results may be summarized as follows:

1. All 12 subjects permitted themselves to become hypnotized and, apart from the items specifically resisted, showed hypnotic responsiveness essentially equivalent to that shown previously. That is, the attempted resistance on two items did not reduce responsiveness to the remaining items.

2. The extent to which the decision to resist neutralized suggestions varied. It might be supposed that, once the decision to resist was made, the hypnotist's suggestions would be ineffective. This was

generally *not* the case. Only one subject of the 12 was able to con-
tradict both suggestions when intending to resist, so that resistance
required no effort, two other subjects "broke the spell" for one item,
but not for the other, and the remaining nine subjects (three-fourths
of the group) reported the suggestions effective so that great effort
was needed to counteract them. That is, when the arm was said to
be heavy it became heavy, and the problem in resisting was then to
lift this heavy arm; when the arm was said to be rigid, it felt rigid,
and became most difficult to bend, even though it might eventually
be bent. As one subject put it ". . . there was a force pulling my
hands apart. I felt like there was an actual force there, and I was
fighting it. . . . I had to concentrate on fighting it."

3. By marshaling effort most subjects had some success in counter-
acting the suggestions even though the original suggestion (stiffness,
etc.) was effective. Only one of the subjects was unable to succeed
on either of the items chosen for resistance, and five of them failed
to resist on one selected item but succeeded on the other. Thus half
of the subjects showed sufficient inability to resist that they scored
a "pass" by standard criteria on at least one of the two items chosen
for resistance. The other six subjects, often by making very great
effort, overcame the suggestions sufficiently to be successful in their
resistance of both items.

In general, among these moderately hypnotizable subjects, in a
relatively permissive situation, the impression was that the difficulties in resisting were decidedly greater than the subject's beliefs about
his capacities to resist.

We tried to find out by subsequent questioning what techniques
the subjects had used in trying to resist. Reports of this kind, like
the retrospective accounts of the secrets of success of self-made men,
are always a little ambiguous, but the methods by which subjects
thought they had resisted fell into four chief categories:

1. Sheer effort or determination overcame the obstacles to response
(two subjects).

2. The thought helped that a cooperative subject would serve the
purposes of the experiment if he made the effort to resist (three subjects).

3. Autosuggestions were used to counter the hypnotist's suggestions (three subjects).

4. Deliberate inattention to the suggestions of the hypnotist weakened their effect (two subjects).

These four reasons accounted for the methods adopted by 10 of the 12 subjects. The other two reported as follows: "I was not surprised to be able to resist," and (the subject unable to resist either item) ". . . it takes a lot of effort . . . it seems you don't really want to . . . I was angry at myself that I was unable to resist."

As pointed out earlier in this chapter (pp. 97–100), the communications in hypnosis are very complex, and in an experiment of this kind they are even more complex than usual, for the subject is asked (1) to become hypnotized, (2) to respond as a hypnotized person when once hypnotized, and (3) to resist responding like a hypnotized person on some occasions. The instructions were, in fact, highly conflictual for some subjects. Several complained that they did not want to resist, it spoiled all the fun of hypnosis, it was like insisting that a child do something he does not want to do. When the resistance period was over (the second resisted item now a thing of the past), and the hypnosis proceeding as usual, there was uniform relief that this great effort was no longer called for. There were many behavioral evidences of conflict during attempted resistance: hands alternately being pulled apart and brought back together in resisting the moving hands suggestion; fingerlock broken but clonus in the forearms when the hands were separated; violent expressions of anger or disappointment. It is not at all surprising that under some circumstances the subject will prefer not to resist at all.

THE FACILITATION OF VOLUNTARY RESPONSE

One kind of communication is not represented in the foregoing accounts. The positive responses called for thus far have been involuntary responses to direct suggestions; voluntary response was either inhibited (as in the challenge items) or set in conflict with suggestions. Another possibility is to *enhance* voluntary responses by combining them with suggestions.

There is an old problem in this, whether or not under hypnosis one can transcend normal capacity and produce responses beyond those that can be made in the waking state. In motor responses this would be a matter of precision, strength, speed, or endurance. The literature is very confusing. Most of the recent studies have shown that with a high order of task motivation, responses can be made in the motivated waking state equivalent to those within hypnosis.

For example, using motor performances, London and Fuhrer (1961), Slotnick and London (1965), and Levitt and Brady (1964) all found no superiority for performance under hypnosis as compared with waking performance. In experiments somewhat more naturalistic, using athletic-type performances with athletes under controlled laboratory conditions, Johnson, Massey, and Kramer (1960) and Johnson and Kramer (1961) found no gains under hypnosis or under posthypnotic suggestion for strength, power, and endurance tests.

These laboratory results run counter to the beliefs of many practicing hypnotists, and counter to some quite well-established clinical observations. For example, Kelsey and Barron (1958) report the three-week maintenance of an awkward posture without discomfort by a patient undergoing plastic surgery, this performance being made possible by hypnosis.

There are major difficulties in doing definitive experiments in this area, chiefly because of the puzzling relationship between hypnosis and task motivation. That is, in comparing waking and hypnotic performances it is necessary to deal with achievement motivation, optimum tension, inhibitory factors such as anxiety and lack of self-confidence, and with the comparability of these aspects inside and outside hypnosis. It cannot be assumed that hypnosis is itself a highly motivated state leading to effortful action merely because there is a tendency for the subject to please the hypnotist, for many of the hypnotist's suggestions are followed reluctantly because of the subject's preference for not making very much effort under hypnosis. Thus in the experiments of Schulman and London (1963a), in which verbal performances in hypnosis were poor, the subjects in the hypnotic state were rather groggy, a condition unfavorable to rote memorization. A related rote memorization experiment in this laboratory is being conducted under the traditional hypnotic instructions emphasizing drowsiness and sleepiness and alternatively under equally effective hypnotic instructions stressing concentration and alertness. The results to date show a statistically significant gain in performance within the alert hypnotic state over the passive hypnotic state, though it is not yet clear that this performance will exceed that of an alert waking state (Liebert, Rubin, and Hilgard, 1965).

Another puzzling variable has been introduced into experiments on performance because of the reported differences between the non-hypnotizable control subjects and the hypnotizable experimental subjects prior to attempted hypnotic induction. Thus London and Fuhrer (1961) found nonhypnotizable subjects to perform better than hypnotizable ones on some motor learning tasks before hypnosis; although such prehypnosis differences favored the hypnotizable subjects in a later study by Rosenhan and London (1963b) the two studies agreed in finding greater learning improvement under attempted hypnosis for the *nonhypnotizable* subjects. Thus the general relaxation of the hypnotic induction procedures may facilitate learning more among those who do not drift into the hypnotic state than among those who do.[5]

In related studies, not depending on differences between susceptible and nonsusceptible subjects, Scharf and Zamansky (1963) and Zamansky, Scharf, and Brightbill (1964) have shown that word-recognition thresholds can be reduced under hypnosis, but this is an artifact of the *raising* of the thresholds prior to hypnosis by those who know that they are later to be hypnotized. While the authors interpret their results to mean that the subjects "held back" in some manner in the waking state in order to permit their improvement under hypnosis, an alternative hypothesis is that the expectation of hypnosis in some way aroused anxiety in the waking state with elevation of thresholds. Whatever the explanation, a serious problem of experimental control is involved.

Slotnick and London (1965), working in our laboratory, found an interaction between the hypnotic state and motivating instructions. While under traditionally induced hypnosis alone, subjects performed less well than in the waking state; when "exhortation" was added to hypnosis, the hypnotic subjects made greater gains as a consequence of exhortation than the waking subjects did as a consequence of adding exhortation to their instructions.

Because all manner of instructions can be used in hypnotic experiments, there is little point in picking some new form of instruction

---

[5] These experiments point to the importance of knowing how susceptible a patient has to be in order to profit from hypnotherapy. It has been known since Bernheim (1888) that very light stages suffice for suggestive therapy. Platonov (1959, page 426) refers to psychotherapy by the Bekhterev–Bernheim method in which only the very lightest of Katkov's nine degrees of depth is involved (patient awake and at rest with eyes closed) when suggestions are given.

at random and then seeing what happens. Telling a subject he is a member of a control group, for example, is comparable to telling him not to let himself become hypnotized, and he does in fact make poorer scores than if he is told in a comparable setting that he is a member of a hypnotic group (Barber and Calverley, 1964d). By now we have a great many such experiments leading to consonant conclusions. For experiments on motor performance the preferred present tactic is to see if an upper limit or asymptote can be reached by increasing the motivation; the question then becomes whether this asymptote is higher inside hypnosis than outside it.

Although we do not believe that we have yet approached an asymptote, the main features of such an experiment have been approximated in an experiment from this laboratory (Slotnick, Liebert, and Hilgard, 1965), built upon the earlier Slotnick–London experiment. To the "exhortation instructions" were added another set of instructions which we have called "involving instructions."

The exhortation instructions were essentially those used by London and Fuhrer (1961) and Slotnick and London (1965). Some excerpts are given here for illustrative purposes:

> . . . Psychologists have learned that most people tend to underestimate their own capacities. This is especially true of women asked to perform muscular tasks. [Note: All subjects were women.] . . . before we start I am going to tell you some things that will help you to discover the real extent of your abilities. . . . I wonder if you are really acquainted with the fact that really desiring and striving to do something helps one to overcome any difficulties that may ordinarily be in the way of doing it . . . in order to perform at your maximum you must imagine what it is like to do the task to the best of your ability and that, thinking this, you will actually begin to feel stronger, steadier, and more capable, enabling you actually to perform at your best. . . .

While these instructions are fairly strong and yielded distinct gains in endurance in muscular tasks we decided to go a step further by adding to these the "involving instructions" that follow:

> Today you will think of yourself as stronger and more capable and you will actually become stronger and have greater endurance. You will have an unusually strong desire to do well. You will do extremely well. In a moment I am going to count from one to ten, and as I count you will actually begin to feel yourself becoming stronger and stronger. Your desire to be stronger and to do well will increase with each number that I say. One . . . you are getting

stronger . . . two . . . three . . . your desire to do well is increasing . . . four . . . you can feel your entire body becoming stronger and stronger . . . five . . . six . . . seven . . . stronger and stronger . . . eight . . . a greater and greater desire to do well . . . nine . . . ten.

Can you feel that you have additional strength and endurance because of your great desire to do well? (Wait for "Yes.") Now I want you to repeat after me: "I can feel that I am very strong. . . . I want very much to be strong . . . so that I can perform physical tasks well . . . my concentration has made me very strong." (Insist upon repetition by subject.)

It will be noted that there is quite a shift in flavor between the exhortation instructions and the involving instructions. The exhortation instructions have the quality that Gill and Brenman (1959, p. 10) call rational magic, that is, to try to give good reasons for improved performances on the basis of what psychologists have found, while the involving instructions use what they call irrational magic, based on direct suggestions emphasizing the power of hypnosis, without appeal to evidence or reason.

The results were striking, and reach statistical significance even with but six subjects in the comparison groups (Table 31). The groups were made essentially alike on the first day under hypnotic induction and exhortation, all subjects having been selected as highly hypnotizable, and having been assigned to the groups through matching of their performances on the first day. Because of the wide individual variability exact matching was not possible, but the mean differences on the first day are not significant.

On the second day, involvement instructions were added to exhortation instructions, but under hypnosis for Group I and in the waking state for Group II. All subjects gained substantially as a consequence of the involvement instructions; note that this means that *in the waking state,* too, all subjects did better than they had *within hypnosis* under exhortation instructions. The power of the involvement instructions is thus evident. However, and this is the point of the experiment, the interaction with hypnosis is such that the involvement instructions produced significantly greater gains within hypnosis than within the waking state. If we think of the hypnotic mean as approaching an asymptote, it is at a mean value of 173.7 seconds; if the waking-state mean is taken as near its asymptote it is at 121.0 seconds. Thus within these roughly equated groups, the hypnotized

TABLE 31. EXHORTATION AND INVOLVING INSTRUCTIONS IN RELATION TO
PERFORMANCE IN HYPNOTIC AND WAKING STATES (SLOTNICK, LIEBERT,
AND HILGARD, 1965)

	Weight-lifting endurance in seconds	
	Group I (N = 6)	Group II (N = 6)
	Hypnotic induction under exhortation	*Hypnotic induction under exhortation*
Mean	106.3	94.2
SD	48.7	36.4
	Hypnotic induction under exhortation and involvement	*Waking state under exhortation and involvement*
Mean	173.7	121.0
SD	28.6	33.8
Mean gain	+67.3	+26.8
SD	27.3	10.5
t	5.53	5.73
p	< .01	< .01
Difference between group mean gains	40.5	
SD	27.0	
t	3.36	
p	< .02	

subjects hold the weight up for nearly three minutes, half again as
long as the waking subjects who hold it up for two minutes. These
performances, for women subjects, despite known sex differences, are
equivalent to the performances of exhorted male subjects in an experiment by Rosenhan and London (1963a). Although no one experiment can settle the question, it now becomes more plausible that
at the asymptote highly motivated performances under hypnosis may
exceed those in the motivated waking state.

CONCLUSIONS ON MOTOR RESPONSIVENESS

Although responses to direct suggestion motor items are easy and
can be given by a high proportion of subjects within waking sugges-

tion, they still help to characterize the hypnotizable person. The fact that they can be given in the waking state makes them useful in the transition to the hypnotic state that takes place in hypnotic induction. The challenge-type item, testing the inhibition of voluntary motor control, is more difficult than direct suggestion, and hence is representative of a greater degree of hypnotic susceptibility, whether tested in the waking or in the hypnotic state. The hypnotist who uses such items (for example, finger lock) in selecting subjects for hypnotic experiments or demonstrations receives ample justification within our findings. As we shall see later, however, there are aspects of hypnotic behavior little related to these motor effects.

The problems of voluntary and involuntary control of behavior, including both inhibition and facilitation of movement, are brought to the fore by the study of the effects upon these responses within hypnosis of variations in communications and in motivation generally. Elucidation of the psychophysiological and psychosocial issues implicit in these responses will ultimately make an important contribution to our knowledge of human behavior.

CHAPTER 6

The Reduction of Pain
and the Production of Hallucinations

In the previous chapter we considered motor phenomena in response to suggestion; now we are prepared to look at sensory effects. One reason Charcot thought he detected a similarity between hypnosis and hysteria was that the responses within hypnosis often showed the kinds of motor and sensory disturbances that he saw in hysteria. The classical hysterical patient often had an arm that was paralyzed, and the same arm was commonly anesthetic. Stanley Lindley and I once treated such a patient whose "dead arm" was dead in both these respects and had to be treated in both respects before the symptoms disappeared and the arm could again be used normally.[1] We now know, contradicting Charcot, that it does not require an hysterical personality to become hypnotized; yet many susceptible subjects readily reproduce the symptoms of hysteria through suggestion under hypnosis.

THRESHOLDS, ILLUSIONS, AND HALLUCINATIONS

Among the sensory effects that have interested students of hypnosis are changes in sensory thresholds, both hyperesthesia (increased sensitivity) and anesthesia or analgesia (decreased sensitivity generally, or especially to pain), positive hallucinations (things perceived as if influencing the senses in the absence of appropriate stimuli), and negative hallucinations (things not perceived, although adequate

[1] The case is described briefly in Hilgard and Marquis (1940, p. 297 f.)

environmental stimuli are reaching the sense organs). Before considering such evidence as we have regarding these effects, there are a few distinctions requiring discussion.

What is meant by a change in threshold is clear enough from the standard psychophysical experiments that have been part of pyschology ever since it emerged as a scientific discipline. A raised threshold (decreased sensitivity) means a kind of blunting of the detection processes, such as might occur under a local anesthetic, or in the presence of distraction (noise). If a threshold is raised within hypnosis, then more intense stimuli should be detected, while less intense ones go unnoticed. Very often the sensory defect within hypnosis is not organized in quite this way; for example, instead of developing a hearing defect that makes him sensitive only to louder sounds, the subject is often made selectively deaf, so that he hears the voice of the hypnotist clearly but does not hear other voices or other sounds in the experimental room. This classifies as a negative auditory hallucination rather than as a threshold change. These distortions (thresholds and negative hallucinations) have something in common, yet the possibility exists that their physiology and their consequences in other respects differ in significant ways.

The distinction between an illusion and an hallucination is also not a sharp one. An illusion results when a stimulus pattern is misinterpreted, for example, when in a hall of mirrors in an amusement park one does not distinguish between an open corridor and a piece of silvered glass. Nobody would call this an hallucination, for the stimuli are arranged so as to be difficult to interpret realistically. A full-fledged hallucination appears when there is nothing out there at all, as when one sees a dog in the corner of an empty room. In extreme cases there is no problem of definition, but there are many transitional situations. If there are a coat and hat hanging appropriately on a hall-tree, an illusion that there is someone standing there is understandable, but suppose there is merely a shadow on the wall cast by the hall-tree. If that is seen as a person is it an hallucination? The main point is that hallucinations, although they may be triggered by stimuli, add so much content that one is not inclined to interpret them according to input from the stimulus, but instead according to contributions from the subject. Hypnotists have worked with both illusions and hallucinations, but the distortions suggested are usually classifiable as hallucinatory, even if some stimulus supports are provided. Thus when a subject is given a stick and told that he is holding a bouquet of flowers this is classified as a positive hallucination because so much sensory content is added beyond what the stimulus provides.

Our own work on threshold changes as such is very limited, although we will have something to say about the effects of stimulus intensity on efforts to block out the perception of electric shocks and odors. We have sampled fairly widely various positive and negative hallucinations.

ANESTHESIA AND ANALGESIA

Anesthesia refers to general reduction in sensitivity, while analgesia refers specifically to reduction in experienced pain. The suggestions that we have used have not distinguished sharply between these, for our purposes in this instance were not to be analytical about the specific kinds of insensitivity produced, but rather to study the individual differences in the ability to show effects in the general area of reduced sensitivity to stimulation of various kinds. We have used as one representative of these areas suggested anosmia to household ammonia (and, in some samples, to acetic acid). Both of these are pungent odors, with a painful component, so that the test is perhaps one of analgesia as well as anesthesia, but to pass it the subject must not only fail to be annoyed by it, he must fail to recognize the odorous substance presented.[2] The other test that we have used is an electric shock administered to the hand; this is a test of analgesia, for many subjects whom we scored as "passing" felt "something" but it was not painful and not recognized as shock.

The general level of responding, and some intercorrelations, are presented in Table 32. While tetrachoric correlations in samples of this size are quite unstable, the intercorrelations are close to reliability estimates for these items, so that it appears that essentially similar psychological processes are involved in the blunted reactions to ammonia, acetic acid, and shock.

Anosmia. While there may be some ambiguity about exactly what is measured in the olfactory insensitivity tests, in view of the pungent and painful components in the odors we used (Brady and Levitt,

---

[2] It would burden the text too much to discuss various part-scores used from time to time. Hence scoring will refer to the standards of the published scales unless otherwise indicated.

TABLE 32.   SUSCEPTIBILITY TO ANESTHESIA–ANALGESIA

Test item		Percentage passing[a]	Anosmia–acetic acid	Analgesia–shock
Anosmia to	SPS, Form I	35 ($N = 60$)		.52 ($N = 60$)
ammonia	Form C	20 ($N = 35$)[b]	.50 ($N = 35$)	
Anosmia to				
acetic acid	Form C'	28 ($N = 35$)		Not available

[a] Two samples are involved. The one ($N = 60$) is the SPS, Form I whole-population sample; the other ($N = 35$) consists of hypnosis-hypnosis subjects from the study by Hilgard and Tart (1966) who had ammonia on one day and acetic acid on the next.

[b] The reported sample is that used in comparison with acetic acid. In the standardization sample for Form C the percent passing was 19 ($N = 203$); thus the two samples agree.

1964), our scoring was on the basis of inability to detect and identify the odor and not giving any overt reactions to its painfulness.

The question raised earlier as to whether or not this kind of insensitivity shows ordinary elevated threshold properties or whether, perhaps, it is more an off–on effect relatively independent of stimulus intensity is answered by the data plotted in Figure 3. It is evident that there are some of the properties of elevated thresholds, in that some subjects who were anosmic at the lower concentrations began to detect the ammonia when the concentration was increased. It should be pointed out that these concentrations are far above the levels at which the waking subject can detect ammonia; this was not a threshold experiment in the ordinary sense. The increasing order was used in all cases; this, if anything, should have anesthetized the nasal membranes, making it more difficult to detect the higher intensities. We do not consider this to be a refined psychophysical experiment, but it suffices to show that the reduced sensitivity can in fact be studied in relation to stimulus intensity and will result in orderly relationships.

The acetic acid was used as an alternative to ammonia in Form C' in only one concentration, judged to be roughly equivalent in pungency to the concentration of ammonia being used. That we were reasonably successful in the choice of concentration is indicated in Table 32, which shows that 7 of 35 subjects were anosmic to ammonia at that concentration, and 10 of 35 were anosmic to acetic acid at that concentration.[3]

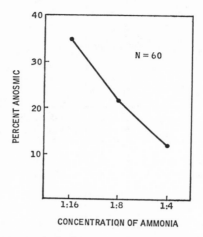

FIGURE 3. DECREASING ANOSMIA WITH INCREASING CONCENTRATION OF AMMONIA. The concentration refers to parts of U.S.P. 27 percent stronger ammonia diluted with distilled water as shown.

Analgesia to shock. We may ask the question also about analgesia as a function of shock intensity. The shocks were given as single brief pulses, unpleasant to most subjects at all levels, and so annoying and painful at the highest level as to be scarcely tolerated in the waking state. The resulting curve of decreasing percentages of subjects who remained insensitive as the shock increased is very similar to that for anosmia to ammonia (Figure 4).

By being insensitive to shock we mean that the subject, while he may have felt "something," did not feel pain, and did not identify the "something" as shock. In this situation the number who feel nothing at all is very few indeed; in this sample of 60 subjects there were only two who felt nothing at all during the suggested anesthesia–analgesia, although an additional seven felt no pain and did not recognize the stimulation as shock, even at the highest intensity. The hypnotic reduction of pain is one of the best-established findings

[3] The acetic acid was used at a concentration of one part of glacial acetic acid to one part water.

within hypnosis, as attested by experiences of anesthesia suitable for major surgery, childbirth (including Caesarean section), the relief of pain of burns, and the relief of pain in terminal cancer. It is at the same time one of the most controversial, as far as the experimental literature is concerned. The controversy centers primarily over the physiological correlates of the pain reduction, *not* over the relief that

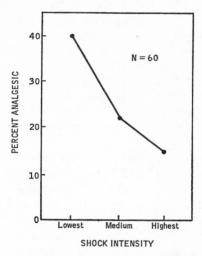

FIGURE 4. DECREASING ANALGESIA WITH INCREASING SHOCK. The shock intensities are graded from a barely perceptible shock at the lowest level to one that most subjects find quite painful in the waking state. For calibration data, see Hilgard, Lauer, and Morgan, 1963, pp. 71–75.

the subject feels as his subjective experience of pain disappears or is greatly attenuated. Another problem, as with all hypnotic phenomena, is the extent to which the pain reduction can be brought about by direct suggestion, without hypnotic induction.

Before turning to the critical problems of physiological correlates and of analgesia produced through waking suggestion, a word or two should be said about spontaneous anesthesia or analgesia appearing within hypnosis. In our experiments we suggest specifically that the hand will become insensitive to pain, but this is not the only way in which anesthesia can be brought about. Another method is to produce a kind of dissociation, so that the arm (or other bodily member, or even the whole body) is interpreted as being somewhere other than where it is. Normally painful stimulation of the sensitive area where it is interpreted not to be tends not to be reacted to. For example, let a highly susceptible subject under hypnosis hold up his forearm, the elbow resting on the arm of the chair or a table. Now the hypnotist proposes to move the hand and arm into the subject's lap, and the subject hallucinates the movement, although the hand remains suspended in the air. The subject now folds his other hand over the hallucinated hand in his lap, so that he feels comfortably sure that both hands are in his lap. *At this stage the hand suspended in the air will often prove to be anesthetic,* although nothing whatever has been said about anesthesia or analgesia.[4] A related method, which I first saw demonstrated by Charles Tart in our laboratory, is to produce a posthypnotic suggestion of an absent arm. A young woman subject found the fact of a missing arm more amusing than annoying after she was aroused from hypnosis, but she paid no attention whatever when the arm that "was not there" was quite severely pinched, and reported that she felt nothing. The method has indeed been used to produce analgesia for childbirth, the woman in confinement being given the hallucination (delusion?) that she is sitting in a chair across the room, watching the baby being delivered from someone else. The method is reported to be quite successful with expectant mothers who are sufficiently hypnotizable.

A susceptible subject is able to produce anesthesia through autosuggestion. An interesting account of a tooth extraction upon a prominent medical hypnotist, Ainslie Meares, done by a reputable dental surgeon who does not use hypnosis in his practice, has appeared in a medical journal (McCay, 1963).

The dental surgeon gives the details of the operation, which included incision of the gums, then the bone over the third molar was removed with a bone chisel, exposing the roots of the tooth near the apices, after which the tooth was removed by forceps. His patient, who is in fact normally sensitive to pain, showed no signs of pain or discomfort whatever, and in preparing the report for publication he asked the patient to write down his subjective impressions. Meares (the patient) has published widely on therapy, has been president of the International Society for Clinical and Experimental Hypnosis, and his integrity is beyond question. He writes, in part:

---

[4] I first witnessed this demonstration by Milton Erickson in the living room of my home, and am grateful to him for calling it to my attention. I have since repeated it myself with other subjects.

. . . When I sat in the dental chair I explained that when I let my arm fall in my lap I would be ready; and I explained that if I raised my arm during the procedure it would be a signal to stop dental work and allow me to regain my relaxation. In retrospect I realize that the thought of raising my arm to halt the dental work never once occurred to me. I was aware all the time as to what was going on; but the awareness was rather vague. When I realized that the bone was being chiselled and that I was not experiencing any pain, for the moment I felt myself becoming angry, as I thought that I must have been given an injection without my knowing it. I then realized that I would not be deceived in this way, and my momentary anger passed off. During the actual extraction I was aware of what was happening and experienced some sensation in that area. This sensation might possibly be described as pain without the hurt of it. There was practically no bleeding. There was not a spot of blood on my handkerchief when I returned home. After the extraction I was surprised at the completeness of the anesthesia, and the thought came to me that I might experience some after-effects. However, I had no after-pain at all. When I arrived home I remember trying to assess my mood, and I decided that I was neither elated nor depressed, but quite normal in my mood and comfortable in myself; and in fact I took my family to dinner at a restaurant and spent the evening at the theatre with no discomfort in my mouth whatsoever.

With this background, it is surprising on what uncertain ground the scientific aspects of hypnotic anesthesia rest. Shor (1962a) finds the earlier studies unconvincing about physiological correlates, and when he tried an experiment of his own he found that the usually studied physiological correlates of pain practically disappeared in both the waking and the hypnotic states when the experimental conditions were such as to minimize anxiety (Shor, 1962b).

About the same time, Barber and Hahn (1962) found no significant difference in the degree of analgesia experienced among two groups of suggestible subjects, each subject in one group having analgesia suggested in the waking state, using imagination instructions to distract attention from the pain of keeping a hand in ice water for 3 minutes, while each subject of the other group was hypnotized and given analgesic instructions. Both physiological and subjective measures were included.

The failure of Barber and Hahn to find differences in analgesia between a waking-imagination condition and a hypnotic condition is inconclusive on at least two grounds. First, the subjects were selected on the basis of their high responsiveness to waking suggestions. Examination of Fig. 1 in Chap. 2 (p. 29) shows that subjects high in waking responsiveness are also high in hypnotic responsiveness, but because they are already scoring high in the waking condition, differences between the two states will necessarily be slight. More striking differences occur for a few subjects who are little responsive in the waking state but who are quite responsive within hypnosis; the method of subject selection eliminated these from the Barber and Hahn sample. Second, the subjects did not serve as their own controls. Small samples and a high correlation between responses in the waking and hypnotic states make even more difficult the finding of significant differences, even if they exist. Furthermore, many moderately hypnotizable subjects do not experience analgesia in the hypnotic state; it is clear that some of the Barber–Hahn subjects did not experience analgesia after hypnotic induction. There is some doubt about including them in a study of this kind, for no one would expect them to differ from waking to hypnosis if hypnosis is ineffective. The real question is whether or not, for highly susceptible subjects who can experience analgesia under hypnosis, the fact of hypnotic induction makes a difference. The Barber and Hahn study is not definitive in answer to this question.

Tart and I have done some preliminary experimentation in the effort to replicate and improve upon the Barber and Hahn study, but many additional difficulties have arisen, among which the following may be noted: (1) the subjective reactions to a hand in ice water (the painful stimulus used by Barber and Hahn) vary enormously from subject to subject in the waking state; for some subjects it was not a sufficiently painful stimulus to serve as an effective test of analgesia; (2) the physiological indicators which change as a result of immersing the hand in ice water vary greatly from subject to subject in the waking state; and (3) when highly susceptible subjects are used, some of them, according to their state reports, drift into hypnosis under the imagination instructions, and for them it is doubtful to classify this as a waking state. Thus a definitive experiment either will have to use the subject as his own control, determining whether or not he becomes hypnotized under the non-hypnotic instructions and whether or not he can experience analgesia following the hypnotic induction, or will have to use carefully matched subjects (matched on the basis of subjective sensitivity and physiological responsiveness to the painful stimulus in the waking state; matched on hypnotic susceptibility and ability to experience analgesia under hypnosis). In any case, moderately large samples will be needed. The present literature on the experimental study of hypnotic analgesia does not at present contain any studies meeting these specifications.

In view of these many difficulties, we would not make too much of our preliminary studies. We studied 11 subjects representing relatively high hypnotic susceptibility but ranging more widely than the Barber and Hahn subjects in their responsiveness to waking suggestions. Using the subjects as their own controls, and guarding against spontaneous hypnosis under waking conditions, the subjective pain reports with the hand in ice water were higher in the waking condition than in the hypnotic condition ($t = 2.37$; $p < .02$, one-tailed test). This is not an impressive difference, but it points to an experimental confirmation of a difference in the direction well attested by the use of hypnotic analgesia in childbirth and in surgery.

POSITIVE HALLUCINATIONS

The hypnotized subject, in the absence of appropriate physical stimuli, is able, under suggestion, to exercise his imagination so vividly that he is able to perceive and interact with objects that are not there. We refer to such perceptionlike experiences as positive hallucinations. In the course of our studies we have collected data on hallucinations in a number of sensory modalities: an hallucinated fly (or mosquito) combining visual, auditory, and tactual modalities; a visual hallucination of a second light on a box that in reality has a single light mounted upon it; an auditory hallucination of a voice that is not there, and another of music from a nonexistent record player; hallucinated tastes and smells; and finally, the hallucination of heat building up in a rod held in the hand.

The overall results of these tests, within a sample in which all subjects had an opportunity to attempt them all within one form or another, are summarized in Table 33. The tests are all rather difficult. The auditory hallucinations show as the most difficult, but if the second light hallucination were limited to those who had the hallucination with eyes open it would be still more difficult than the auditory one (only 2 of this sample of 60, or 3 percent, passing it). All items

TABLE 33. PASSING FREQUENCIES AND INTERCORRELATIONS OF POSITIVE HALLUCINATION ITEMS[a] ($N = 59-61$)

Experimental object hallucinated	Modality	Percent passing	Intercorrelations (r_t)					
			Second light	Secretary's voice	Music	Tastes	Ammonia	Heat in rod
Fly (or mosquito)	Several	40	.40	.50	.66	.86	.44	.57
A second light (eyes closed)	Visual	34		.35	.85	.42	.34	.37
Secretary's voice	Auditory	13			.70	.63	.32	.42
Music	Auditory	17				.59	.42	.68
Sweet, sour, salt, bitter	Gustatory	42					.43	.54
Ammonia	Olfactory	36						.74
Heat in rod	Tactual	46						

[a] The percent passing is based on the *first* test with this suggestion.

are positively correlated, showing that some common factor runs throughout the ability to have positive hallucinations under hypnosis.

Fly or mosquito hallucination. This item, which appears in SHSS, Forms A, B, and C, is satisfactory from a psychometric point of view, but as used in the scales does not require a very rich hallucination in order for the item to be passed. The scoring is done merely on the basis of overt behavior, such as grimacing, brushing off the imaginary insect, and so on, and such movements are strongly suggested by the hypnotist. Therefore it is of some interest to learn what subjects say about their experience in the interrogatory which follows the experience. The comments of 142 subjects scored as passing this item, among 447 tested, have been coded, with the results presented in Table 34. The subjects have been subdivided into those

TABLE 34. REALITY OF FLY OR MOSQUITO HALLUCINATION FOR LESS AND MORE SUSCEPTIBLE SUBJECTS WHO PASSED THE ITEM[a]

Reality of fly or mosquito	Less susceptible (Score of 7 or below on initial test with Forms A or B)	More susceptible (Score of 8 or above on initial test with Forms A or B)
	Percent	*Percent*
Not real at all	33	17
Definite sensory experience, but short of complete realism	35	52
Just something annoying to be got rid of	9	7
A matter of belief rather than sensory experience	15	12
Very lifelike and real	2	5
Not ascertained	6	7
	100	100
	($N = 54$)	($N = 88$)

[a] The 142 cases here listed were scored a "pass" on the basis of overt movements in response to the suggested fly or mosquito; they represent 32 percent of 447 cases from several Stanford samples.

more highly susceptible and less highly susceptible to hypnosis as measured by the scale as a whole, in order to see how their subjective experiences may have differed.

As we surmised, the hallucination was not very real at all for some of the subjects who "passed" by the motor reaction criteria; these amounted to one-third of the lower-scoring subjects, and one-sixth of the higher ones. For the rest there was either sensory experience or some sort of belief (delusion) about being bothered by a fly or mosquito, with sensory experiences more prominent among the more highly susceptible group. The experience was reported spontaneously as very lifelike and real in only a very few cases in either group.

Those who reported sensory experiences had a great variety of them. More heard the fly or mosquito than reported that they either saw or felt it, and more felt it (darting against the forehead, or alighting on the hand) than saw it. Nobody reported seeing it without also reporting either hearing or feeling it. The delusional type of experience was somewhat unexpected, in which there was some assurance that there was a fly or mosquito present, leading to a compulsive movement to get rid of it, without any direct sensory experience of the fly or mosquito.

The delusional type of experience was dramatized in one subject who had the experience recur the night following the hypnotic session. Around the bed a fly (known to be an imaginary one) was buzzing so that there was no hope of getting rid of it. This naturally was a very disturbing experience to the subject, although following an interview and another hypnotic session the matter was cleared up, and there was no further trouble.[5]

Hallucinated second light. One of the tests of positive hallucination that has proved to be very interesting is that of a second light hallucinated to be at one end of a small metal box which has one light (turned on) at the other end. The hallucination is first tested with the eyes open; the task is very difficult, and was passed by but 11 percent of the selected subjects who were given the profile scale and by 3 percent of unselected subjects. If failed with the eyes open the suggestions are repeated and the opportunity is given to report the hallucination with eyes closed. Within the same sample from which the 11 percent for eyes open was derived ($N = 173$), 35 percent were able to report the hallucination of two lights with the eyes closed. The arrangement of the box and light is pictured in Figure 5 (from Hilgard, Lauer, and Morgan, 1963, p. 77).

[5] This case has been reported by Hilgard, Hilgard, and Newman, 1961, p. 470 f., as the case of Margaret; also, in Chapter 3, page 57.

For the 19 subjects who reported seeing the two lights with their eyes open, we were interested in their own descriptions of the experience and in the reality of the hallucinations reported. Some of these reports are summarized in Table 35.

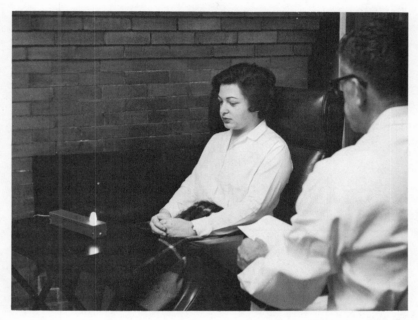

FIGURE 5. ARRANGEMENT FOR HALLUCINATION OF TWO LIGHTS. The subject, before opening her eyes, has been told that she will see two lights, one near the right and one near the left of the box.

As noted earlier (p. 18) and in agreement with Orne (1959), there are many degrees of reality in reported hallucinations. About half the subjects (10 of the 19) felt confident that they knew which light was real, although one of them was mistaken about it. Those who knew which was real usually saw the hallucinated light as dimmer; in some cases as not lighted at all. Among the more interesting replies was that of one who, studying the lights to find a difference, noted that the hallucinated light was not mirrored in the bright metal the way the actual light was, and two others saw it floating as a sort of will-o'-the-wisp above the box, lighted but unconnected to a source of current.

TABLE 35. REALITY OF HALLUCINATED LIGHT WITH EYES OPEN ($N = 19$, 11 PERCENT OF 173 CASES, SPS, FORM I)

Inquiry	Reply	Cases
Two lights reported:		
Can you tell which is real?	Yes	10
	No	8
	Can't answer	1
	Total	19
If "yes:"		
How can you tell which is real?	Real light is the only one turned on, other burned out, not lighted; real light is brighter than other	7[a]
	Hallucinated light fails to show a reflection in metal surface	1
	Hallucinated light floats above box, is not connected by wires	2
	Total	10
If "no" or can't answer:		
Is subject's guess correct?	Yes	7
	No	2
	Total	9
Subject's basis for guessing (whether right or wrong):	No basis; just a guess	1
	One light dimmer or burned out	5
	Inferred from location of cord or switch	2
	Noted intensity of light from one side on closed eyelids	1
	Total	9

[a] One subject was sure that she knew which was correct because one was dimmer. She saw the actual light as dimmer and hence was in error.

Those who were unable to tell which was real and had to guess were commonly successful in their guessing, and they used somewhat the same reasons as those who were confident from the start: the hallucinated light was not as bright as the real one. A new set of rationalizations emerged, based on the side of the box where the cord was attached, or where the switch was placed, the assumption being that the true light would be near there; the form in which the inference was made proved correct for one subject, incorrect for another. An ingenious discovery was made by one of these subjects, which was that the light that was shining on her closed eyelids came more from one side; thus she judged that this sensory reality was correlated with a source of stimulation, which it proved to be. With her eyes open she was so much under the influence of the hallucination that she was unable to tell the real light from the hallucinated one.

Hallucinated voice and music. Among members of a patient population there is a difference between those who have auditory hallucinations and those who have visual hallucinations, although, of course, there are always a few who have both; characteristically drug effects (alcohol, vitamin deficiency, mescaline, LSD-25) produce predominantly visual hallucinations, while among schizophrenics (and the related alcoholic hallucinosis) the hallucinations are more frequently auditory. Because of the possibility of producing hallucinations fairly readily under hypnosis, plus the fact that some subjects produce one kind more readily than another, the possibility is open of throwing light on the problem of differential hallucinatory tendencies by way of hypnosis. Our experiments thus far are confined to a normal student population, but this need not blind us to an eventual broader relevance.[6]

The auditory hallucinations upon which we have most data consist of a music hallucination, the music coming from a nonexistent record player while the subject sits with eyes closed,[7] and a voice hallucination, in which the subject hears a nonexistent voice coming over a nonexistent intercommunication system, and answers the questions the voice asks him, again with eyes closed. We have already noted

[6] Some preliminary work with schizophrenics by Errol D. Schubot of our laboratory indicates resistance to artificially induced auditory hallucinations by patients who have such hallucinations as part of their pathology.

[7] In an earlier version, the hallucination was continued with the eyes open, the subject now being required to see the record player as well, and to adjust the controls until the music pleased him better. While this makes a very interesting demonstration, it required too much time for the added information it yielded in a test situation. Of those who heard the music well, about 40 percent were able to combine it with the visual hallucination. Of those unable to hear the music a few were able to hallucinate the record player when they opened their eyes.

(in Table 33, p. 130) that these two auditory hallucinations are correlated.

Music hallucination. The music hallucination provides an opportunity to show that the development of an hallucination takes time, and a hurried test is likely to be unfair to some subjects. We suggested that the volume of the music was being turned up slowly,

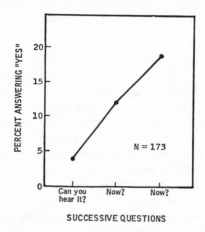

FIGURE 6. RESPONSE TO REPEATED QUESTIONING ON MUSIC HALLUCINATION. The successive questions, indicated along the baseline, follow suggestions that the loudness has been increasing.

so that this justified delayed acknowledgment of hearing the music; at intervals we asked: "Do you hear it now?" Each time we asked, a few more subjects said "Yes," and an examination of their records showed that those who did not acknowledge the hallucination until the third question were fully as high scoring on other tests of susceptibility as those who answered more promptly. The increase from question to question is plotted in Figure 6.

Because of the ease with which most of us recall "tunes running in our heads" it is somewhat surprising to find how difficult an auditory hallucination is. At the same time this very difficulty gives some assurance of the cooperativeness and honesty of hypnotic subjects, for if a subject says he hears a tune, there is no way of checking on him; if his desire were merely to please, one would expect a higher proportion of positive responses. The statements about how the music sounded also give assurance of careful reporting. Of 39 subjects among 173 who received credit for some degree of auditory hallucination, only 9 reported the music as fully clear and satisfactory as heard; 18 reported it faint, or unclear, or as if coming from a distance (usually from outside the room); 8 more found imperfections in the record, so that some of them heard more scratching than music; of the remaining four, 2 lost the music after having heard it for a while, one was disappointed to hear only singing voices, unaccompanied by instruments, and the report of one went unrecorded. There is little evidence here of simulation.

Hallucinated voice. There is some advantage in having the hypnotic subject become involved in what is being suggested, and having him answer the hallucinated voice made the situation more real than having him merely sit back and listen to it. Of 18 subjects who received credit for the hallucinated-voice item among the standardization sample of Form C ($N = 203$), those who replied to the initial question (asked by the nonexistent voice) for the most part continued to reply. Only one stopped replying after the first supposed question, and only one after the second; three quit responding after the third question; all the rest kept right on answering until the hypnotist said that it was enough. The conversation was often very orderly, with detailed explanations about early health history or sibling rivalries that presumably might interest an interviewer.

Hallucinated taste and smell. Some degree of hallucination of taste and smell is easier to obtain than visual or auditory hallucinations. The reasons for this are several: the senses are somewhat primitive, and we are accustomed to some vagueness in discriminations based on them; they are also "organic," in that our own bodies produce substances that can stimulate taste and smell, and so sensation, illusion, and hallucination become intermingled.

The ability to hallucinate sweet, salt, sour, and bitter is very much a common ability, as attested by the intercorrelations of reported hallucinations in each of these aspects. We have only a small sample ($N = 35$) in which the four tastes were all tested; there is incomplete rotation of the order, so that too much is not to be made of it. All had two tastes on each of two days, one pair being sweet and sour, the other being salt and bitter. Some had one pair on the first day, some the other. The within-day correlations turn out to be for sweet and sour $r_t = .85$ and for salt and bitter $r_t = .65$. Illustrative between-day correlations are for sour and salt $r_t = .73$ and for sweet and bitter $r_t = .83$. Thus the reliabilities are satisfactory. The distributions turn out to be quite similar, as shown in Table 36.

TABLE 36. HALLUCINATED TASTES

Report	Sweet		Sour		Salt		Bitter	
Strong	3		7		7		5	
		12		12		18		14
Weak	9		5		11		9	
Vague	10		8		9		4	
		23		23		17		21
Absent	13		15		8		17	
Total	35		35		35		35	

The positive smell hallucination that we have most often used is that of ammonia, because the subjects are known to be acquainted with this odor, having experienced it previously in the laboratory. Alternatively we have used the odor of gasoline. The two olfactory hallucination tests (ammonia and gasoline) are passed by some 34 percent of the subjects and in a small sample they correlate $r_t = .39$ ($N = 35$).

It is quite clear that in producing taste and smell hallucinations subjects draw on their memory and tend to think in terms of the taste of substances and the odors of things, rather than of taste and odor in the abstract. One young woman said that she was able to produce a sour taste only by remembering the lemon in her iced tea of the day before, and in her imagination she put too much lemon in the tea. To smell gasoline, a subject may call up an image of a filling station. This is not to imply that hallucinations and imagery are alike; many subjects rich in visual imagery are not able to have visual hallucinations under hypnosis. It may even be that a subject accustomed to recognizing his own images will distinguish more clearly between ordinary images and hallucinations than one less accustomed to examining his own images.

Heat hallucination. The heat-hallucination test (or heat-illusion test, perhaps, because of the presence of a rod that might contribute to the experience) has been the subject of some debate ever since Eysenck and Furneaux (1945) reported that it, in combination with postural sway, correlated .96 with later susceptibility to hypnosis. Because neither test has a reliability of .96 their figure is subject to some skepticism; it was arrived at by applying mechanically a multiple correlation formula to unstable correlations arrived at through fourfold tables, and does not by any means account for as much of the variance of hypnotic susceptibility scores as such a high correlation implies. Still, the result makes the heat hallucination interesting.

Our test of the heat hallucination is made within hypnosis (rather than in the waking state) so that our results do not bear on the issues raised by Eysenck and Furneaux, except to the extent that there is always a fairly high correlation between responsiveness to a suggestion of this kind in the waking state and in hypnosis. Our heat illusion item turns out to be positively correlated with all other positive hallucinations, the highest correlation being $r_t = .82$ with hallucinated light ($N = 112$). We ask our subjects not only to report when the rod is getting warm, but to drop it when it gets too hot to hold; thus there is some scaling of the response. In our SPS standardization sample, although 71 of 112 (63 percent) gave some indication of the illusion, only 34 of these (30 percent) went on to drop the hot rod. Even so, this makes this one of the easier hallucination items, while it is at the same time representative of the other positive hallucinations.

The hallucinations produced are sometimes very realistic, as in the case of one female subject who felt that she had held the rod too long and had burned her hand. The hypnotist went on to the usual termination and said: "I've taken the rod away now. . . . Your hand is quite normal. . . . It feels just as it did before I gave you the heating element. . . ." He noted, however, that she was still shaking her hand. On questioning she said she had burned her hand, and that merely saying it was better would not cure it. She did, however, accept the prompt curative power of an hallucinated salve!

The several positive hallucinations that we have considered in this section all show kinds of cognitive distortion possible within hypnosis. We turn now to the other side of the coin, to the negative hallucinations.

NEGATIVE HALLUCINATIONS

The three test items to be considered here are more clearly negative hallucinations than the analgesia and anosmia ones because in each of these some aspect of normal perception is inhibited while other aspects are preserved. Two examples are from vision; in one of them, three boxes on a table are perceived as only two, while in the˙ other an intact watch is seen as though its hour hand were missing. The third example is from hearing in which there is selective deafness to the ticking of a watch while the subject continues to hear the voice of the hypnotist. The visual negative hallucinations require maintaining the hypnotic state with eyes open, and hence are quite difficult; blocking out the sound of the watch is difficult also (Table 37). The intercorrelations of these items are relatively high even within this small sample.

TABLE 37. PASSING FREQUENCIES AND INTERCORRELATIONS OF NEGATIVE HALLUCINATION ITEMS ($N = 59$)

Environmental stimuli negated	Percentage passing	Correlations (r_t)	
		Watch hand	Ticking of watch
1 of 3 boxes	10	.55	.89
Watch hand	17		.68
Ticking of watch	22		

Failing to see one of three boxes. This hallucination, like most others, can be experienced in degrees. Some see the third box very briefly and then it disappears (in some cases to reappear intermittently); some see a shadow or discoloration on the table where the third box actually is. Those who have the full-fledged negative hallucination appear to be totally unaware of the third box. In the early testing with this item we further probed for the reality of the hallucination by requesting the subject to place a one-cent piece in "the middle box" after establishing the hallucination that there were only two boxes. The subject, if he had an adequate hallucination, was disturbed by this request, usually indicating that the request made no sense because there were only two boxes, occasionally placing the coin between the two boxes perceived. It is of interest that it is invariably one of the end boxes that is not perceived, so that the two remaining boxes are always adjacent. While the behavior in this portion of the test proved interesting, in an effort to save time testing with the coin was dropped when the SHSS, Form C, was standardized. Although this item is passed by only a small fraction of the subjects, it is reliable, and the subjects who pass it are highly susceptible subjects in other respects.

The missing watch hand. The subject is told that when he opens his eyes he will see a defective watch, one in which only the long minute hand remains, while the hour hand is missing. When he opens his eyes and looks at the watch he is asked to tell the time. Nearly half of those who have the hallucination do not try to tell the time (because the watch is broken); for others this request cancels the hallucination, so that, usually after considerable hesitation, they tell the time correctly. Others announce some incorrect time.

For about a tenth of those who experience the hallucination (7 of 74 cases), a very interesting kind of behavior occurs, in which the subject makes use of the perception of the watch as he sees it in order to tell the time. The most literal interpretation of what he sees is that the two hands must be one on top of the other. Thus if the minute hand is at 10, the time can be read as "10 minutes to 10" no matter where the missing hour hand really is, or if the minute hand is at two, the time can be read "10 minutes past two." This is exactly what these subjects report, and they do it unhesitatingly when asked to tell the time just after their eyes are opened. This is a kind of spontaneous behavior most unlikely in one being asked to act like a hypnotized person, for such a "cooperative" simulating subject would recall the suggestion that the watch was missing a hand—the basis for the trouble in reading the time. The subjects who ignore the fact that the watch is defective and act as if the hallucinated defective watch is a sound one, illustrate the peculiarities of "trance logic" mentioned by Orne (1959). The logical processes are there (as a kind of "rationalization" of the situation), yet action is taken very much on the basis of the contemporaneously experienced phenomena, rather than upon the total causal nexus giving rise to them. The response to the watch is in this respect similar to the rationalizations that are often made to account for the compulsive behavior elicited through posthypnotic suggestion.

Selective deafness. In order to produce selective deafness, the subject is told to cover his ears with his hands, so that he learns that he can no longer hear the ticking of a watch, while at the same time he can still hear the words of the hypnotist while his ears are covered.[8] We then suggest that this same difference between hearing the watch and hearing the hypnotist's voice will persist after the hands are removed. This approach might be called that of "rational

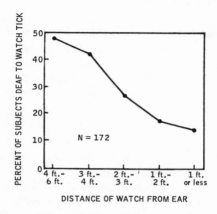

FIGURE 7. SELECTIVE DEAFNESS AS A NEGATIVE AUDITORY HALLUCINA-TION. The subject, after suggested selective deafness, reports when the ticking of a watch can be heard as it is brought in slowly from a distance of six feet. All subjects normally heard the watch at six feet. The sample of 172 cases combines several SPS, Form II, samples, excluding subjects of very low hypnotic susceptibility.

magic," in the words of Gill and Brenman (1959), because it makes the selective deafness plausible, whereas a direct suggestion that the subject could hear one thing and not something else would be "irrational magic." The suggestion of total deafness is anxiety-provoking for many subjects, but this kind of partial deafness is not at all threatening, particularly because it is so close to the normal experience demonstrated with the hands over the ears. The negative hallucination, in its full-fledged form (not hearing the watch at a distance of 1 foot from the ear) is difficult, of the same order of frequency as the negative visual hallucinations, although some slight

[8] We are indebted to Martin T. Orne for suggesting this approach to testing hypnotic deafness.

effect is shown by a greater number of subjects. The somewhat crude threshold method used in the test situation was to bring the watch in from a 6-foot distance, inquiring at every foot whether or not it could be heard. The farther from the ear at which it is first heard, the less effective the suggested deafness, but the more subjects who show some signs of deafness (Figure 7). Because all subjects could still hear the watch at six feet when not given deafness suggestions, non-hearing at this distance under suggested deafness was taken as a sign of partial deafness, even though the watch was heard when placed closer to the ear. The crudely tested selective deafness is satisfactory enough as a time-limited test within a susceptibility scale, although suggested deafness deserves a more careful study with audiometric equipment.

PARAMETERS AND CORRELATES OF HYPNOTIC HALLUCINATIONS

The investigation of hallucinatory behavior presents many knotty problems. Among the topics of interest are those common to other hypnotic phenomena: How important is hypnotic induction in producing the effect? What are the physiological concomitants? What is the role of learning in producing or enhancing the effects? We may consider briefly some of the fragmentary evidence now available.

The effects of induction. Barber and Calverley (1964e) have shown that a certain amount of hallucinatory behavior can be produced by suggestion in the waking state, and in fact they conclude that no significant difference is produced by hypnotic induction over task-motivating instructions. We included two hallucinatory items in the experiment on effects of induction previously referred to (Hilgard and Tart, 1966), a taste hallucination and a negative visual hallucination. The results are given in Table 38.

Although significant gains are found between the waking state and hypnosis for the easier positive hallucination (taste), the gains with the more difficult negative hallucination (missing box; seeing only two of three boxes) are not significant. This is in part due to the few cases who yield positive results, but it is not to be overlooked that despite the difficulty of the item, it can be passed by some subjects in the waking state or in the state engendered by aroused fantasy.

TABLE 38. CHANGES IN RESPONSIVENESS TO HALLUCINATORY ITEMS BETWEEN SUGGESTIONS IN WAKING CONDITION AND SUGGESTIONS FOLLOWING ATTEMPTED HYPNOTIC INDUCTION (HILGARD AND TART, 1966)

	Taste hallucination (positive)	Missing-box hallucination (negative)
Experiment I ($N = 60$)		
Waking suggestion	11	4
Hypnotic induction	19	8
Gain with hypnosis	+8	+4
Significance of gain (one-tailed test)	.05	n.s.
Experiment II ($N = 52$)		
Waking-imagination condition	5	3
Hypnotic induction	15	4
Gain with hypnosis	+10	+1
Significance of gain (one-tailed test)	.01	n.s.

Physiological concomitants of hypnotic hallucinations. The pronounced modification in perceptual processes brought about by suggestion (whether in the waking state or under hypnosis) indicates that something must be going on inside the nervous system of the subject, and surely there ought to be some way of detecting these changes.

The effects of hypnosis commonly take place at such a high level of cognitive function that simple physiological correlates are not to be expected. Thus to perceive the watch face and the minute hand, while the hour hand is blotted out, requires some sort of discrimination to select the minute hand as the one to see; to the extent that this is the case, it is scarcely likely that some indicator, such as the blocking of evoked potentials in the cortex, will reflect this kind of selectivity in perception.

It may be, however, that in some more massive types of hallucination (positive or negative), physiological measures will prove useful. Two examples from ongoing work may be cited.

Consider the positive hallucination of a swinging pendulum. In the waking state, the pursuit movements of the eyes are adequate, and will follow the pendulum in sine-wave motion, with minor corrective movements. The attempt to do this by a waking subject with eyes closed fails, because the eyes jump, making what are called saccadic movements instead of the smooth movements of pursuit. The question arises: Can the hypnotic subject, hallucinating a swinging pendulum, make pursuit movements, as though the pendulum is actually seen? An investigation by Deckert (1964) suggests that perhaps he can.

As a second illustration, consider total hypnotic deafness. The response to a click can be detected with modern equipment in the form of evoked cortical potentials. What will happen to such an indicator when the subject reports that he cannot hear the click? Preliminary experiments by Gordon Bower and Karl Pribram at Stanford indicate that the effects of such a stimulus get through to the cortex, but quite probably at longer latency and reduced potential. If these results hold up, there will be direct confirmation of some sort of cortical inhibition associated with the suggested deafness.

Hypnotic hallucinations and drug effects. The correspondence between hallucinations obtained under hypnosis and under LSD-25 has been pointed out by the case of Fogel and Hoffer (1962), cited earlier, in which hypnosis could produce the same sorts of hallucinations as the drug, or cancel the effectiveness of the drug in producing the hallucinations. The possibility exists that the drugs produce a hypnoticlike state, in which the subject is unusually responsive to suggestions.

A Stanford doctoral dissertation by Sjoberg (1965, in progress) has compared hypnotic susceptibility (not merely hallucinatory behavior) following various drug ingestions in a controlled series of experimental sessions. Some of Sjoberg's results are summarized in Table 39.[9] The 17-item suggestibility scale is that developed and used earlier by Weitzenhoffer and Sjoberg (1961). The gain between waking and hypnosis in this study is essentially the same as that earlier found. It is of interest that two of the drugs (mescaline and LSD-25) produce about the same increase in suggestibility that induction of hypnosis does, while psilocybin has no appreciable effect on suggestibility. The drugs do not have any enhancing interacting

[9] The study has been conducted at the Palo Alto Veterans Hospital under the direct supervision of Leo E. Hollister, who controlled the drug dosages and other biochemical and pharmacological aspects of the study. Acknowledgment is due both to him and to Bernard Sjoberg for permission to use these as yet unpublished results.

TABLE 39. CHANGES IN RESPONSES ON A 17-ITEM SUGGESTIBILITY SCALE FROM A WAKING PRETEST TO A TEST UNDER HYPNOSIS AND UNDER VARIOUS DRUGS[a] (N = 24, SAME SUBJECTS THROUGHOUT) (COURTESY BERNARD SJOBERG)

	Nondrug nonhypnosis pretest mean	Mean under stated condition	Gain	Significance of gain[a]
Hypnosis	2.79	4.67	1.88	.005
Mescaline	3.33	5.50	2.17	.005
LSD-25	3.63	5.17	1.54	.025
Psilocybin	3.46	3.54	.08	n.s.
Combination of three drugs	3.33	4.75	1.42	.005

[a] The significance represents the probability as estimated from the Wilcoxon Matched-Signed-Ranks Test.

effect; at least the combination tried had no greater effect than single component drugs.

Conditioned hallucinations. It is possible to generate hallucinations in the hypnotic subject by using the paradigm of simple associative learning (conditioning). The method was first proposed by Leuba (1940) and has been extensively carried on by Naruse and his associates in Japan (for example, Naruse and Obonai, 1953; Naruse, 1962a, 1962b).[10]

The arrangements are essentially quite simple. The subject is seated before a small easel or a projection screen, at a desk or table on which he can draw what he sees on the easel or screen before him. He is then hypnotized and told simply to open his eyes and look at the screen when he hears a buzzer sound, and to close them when the buzzer stops sounding. When he opens his eyes he sees something on the screen, say, a circle. He presumably forms a simultaneous association between the buzzer and the circle that appears on the screen, hence a sort of conditioned perception. Now the subject is given a suggestion of amnesia for the experience and is tested

[10] I wish to acknowledge my gratitude to Gosaku Naruse for demonstrating his methods in our laboratory, and thus making it easier for us to proceed with some experiments along the same lines.

posthypnotically. With a blank card or blank screen in front of him, he is asked what he sees and reports that the screen is blank. Now the buzzer is sounded as before for several seconds, corresponding to the time he previously had his eyes open and looked at the screen. He is now asked to draw what he sees, if anything appears on the screen. What commonly happens is that he draws some fragment of the figure that was on the screen, perhaps the arc of a circle, rather than a full circle. As the buzzer is sounded again, the figure develops further, and perhaps by the fourth sounding of the buzzer he will draw a full circle. This represents, then, the kind of "conditioning" under consideration. By the use of a discriminably different sound, some other figure can be "conditioned," and when the two sounds are presented together, he may integrate the two figures, perhaps fitting an X into a circle as the spokes of a wheel. Naruse and his collaborators have tried various combinations, including fitting hallucinations with perceptions, as when a half-circle has been "conditioned" and then the other half appears as a drawing on the screen. When the buzzer sounds, the subject is quite likely to perceive a completed circle.

That this experiment is indeed reproducible with a substantial number of subjects who are able to sustain posthypnotic amnesia has been demonstrated in our laboratory in an investigation conducted by Michael B. Conant (unpublished). Some of his results are presented in Table 40. This is essentially a confirmation of the work of Leuba

TABLE 40. "CONDITIONED" VISUAL HALLUCINATIONS UNDER HYPNOSIS BY SELECTED SUBJECTS AMNESIC AND NONAMNESIC FOR THE EXPERIENCE (COURTESY MICHAEL B. CONANT)

	Amnesic ($N = 11$)	Nonamnesic ($N = 6$)
Experienced "conditioned" hallucination	10	2
Drew image during test session	8	1

and of Naruse and his associates. Further experimentation with the method is planned. The importance of posthypnotic amnesia in the production of the experience is evident, the hallucinations appearing for 10 of 11 amnesic subjects but only in very limited form for 2 of 6 nonamnesic ones, although all were relatively high scorers on hypnotic susceptibility tests. The failure of the nonamnesic subjects to yield the phenomena shows that "demand character" alone is not enough to produce them.

It is doubtful whether these experiments should be classified as conditioned responses in the ordinary sense, although they illustrate a variety of associative learning. The criticism of these experiments by Fisher (1955) is that the so-called conditioned responses are essentially like responses to explicit posthypnotic suggestions. The fragmentary nature of the hallucinations reported makes his interpretation an incomplete account of what actually happens. The unstructured responses that he used (olfactory hallucination and coughing) would have made him less likely to detect the disintegration of pattern that occurs.

CONCLUSIONS REGARDING SENSORY AND HALLUCINATORY EFFECTS WITHIN HYPNOSIS

The only threshold modifications we have been concerned with are those reducing sensitivity, as in analgesia to shock, anosmia (and analgesia?) to ammonia and acetic acid, and hypnotic deafness. While the psychophysical methods used were all somewhat crude, in each case it was evident that there was a marked change in the threshold of reporting the stimulus, and that this was related to the intensity of stimulation, in the sense that more subjects could blot out a less intense stimulus than a more intense one (even though the less intense stimulus was well above the normal waking threshold).

We have not experimented with hyperesthesia, although the reports in the literature indicate that little is to be expected in the way of improved sensitivity within hypnosis (for example, Weitzenhoffer, 1953, p. 163). The recent experiments by Scharf and Zamansky (1963) and Zamansky, Scharf, and Brightbill (1964), concerned with word-recognition thresholds, show that great care has to be exercised in such experiments, for without proper controls there appears to be a reduction in threshold (that is, increased sensitivity) under hypnosis, while with more careful controls this advantage for hypnosis disappears.

The hallucinations produced through suggestion in various senses, whether positive or negative, have high validity (that is, are fully perceptionlike) for a very few subjects, but many others share the experiences to varying degrees. Where comparisons can be made appropriately, the hallucinations appear to be very similar to those evoked by drugs.

The manipulation of hallucinatory behavior through procedures similar to conditioning seems promising, and physiological studies may soon tell us more about what is happening in the nervous system when some kinds of hallucinations are experienced. The subtlety of some of the experiences, particularly selective negative hallucinations, makes it unlikely that satisfactory physiological explanations of them will be forthcoming in the near future.

CHAPTER 7

Hypnotic Dreams

A dream is an hallucinatory experience that is common to normal people, requiring nothing more unusual than sleep to elicit it. To find that dreamlike hallucinations are produced within hypnosis is therefore not surprising.[1]

WHY HYPNOTIC DREAMS ARE NOT THE SAME AS NIGHT DREAMS

The usual method of obtaining dreams under hypnosis is for the hypnotist to tell the subject that a dream will come when he gives some sort of signal, that the dream will be on such-and-such a topic (or the topic may be unspecified), and that the subject will remember the dream upon being aroused from hypnosis. Under these circumstances, some differences between hypnotic dreams and night dreams are to be expected. To be more specific:

1. *The hypnotic state is not the same as sleep.* While the hypnotic state in general shows waking electroencephalograms (EEGs), it is more pertinent that the state during which the subject has hypnotic dreams is also one of waking EEGs (Schiff, Bunney, and Freedman, 1961; Sirna, 1945; Tart, 1964). There may be occasional exceptions, as when the subject actually falls asleep within hypnosis, or

[1] I wish to express my appreciation to Charles T. Tart, Public Health Service Postdoctoral Fellow in our laboratory during the years 1963–65, for making available to me prior to their publication some of his manuscripts on hypnotic dreams, including a review of the literature upon which I have leaned heavily (Tart, 1965). Some of the analyses of the data previously collected in our laboratory were also analyzed under his supervision, with the advice and help of Kenneth M. Colby, whose aid is also gratefully acknowledged.

perhaps when he has a posthypnotic dream while asleep at night, but these exceptions are not typical and do not apply to the circumstances under which we have collected the dreams to be reported in this chapter.

2. *The topic of the dream is often one specified by the hypnotist.* This places an artificial constraint upon the "spontaneity" associated with night dreaming. While unconscious determination (in the Freudian sense) could color a dream upon a suggested topic, some differences in this respect between a suggested dream and an ordinary night dream would be understandable.

3. *The time of dreaming is set by the hypnotist.* A spontaneous dream awaits both the appropriate type of sleep and whatever other conditions determine the rhythm of dreaming during the night. These normal rhythms are cut through by the suggestion of dreaming forthwith, and there is usually little time for an appropriate dream state to be reached.

4. *The subject knows that he is to report his dream.* Whatever privacy there is in ordinary dreaming is invaded in advance by the hypnotist's statement that a dream report is to be called for. While there is commonly concern lest the "demand characteristics" of the situation produce an expected result (Orne, 1962b), the demands may also have an inhibiting effect. It may be that a therapist with whom a confidential relationship has been established will elicit a different kind of dream than an unknown hypnotist conducting an experiment.

There is little point, then, in getting worried lest there be some differences between hypnotic dreams and night dreams. A more interesting point is that they are often quite similar, and this fact of overlap is itself important. Night dreams are not all cut of the same cloth, either, and some hypnotic dreams and some night dreams will prove indistinguishable in content. The typical dream mechanisms pointed out by Freud, such as condensation, displacement, symbolization (including disguised sexual references) may all occur in some hypnotic dreams.

THE FREQUENCY AND QUALITY OF DREAMS UNDER HYPNOSIS

Among our student samples, something over two-fifths will report some sort of dreamlike experience under hypnosis on their first opportunity, and repeated opportunities (within the arrangements of an experimental test situation) do not change the proportion dreaming (Table 41). Those who dreamed on successive days were not all the

TABLE 41. FREQUENCY OF REPORTED DREAMS FOLLOWING SUGGESTION TO DREAM WITHIN HYPNOSIS

Opportunity to dream	N	Percent dreaming[a]
Standardization sample, SHSS, Form C	203	44
Special sample given Forms C and three SPS forms		
First opportunity (SHSS, Form C)	59	48
Second opportunity (SPS, IA or IIA)	59	49
Third opportunity (SPS, I or II)	59	44
Fourth opportunity (SPS, II or I)	59	47

[a] The passing criterion for Form C is roughly equivalent to a score of 2 or 3 on the profile scales, and has been so interpreted for the purposes of this table.

same subjects; of the sample of 59 cases for whom there were four opportunities to dream, let us consider what happened on the last two days. On these two days 34 subjects had a dream on one or both days; of these, 6 subjects who dreamed on the first day failed to dream on the second, and 8 subjects who failed to dream on the first day dreamed on the second; this leaves only 20 subjects who had dreams on both days.

Thus to say that a subject does or does not dream under hypnosis is something like asking whether he does or does not dream at night; the answer may well be: "It depends." For any precise estimate of hypnotic abilities it is important to test a subject more than once, especially if one wishes to know just what things he can do under hypnosis.

To inquire about the quality of the dreams reported, we made use of a scale designed by Charles T. Tart in which the "low" end is just thinking or daydreaming about things, then like watching a movie, with visual imagery, and, finally, at the "high" end, the experience is reported to be like a real night dream, in which there is not only visual imagery but the subject feels himself physically involved, instead of sitting in a chair watching. In a sample of the dreams of 39 subjects, the responses of all but two subjects could be classified according to this qualitative scheme. It was interesting to compare the reality of the dream with the susceptibility to hypnosis and the reported dream quality as related to hypnotic scores. The results are reported in Table 42. We found, as expected, that

TABLE 42. DREAM QUALITY AS RELATED TO HYPNOTIC SUSCEPTIBILITY AMONG THOSE WHO REPORT DREAM EXPERIENCES ($N = 39$)[a]

	Susceptibility to hypnosis			
Dream quality	Lower third (0–4.5)	Middle (5–6.5)	Upper third (7–10)	Total
Just thinking and day-dreaming	5	8	1	14
Like watching a movie, with visual imagery	4	3	7	14
Like a real dream	1	3	5	9
Not ratable	1	—	1	2
Total	11	14	14	39

[a] Among 60 Ss from the sample of Hilgard and Tart (1966) for whom information was available. The susceptibility scores are from the shortened SHSS, Form C, with a maximum score of 10.

many of the dreams reported were lacking in full dreamlike quality, from the point of view of the reporting subject, but 9 of the 39 dreams (23 percent) were reported by the subject to be "like a real dream," by which he meant such a dream as he dreams at night, with visual imagery and himself physically present in the action. It may be noted that only one of 10 ratable dreams yielded by the least susceptible subjects felt in the "like a real dream" category, with five in the "just thinking and daydreaming" category, while, by contrast, for the most susceptible subjects, five of 13 were in the highest category and but one in the lowest. Thus the more hypnotizable subjects are found to give the most "dreamlike" dreams and to dream at higher frequency than the less hypnotizable when a dream is suggested within hypnosis.

EFFECTS OF INSTRUCTIONS ON THE CONTENT OF HYPNOTIC DREAMS

Although many experimenters have used specific instructions with a few subjects, telling the subject what he should dream about, we have gathered a fairly large sample of hypnotic dreams, two per subject, under two sets of instructions. Thus, perhaps for the first time, a statistical comparison is possible of the influence of the instructions on the hypnotic dreams of a substantial number of different individuals. One set of instructions left the topic unspecified:

> Now I am going to allow you to rest for a little while and you are going to have a dream . . . a real dream . . . just like you have when you sleep at night. When I stop talking to you very shortly, you will begin to dream. Any kind of dream may come. . . . Now you are falling asleep, deeper and deeper asleep, soundly asleep. As soon as I stop talking you will begin to dream [Weitzenhoffer and Hilgard, 1963, p. 18].

The other set of instructions indicated that the dream would be about hypnosis, and it implied that there might be some symbolism:

> We are very much interested in finding out what hypnosis and being hypnotized means to people. One of the best ways of finding out is through the dreams people have while they are hypnotized. Some people dream directly about the meaning of hypnosis, while others dream about this meaning in an indirect way, symbolically, by dreaming about something which does not seem outwardly to be related to hypnosis, but may very well be. Now neither you nor I know what sort of dream you are going to have, but I am going to allow you to rest for a little while and you are going to have a dream . . . a real dream . . . just the kind you have when you are asleep at night. When I stop talking to you very shortly, you will begin to dream. You will have a dream about hypnosis. You will dream about what hypnosis means. . . . Now you are falling asleep . . . deeper and deeper asleep . . . very much like when you fall asleep at night. . . . You will begin to dream. . . . [Weitzenhoffer and Hilgard, 1963, p. 40].

While the request for a dream was very different within these two sets of instructions, it was not self-evident that the dreams would differ under the two sets of instructions; it could be, for example, that the dream with topic unspecified would also be about hypnosis. From some samples of subjects tested with SPS, Forms I and II, we found 33 subjects with dreams recorded under both sets of instructions.[2] The first step in determining whether it was fruitful to analyze these dreams further was to have them uniformly typewritten without identifying material and then to give them to judges to

[2] The analysis made use of here was undertaken by Colby and Tart, with the help of Charles Imm.

sort "blindly" into two piles, one for the dreams judged to ⌐
lowed the topic-unspecified instructions, the other the instruc
dream about hypnosis. While there were a number of small
tions of differences, if very obvious dreams about hypnosis were eliminated, the differences did not reach significance for the small sample. Actually there were fewer "obvious" dreams than one might have
expected, only 7 among 33 dreams when the subject was instructed
to dream about hypnosis and 2 among 33 when the dream was given
under topic-unspecified instructions. Thus, within the limits of this
study, the dreams under the two sets of instructions were not very
different. Two major interpretations are possible: first, that the instruction to dream about hypnosis was not very powerful, so that the
dream was determined in both cases more by the subject's experiences outside hypnosis; second, that a dream within hypnosis very
naturally reflects something about the hypnotic relationship, without
any instructions to that effect. The study reported here is being carried further, for with larger dream samples some differences may
reach significance.

SOME SPECIMEN DREAMS WITHIN HYPNOSIS

As already indicated, some subjects have dreams that are not very
dreamlike at all, that perhaps review an experience of the previous
weekend, or correspond more to a daydream. Some, however, have
dreams that have very much the quality of night dreams, and the
following illustrations are given to make this observation more concrete. A deeper analysis of the significance of these dreams to the
dreamer would require associations with the dreams; because these
dreams were obtained in the midst of regular test procedures there
was not time for this, and special studies will have to be designed
for this purpose. Even so, the affective coloring is often clear, and
sometimes the symbolic references to hypnosis are transparent.

Dream 1. With pleasant affect. Female subject: "I saw woods—
pine tree woods—very green—a stream. I was there, younger; my
little brother was there, too. We had a picnic lunch and we were
fishing. We put down our poles and ran around playing tag.

"I was about 9 or 10 but my little brother was his present age."

This dream illustrates not only a generally pleasant affect, but also
a not infrequent tendency for the reference to be back to an earlier

period of life. The more nearly equated ages of brother and sister doubtless have some personal significance.

Dream 2. With unpleasant affect. Female subject: "I was in front of the post office; had gone to get mail. Saw a small car (Volkswagen) in front of the bookstore, with a woman inside. She tried to pull me inside the car. I struggled, but I don't know whether or not I actually got in. She kept saying: 'Get in the car!'

"I don't know why I didn't want to get in, but I was terrified at the thought of getting in."

It is quite possible that this is a concealed reference to being drawn into hypnosis, which frightens her as the hypnotist continues to tell her what to do. The fact that the hypnotist was male could make of the woman a thin disguise.

Many dreams in hypnosis have the quality of defying gravity, of floating, sailing, falling, without getting hurt. This leads to a certain Alice-in-Wonderland quality about many of the dreams, of which the following two are illustrative.

Dream 3. An Alice-in-Wonderland dream. Male subject: "First a genie came out of a lamp and hypnotized my sister and me. He made us small and we went inside the lamp with him. Then everything changed. My friend Bob and I were up in a tree and we watched a truck go by that was carrying a mountain lion. We came down to watch the 'ant lions.' One ant lion came out of his hole and hypnotized us. He made us so small that we fell into the hole just like ants. Ant lions are usually mean, but this one was nice to us. He showed us around. There were tree roots penetrating the hole and he would use these to hang up his clothes. Some of the roots had spigots and he could get hot and cold water from them. We were very small and in the hole nobody could find us. The ant lion helped us get out and we were big again. We had been playing with trucks before the ant lion came out and hypnotized us."

Dream 4. Another Alice-in-Wonderland dream. Female subject: "I was walking along, and noticed a hole in the ground; couldn't see inside. It was a large hole, covered the whole pathway, no way to get around it, too big, sort of black. . . . I had to go into the hole —steps inside—I walked on the steps, slipped—some grass or something, but couldn't hold on to it—was falling, not falling straight, but turned around, brushed along, but nothing to hold on to when I reached out, wasn't any bottom. . . .

"I just let myself go, falling; didn't feel like screaming or anything."

The subject who dreamed the preceding dream had the feeling that she had dreamed something like it before, only earlier it had been terrifying. We have had several instances in which the instruction to dream under hypnosis' led to the repetition of earlier night dreams. Here is one illustration.

Dream 5. Repeated dream. Male subject: "Like I'm in a big room. It's so big—I can't describe it. Then it comes in close to me, makes me feel sort of sick. . . .

"I've had this dream before—the prominent color in it is red."

References to hypnosis come into the dreams in a variety of ways. The content of the prior hypnotic items may in some cases provide "day residues" that are fitted into the hypnotic dream, as illustrated in the next dream.

Dream 6. The missing watch-hand as a day residue.[3] Male subject: "I was walking down—over a meadow—there was a single flower that somehow reminds me of a girl. At the end of the meadow there is an elliptical cloud, with a hollow place in the center. I enter into this hollow, looking only to the left, because somehow I don't want to look to the right. There is a door on the left, and I go through and shake hands with someone. I think I've done wrong, and I return through the door, this time looking to the right, but there's nothing there. I retrace my steps through the cloud and I go back; the flower has wilted."

The subject had previously passed an item in SPS in which he is told that he will see a defective watch, one in which the hour hand is missing, and only the long minute hand remains. The watch was actually set at 10 minutes to 2, so that the missing hand was on the right, at 2. He opened his eyes, and read the time promptly as 10 minutes to 10, which would have been the time had the two hands overlapped where the single minute hand appeared, on the left side of the watch.

A possible interpretation is that the watch is the equivalent of a "day residue" that provides the background for the dream in which there is orientation to right and left within the cloud. On the left he "shook hands" which may be a dimly concealed statement of having one hand of the watch on top of the other at 10 minutes to 10.

[3] This dream has also been reported in Hilgard (1964).

He felt something was wrong, and looked to the right (where he had blanked out the hour hand), but when he saw nothing he was reassured. There are, of course, many more things that can be said about this dream in terms of sexual symbolism and personal references, but it is presented here to illustrate the point of incorporating aspects of the hypnotic performance into the dream in symbolic form.

The dissociative aspects of hypnosis may be represented in the Alice-in-Wonderland dreams, but sometimes they are more overtly indicated in dreams in which part of the self separates itself off from the rest. The extreme form of this is the complete duplication of the self, as in the following dream.

Dream 7. The subject duplicated. Male subject: "The two of us [subject and hypnotist] were here in the room. There was a knock at the door—I was standing at the door and saw myself in the chair. I asked you who was in the chair—you said it was I. I couldn't believe you, but the one in the chair said he was I. So you hypnotized me, too. We both sat next to each other and listened to you. Dream ended."

Query: "Were you annoyed?"

"No, it felt good."

This illustration of "trance logic" seemed to cause no difficulty for the subject. While further associations were not obtained, the possibility that this represents in some way the feeling of a divided self makes good sense.

The direct references to hypnosis come into the dreams in many forms—as in being hypnotized by the ant lions in Dream 3, or the reproduction of the laboratory in Dream 7. There are many references to nonprofessionals hypnotizing each other, to mysterious strangers.

Dream 8. Mysterious hypnotists all around. Male subject: "Some man, I can't see, seems to be outside the general picture. He hypnotized someone who seems to be walking in his sleep. His arms are outstretched in front of him. The man who is hypnotized is following the hypnotist around. A man is in a bar and he is laughing. He stops laughing and suddenly walks out of the bar as if he were hypnotized and goes out in the dark. Some person dressed in black, outside the bar door, in the dark, hypnotizes the man."

Dream 9. A brother as hypnotist. Male subject: "There were two little boys—I was one of them—at Grand Canyon at a lookout place.

One boy was at Grand Canyon walking with his hands in his pockets. The other boy was the hypnotizer and he had hypnotized his brother and had him walking along the edge. Then the parents came along and told them to stop it.

"I was the little boy and my brother was the big boy."

Dream 10. A caricature of the hypnotist. Male subject: "First I saw a ghost (a skeleton) covered with a white sheet (like those in the movies); he was bowing down to the audience and motioning with his hands to induce them to do something; he looked "good," . . . er . . . happy, from a distance, but when he danced up close I could see that he was really ugly and dangerous, even though from a distance he looked pleasant and happy."

Hypnotic dreams are rather like projective tests, and their interpretation runs the same hazards. It takes little acquaintance with "primary process" thinking to detect a reference to hypnosis in some dreams that in overt content are far from it. This is the final illustration.

Dream 11. Staring too long at the tank. Male subject: "Oh, I was flying a ground support mission in Germany, leading a flight of two, strafing a tank. I pushed my limit and almost hit the tank . . . (long pause) . . . but I got out of it all right and got back.

"I stared at the tank too long I guess. I almost didn't pull out in time."

Hypnosis in this case had been induced by "staring at a tack," and if "tack" is substituted for "tank" in the final statement of the subject, one gets an interesting parallelism between the flight into enemy territory and the flight into hypnosis.

THE POSTHYPNOTICALLY INDUCED DREAM

Although the experiments in our own laboratory have not thus far dealt with posthypnotically induced dreams, they deserve mention because of some special problems and opportunities that they pose.

When within hypnosis the hypnotist suggests to the subject that he will have a dream when asleep at night, that the dream will reflect a particular content, and that he will remember the dream upon waking, the stage is set for something similar to the usual hypnotic dream, but in a somewhat more favorable context, in that the time of dreaming may fit in better with the subject's own dream rhythm during sleep.

From the point of view of sleep background, two main possibilities exist: (1) when the posthypnotic suggestion operates, the subject may awaken from true sleep, be again in hypnotic sleep, and thus dream as in the ordinary hypnotic session, or (2) the posthypnotic dream may take place as a regular dream, with the EEG background of more usual night dreaming. While it may be that sometimes one and sometimes the other of these effects occur, few studies give precise information about it. At least in some cases dreams that occur in EEG-Stage 1, where most night dreams occur, can be shown to be influenced by posthypnotic suggestions (Stoyva, 1965; Tart, 1964, 1966). Even those dreams that are affected by the posthypnotic suggestions commonly show considerable spontaneous supplementations: elaborations, intrusions, or irrelevancies. The posthypnotic suggestions may also affect the non-Stage 1 experience, on the borderline between thinking and dreaming (Stoyva, 1965).

THE PSYCHODYNAMICS OF THE HYPNOTIC DREAM

Whether or not the "dream work" that accounts for the construction of the hypnotic dream is similar to that of the night dream is a subject of some controversy, as, indeed, is the dream work of the night dream itself.

Most of the studies done by those under the influence of psychoanalytic theory found much in common between the hypnotic dream and the night dream. Thus the disguise of the true meaning of the dream within the hypnotic situation can be inferred from the statements of Farber and Fisher, 1943; Fisher, 1953a, 1953b; Mazer, 1951; Nachmansohn, 1925; Newman and others, 1960; Roffenstein, 1924; Rubenstein and others, 1957. However, the problem of disguise turns out not to be so straightforward when subjected to experimental study. Thus Tart (1964) found little or no evidence of disguise in his posthypnotically suggested dreams. Sweetland and Quay (1952) found the amount of disguise unrelated to the emotional impact of the substance of the dream; Moss (1961), also, using the semantic differential method to measure degree of disguise, found no relation to the emotion-arousing nature of the dream suggestion.

Because of the similarity between "rapport" and "transference" it might be supposed that one could find many representations of the hypnotist, both direct and indirect, in the hypnotic dreams. While the direct references are few (even in dreams "about hypnosis") the indirect references are harder to assess. They are undoubtedly present in some instances; when less evident, they would have to be determined through the associations to the dream that we do not have in the course of our ordinary testing. However, there are some experimental approaches that throw light on these problems.

The induction of artificial conflicts through hypnosis has had a long history, and the method is a promising one for the study of many problems, including symbolic distortion in dreams, the engendering of psychosomatic reactions, shifts in defense preferences, and so on. Studies of this type typically produce in the subject a falsified memory (paramnesia) of some distressing event the recall of which produces remorse, anxiety, or hostility. He is then given amnesia for his paramnesia, but told that the event will continue to bother him. If, a little later, he is told to dream under hypnosis, the chance is good that the dream will have some derivatives of the paramnesic experience (e.g., Barron, 1963, pages 231–32).

A study of this kind is now under way in our laboratory as a doctoral investigation (Imm, 1965). Having been selected as high-scoring on the basis of SPS, Forms I and II, each subject goes through the following procedure. First the subject is hypnotized and regressed to the age of 5 or 6. Then, while reliving the experiences of that age, he is given a falsified account of an experience likely to produce guilt or anxiety or both, but the experience is of course suggested as though it actually had just happened (at this regressed age). The experience is either one of hostile impulses toward a playmate while playing with forbidden fire and matches, or one of sexual curiosity aroused by the primal scene noises coming from the parental bedroom. Alternative versions are involved, in which the parental reactions to discovering the listening child are punitive, on the one hand, or understanding on the other. In the former case the conflict is unresolved, in the latter case it is presumably resolved or at least lessened. In one condition amnesia is suggested for the whole experience; in another condition memory is retained. The whole experiment is thus rather complex, and includes a control session in which nothing conflictual is introduced into the regression session. The regression is removed, and the subject is again his own age (college-student age); now a dream is suggested under hypnosis. This fulfills Reyher's paradigm of setting up a situation in which something is likely to influence a dream, but how the dream is put together is not suggested (Reyher, 1962). Let us look at some dream fragments that followed the unresolved sexual curiosity experience:

"And this time there was this rubber tire over there, and the man that was dressed as a cigarette and the rubber tire—they just danced a kind of a, a jig or something. And then the lights went out."

"I'm sticking a piece of conduit into this pipe, but the conduit is only half the size of the pipe."

"Big silver airplane, sparkling, flying into the sun, all around. I was standing there watching. So big I could see it fairly well even though it was up so high. Almost like it were a toy airplane going back and forth, back and forth."

It does not require a very fertile imagination to see in these dreams from three different subjects symbolic representations of the suggested episode, with references both to copulatory movements and to watching. Sometimes the sounds are also represented, and anxiety is more overt, as in the following dream from another subject:

"The train started to come. We could see the light before we heard the noise. The music in the background got softer and then started to build up again. And the light got brighter as it came closer and closer. And then we could hear the wheels, feel the vibrations in the ground through the tracks we were standing on. We were still inside the tunnel. Was really long. It took a long time for it to come. And then, the music got louder and I was worrying about getting out in time, before the train came."

Sometimes the sound and anxiety are represented, without the sexual symbolism being quite as clear:

"I was lying on the floor, studying, with my head up. . . . This stereo, with my head sort of between the amplifiers, even with the front of the record player. Music was playing pretty softly. But all of a sudden. . . . I dreamed that the speakers were closing in on me and were going to crush my head. And I screamed and woke up."

In general, the sexual situation produced more dreams with clear references to it than the hostile one produced; the results of the investigation will eventually appear, but now the point is that hypnosis permits manipulations in which the source of the conflict is known and the dream processes can be related to it.

CONCLUSIONS REGARDING HYPNOTIC DREAMS

Although hypnotic dreams are not night dreams, the two dream categories overlap and they undoubtedly have much in common. Barber's (1962a) interpretation that hypnotic dreams are merely fabricated to please the hypnotist is an extreme one, unjustified particularly by the dreams dreamt in sleep as a result of posthypnotic suggestion. Even though some amount of fabrication goes on, it may be revealing, as indeed the deliberate fabrication of a TAT story is. In any case the dreamer is the author of his own dreams; how deeply "unconscious" any dream production is can only be a matter of speculation at the present time. All evidence points to the fruitfulness of hypnotic dreaming as an area of investigation.

CHAP... **8**

Restored Memory and Age-Regression

The fixation and storage of memories and their later retrieval constitute an area of very great psychological importance, for memory of things past, perception of things present, and the imaginative foreseeing of the future permit man to live in a world of time transcending the present and binding the past to the future. Hypnosis enters this important area because of some evidence that the past is more available in hypnosis than in the ordinary waking state. Memories can be revived under hypnosis either directly, through the hypnotist's suggestion that the forgotten material can be recalled, or indirectly, through returning imaginatively to an earlier time, the old memories then arising through the reconstruction (or reliving) of these earlier events. The improvement of recall falls under the general category of *hypermnesia,* that is, heightened memory; the method of recall through reliving comes under the general category of *age-regression,* implying a return, in some sense or other, to an earlier time. Of course age-regression might occur even though no unforgotten material was recovered, and one might enjoy reliving an experience the details of which are still subject to recall, just as one may enjoy rereading a familiar book. Hence hypermnesia is one of the accompaniments of age-regression, but not the only sign that age-regression has taken place.

THE INTERRELATION BETWEEN HYPERMNESIA AND AGE-REGRESSION

In our laboratory the tasks labeled hypermnesia are those involving fairly recent memories, such as a meal eaten on a specified night a week or two ago, or an academic lecture listened to at a specific time a short while ago. Of course there may be a mild regression involved in even such recall, as the subject places himself back into the situation he is trying to reconstruct, but it is a normal kind of regression commonly used to facilitate recall, as in saying: "Let me think, just where was I when I last used my fountain pen?"

For age-regression that goes back more years, into childhood, we have used several "targets"—such as school grades, or birthdays, or Christmases. Some specimen results for hypermnesia and age-regression, for subjects having all these experiences, are given in Table 43.

TABLE 43. PASSING FREQUENCIES AND INTERCORRELATIONS OF SUGGESTED HYPERMNESIA AND AGE-REGRESSION ($N = 28$–32, EXCEPT AS INDICATED)

	Percent-age passing	Intercorrelations (r_t)		
		2. Lecture	3. Birthday	4. Christmas
Hypermnesia				
1. Recall of meal	50	.85	.62 ($N = 59$)	.30
2. Recall of lecture	66		.64	Not available
Age-Regression				
3. To early birthday	55			.64
4. To early Christmas	79			

Although the numbers in this table are small, the correlations are large enough to be significant and to indicate some overlap between the hypermnesia items and the age-regression items in the abilities they tap.[1]

HYPERMNESIA

When asked to recall an earlier meal as a pretest, before induction of hypnosis, most subjects were quite baffled in trying to pick

[1] In order here is a word of caution that applies to all the correlation tables of this kind. There is a common factor running through *all* hypnotic suggestion tests, so that correlations between any pair of items must be interpreted in the light that all they have in common may be the subject's general factor of hypnotic susceptibility. For a better estimate of what the items have in common, the more complete intercorrelation tables, with their factor analyses (to be found in Chapters 11, 12, and 13) must be consulted.

out one meal from others of the preceding week, though they tried, by recalling where they went after the dinner was over, and so on. Under hypnosis, those who succeeded commonly added a great deal of detail about the food, their companions, and the dinner conversation. We made no effort to ascertain whether or not their reports were veridical by attempting to recover actual menus, as one might in an experimental investigation of these phenomena. For our purposes it sufficed that those who felt the subjective assurance that their recovered memories were genuine were the ones who proved to be more susceptible to hypnosis by other criteria.

Confidence by the subject in the accuracy of recovered memories does not guarantee their accuracy. In a careful experiment, Stalnaker and Riddle (1932) tested the ability of 12 university students, all highly hypnotizable, to recall prose or poetry learned at least a year earlier. Recalls were done in the A–B–B–A order, that is, some material in the waking state (A) and some in the hypnotic state (B), in order to counterbalance practice effects. Their results showed much more successful recall under hypnosis for every one of the 12 subjects as measured by the number of words correctly recalled in the trance compared with the waking state. Stalnaker and Riddle noted that subjects in the trance state were somewhat less critical of the material they produced than they were in the waking state, with the result that, instead of stopping their recall when they made an error, they went right on. One example that they cite, quoted also by Hull (1933, p. 113), is an attempt to reproduce the second verse of Longfellow's poem, "The Village Blacksmith," which goes:

> His hair is crisp, and black, and long,
>> His face is like the tan;
> His brow is wet with honest sweat,
>> He earns whate'er he can,
> And looks the whole world in the face,
>> For he owes not any man.

One of the subjects was quite satisfied to have written:

> The smithy whistles at his forge
>> As he shapes the iron band;
> The smith is very happy
>> As he owes not any man.

Such a reply would get a substantial word-accuracy score as against not attempting the verse at all, and this willingness of the hypnotic subjects to plunge ahead may have helped their score gains under hypnosis. The subject who wrote this had omitted it entirely in the waking state.

Dorcus (1960) has given an interesting account of the recovery under hypnosis of events that were not subject to waking recall. He reported eight cases of which four dealt with the attempt to find misplaced or lost articles of value and four with information related to crimes. While none of the lost articles cases was successful, it is not clear that there was actually pertinent information to be recovered. For example, a watch accidentally lost in a hedge (and recovered there a year later) may well have slipped off without any awareness on the part of its owner, so that there was no memory to be recovered. Three of the four crime-related cases yielded information of help to the police, although the actual information recovered was very fragmentary. The following case is illustrative:

> This case involved a witness of a tavern holdup. She was a young woman in her late twenties who worked as a waitress in the tavern. The circumstances that she could recall for the police were as follows. While she was working one evening a man entered and demanded money from the barkeep, threatening to shoot if the barkeep refused. She recognized the holdup man as a person who had been in the tavern several weeks earlier and who had "struck up" a conversation with her. He had on the previous occasion shown her a union card which gave certain information about him. The waitress was able to describe him but could not remember very pertinent information which she had previously seen on the card. Under hypnotic recall she was able to add some additional information which was very helpful to the police. For legal reasons the additional information cannot be supplied in detail here [Dorcus, 1960, pp. 58–59].

Dorcus believed that in this, and other cases, hypnosis was of value in overcoming some emotional blocking associated with the original experience, thus facilitating recall.

AGE-REGRESSION

When a particular sample of behavior is used as part of a measuring instrument it is necessary to decide arbitrarily on some kind of indicator to use for purposes of scoring the presence or absence of the behavior called for. In age-regression one might use any of several indications that the subject was in fact acting as if younger (when being younger was suggested), such as manner of speech, description of clothing and surroundings, or age-appropriate intelligence test items. We found in our pretesting that a handwriting change was so often associated with age-regression that in SHSS, Form C, we adopted such a handwriting change, at one of the suggested ages to which the subject was presumably regressed, to diagnose the regression. In the process of suggesting the regression, we obtained other information that did not contribute to the recorded score, and it is of some interest to see how well the handwriting change reflects the other changes observed. The other changes were judged by the hypnotist on the basis of answers to a number of questions at the time of the supposed regression: How old are you? Where are you? What are you doing? Who is your teacher? (Weitzenhoffer and Hilgard, 1962, p. 36). The hypnotist then rated the regression at each of two ages as good, fair, or none. The relationship between these ratings and the handwriting change is indicated in Table 44. If we dichotomize the ratings based on subject reports into fair and good regression on the one hand, and no regression on the other, the correlation with the handwriting evidence turns out to be $r_t = .78$ for the fifth-grade regression and $r_t = .83$ for the second-grade regression, indicating that the handwriting evidence alone is fairly satisfactory as an evidence of regression. We have, however, given some weight to the other evidence in SPS, Forms I and II. This kind of evidence does not distinguish between regression in the sense of primitivation ("seeming younger") and in the sense of actual return to the experiences of a target age ("reliving" again an actual birthday). These distinctions do not turn out to be black-or-white in any case, for true memories can be involved even when there is considerable elaboration through role-playing. Our interest at this point is in individual differences, some subjects showing an age-regression type of behavior (in one or more of its various forms), others not exhibiting any at all.

An interesting aspect of the handwriting change, apart from a generally "juvenile" appearance of the writing at the supposed earlier grade levels, was a tendency to shift to printing at the second-grade level. It is a very widespread practice in American schools to teach

TABLE 44. HANDWRITING CHANGE AS AN INDICATOR OF AGE-REGRESSION (SHSS, FORM C, STANDARDIZATION SAMPLE)

Quality of regression rated by hypnotist on basis of subject's replies to questions	Regression passed by handwriting criteria[a]	Regression failed by handwriting criteria
Fifth grade		
Good regression	24 ⎱ 72	6 ⎱ 37
Fair regression	48 ⎰	31 ⎰
No regression	9	74
Not ascertained	6	5
Total	87	116
Second grade		
Good regression	23 ⎱ 73	5 ⎱ 30
Fair regression	50 ⎰	25 ⎰
No regression	8	81
Not ascertained	6	5
Total	87	116

[a] A ratable change in handwriting at either of the regressed ages was accepted as evidence of regression.

children to print ("manuscript writing") before they are taught cursive script; the change to cursive script ordinarily occurs in the third grade. Hence the printed name would be characteristic of the second grade. The actual printing is often somewhat too mature for the age, but the compulsion to print may be felt strongly. Illustrations of normal and regressed signatures are shown in Figure 8. Among the 73 subjects who passed regression, 50 printed their names at second grade level, while 23 used cursive script. One interesting case was that of a boy raised in China, who handled the pencil as though it were a brush and wrote his name in Chinese characters. He was quite surprised on awakening to find that his name, written in Chinese, was written more nearly to fit a perfect square (as he had been taught as a child) than to have the slant with which he today writes his name in Chinese characters. He made the observation, also, that he was surprised, during the regression, to be able to understand the English of the hypnotist, for "he did not know" that he could understand English.

Most subjects preserve some kind of "observing ego" even though the regression is quite real to them; something of this sort must be present or it would not be so easy for the hypnotist to continue to be in charge, and to have the "child" grow up again at his suggestion. As one test of how much this normal orientation to the hypnotist was retained, we asked the question "Who am I?" during the suggested regression to see whose questions the "child" thought he

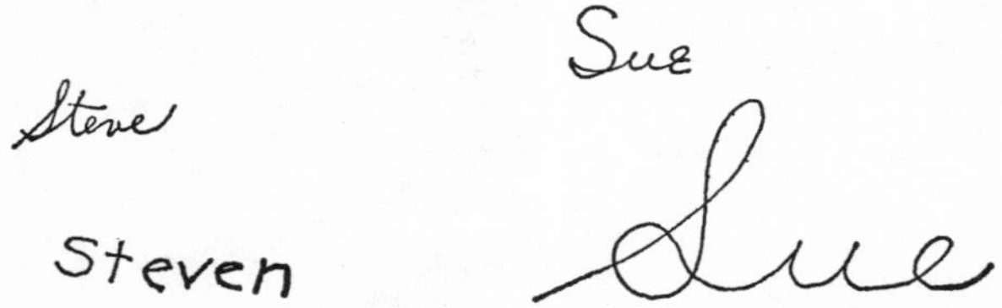

FIGURE 8. TYPES OF REGRESSED HANDWRITING. The "normal" and "regressed" signatures were both obtained with eyes closed and under hypnosis.

was responding to about where he was, what he was doing, and so on. The replies, as summarized in Table 45, are quite informative. Some two-thirds of those judged to show little or no regression found it easy to identify the hypnotist; the one subject in the nonregressed group who made him a friend of the family was perhaps playing a role according to the demand characteristics of the situation, yet he showed no other sign of regression. A very few, 12 out of 66, who showed fair to good regression identified the hypnotist as such, the others all assigning him some other role as friend of the family, stranger, or someone else. The two cases classified as "specified other" called him in one case a headmaster from school and in the other case, a custodial worker, picking up papers around the picnic area where a birthday party was being held. The latter subject found it a little odd when this janitor-type person suddenly became a hypnotist and told her to grow up again!

The preservation of an observing ego within age-regression is illustrated by the experience reported by one of my subjects in the

TABLE 45. REPLIES TO QUESTION "DO YOU KNOW WHO I AM?" ASKED BY HYPNOTIST IN SUGGESTED AGE-REGRESSION (SPS, STANDARDIZATION SAMPLE, $N = 112$)

Person hypnotist said to be in reply to question	Quality of regression				
	None	Some	Fair	Good	Total
1. Himself (the hypnotist)	19	11	6	6	42
2. Someone else					
a. Friend of family	1	1	4	8	14
b. Stranger	0	5	16	21	42
c. Specified other	0	0	0	2	2
Not ascertained	8	1	2	1	12
Total	28	18	28	38	112

study in which an effort was being made to modify hypnotizability, so that some kinds of experiences were followed for a longer period than the usual testing situation permitted (Ås, Hilgard, and Weitzenhoffer, 1963).

The regression under hypnosis had taken place to a childhood experience in which she had accompanied her mother and grandmother on a shopping expedition, and now found herself in a department store. She became separated from her adult companions, and was quite frightened, but the hypnotist, in the role of a sympathetic stranger, comforted her and assured her that her mother would soon come. She saw her mother come to meet her, and was happy again. Grandmother bought her a balloon; she held tightly to hers because she saw a little boy lose his in the wind. The reason for telling this little story was her account of it after she was aroused from hypnosis:

"I felt so sorry for that little girl," she said, "because I knew all the time that her mother was going to find her, but *she didn't* know it."

Here we have almost a multiple-personality type of dissociation between the regressed ego (that of the child) and the observing ego (that of the watching adult), both belonging to the hypnotized subject.

EXPERIMENTAL STUDIES OF AGE-REGRESSION

All topics within hypnosis have been the subject of controversial studies, and age-regression is no exception. Reviews of the literature by Barber (1962b), Gebhard (1961), and Yates (1961) assess the literature as it bears upon the two divergent theories of role-enactment on the one hand, and "ablation" on the other. The "ablation" theory supposes that all memories later in time than those of the regressed age have been functionally destroyed. Weitzenhoffer (1953) earlier made the distinction among three types of regression: *Regression I* being strictly a dramatization of the suggested age, *Regression II* implying a psychophysiological return to functioning at that age, and *Regression III* being a mixed type. Regression II would presumably be brought about through a process of revivification (Erickson and Kubie, 1941), but, according to Weitzenhoffer, we do not really find pure cases of Regression II; what we are more likely to find is the mixed type. Many of the studies with which these reviews are concerned have endeavored to see how accurately the subject hit the "target age" assigned for the regression. Here the evidence all points in the same direction: there will be regression as tested by various psychometric procedures, but the results will tend to correspond to those of an age somewhat more mature than that to which the subject is presumably regressed. On the basis of some qualitative evidence within his study, Orne (1951) observed that much of the regressed behavior showed "sophisticated oversimplifications." Thus the notion of a full revivification, or of ablation, is too extreme to support; at the same time the theory of role-enactment does not account fully either for the subjective reality or the compulsive quality of the regressed behavior (Edmonston, 1962).

Among the more interesting studies of age-regression in relation to hypermnesia is that of Reiff and Scheerer (1960) in which a small group of subjects was regressed and tested for age-appropriate behavior by tests of the Piaget type, and their memories tested for recall of schoolmates and teachers whose names were inaccessible to them in the waking state. Considering only the latter aspects, they were successful in checking the accuracy of recall by going back to old school records and substantiating the names of teachers and pupils. The study has been attacked on methodological grounds by Orne and O'Connell (1961), but the target of their attack centers more on the reality of the childhood behavior under regression than on the hypermnesia. O'Connell has gone on to an experimental replication of much of the Reiff and Scheerer study, but unfortunately only preliminary data are available at the time of writing.[2] He has made use of Orne's technique of simulators to try to produce the appropriate regressed behavior, the hypnotist present not knowing which subjects are genuinely hypnotized and which are simulating. One preliminary finding is that those judged to be "real" (and only about half of those so judged were) produced the kind of evidence that Reiff and Scheerer accepted for regression, while those judged to be simulating (again half of them were not) failed to produce age-appropriate behavior. It is not entirely clear at this time just how these results are protected from being circular, for those who regress successfully may be the ones judged to be hypnotized; in any case the question of the reality of hypnotic regression is left open if some nonhypnotized subjects yield about the same results as some hypnotized ones, and some of each are unable to regress convincingly.

In view of the many puzzling problems, a closely related investigation was undertaken in the Stanford laboratory by Suzanne Troffer (1965).[3] The experiment was done with the aid of an assistant who was somewhat misinformed about the experiment, although the task assigned her was genuine, so that puzzled guesses about the experiment on her part were not evoked. The assistant was given the task of maintaining certain conditions and testing subjects one at a time, *each* of the subjects presumably having been hypnotized and regressed by the responsible experimenter. Actually each subject came without the assistant's knowing it from one of three groups: regressed subjects, highly hypnotizable subjects simulating the role of regressed subjects, and nonhypnotizable subjects simulating the role. The assistant's duty was to test the subject with some of the Reiff and Scheerer tasks under one of two conditions (these two conditions being germane to the experiment, but from her point of view the sole significant parameters). Under one of these conditions she gave high role support, interacting with half of the subjects (actually half from each of the three groups) in a manner appropriate for an adult speaking to a child in a friendly and supportive manner. Under the

[2] Thanks are owing to Donald N. O'Connell for making some of his tabular material available in advance of publication.

[3] Mrs. Troffer has kindly permitted the use of the following summary prior to the completion of her dissertation.

other condition she gave low role support, interacting minimally with the subject, maintaining more of an observer role.

The analysis of these data is not yet complete, but some results are apparent from preliminary examination of the protocols. The hypnotizable subjects do not differ very much in their role-playing effectiveness, whether they are hypnotized or simulating. In fact, on some of the tasks the hypnotizable role-players give more childlike performances than the actually regressed subjects. This is in line with the hypothesis that highly hypnotizable subjects have greater access to their earlier experiences than less hypnotizable subjects, whether or not they have gone through an induction and regression procedure. The unhypnotizable role-players gave less childlike performances than the other two groups.

The most consistent finding of the experiment had to do with the effect of high and low role-support conditions. For all three groups, the high role-support condition yielded more childlike performances than the low on all tasks. The support that the experimenter gives a subject for acting like a child is crucial in helping the subject, *whether regressed or role-playing,* to maintain the illusion that he is indeed a child.

The hypnotized and regressed subjects showed clear difference from the simulators only in their subjective reports about the experience. As a whole, as judged from interviews after the experiment was over, the regressed subjects experienced the regression as more real and consistent than the role-players. Some subjects within the simulating groups reported, however, that they became so involved in their acting that they lost awareness of their adult age and felt as though they were actually children. Thus they may actually have drifted into a hypnoticlike condition.

While the difficulties in experimental control are very great, and the results to date leave some uncertainties about the precise nature and boundaries of age-regression phenomena, case reports continue to be interesting. Thus in one case studied in our laboratory some progress was made in recovering a lost childhood language through regression (Ås, 1962b). The subject, now a college student, had been brought up in Finland where he learned a Finnish-Swedish dialect. Upon the death of his father when the boy was 5 years old, he moved to America and heard the dialect a little until the age of 8, because his first stepfather spoke it. At that age the stepfather died; the language of the home had already become primarily English, and the new stepfather did not speak the original dialect, so the subject heard it no more. Another Finnish student was located who was familiar with the Finnish-Swedish dialect, and he served as an assistant. Under attempted hypnotic regression the subject made gains in comprehension of the language over a pretest in the waking state, answering a number of questions directed to him that were totally baffling to him in the waking state. It is of interest that the conversation went on in terms such as the following. Question (in Swedish): "Where are you?" Subject (in English): "In class." Question (in Swedish): "What is the name of your mother?" Subject (in English): "She is working." Thus the language was by no means completely recovered; he understood it better under hypnosis than in the waking state, but still made mistakes in comprehension, and even when he comprehended he replied in English.

CONCLUSIONS ON HYPERMNESIA AND AGE-REGRESSION

There is little doubt that hypnosis is useful in facilitating recall, although the results are not as striking as some popular accounts lead one to expect. Furthermore, there are other techniques, not involving hypnosis, which may work as well, so that the *uniqueness* of hypnosis in this respect has yet to be established.

Age-regression is related to hypermnesia in that the regression technique is often used as an aid to the recovery of memories. Many subjects experience very vivid age-regressions, although for most of them an observing ego is maintained so that the regressed state represents a partial rather than a full dissociation from present awareness. The notion that regression is a complete revivification of an earlier experience, and shows an "ablation" of all subsequent memories, is too extreme to be supported by acceptable studies.

CHAPTER 9

Posthypnotic Amnesia and Other Posthypnotic Responses

B y amnesia we mean a temporary (or recoverable) forgetting, thus distinguishing between it and a permanent forgetting; the test of recoverability is implied even though it is not universally applied. Amnesia for events that transpired within hypnosis has been the most recurrent sign of deep hypnosis ever since posthypnotic amnesia was first discovered accidentally by the Marquis de Puységur in 1784. He "mesmerized" a young shepherd who fell into a sleeping trance and then engaged in a kind of sleepwalking behavior for which he afterward had no memory. Thus hypnosis came to be thought of as an artificial somnambulism, and posthypnotic amnesia was noted as one of its distinguishing characteristics. Braid identified hypnosis with "nervous sleep" and ever since his time the metaphor of sleep has been applied to hypnosis. This metaphor may itself be enough to suggest amnesia, for the subject doubtless has picked up from the folklore that a sleepwalker does not remember what he did while "somnambulistic." Hence the statement that posthypnotic amnesia often is spontaneous must be taken with a grain of salt; nevertheless the word *somnambulist,* applied to a deeply hypnotized person, meant in early usage that he was automatically amnesic for what he did within hypnosis. This meaning has drifted somewhat, so that practicing hypnotists often use *somnambulist* to refer to any subject who is deeply hypnotizable, without specific reference to the amnesia formerly associated with the term. In our experimental work we have preferred to be unambiguous about the occasion for amnesia by making direct suggestions that it will occur; under such circumstances it is very representative of hypnotic performances generally, and its further study is likely to prove profitable.

It is possible to suggest posthypnotic responses other than amnesia for the events that have occurred within hypnosis. The suggestions that lead to responses to be carried out after the subject is aroused from hypnosis are called *posthypnotic suggestions,* and they are usually given accompanied by the suggestion that the subject will not recall that he is initiating an activity that he was told to perform.

Thus posthypnotic suggestions commonly imply amnesia, and it is appropriate that we should study at once posthypnotic amnesia and responsiveness to other posthypnotic suggestions. It should be noted, however, that posthypnotic responses may be undertaken through a feeling of compulsion, even though the subject remembers clearly that he was told what to do while under hypnosis. Many hypnotists recommend that the subject be encouraged to carry out the posthypnotic suggestion even if he remembers the instruction and hesitates to comply, because it then leaves no "unfinished business" and he may feel better for having done it.

We have some information on both amnesia and posthypnotic suggestion from our SHSS, Forms A and B, and information on either amnesia or posthypnotic behavior in the other scales. The items include posthypnotic amnesia for the various tests that were given within hypnosis, the posthypnotic motor response of moving from one chair to another, standing up and stretching, or (in the Harvard group form) reaching down from a seated position to touch an ankle; additional posthypnotic items in SPS, Forms I and II, include a compulsion to say "February" to the number "3," and, in the alternate form, posthypnotic automatic writing in which the hand writes "No" when the subject verbally answers "Yes" to a question and writes "Yes" when he answers "No," these written responses going on outside his awareness. For subjects who took SHSS, Form A, and SPS, Forms I and II, and hence had all these experiences, some results are given in Table 46. While all items are positively correlated, it is evident that amnesia correlates less well with the other posthypnotic items than they correlate among themselves. Therefore it is improper to equate posthypnotic amnesia and other posthypnotic items, despite their overlap as representative tests of hypnotic susceptibility. The amnesia and posthypnotic movement items were tested on the same

TABLE 46. PASSING FREQUENCIES AND INTERCORRELATIONS OF POSTHYPNOTIC AMNESIA AND OTHER POSTHYPNOTIC RESPONSES ($N = 59$)

		Intercorrelations (r_t)		
Item	Percentage passing	Posthypnotic movement	Verbal compulsion	Posthypnotic automatic writing
Amnesia (SHSS, Form A)	31	.61	.10	.20
Posthypnotic movement (Form A)	53		.84	.67
Posthypnotic verbal compulsion (February) (SPS, Form I)	28			.75
Posthypnotic automatic writing (SPS, Form II)	34			

day, yet they correlate no more highly (actually numerically lower) than posthypnotic movement correlated with the posthypnotic items tested at a later date.

POSTHYPNOTIC AMNESIA

We score amnesia in our tests on a pass–fail basis. A pass requires that the subject remember not more than three of the test items presented during the course of hypnotic testing, after his eyes have closed at the end of the induction. In our records, however, we have noted exactly how many items were recalled, and the order of their recall, and we have other indications of the nature of the amnesia from the subject's point of view.

Distribution of individual differences in amnesia. When scores are plotted according to the number of items forgotten, so that high scores mean high amnesia, the resulting distribution for amnesia scores is distinctly bimodal and resembles the general distribution of hypnotic-susceptibility scores. What this distribution means is that among the small group of subjects who remember very few of the items that they experienced in hypnosis there are more who remember *none at all*

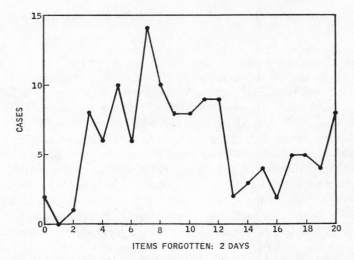

FIGURE 9. DISTRIBUTION OF POSTHYPNOTIC AMNESIA, SHOWING BIMO-DALITY. The scores are plotted according to items forgotten, with a possible of 10 on each of two days of hypnosis ($N = 124$). From Hilgard and others, 1961, p. 15.

than who remember one, two, or three items out of 10 (that is, one to six on two days).

Day-to-day effects. There tend to be slight *gains* in recall over two days of practice (thus a *reduction* in amnesia) although the usual practice effect expected in hypnosis is for the subject to become *more* hypnotizable with practice. Thus, in the case of amnesia, we might expect him to recall *less* with practice instead of more. Our results are probably the consequence of very similar items on the two days. For the many subjects who are not amnesic at all the practice effect (that is, increased recall) would be expected to operate. Even for the amnesic subjects, memory is restored before leaving on the first day. Hence in the amnesia test of the second day they have the remembered tests from the first day to help facilitate recall. It seemed fairly plausible that the amnesic subjects should make less gains than the nonamnesic ones as a result of practice effects, but it turned out that the more-amnesic subjects gained 1.76 points, the slightly amnesic subjects .94 points, and the nonamnesic subjects *lost* .69 points between the two days. These results are deceptive because they have concealed within them some facts of statistical regression.

The effects of statistical regression on amnesia scores. When changes are studied between two sets of correlated scores, it is always predicted that both high and low scores on the first measure will "regress" toward the mean on the second, high scores becoming lower and low scores becoming higher. The best-known example of this is that fathers taller than the average tend to have sons shorter than themselves and fathers shorter than the average tend to have sons taller than themselves, although the mean heights of the fathers and the grown-up sons have not changed between the two generations. The situation we are studying is two sets of recall scores that correlate $r = .67$; those who have high scores are less amnesic than those who have low scores. Hence if we take the high scorers (those little amnesic) on the first day, we expect their scores to decrease somewhat on the second, through statistical considerations alone. This is what we reported to have found empirically, but the question remains whether there is anything *other than* statistical regression involved.

A fairly straightforward way to go at this is to predict the scores that would be yielded *through statistical regression alone,* if the means and standard deviations of the two days remained alike. These have been computed and are shown in Table 47 as the expected means on the second day by regression. Note that we expect the low scores of the more amnésic subjects to rise from 1.26 to 2.10 by regression and the high scores of the nonamnesic subjects to fall from 7.69 to 6.42 by regression. The "true" differences, as a practice effect beyond statistical regression, can then be obtained by subtracting these "expected" scores from the obtained second-day scores. Then all differences become positive and lie between half a point and one and a half points for the groups differing in amount of amnesia.[1]

Subjective aspects of amnesia. We have tried to get subjects to tell us what amnesia is like. Often they reply sensibly enough that they have the helpless feeling that one has when trying to think of a name that doesn't come, but there are many variations. Some "see"

[1] An alternative method of dealing with the same problem, through correlation between initial score and gain, corrected for regression, is given by Mc-Nemar (1962), pp. 158–61. The method illustrated in Table 47, while not as elegant, shows quite clearly what is happening.

TABLE 47. EFFECT OF REPEATED TESTING FOR AMNESIA OF SUBJECTS DIF-
FERING IN AMNESIC RESPONSE ON THE FIRST TEST ($N = 220$)

	Subjects classified according to items recalled on first test				
	More amnesic (0–3) ($N = 91$)	Slightly amnesic (4–6) ($N = 100$)	Not amnesic (7–9) ($N = 29$)	Total ($N = 220$)	
	Recall Mean	*Recall Mean*	*Recall Mean*	*Recall Mean*	*SD*
First test	1.26	5.10	7.69	3.85	2.52
Second test	3.02	6.04	7.00	4.91	2.79
Difference	1.76	0.94	−0.69	1.06	
Expected mean on second day by regression[a]	2.10	4.69	6.42		
Corrected difference	0.92	1.35	0.58		

[a] Based on assumption that the two-day correlation ($r = .67$) holds, but that the mean and standard deviation overall are the same on the second day as on the first day.

the activities but cannot put them into words; others find that they do not want to make the effort to recall. Many report the "almost" recall, in which they know vaguely that something is there, just about ready to emerge into open recall:

"It was like being on a merry-go-round and reaching for a ring. It's gone before you get a chance to grab it, and on the next time around, you almost get it, but not quite. It's always just out of reach."

"It was like all the information was behind a curtain on the stage. I knew it was there, but couldn't see it. When you said 'now you can remember everything,' it was as if the curtain just fell away."

"It was like someone's name that is on the tip of your tongue. You know it and you know you know it, but you just can't bring it into focus."

"It was like trying to recall a very vivid dream, when the details keep eluding you."

SPECIAL STUDIES OF AMNESIA

Kinds of amnesia. Amnesia lends itself to several types of study. One of these is concerned with the various kinds of amnesia within hypnosis. A distinction can be made between *spontaneous* amnesia and *suggested* amnesia. While a number of investigators have used spontaneous amnesia for events within hypnosis as an indicator of hypnosis, it seems quite likely that such amnesia is indirectly suggested by the expectations of the subject. In the work of Evans (1963a), for example, such spontaneous amnesia was exhibited by 12 to 18 percent of the subjects, a result that is about half of the 32 percent whom we report as showing posthypnotic amnesia as a consequence of our suggestions. In some work currently under way in our laboratory we are finding also that if there is no suggestion of amnesia the reported amnesia (that is, spontaneous amnesia) is under half that found when the suggestion is made that there will be amnesia on arousal from hypnosis. Another kind of amnesia, noted by Evans and Thorn (1966), is called *source* amnesia. Something may be learned under hypnosis and the result of the learning retained in the waking state, while there may be amnesia for *the fact that it was learned under hypnosis.* We have found it easy to demonstrate this effect. For example, I taught a subject under hypnosis the population figures for several moderate-sized cities whose population she was most unlikely to know, with the suggestion that she would not remember that we had talked about these cities. Then in the waking state she had no trouble in reciting the figures, but was a bit puzzled that she knew them, until she recalled (probably a slightly falsified memory) that she had listened to a discussion about television stations in smaller cities, and she believed that these cities must have been mentioned as illustrations of smaller places with television stations. She thus illustrated not only source amnesia but the common tendency for posthypnotic behavior to be "rationalized." There are other kinds of amnesias within hypnosis, some of which are not posthypnotic at all, but are within the hypnosis itself, as in response to the suggestion that something just learned within hypnosis will be forgotten then and there. Another posthypnotic kind is the deliberately suggested "partial amnesia," in which the subject is told that he will forget some but not all of what he has learned. An illustration of this will be given presently.

When amnesia is incomplete, what kinds of items are recalled?
Because many subjects recall a few items from their hypnotic experience, even though they are somewhat amnesic, we decided to review our data to find out what kinds of items tended to be selected for recall by the incompletely amnesic subject (Hilgard and Hommel, 1961). A natural conjecture is that while passing an item, that is, while behaving like a hypnotized person, one ought to be in the state that would produce amnesia, and, contrariwise, while failing an item (behaving like an insusceptible person) one ought to be in a state favoring recall. In general this is true; that is, the more susceptible subjects are more amnesic than the less susceptible ones. In another sense, however, the reverse turns out to be true. When some items break through a partial amnesia, *they are disproportionately the ones that were passed,* that is, the ones on which the person had acted as if hypnotized. This puzzled us and led us to propose two noncontradictory hypotheses. The first of these supposes that there is a sense of failure in not coming up to expectations as a hypnotized person when an item is failed, so that the failure item is repressed; the other conjectures that the unusual experience of succeeding, of finding that an arm cannot be bent, for example, is so dramatic that its memory value is enhanced. While we had no strict basis for choice between the repression or the enhancement hypothesis, we are now inclined to favor the latter one, partly on the ground that the effect is just as pronounced for the relatively insusceptible subjects who must be "passing" items in essentially a waking state as it is for the more susceptible (see Figure 10). Since these "passed" items are enhanced for them also, any special relationship to the hypnotic state appears remote. It is possible, however, that they are "disappointed" also in failing to enter hypnosis, so some sort of normal repressive process (not specific to hypnosis) might be operating.

In favoring an enhancement interpretation over a repression interpretation for this particular phenomenon, nothing is inferred regarding the interpretation of the more general aspects of amnesia. Note that this has to do only with the breaking through the amnesia of some items over others; for the highly hypnotizable subject all items are forgotten, and these forgotten items are mostly successful ones. Hence we are here considering some aspects modifying the amnesia, not the amnesia itself. A repression interpretation does seem suitable to the amnesia itself, as we shall see.

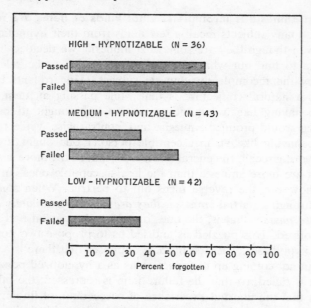

FIGURE 10. ITEMS FORGOTTEN IN POSTHYPNOTIC AMNESIA AS A FUNC-
TION OF PASSING OR FAILING DURING HYPNOTIC INDUCTION. A larger fraction of the failed items were forgotten than of the passed items, regardless of the level of hypnotizability. The more highly hypnotizable were of
course the more amnesic and forgot more of both kinds of items. Plotted
from data of Hilgard and Hommel, 1961, p. 209.

Amnesia as repression. An investigation in our laboratory in which
posthypnotic amnesia did turn out to show many of the characteristics
ordinarily attributed to repression was conducted by Clemes (1964).
He hypothesized that in a partial amnesia the "target items" for the
amnesia might be topics that would, on psychodynamic grounds, be
candidates for repression, and thus such items would be more often
forgotten than other ones that, in terms of experimental arrangements,
would be equally available for forgetting. To test this hypothesis he
needed some way of specifying the preferred "targets" for repression,
and then some way of introducing them, along with "neutral" items,
when partial amnesia was suggested. He decided upon an experiment
in verbal learning and retention, and selected the "target" words as
those that the subject found troublesome in a word-association experiment of the kind made familiar by Kent and Rosanoff (1910). He

relied chiefly upon long reaction times to separate out the "target" words from the "neutral" ones, but secondarily used such "complex indicators" as repetition of the stimulus word and bizarre responses. In this manner he individually tailored a list of 18 words, half "target" words and half "neutral" words for each subject. The association experiment and the later memorization experiment were separated in time so that the subject did not suspect their connection. The subjects for the main experimental group were selected on the basis of prior testing to be capable of posthypnotic amnesia. The procedure was for each subject to learn his list of 18 words to mastery under hypnosis, and then to be given the posthypnotic suggestion that he would be able to recall only half of the words upon being aroused from hypnosis. He was then awakened and tested for recall. Now the amnesia was removed at a signal that had been earlier arranged, and the list again recalled.

The experiment worked quite well. The subjects did indeed forget about half the list, and when the amnesia was removed they recovered a substantial part of what had been lost. Thus the characteristic of repressed memories as *recoverable* memories was sustained.

While this much of the experiment was itself illuminating as to the possibility of a suggested partial amnesia, the main hypothesis that the items selected for amnesia would be the "target" words also received support. Accepting in evidence only words that were forgotten in the amnesia test and recovered when the amnesia was removed showed that a significantly higher proportion of these words were "target" words than "neutral" words, thus further supporting the analogy between hypnotic amnesia and repression.

The reality of posthypnotic amnesia. The general skepticism with respect to hypnosis has been extended as might be expected to posthypnotic amnesia (Barber, 1962c), but, as in other areas, this skepticism is met by evidence supporting the reality of the phenomena.

In a carefully designed experiment Williamsen, Johnson, and Eriksen (1965) set out to determine the quantifiable differences in the amnesic characteristics of subjects high and low in hypnotic susceptibility under conditions of hypnosis, simulation, and control. There were 10 female subjects in each of the six groups. Under the experimental conditions each subject, studied individually, learned a list of six words (butter, dark, soft, king, slow, cold), and then was told that the words would be forgotten after the experiment until told "The experiment is over." In the simulation condition the same words were learned and the subject was told to be as good an actress as possible, so that the experimenter doing the posthypnotic test would believe she had been hypnotized and given amnesic instructions. The control treatment simply served as a check on normal forgetting, when the words were learned and tested later with no suggestions of amnesia.

The posthypnotic amnesia was tested in several ways. First, the subject was asked if she had learned any words while hypnotized. If she replied affirmatively, she was then asked to recall as many of the words as she could. Next she was given a partial-word recognition test, in which 12 skeleton words were projected, the distortions making the word recognizable to between 20 and 50 percent of a pilot group; six of these were the words previously learned, intermingled with six control words. Then an association test was used, calling for the first word to come to mind when a stimulus word was presented. The stimulus word was the most prominent association to the experimental and control words in tables of associative responses. Finally, a direct word-recognition test was given. The hypnotic group turned out to be more amnesic than the controls in the original recall test and the word-recognition test, but not in the partial recognition test or the word-association test. The simulators overplayed their roles, and were more amnesic than the true hypnotic subjects. The authors conclude that they have found quantitative differences between hypnotic behavior and that of simulators as well as that of highly susceptible but non-hypnotized controls, thus supporting the reality of hypnotically induced amnesia.

As previously shown, with practice on similar tests there is a general tendency for subjects to recall more (to become less amnesic) on the second day. We have found, for example, that a change from waking suggestion to hypnosis may actually result in a *decrease* in the amount of amnesia, which, on the surface, leads to the inference that there is less amnesia under hypnosis than in waking suggestion! The reason lies in the rehearsal that is provided in the waking states, so that the items to be recalled are very familiar. This does indeed make it more difficult to forget them under hypnosis; with this knowledge, greater care will have to be given in later experiments to use entirely unrelated items on the two days if this effect is to be avoided. Even so, it is noteworthy how nearly equal amnesia can be as a result of direct suggestion without induction and after hypnotic induction (Barber and Calverley, 1962).

OTHER POSTHYPNOTIC RESPONSES

It will be recalled from Table 46 (p. 178) that there is a low positive correlation between posthypnotic amnesia and other posthypnotic responses. This means that there are subjects who give posthypnotic responses who are not scored as amnesic. The correlations of Table 46 are based, however, on dichotomized scores, so that when it is indicated that a subject gives one of the responses and not the other it means only that he does not meet some arbitrary criterion in both; the finer grain of the items tends to be lost. It is of some interest to compare posthypnotic amnesia and other posthypnotic responses when the finer gradations of response are taken into account. It is possible to do this with amnesia because the record has been kept of the number of items recalled; it is possible to do it with the posthypnotic compulsion items of the profile scales because these items, too, permit a counting of the number of responses yielded. For example, the opportunity to say "February" to "three" as a stimulus occurred eight times; while most subjects did not respond at all, some responded only once, caught themselves, and said "Feb-

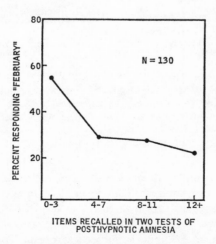

FIGURE 11. RELATIONSHIP BETWEEN POSTHYPNOTIC AMNESIA AND A POSTHYPNOTIC COMPULSION. The more amnesic subjects (recalling fewer items) more often yielded the posthypnotic response "February" when a "three" was presented, but some of the nonamnesic subjects also gave the posthypnotic verbal response.

ruary" no more to "three" as a stimulus; others kept on saying "February" at each opportunity until the testing was terminated with the eighth time. Those who said "February" at least once were prominently those who were most amnesic, but about a fourth of those at each other level of amnesia also responded at least once (see

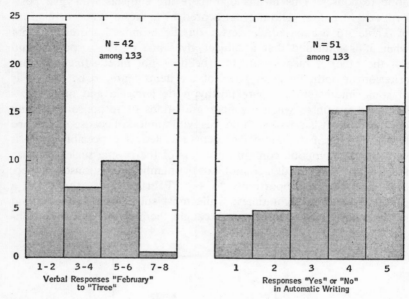

FIGURE 12. DISTRIBUTIONS OF RESPONSES WITHIN POSTHYPNOTIC SUGGESTION OF THOSE WHO RESPONDED. The responses plotted are of those who yielded one or more responses, thus omitting the 91 subjects who failed to respond with "February" and the 82 who failed to write within automatic writing. The distributions show the tendency to cease responding with "February" but to continue responding with "yes" or "no" in automatic writing.

Figure 11). The actual number of responses, for those who responded at all, was not correlated with amnesia; this mean was near three responses of "February" regardless of the level of amnesia.

The results for automatic writing are somewhat similar. That is, 65 percent of the most amnesic subjects wrote at least one response of "yes" or "no," while only 16 percent of the least amnesic subjects did so. There was a difference, however, in the continuation of the responding under the two posthypnotic instructions (Figure 12). Many of those who said "February" to "three" caught themselves and ceased after one or two responses, while many more of those who wrote in the automatic-writing test continued to write through five responses. This might very well have been due to the greater awareness involved in saying "February" in an incongruous situation; there had been no suggestion that the subject would not know what he was doing, only that he would forget that he had been told (a kind of "source" amnesia). In the case of automatic writing he was told that he would not only forget his instruction, but would also not be aware of the fact that he was writing.

Some comments made after the automatic writing item are illuminating.

"For a split second, at first, I started to write and didn't know what I was writing, then I became aware of writing, so I *knew* there was a pencil there—there had to be a pencil in my hand because I had written something. . . ."

"It seems like it was detached from me. Somewhere I knew I was writing. I could have gotten to it if I had to. It wasn't completely unconscious, but it wasn't at the front of my mind."

"I could feel the pencil in my hand after you told me to look at it. I could feel it before I could see it."

"It was just like I was doodling. After I looked down and saw the pad and pencil, I remembered you told me to."

THE DURABILITY OF POSTHYPNOTIC RESPONSES

The possibility of influencing behavior posthypnotically has both benign and sinister implications. Symptom suppression and habit strengthening are possible beneficial results; imposing antisocial attitudes or even suggesting crimes are among the feared potentials. Reviews of the literature and experiments on suggested antisocial behavior are reassuring; although there is always the possibility that someone might be led to do something violent or destructive, if he is inclined to do it without hypnosis, there is little likelihood of producing antisocial behavior through hypnosis that cannot be produced without it (Barber, 1961; Orne, 1962c).

The problem of the durability of posthypnotic suggestions has been investigated by Edwards (1963). He found many variations from individual to individual in the decay effects of a posthypnotic finger response to a buzzer, but found at least some evidence of response at 405 days, the longest interval tested.

The problem of how long something endures must obviously depend on what that something is. Thus a response to some signal from the experimenter, if it is not the kind of signal likely to be met outside his laboratory, is quite likely to be long retained. This is true, outside hypnosis, for such laboratory responses as those on the pursuit rotor or in conditioning experiments. Hence the relatively long retention of posthypnotic responses in the Edwards experiment is not surprising.

Other kinds of posthypnotic response require the subject to do more, that is, to seek out the stimuli to which to respond. Such a task is more difficult, and a typical forgetting curve would be likely to be found. Existing experimental studies of posthypnotic response over time do not permit a comparison of tasks graded for complexity or difficulty, but a recent experiment reported by Orne (1963) illustrates what happens with a task quite different from that which Edwards used. Workers in Orne's laboratory gave subjects posthypnotic suggestions to mail in a postcard daily from a stack of 50 of them provided. Thus the subject had to take the responsibility daily of locating a postcard from his supply and mailing it, a task obviously different from being handed a card after a month or so to see what he would do with it. Under these instructions the daily receipts fell off gradually, long before the 50 cards were mailed. Interestingly enough, a control group, invited without hypnosis (but under monetary incentive) to send in a card each day performed much more faithfully than the posthypnotically instructed subjects.

The results of this experiment reduce the fear that posthypnotic behavior will be continued indefinitely, and they raise doubts that it is more effective than other means of social control. As Orne points out, the experiment also bears on the issue of "demand characteristics" and the "cooperativeness" of the hypnotic subject, and it shows that one has to be cautious about asserting too much about the subject's desire to please as the reason for his cooperative behavior under hypnosis, for in this case the hypnotized subjects were *less* cooperative than the nonhypnotized ones.

CONCLUSIONS ON POSTHYPNOTIC EFFECTS

The psychological situation in posthypnotic amnesia and in carrying out posthypnotic suggestions is a complex one, involving both the compulsive quality of posthypnotic responding, and the altered awareness that amnesia suggestions produce. Any given behavior may mix these aspects in different proportions, as in the difference between the verbal compulsion (saying "February" to any reference to "three") and the motor compulsion of automatic writing (the hand writing "yes" or "no" opposite to what the subject was saying). Because the subject was fully aware of the compulsion to say "February," and heard himself saying it in an incongruous manner, he often checked himself and ceased responding; because in automatic writing the response was out of awareness, no such checking went on, unless the amnesia was broken when the incongruity became evident. For some subjects the tasks were no doubt highly similar, while for others they were quite different; the positive correlation between them reflects what they have in common but allows room for these many individual differences.

Many puzzling problems remain. There is an old contention that the subject re-enters hypnosis while carrying out the posthypnotic suggestion. It is difficult to get clear evidence on this, and we do not have evidence for or against this contention. If it were true, then one might suppose that a state in which a posthypnotic amnesia is retained is also a partially hypnotized one. We do not know the answer to this, but in our laboratory we prefer to terminate posthypnotic amnesias with full recall, just as we terminate posthypnotic suggestions by having the subject fulfill them and recall the instructions that led to them. In other words, until we know more, it seems better to have the subject leave the laboratory as he entered it, without doubts as to what happened there, and without unfulfilled demands upon him of which he is unaware.

CHAPTER 10

Distortions of Meaning, Affect,
and the Image of the Self

A person can distort reality in a number of ways. He may discriminate inaccurately because of sensory defects, as when the colorblind mistakes one color for another. He may see a straight line as curved because of the background against which it is placed, as in the many optical illusions. Such distortions (of sensory defect or of illusion) can be accentuated through suggestion. Then there are the distortions of positive and negative hallucinations, when what is perceived bears little resemblance to the presented stimuli. Finally, and these are the distortions with which this chapter deals, there are distortions of meaning, when all the "givens" from the stimulus may be accurate; although there is no distortion of shape, or contour, or color, or sound, there is distortion of reference, so that, for example, a clearly perceived object may not be recognized for what it is, or may be given a wrong name. We have no single word such as illusion or hallucination to refer to these distortions beyond perception; the word *delusion,* because it means false belief, is appropriate, but common usage makes it too strong a word. Hence the expression *distortion of meaning* is used here to cover this realm of cognitive inaccuracy beyond illusion and hallucination.

DISTORTIONS OF MEANING ILLUSTRATED BY SELECTED TEST CONTENT

In selecting content to sample distortions within hypnosis beyond illusions and hallucinations, we chose as part of our testing program two aphasia-agnosia items, one affective-distortion item, and one item reflecting a change in personality.

Cognitive distortions that involve the failure to recognize familiar objects even though they are clearly perceived, or the inability to name them even though they are recognized for what they are, fall in the general area of *agnosias* (losses of ability to recognize familiar objects) or *aphasias* (disturbances in the use or understanding of speech). Although our experiments with tests in this general area began with the suggestion for nominal aphasia (that the familiar name would seem like a word from a foreign language), the typical hypnotic subject was not that analytical and often produced broader kinds of distortion. Hence we have come to speak of our tests as those of agnosia rather than aphasia, although we are not in fact distinguishing at all sharply between aphasia and agnosia. The hypnotic subject is said to be very literal-minded, interpreting a suggestion for exactly what it is; this is true in some sense, in that suggestions tend to be little criticized, but in another sense it is not true, for the subject readily imposes his own interpretation upon a suggestion in accordance with the kind of behavior he perceives the hypnotist as having in mind when he gives the suggestion.

We have used two items, one in SPS, Form I, the other in SPS, Form II, intending them to represent the same domain but in somewhat different detail. One of these calls for loss of meaning of the word *house,* tested by pictures of various kinds of buildings and other objects, the other for loss of meaning of the word *scissors,* tested with actual objects presented on a tray for identification and handling. Subjects who were not expected to understand the word *house* occasionally interpreted this to mean that they could not understand *home* either, thus converting a specific word loss to a more general concept loss. Correspondingly, some subjects showed extreme awkwardness when trying to demonstrate the *use* of scissors, although they were told only to forget scissors as a *name* for the instrument.

Meanings have their affective components also. Thus a situation is interpreted as happy, sad, innocuous, moving, or amusing. In order to study distortion in this aspect of experience, we presented the subject with a "joke" that was not at all funny, with the suggestion that he would find it very amusing:

I am going to read you a very funny statement. I think after you hear it you will agree that it is very funny and humorous, the kind of statement that gives people a good laugh. I hope very much that you will enjoy it to the fullest [Weitzenhoffer and Hilgard, 1963, p. 20].

After this promise the "joke," to a nonhypnotized person, is something of a letdown, no matter how amusing the hypnotized subject finds it:

The whale is undoubtedly one of the largest mammals alive today.

The subject is scored depending upon how much he laughs or chuckles.

The final area of distortion consisted in a suggested alteration in personality. The subject is to see himself as someone else, of a lower station in life, and of lower mentality:

> When I next clap my hands like this (*clap audibly but not too vigorously*), you will no longer be the person you are now. You will have a different name and background. You will be an illiterate, dull, slow-witted individual, a peasant of low mental caliber, a clod. You will attend to me at all times and it will seem quite natural that I should be asking you to do various things. . . . You will remain this person until I next say, "Thank you, that will be all for today" [Weitzenhoffer and Hilgard, 1963, p. 43].

The success of this suggested alteration of personality is determined by testing, both with a few questions about the new identity and some selected items from the Wechsler Adult Intelligence Scale.

Before turning to some details about the individual items, we may examine the successes achieved and the intercorrelations (Table 48).

Although the agnosia items and the personality change appear to belong together, the affective distortion item (nonfunny joke) shows low correlations with the others. This may reflect a rather low reliability for this item; on a retest with an alternate form (a giraffe substituted for the whale), the correlation between the two forms was only $r_t = .31$ ($N = 32$). We turn now to consider the individual items in greater detail.

APHASIA AND AGNOSIA

Our reasons for some confusion as to whether we are testing aphasia or some broader distortion of understanding (agnosia) will be clearer when we discuss what the subjects actually did.

TABLE 48. PASSING FREQUENCIES AND INTERCORRELATIONS OF ITEMS RE-
FLECTING DISTORTIONS OF MEANING AND OF THE IMAGE OF THE SELF ($N = 59$)

	Percent passing[a]	Intercorrelations (r_t)		
		Agnosia II: scissors	Affective distortion	Personality change
Agnosia I: House	17	.84	.30	.90
Agnosia II: Scissors	10		.32	.76
Affective Distortion:				
Nonfunny Joke	29			.34
Personality Change				
Toward Stupidity	22			

[a] For this purpose, percents represent those who scored the maximum on the agnosia items (a score of 3); scores of 2 or 3 are included on the other two items.

Disturbances over the word *house*. The test for *house* was conducted in two parts. First the hypnotist asked the subject to point
to individual pictures on a card as he (the hypnotist) named them
one at a time. The standard card, as pictured in Figure 13, has six
pictures (a barn, an automobile, a dog, a building, a house, and a
tree). The suggestion had already been given that the subject would
not understand the word *house*, and passing this part of the test
required inability to point out the house on the card. In the second
part of the test the hypnotist did the pointing and the subject was
asked to do the naming. Passing this part of course required the
subject to fail to use the word *house* in naming that picture, although
he might use some other word such as *dwelling* or *home* and still
satisfy the requirements. There were essentially no errors on the
noncritical control pictures, so our analysis is only of responses relevant to *home* and to *house*. What the subjects did and said is indicated
in Table 49. A few subjects generalized their inhibition to the word
home as well, but most of the subjects who passed the item made a
distinction between the two words.

What happened throughout made items of this kind suitable for
inclusion in susceptibility scales because the generally more susceptible subjects more frequently gave the distorted responses, with
proportions graded in rough agreement with the level of susceptibility.

FIGURE 13. Pictures Used in *House* Agnosia Test. From Hilgard, Lauer, and Morgan, 1963, opposite p. 80.

TABLE 49. REPLIES RELEVANT TO "HOUSE" IN AGNOSIA TEST

	High subjects[a] (N = 44)	Medium subjects (N = 50)	Low subjects (N = 48)	Low-low subjects (N = 15)
	percent	*percent*	*percent*	*percent*
Subject's pointing				
a. "Home" (control)				
Points promptly	64	76	94	87
After hesitation	27	24	6	13
Fails to point	9	0	0	0
	100	100	100	100
b. "House" (critical)				
Points promptly	9	51	73	80
After hesitation	11	20	21	13
Fails to point	80	29	6	7
	100	100	100	100
Subject's replies to hypnotist's pointing to house				
"House"	5	50	75	87
"Home"	46	36	17	13
"Building"	25	4	2	0
Other	10	10	6	0
No response	14	0	0	0
	100	100	100	100

[a] The subjects are classified into high, medium, and low by approximate thirds within total scores on SPS, Form I or II; the low-low group scored 0–3 on SHSS, Form A, and is not normally tested within the SPS sample.

The test suggestion, as worded, states that the reference is to the meaning of the word *house,* not to the general recognition of a house:

> When I reach the count of five, and after that until I tell you otherwise, you will no longer know what the word *house* means. It will be as if you had never heard the word before. When you hear the word *house* you will have the same feeling you would have if you saw or heard a foreign word with which you had no familiarity or knowledge. It will mean absolutely nothing to you! [Weitzenhoffer and Hilgard, 1963, p. 19].

Note the absence of any reference at all to recognizing a house when you see one. Still, when asked to name an object to which the hypnotist pointed, if it happened to be a house, many subjects simply failed to assign any name to it at all; others, who were "literalists" with respect to the suggestion, used alternative words that would be quite appropriate if the only trouble was that *house* was a foreign word. One subject who made use of this literal linguistic loss of meaning of the word house replied, when the hypnotist pointed to the house, that he knew that in German it was called H-A-U-S, but because he had never studied German he did not know what the word meant, so that he could not give either an English spelling or an English translation.

Disturbance over the word *scissors*. Roughly the same behavior occurred with *scissors,* although here there was an opportunity to handle the scissors as an object. The same general suggestion was given as for the word *house,* only the word *scissors* was substituted. The test was presented in two parts as before. First, the hypnotist named the objects on a tray, asking the subject to pick up each object as named. Some subjects, mildly aphasic, said they were able to pick up the scissors because it was the only unfamiliar object on the tray; a better test would involve some related, less familiar objects, such as hemostats or forceps, but even so, many subjects were confused and failed to pick up the scissors. If the subject failed to pick up the scissors, it was handed to him, with a piece of paper, and he was asked to demonstrate its use. Because the suggestion had said nothing about use, we supposed that this might be of some interest in determining how literally the subject took the loss of name; actually many took the loss of name to be general loss of familiarity with scissors, and showed great awkwardness in trying to use the scissors. The second part of the test was a naming test, the hypnotist doing the pointing, the subject the naming. The same objects were used. Here the subject again had the option of leaving the scissors nameless, or substituting some name, such as shears, paper cutter, and so forth. The results of this test are given in Table 50.

The main effect (failing to pick up the scissors when they are named) comes out clearly with 86 percent of the high-scoring hypnotic subjects, 16 percent of the medium subjects, and none of the low or low-low subjects failing to pick them up. The generalization to the use of scissors (as well as to their name) occurs with nearly half of the high subjects, if one counts awkwardness as an effect; not counting awkwardness, there are still 29 percent of these subjects

TABLE 50. REPLIES AND BEHAVIOR RELEVANT TO "SCISSORS" IN AGNOSIA TEST

Behavior relevant to scissors	High subjects[a] (N = 44)	Medium subjects (N = 50)	Low subjects (N = 48)	Low-low subjects (N = 16)
	percent	*percent*	*percent*	*percent*
When asked to pick up				
Picks up easily	2	74	96	88
Hesitates, picks up	14	10	4	12
Fails to pick up	84	16	0	0
	100	100	100	100
When asked to show how to use with paper				
Uses to cut naturally	47	89	98	94
Uses to cut awkwardly	24	7	2	6
Uses in some other way	22	0	0	0
Refuses to use	7	4	0	0
	100	100	100	100
When asked to name objects on tray (including scissors)				
Names scissors	9	84	100	100
Names or describes as cutting tool	42	4	0	0
Names something else	6	2	0	0
Ignores or can't name	43	10	0	0
	100	100	100	100

[a] See footnote to Table 49.

who use the scissors as a dagger, or pencil, or in some way other than cutting, or who refuse to use them at all. When it comes to naming the objects on the tray, 91 percent of the high subjects, 16 percent of the medium subjects, and none of the rest avoid using the word "scissors," although many substitute *shears* or reference to some other cutting tool to indicate knowledge of use. Thus the instructions, which really call for an aphasia, are converted by many to a fuller agnosia.

The subjective reactions were quite varied. The following quotation shows how hard it is to put into words just what actually goes on:

"I felt compelled to tell you that I didn't know what 'scissors' were, although I did know. However, when I tried to tell you, the knowledge went away."

Speech disturbances within and following hypnosis. The role of speech in hypnosis is a most important one; with practice a subject can enter a trance quickly at a verbal signal, and all sorts of effects, autonomic and peripheral, can be produced by the hypnotist's words. It is quite possible that the hypnotist takes over some of the talking-to-himself behavior of the subject, as pointed out by Miller, Galanter, and Pribram (1960).

One of the "challenge" items that appears in SHSS, Forms A and B, is a "verbal inhibition" item, which appears in the form of inability to say one's own name (in Form A) and inability to name one's home town (in Form B). The inhibition is very real, the subject often making strange facial contortions, including the lips and tongue, in the effort to speak what is a normally familiar and easy word. Some 23 percent of the standardization sample responded to this item with inability to say the asked-for word within 10 seconds. Most of them could think of the word but could not say it; a few reported that they had a lapse of memory, and did not know what they were supposed to try to say. The inhibition is readily removed by the hypnotist's words: "You can say your name easily now. . . . Go ahead and say it."

Very occasionally a subject who has been through hypnosis, and given a suggestion of posthypnotic amnesia, will be unable to talk, even when he is told that his memories are restored. The following case, from our regular laboratory sample, illustrates this:

Case 11. Jerry, who could not talk following suggested amnesia. This political science student came to participate in our experiments and responded moderately well on the first day of hypnosis with SHSS, Form A, (7 of 12 possible), and better on the second day with SHSS, Form B, (11 of 12). He returned for two days of SHSS, Form C, scoring 7 and 9 on the two days (out of a possible 10 each day). The most interesting aspect of his behavior, *repeated on all four days,* with three different hypnotists, was his inability to speak when awakened, following the suggestion of posthypnotic amnesia.

After being awakened from hypnosis on the first day he was totally unable to form words. He was rehypnotized, and given assurance that he could speak, but he still found it difficult. "You told me not to remember." The hypnotist then reminded him that a signal had been mentioned, that when the hypnotist said, "Now you can remember everything," he should remember everything again; that the suggestion to forget was no more important than the suggestion to remember again. He now began to speak somewhat more easily. He said he felt "funny," relaxed, different from the way he usually felt, but felt good. On the next day, the same thing happened, and he again had to be rehypnotized. He finally recalled a few of the items and remarked: "I didn't forget, but I couldn't say it." These two days were with the same hypnotist. The following week he came back for two more sessions, each with a different hypnotist, and on both days was again unable to speak until rehypnotized, despite all the reassurances he had had that this was not the behavior called for. On the final session he again repeated that he could remember things but he could not speak while the amnesia instructions were in effect.

Erickson (1943) lists speech disturbances as among the spontaneous psychosomatic accompaniments of hypnosis. Gill and Brenman (1959, p. 25 f.) report two cases of spontaneous loss of control of motor speech during induction. The first case is that of a young woman patient who had come for treatment of a depression. When asked a routine question during induction, they report that the movements of mouth, lips, and tongue made it evident that she was trying to speak, but unable to answer the question. When the hypnotist gave a strong suggestion that her voice should return she seemed "a trifle confused, even dazed, and soon began to talk normally." The second case was that of a psychiatric resident who, without any specific suggestion to that effect, lost control of his tongue and lips, later reporting the experience as a "frozen" feeling.

Various disturbances of speech and vocalization are met in psychotherapeutic practice. This then presents the other side of the coin: the opportunity within hypnosis to alleviate speech symptoms. Thus Kirkner, Dorcus, and Seacat (1953) present a case in which an organic motor aphasia was motivated to improve under speech retraining by means of hypnosis; Kroger (1963) presents the case of a radio announcer who lost his voice (and almost his job!) until aided by hypnotherapy.

DISTORTED AFFECTIVE MEANING: IS THE JOKE FUNNY?

It is not difficult to produce various affective changes under hypnosis. This has often been tried, and with considerable success; the only problem that haunts these investigations is that nonhypnotized subjects can produce many of the same effects (for example, Damaser, Shor, and Orne, 1963).

Our one test item, the nonfunny joke, was not entirely successful, probably because it was too "intellectual" in one sense, requiring an interpretation that a presented object is sufficiently incongruous to be "funny," and was too impersonal, calling for too little involvement of the subject. Thus our joke did not evoke sympathy, or fright, or other compelling emotion; there was none of the "sudden burst of glory" sometimes associated with the appreciation of humor. In any case, a certain number of our subjects found the joke very funny, and for them it evoked side-splitting laughter; unfortunately, a few of the nonhypnotized were so amused at our presenting the nonfunny joke as funny that they smiled or chuckled at the incongruity in the total setting, for there is something amusing about presenting a nonfunny statement as funny. The findings are summarized in Table 51.

TABLE 51. REACTIONS TO NONFUNNY JOKE SUGGESTED TO BE HUMOROUS ($N = 58$)

Reaction to joke	High subjects[a] ($N = 14$)	Medium subjects ($N = 15$)	Low subjects ($N = 14$)	Low-low subjects ($N = 15$)
	percent	*percent*	*percent*	*percent*
Impassive	7	40	42	60
Smiles	57 ⎫	20 ⎫	29 ⎫	20 ⎫
	⎬ 93	⎬ 60	⎬ 58	⎬ 40
Laughs	36 ⎭	40 ⎭	29 ⎭	20 ⎭
	100	100	100	100

[a] See footnote to Table 49. This analysis was made on a somewhat smaller sample, but of the same kind.

Although many more of the high subjects responded with smiles and laughter than the others, the item does not discriminate at all clearly between the medium and low subjects. From a statistical point of view it is one of our least satisfactory items because of low reliability and low correlation with other items, although it still has some discriminating power. Subjects who laughed at the nonfunny joke, even though they were not hypnotically susceptible, said such things as: "Whales are funny looking." "The whale is not a mammal" [sic]. "Any well-known fact sounds humorous when placed in an inappropriate context." A responsive subject yields a very wholehearted and delightfully genuine response to an item of this kind. I recall a demonstration before one of my classes in which I repeated one of the tasks used in a film version by Lester Beck. Two subjects were hypnotized at once, and together studied a picture magazine before them under the instructions that one would find the left-hand page amusing, the other the right-hand page. The joy shown by one of the subjects in particular when attention was directed to "his" side and impassiveness when attention was directed to the other, was most impressive, and led to a kind of contagious response to his mood by the class.

DISTORTED SELF-IMAGE: THE SELF AS A STUPID PERSON

Stage hypnotists commonly capitalize on the readiness of the hypnotized subject to adopt an unusual role: to become a rooster, and flap his "wings" and crow, to become a ballet dancer, or to become a political orator. The hypnotized person thus demonstrates his willingness to undergo, temporarily, a personality change, and to act in out-of-the-ordinary ways. This behavior may be quite superficial; thus the same sort of behavior may occur, outside hypnosis, at a costume ball, or at a party in which adults dress and act like children, a so-called "kid party." At the same time, it may go much deeper, as the hypnotized subject becomes involved in his role as though it were the only reality.

We have not sampled this behavior in its most dramatic forms, partly as a matter of keeping good faith with our experimental subjects so that we do not ask them to do things either that would embarrass them or that are likely to make contact with disturbing experiences in their past. In asking the subject to perceive himself temporarily as a stupid and somewhat degraded person we did, in fact, threaten the self-esteem of a few subjects; however, the indication given in the instructions that there would be a clear termination softened the blow for most subjects. That it is time-limited is, of course, one of the marks of any "regression in the service of the ego."

We have a good deal of information about what happened in the midst of the suggested personality alteration that is not reflected in the quantitative scores. The initial questions that we asked, after the alteration was supposed to have taken place, were these:

What is your name?
How old are you?
How do you earn your living?
With whom do you live?

If this is merely some sort of game, in which the cooperative subject wishes to please the hypnotist, it would be easy for a subject to "play the game" and conform to expectations across the board. This did not happen, however; only the more highly susceptible subjects showed the expected responses. How these responses hang together is shown in Table 52.

TABLE 52. INDICATIONS OF PERSONALITY ALTERATION OTHER THAN INTELLIGENCE TEST SCORES IN RELATION TO GENERAL LEVEL OF HYPNOTIC SUSCEPTIBILITY

Personality alteration	High subjects[a] (N = 45)	Medium subjects (N = 50)	Low subjects (N = 48)	Low-low subjects (N = 16)
	percent	*percent*	*percent*	*percent*
Changed name	80	60	8	0
Changed age	64	44	4	0
Changed mode of earning living	76	56	6	0
Changed with whom living	71	56	6	0

[a] See footnote to Table 49.

The further evidence of personality alteration in the direction of lowered mentality was reduced scores on some items (information, comprehension, similarities) from the Wechsler scale.

The corresponding results for the intelligence test items from the Wechsler test are plotted in Figure 14. Again, it is easy to see that the most striking changes were made by the subjects most susceptible to hypnosis in other respects.

It is of some interest that when the Wechsler items were given in control form to subjects in the hypnotic state, there was no depression of scores. This is not what one would expect if that state were a generally "regressed" state intellectually—one might then expect a depression of scores. Instead we found that subjects gave intelligent answers under hypnosis and gave "stupid" answers only after the suggestion that they were stupid.

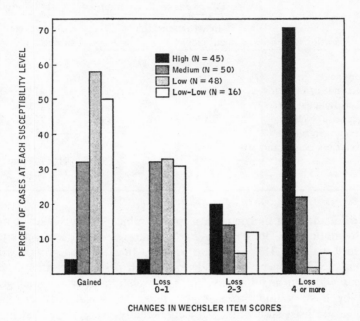

CHANGES IN WECHSLER ITEM SCORES

FIGURE 14. EFFECT OF SUGGESTED PERSONALITY ALTERATION ON INTELLIGENCE TEST ITEMS AT DIFFERENT LEVELS OF HYPNOTIC SUSCEPTIBILITY. The score losses of 4 or more points are predominantly by the subjects most susceptible to hypnosis, while many subjects low in susceptibility actually gained a few points when tested following the suggestion of personality change.

The test questions are too few to make adequate comparison with published norms, but one approach to the problem is to compare the scores of the least susceptible subjects with the most susceptible subjects, *prior* to the suggestion of change. The argument is that the least susceptible subjects ought to be giving their more nearly "normal" responses, while the most susceptible subjects are giving "hypnotic state" responses. Such a comparison is made in Table 53. If this argument is correct, then the fact that the average intelligence test scores before the suggested personality change are essentially

TABLE 53. CONTROL SCORES ON WECHSLER ITEMS AND SCORES AFTER SUGGESTED PERSONALITY ALTERATION BY LEAST SUSCEPTIBLE AND MOST SUSCEPTIBLE SUBJECTS

	All scores within attempted hypnotic induction			
Wechsler item score	Least susceptible subjects ($N = 64$)		Most susceptible subjects ($N = 45$)	
	Mean	SD	Mean	SD
Before suggested personality change	7.39	1.92	7.47	1.67
Following suggested personality change	8.06	2.36	2.96	2.36
Difference in means	.67		−4.51	
Correlation, before and after	.52		.06	
t	3.32		−10.74	
p	.01		.001	

alike for the least and most susceptible subjects means that being in an hypnotic state does not *in itself* lower responsiveness on intelligence test items. This argument assumes that the two groups would be equally intelligent outside hypnosis, an assumption that is consistent with our inability to find a correlation between intelligence and hypnosis within our samples. After the suggested personality change the least susceptible subjects actually make somewhat higher scores, but it may be that the alternate before-and-after short forms are not exactly equivalent. In any case the contrast with the highly susceptible subjects is striking, for their *loss* in score is highly significant.

HYPNOSIS AND MULTIPLE PERSONALITY

The possibility of becoming so involved in an alternate role that it becomes, temporarily, the "real" personality is implied in fugues, in which a strange personality is adopted for some time, or in alternating or multiple personalities, in which the individual appears to be now one person, now another.

These, in fullblown form, are quite rare, and our own experience has not included any persistent multiple personalities. The issue within hypnosis is whether hypnosis merely reveals underlying splits within the personality, or whether it *creates* these personalities through suggestion. There is no doubt that such effects appear within hypnosis, however they are produced (for example, Harriman, 1942; Leuba, 1942; Leavitt, 1947; Bowers and Brecher, 1955). In the patient whom they studied, Bowers and Brecher thought they detected that the three underlying personalities had existed prior to hypnosis, although the subject in his ordinary state of consciousness was not aware of them. While Leavitt felt that he had induced the three personalities in his subject, the personalities were at the same time coherent with trends within the normal personality. This is a puzzling matter, and the final answers are not yet ready to be given.

The importance of continuity of memories in maintaining the integrity of personalities cannot be overlooked; many of us act in quite different roles from time to time, but because our memories are continuous, no full "dissociation" is involved. The possibility of amnesia, however, which is commonly associated with the highly hypnotizable individual, permits roles to be unavailable to memory, and in this case multiple personality manifestations may emerge.

Some of our cases of regression are very much like this, including the case cited earlier of the young woman who felt sorry for herself as the child in the regressed incident, for the "child" did not have the memories that "she" had (Chap. 8, page 171).

CONCLUDING COMMENTS ON DISTORTIONS OF MEANING, AFFECT, AND PERSONALITY

Because of the prominence of words in the induction of hypnosis and of verbal suggestions in producing hypnotic behavior of all kinds, distortions of verbal meaning and verbal behavior generally take on special significance for the understanding of hypnosis. Hence further investigations of aphasias, agnosias, and aphonias (loss of voice) would be illuminating.

We have scarcely scratched the surface with respect to affect. Others have found that the production of anxiety under hypnosis is extremely useful in connection with various problems of psychodynamics (for example, Blum, 1961, 1963; Levitt and others, 1964).

The problem of the nature of dissociation has been a bugbear for many years, ever since the notion was given prominence by Morton Prince (1916) and Pierre Janet (1920). Despite the "refutations" of dissociation from time to time (for example, Messerschmidt, 1927;

Rosenberg, 1959) it remains, at a descriptive level, a useful characterization of some aspects of hypnosis in which some of the behavior does appear to be "split off" from the normal memories, the normal standards of criticism, and the normal aspects of self-control. The personality-distortion item, along with regression and automatic writing, dramatize features of what is meant by dissociation.

By including in our scales a few items in which distortion of meaning, affect, and personality can be displayed, we have hoped to represent the domain of hypnotic effects more fully than if such manifestations had been ignored. Because of limits of time to be spent in appraising the susceptibility of a subject, the sample of items from such a rich field is necessarily sparse.

Part III

What the Hypnotizable Person is Like

Nobody can tell whether or not a person who presents himself for hypnosis will prove to be hypnotizable. Still, if people are so unlike in their degrees of hypnotizability, there must be some reason for it. It is the search for these reasons as to why people differ that will occupy us in the next five chapters. Thus there may be differences associated with age or sex or level of anxiety; perhaps the hypnotizable person has had experiences like hypnosis in ordinary life. We shall look at these questions in various ways, examining the results of personality tests and reviewing the clinician's personal interviews with those who present themselves for hypnosis, both before and after their attempted hypnotic induction.

What the Hypnotizable Person Is Like

CHAPTER 11

Effects of Age, Sex,
and Neuropsychiatric Diagnosis

One of the nagging problems in personality appraisal is the difficulty of finding agreement on the appropriate variables according to which people can be classified. From time to time we turn to type theories, categorizing people according to their bodily shapes or facial features or temperaments, or on the basis of such psychological traits as introversion and extraversion. The relative success of intelligence tests encouraged the development of personality tests modeled after them, leading to scales or measurements of the dimensions of personality in preference to characterization by types. Intelligence tests had the distinct advantage that the answers on a test could be scored in accordance with their agreement with truth and fact, so that the technical problems that remained were merely those of having the tests fair to the subject taking the test and of having the items arranged in some sort of difficulty scale. The problems confronting the personality tester were far more difficult. There is no standard of truth and fact whereby to decide that "blushing frequently" deserves a high or low personality score. Of course one can count up complaints or troubles (how many times the subject answers "yes" to a question such as "I often feel just miserable"), but it is not clear that this will distinguish the effective person from the ineffective one in the same way that the number of correct answers will separate the intellectually competent from the intellectually incompetent. The problem is to find simple standards of effective personality that can be measured by a test. Hypnotic susceptibility holds up better than most personality measures. The internal consistency of the test items that sample hypnotizability and the intercorrelations of the various criteria of hypnotic susceptibility provide a kind of anchor against which to reflect other measures; if some of the other measures can be found meaningfully related to hypnosis, they can eventually become more meaningfully related to each other.

There is no guarantee that a stable criterion will produce the kind of understanding of individuality that we seek. Thus body build perhaps corresponds in potential usefulness and measurability to hypnotic susceptibility in the sense that it is personality-relevant and can be appraised quite objectively. Yet the studies of body build have not proved to be solutions, despite the occasional claims made for them. It just happens that body build is not sufficiently related to personality to be the key to its secrets. It may very well be that hypnotic susceptibility is a specialized characteristic that will also fail to tell us much about personality, though there are good reasons why it should be promising. Among these are that it (1) is an interpersonal process, reflecting features of dominant–submissive behavior that are of wide interest, (2) involves the free play of fantasy in a manner that suggests relevance to personality flexibility, autonomy from the environment, and possible relationship to creativity, and (3) bears importantly upon the voluntary–involuntary distinction that is important in relation to initiative, leadership, and planfulness. There is no assurance that these relationships will be found, but it is a rich enough field to be worth tilling.

As we shall see later (Chap. 16) there is some plausibility to the notion that hypnotic susceptibility is not something that has to be acquired specially. It may be an ability that we all have early in life but that some of us lose as a result of training. If that is so, there ought to be heightened hypnotizability in childhood, with reduction later on. Hence one area of exploration is the changes in susceptibility with age. Since dependency relationships are thought to be different in men and women, we might also expect sex differences. Because of the similarity of things done in hypnosis to some neurotic symptoms, a relation to neuroticism would not be implausible. Hence we turn to what evidence there is along these lines before spinning theories about hypnosis in relation to them.

AGE AND SUSCEPTIBILITY

The classical study of susceptibility through the age span is one of Liébeault's, published some 80 years ago (Beaunis, 1887). He found children more susceptible than adults, with the height of susceptibility between the ages of 7 and 14 (Figure 15). There appeared to be a

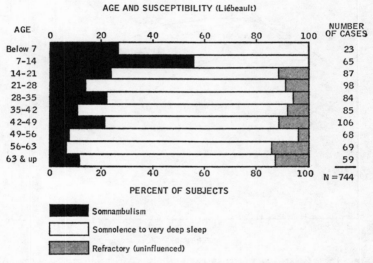

FIGURE 15. AGE AND SUSCEPTIBILITY TO HYPNOSIS. The data are from Liébeault as reported by Beaunis, 1887. From Hilgard and others, 1961, p. 6.

decline in susceptibility through the adult years, but it is slight, if indeed it can be demonstrated at all. Messerschmidt (1933a, 1933b), one of Hull's students, studied the suggestibility of young boys to several waking suggestion measures. In postural sway, which later studies have confirmed to be related to hypnotizability, she found an increase in responsiveness from age 5 to high points at ages 6 and 8, with slow decline thereafter. The next important study was that of Stukát (1958).

Although Stukát, like Messerschmidt, did not actually hypnotize children, he gave them a large number of suggestion tests, some of which classify as tests of "primary suggestibility" and hence may be considered related to hypnosis. There were 319 children in his sample, aged 8 through 14. The three tests of "primary suggestibility" were body sway, arm-lowering, and a Chevreul pendulum. The tests of "secondary suggestibility" included four personal ones (leading questions, majority and authority suggestions, co-judge influence on weight pairs, and responsiveness to contradictory suggestions) and

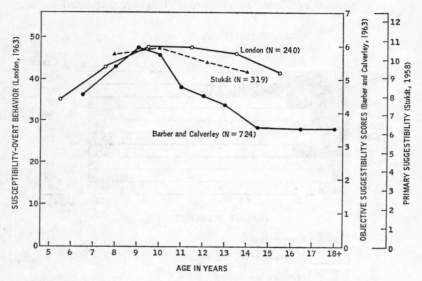

FIGURE 16. CHANGES IN RESPONSIVENESS TO SUGGESTIONS WITH AGE IN THREE INVESTIGATIONS. The subjects in the study by London (1965a) were tested after induction of hypnosis; the others were tested in the waking condition without any formal induction of hypnosis (Stukát, 1958; Barber and Calverley, 1963b).

two impersonal ones (weight pairs, and a sensory hallucination test). Stukát found a marked decline with age from 8 to 14 in the tests of secondary suggestibility, but no significant change in primary suggestibility within this age range.

Recent investigations of hypnotic susceptibility in children began with the work of London (1962b), and Moore and Lauer (1963) who found some differences in responsiveness between children and adults, but failed to find any distinctive age changes within the groups as tested. In a more extensive study, testing 240 children, London (1965a) has found definite changes with age, with the maximum susceptibility between the ages of 9 and 14, falling to adult levels at 15 to 16. A related study, which, like Stukát's, did not use any hypnotic induction, has been done by Barber and Calverley (1963b) with 724 children in the sample. They also found maximum suggestibility about ages 9 to 10, but in their sample the falloff with age beyond that was more rapid than in either Stukát's or London's sam-

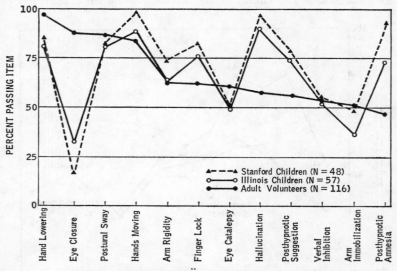

FIGURE 17. DIFFERENCES IN ITEM DIFFICULTY FOR CHILDREN AND ADULTS. The Illinois children were tested by London (1962b), the Stanford ones by Moore and Lauer (1963). The adult volunteers used for a comparison group come from a Harvard study (Shor and Orne, 1963) and a Stanford study (Boucher and Hilgard, 1962). From Moore and Lauer, 1963, p. 171.

ple (Figure 16). It is not implausible that the effects of hypnotic induction are more detectable with increasing age, and that the more rapid falloff in the Barber–Calverley study is a consequence of their not using an induction procedure. Some support for this conjecture comes from the subjective involvement scores which both London and Barber and Calverley report. There tends to be higher involvement in hypnosis at the higher ages; it is conceivable that there could be an interaction effect with induction so that objective scores are increased with the increased involvement when hypnotic induction procedures are used at these higher ages.

What are the differences in responsiveness between children and adults on these tests? Moore and Lauer (1963) asked this question, and pointed out that in both the Illinois data and the Stanford data the distributions for percent passing the various items were quite different between children and adults (Figure 17). The most striking differences lie in the children's dislike for closing their eyes and in

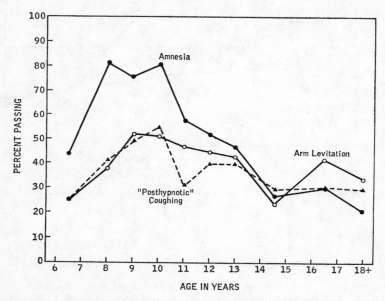

FIGURE 18. CONTRAST BETWEEN AGE CHANGES FOR POSTHYPNOTIC AMNESIA AND FOR OTHER RESPONSES TO SUGGESTION. The data have been plotted from that tabulated by Barber and Calverley (1963b).

the ease with which they have hallucinations and amnesia. Examination of some of the evidence presented by Barber and Calverley (1963b) reveals these differential age trends for specific items (Figure 18). The age trends for amnesia relative to arm levitation and a "posthypnotic" response show amnesia to reach its height earlier and to be much easier than the motor items at ages 8 to 10. At these ages about 80 percent of the children pass the amnesia item, compared with about 50 percent passing the motor items. When the adult level is reached, however, at ages 18 to 22, amnesia has become the most difficult of all the items. Even though these items were tested without prior hypnotic induction, the evidence is coherent with that presented for responses following induction by London (1962b) and Moore and Lauer (1963).

The differences in hypnotic responsiveness of children and adults deserve further study because of their importance in relationship to development and personality theory. It will be recalled that Freud made the supposition that hallucinations were part of very primitive thinking ("primary process" thinking), and he also emphasized childhood amnesia. The prevalence of hallucinatory behavior and amnesia in these samples of children lends some cogency to his comments and perhaps bears on the regressive interpretation of hypnosis in adults.

SEX DIFFERENCES

Probably because of the association between hypnosis and hysteria (Charcot) it was long supposed that women were more hypnotizable than men, but this conjecture has also been denied for many years. Weitzenhoffer (1953), reviewing earlier evidence, agreed that women tend often to score as more suggestible or susceptible to hypnosis than men, many studies reporting slight but nonsignificant differences in this direction. Later studies, however, have tended to deny these differences. In a study comparing the results for 100 men and 100 women, half of each sex hypnotized by a male hypnotist, half by a female hypnotist, no sex difference was demonstrated (Weitzenhoffer and Weitzenhoffer, 1958a). The results from repeated testing in our laboratory have failed to reveal any sex differences, beyond an initial study in which such differences were reported (Hilgard, Weitzenhoffer, and Gough, 1958). For example, the mean of Form A for 272 males from our regular samples is 5.59 (*SD* 3.12), for 261 females 5.65 (*SD* 3.42), obviously a nonsignificant difference between the means. While some subtle sex differences will doubtless be discovered in time, the general burden of evidence at present is that men and women are equally susceptible to hypnosis.

NEUROPSYCHIATRIC DIAGNOSIS

Despite the many years that hypnosis has been used in psychotherapy, little is known about the relative hypnotizability of patients falling into the various categories, nor about the depth of hypnosis necessary for successful psychotherapy. The fact that very light hypnosis suffices for therapy means that the practitioner often cares very little how susceptible his subject is, so long as he gets somewhere in treatment. Bernheim (1888) was clear long ago that patients were responsive to suggestion with very little hypnosis, and he recommended starting therapeutic suggestions before the patient had entered the trance. Platonov (1959), a student of Bekhterev, who also used suggestive psychotherapy with patients very little hypnotizable, refers to the method using very light hypnosis as the Bekhterev–Bernheim method.

The evidence is not very extensive about how different groups of subjects deviating somewhat from the norm fare in hypnotic susceptibility, but such evidence as there is can be noted rather briefly.

Mental deficiency and hypnosis. Mentally deficient subjects have been thought poor candidates for hypnosis because of their lack of verbal abilities and their incapacity for concentration. Sternlicht and Wanderer (1963), however, found 12 of 20 mentally deficient children hypnotizable (ages 7–16; mental age 3.3 to 9.0). Within this small sample there were positive rank-order correlations between subjectively estimated hypnotic depth and both mental age and intelligence quotient (.52 and .77, respectively). Five of the six high hypnotic scores were made by those with mental ages of six and above, one with a mental age of five (chronological age, 9; IQ 56). Thus the minimum intellectual level needed for satisfactory hypnosis appears to correspond to the verbal abilities of a kindergarten or elementary school child.

Neurotic diagnoses. Despite the many years that hypnosis has been used in psychotherapy, little is known about the relative hypnotizability of patients falling into the various categories of disturbance. Charcot's contention that only hysterics could be hypnotized was refuted by many of the early writers on hypnosis. The general summary by Gill and Brenman (1959) was to the effect that neurotics are less hypnotizable than normal individuals, while hysterics are perhaps more hypnotizable than other neurotics, and most schizophrenics not hypnotizable. These conclusions were based on a study by Ehrenreich (1949), which, while based on a large sample (717 patients, mostly psychiatric cases; 180 normal adults in various subclasses), has been very sketchily reported and should be repeated.

There is evidence coming from Eysenck's laboratory that psychiatrically diagnosed neurotics are in fact more suggestible (as measured by the postural sway test) than a normal population (Eysenck, 1943b, 1944; Furneaux, 1946, 1952). The group of neurotic army patients tested by Eysenck and Furneaux (1945) distributed very much the way in which a normal subject group does, however. Hence great differences between normals and neurotics are scarcely to be expected.

Hypnosis among psychotics. Most of the studies recently reported deny the allegation that psychotics are little hypnotizable. The literature has been reviewed by Abrams (1964). The three studies whose quantitative results he reports are those of Wilson, Cormen, and Cole (1949), Gale and Herman (1956), and Heath, Hoaken, and Sainz (1960), all of whom found upwards of 50 percent of the psychotics studied to be hypnotizable, whether they were classified as belonging to the functional or organic groups, or whether or not classified as paranoid schizophrenics. A recent study by Kramer and Brennan (1964) reports the results of testing 25 hospitalized schizophrenic women on SHSS, Form A. The resulting mean score was 8.00 (of a possible 12 points), with a standard deviation of 1.83, as high a mean as found for volunteer samples of college students.[1] In this sample scores below five were missing, and six of the 25 scored between 10 and 12. There is thus no reason to expect psychotics to be any less hypnotizable than normal subjects, with the proviso, of course, that a psychotic patient may not be in sufficient contact for hypnosis to be attempted at all. Abrams believes, as a result of his review of the evidence, that hypnosis may be a useful aid to therapy with psychotics and, with reasonable care, involves few dangers. He has reported the successful treatment of a schizophrenic patient with the aid of hypnosis (Abrams, 1963).

The only counterevidence on the hypnotizability of schizophrenics comes from a study by Barber, Karacan, and Calverley (1964), in which they found schizophrenics little susceptible to hypnosis. They point out, however, that the population studied was a chronic one, and little indication is given of the manner in which rapport was estab-

---

[1] Some concern was expressed by reviewers of the Kramer and Brennan study lest the fact that the patients were on tranquilizers might have influenced their hypnotizability. Studies at Napa State Hospital, where the original work was done, have since shown that phenathiazines do not increase scores on the tests; the only significant difference found for drug effects within a doublebind study was that prolixin enthanate made subjects less cooperative and more of them refused to participate in the hypnotic study (Vingoe and Kramer, 1966).

lished. The patients studied by Kramer and Brennan (1964) were more recent admissions and were in a psychotherapeutic relationship. Not all schizophrenics are alike, and the relationship between hypnotist and patient is particularly important in securing their cooperation. Webb and Nesmith (1964) found normal subjects more suggestible than psychiatric patients on a postural sway test, and psychotics more suggestible than nonpsychotics.

Normal subjects classified clinically. While we have not extended the studies in our laboratory to patient populations, in the course of interviewing our subjects prior to hypnosis, the interviewers formed some impressions of their personalities and recorded these in the form of ratings. One set of ratings permitted the classification of subjects into three groups, a normal-outgoing group, a troubled-withdrawn group, and a borderline group that fell between these two extremes. The troubled-withdrawn group might under some circumstances be classified as neurotic, but it must be emphasized that these were all students carrying a normal class load in a competitive university setting. They were functioning within a normal range, and coming to our laboratory only as part of fulfilling course requirements.

When classified in this way, differences are not striking, though there is a tendency, statistically significant ($p < .025$), for the normal-outgoing group to prove more susceptible than the troubled-withdrawn (Table 54). These results, within the normal range, are in agreement

TABLE 54. HYPNOTIC SUSCEPTIBILITY OF SUBJECTS WITHIN THE NORMAL RANGE CLASSIFIED CLINICALLY ($N = 100$)

Score on SHSS, Form C	Normal-outgoing	Troubled-withdrawn	Total
More susceptible (7–12)	28	10	38
Less susceptible (0–6)	30	32	62
Total	58	42	100

$\chi^2 = 6.2, p < .025$.

with the findings of Ehrenreich (1949) for the contrast between the normal and the diagnosed neurotic.

CONCLUSIONS ON THE GENERAL CHARACTERISTICS AFFECTING HYPNOTIZABILITY

The general characteristics studied here (age, sex, and neuro-psychiatric diagnosis) permit a few assertions.

It may be stated with a high degree of confidence that children in the age range of 8 to 12 respond more readily to hypnoticlike suggestions (with or without induction of hypnosis) than either younger or older children, and that the adult level of responding is reached perhaps between ages 14 and 18. The change in susceptibility with age brings with it a change in pattern of response, most notably the decrease in the proportion of the population capable of posthypnotic amnesia. It is possible, but not clearly proven, that the importance of hypnotic induction in setting the stage for response to suggestion increases after the period of peak hypnotic susceptibility.

Evidence has been mounting for many years that there are no appreciable differences in hypnotic susceptibility to be attributed to sex, whether of subject or hypnotist. A statistical statement of this kind does not preclude many kinds of individual differences, and *some* subjects may of course be responsive to a male hypnotist and others to a female hypnotist; the point is that these personal idiosyncrasies wash out over groups, so that no generalization is possible respecting the relationship between sex and hypnotizability in general other than that there is none.

The evidence with respect to normals, neurotics, and psychotics is not firmly established and in some cases is contradictory. It can be said with confidence that there is no diagnostic category that precludes hypnotic susceptibility; correspondingly there is none that guarantees it. At least two studies (including our own) are in agreement that normal subjects are more hypnotizable than those who border on the neurotic or are frankly neurotic. This should help correct the public image that being susceptible to hypnosis is a sign of weakness or instability.

CHAPTER 12

Hypnoticlike Experiences
Outside Hypnosis

Psychologists are familiar with many experiences that, although they seem unusual, are found to be universal when the conditions for demonstrating them are arranged. Because such phenomena require no practice (or at most very little) they must have been in some way incorporated within daily experiences where they have passed unnoticed. The blind spot is a good example, easily plotted if one eye is kept covered, and the open eye fixed upon a point while a target is moved appropriately across the visual field. People do not ordinarily become familiar with the blind spot because vision is commonly with both eyes open, and in patterned vision the blind spot is phenomenally "filled in." Another example is that of double vision, such that when the two eyes are focused on some near point objects at a distance are doubled, and when focused on a far point near objects are doubled. These double images are usually "neglected," if indeed they are even dimly perceived, but it is easy to demonstrate them, for example, by holding the index finger of each hand upright and in line before the eyes, one six inches in front of the nose, the other six inches further beyond. Then if you look at the near finger the far one is doubled, and if you look at the far one the near one is doubled. Among susceptible subjects who have never before been hypnotized the appropriate experiences come so quickly at their first opportunity (with or even without a short induction) that something of the same sort must be happening as takes place in perception; that is, there must be many similar experiences within daily life that are neglected until attention is called to them by making circumstances appropriate for their demonstration. Probably some of these experiences, like the perceptual ones, are universal; however, individual differences in hypnotic susceptibility lead us to conclude that some people have had more of them than others.

This line of thinking has been followed by a number of investigators who have sought to find in ordinary experience the kinds of behavior that are called for in hypnosis, and from the prevalence of these experiences in a subject's reports have tried to estimate his hypnotizability.

THE CONSTRUCTION OF HYPNOTICLIKE EXPERIENCES INVENTORIES

Systematic work along these lines was first undertaken by Shor (1960). He built a 44-item written questionnaire by means of which to study naturally occurring "hypnoticlike" experiences, which has come to be known, in revised form, as the Personal Experiences Questionnaire (PEQ). Although he made no special effort to categorize the items, they reflected a wide range of experiences, such as being lulled to sleep in a lecture or concert, staring blankly into space, talking or walking in sleep, mystical or deeply religious experiences, especially absorbing experiences, amnesic periods, dissociation of mind and body. He was initially interested in the prevalence of these experiences, hypothesizing that if hypnosis is so readily induced in so many people, some similar kinds of experience must be relatively common. He found this to be so; the median for a group of 80 engineering students at Boston University, all but two male, was 41 percent "Yes" answers favoring such experiences, and for 65 Brandeis University students, mostly female, the median percentage of "Yes" replies was 59. The fact that many people have had hypnoticlike experiences does not yet establish the correspondence between these experiences and hypnotizability, but it makes such a correspondence plausible.

Shor's work was soon carried further by others, particularly by Ås and his associates working in our laboratory (Ås, O'Hara, and Munger, 1962). They adopted Shor's general instructions to the subject, selected 18 of his questions for comparative study on a new sample, and added 42 new questions to construct a 60-item Experience Inventory (EI). In order to test some particular hypotheses about hypnosis, they classified their items into nine categories selected as representing varied interpretations of the phenomenology of hypnosis. The background and some sample items are as follows:

A. *Altered state; fading of generalized reality-orientation.* This category was based in part on suggestions by Shor (1959), and all the items are from his questionnaire. A typical question: "Have you ever actively stared at something and had it slowly (or suddenly) become very strange before your eyes?" (Yes).

B. *Tolerance for logical inconsistencies.* Based in part on Orne's notion of "trance logic" (Orne, 1959), this assumes that a susceptible person ought not be too much provoked or alerted by perceived logical inconsistencies. A typical question in this category: "Do you think that many people in our culture have visions at some time or other?" (Yes).

C. *Role-taking.* This is based on the well-known proposal by Sarbin (1950) that role-enactment is the most characteristic feature of hypnotic behavior. Specimen question: "Have you ever had the experience of telling a story with elaborations to make it sound better and then having the elaborations seem as real to you as the actual incidents?" (Yes).

D. *Dissociation; exclusion of distracting stimuli.* Dissociation is, of course, one of the classical interpretations of hypnosis. In another form it refers to selective inattention—that is, concentrating so much on some part of the field as to exclude others (Barber, 1960; Leuba, 1960). Example: "Have you ever experienced a part of your body move and have the feeling that it was moving without your volition?" (Yes).

E. *Willingness to relinquish ego control.* Turning over at least part of the ego's control to the hypnotist is a frequently asserted aspect of hypnosis, particularly by psychoanalytic writers (A. Freud, 1936; Gill and Brenman, 1959). Illustrative question: "Do you always want to have knowledge and information about what you are doing or taking part in, so that you are not lured into something over which you have no control?" (No).

F. *Tolerance for regressive experiences.* The notion of regression in the service of the ego, proposed by Kris (1952) and used in reference to hypnosis by Gill and Brenman (1959) is here broken into at least two components, of tolerance for regression (this category) and the constructive use of regression (the next category). Tolerance means that regressive experiences (affects, primary-process experiences, infantilisms) do not stir up an inordinate amount of anxiety or guilt, but can be tolerated or even enjoyed. Example: "Would you like to indulge in emotions and sensations with the feeling of just 'letting go'?" (Yes).

G. *Constructive use of regression.* Humor, creativity, and hypnosis may have in common the capacity to make use of a partial regression, and then to return from it with a better solution to a realistic problem. Example: "Have you ever found a sort of fulfillment of yourself in creating something, as in crafts, science, writing, art, or music?" (Yes).

H. *Peak experiences; philobatism.* The idea of peak experiences that are in some way both overwhelming and self-fulfilling comes from Maslow (1959) while the coined word "philobatism" is Balint's (1959) for what is essentially "love of acrobatics," that is, adventure, thrill, controlled danger, willingness to face the unknown courageously. Question: "Have you ever been completely immersed in nature or in art (for example, in the mountains, at the ocean, viewing sculpture, paintings, etc.) and had a feeling of awe, inspiration, and grandeur sweep over you so that you felt as if your whole state of consciousness was somehow temporarily altered?" (Yes). Another: "Do you enjoy roller-coasters, ferris wheels, and similar 'thrills' at amusement parks?" (Yes).

I. *Basic trust; interpersonal relations.* It may be assumed that a subject who can trust the hypnotist will be more likely to become hypnotized than one who can't, according to such a motivational theory as that of White (1941). Specimen question: "Have you usually found it easy to yield to others and to discipline asked by others?" (Yes).

The universality of such experiences among college students is attested by the correspondence between the results obtained on the East Coast by Shor and now on the West Coast. Shor (1960) found a rank order correlation between frequencies at Brandeis and Boston of $+.90$; Ås and his associates found for the 18 items in common within Shor's questionnaire and Ås's a rank order correlation between Brandeis and Stanford equal to $+.84$ and between Boston and Stanford one equal to $+.79$. These correlations refer to the frequencies of positive answers to the various items; they mean that an experience reported frequently at one place was likely to be reported frequently at the other.

At this stage their relationship to hypnosis is still conjectural, but if the questions actually tap abilities related to hypnosis, then the experience inventory becomes a means of hypothesis-testing about hypnosis. Before going on to the study of hypnosis, the Ås group studied the inventory itself in order to determine whether the internal characteristics justified the various categories. By selecting out 24 items that appeared to be most representative of the categories (from 2 to 4 questions from each of the groups), they had a pool of items to serve as the basis for both a cluster analysis and a factor analysis. The cluster analysis was done with the items pooled according to their intended categories; the factor analysis was done by correlating the items individually. The results of the two analyses were consonant in showing mainly two factors underlying the relationships within the responses to the inventory. The first factor, which they called *role absorption,* combined the role-taking items with the peak experience items; the second factor, tentatively described as *early experience of and tolerance of unusual states* included items from altered state, tolerance for logical inconsistencies and for regression, dissociation, and willingness to relinquish ego control. These two factors seem plausible enough; it remained to be seen if they were indeed related to hypnotizability.

The items entering into Ås's detailed analyses were too few from each category to be very clear about the differential effects by category. Hence Evelyn Lee (1965), also working in our laboratory, determined to investigate the consequences of building an inventory with an equal number of items per category, so that subscales could be used in correlations with hypnotic susceptibility. She selected five categories, somewhat related to those of Ås, with 12 questions per category, thus coming out also with a 60-item questionnaire, the same length as the Ås EI. It included 30 of the Ås questions (which in turn included 10 from Shor), but there were 30 new ones added. She called her inventory the Hypnotic Characteristics Inventory (HCI). Her categories were derived, as indeed were Ås's, on the basis of some suggestions coming out of the interview program within the laboratory (see Chap. 18). Her five categories, with specimen questions, were:

I. *Conformity vs. autonomy.* The idea here is that a hypnotized subject ought to be willing to be led, and ought not to value too highly autonomous, self-controlled activity. Some of the items came from the categories labeled by Ås as basic trust and willingness to relinquish ego control; her own items added matters such as competition and leader-ship–followership. Example: "In general, do you prefer to follow rather than to direct?" (Yes).

II. *Trancelike experiences.* All but one of the items came from Ås's role-taking, dissociation, altered state, tolerance for logical incon-sistencies, and peak experiences. The new item was of similar sort: "When you dance, do you feel that the music and the mood are being expressed through your movements, while you yourself fade into the background?" (Yes).

III. *Role-playing.* These items again rest heavily on those that Ås classified as role-taking, but one is included that he classified as a peak experience; the new ones involve other aspects of roles, in-cluding role-flexibility. Specimen question: "While watching a movie or show do you sometimes become so involved that you feel yourself participating in the action?" (Yes).

IV. *Impulsivity vs. rationality.* The thought here is that a successful hypnotic subject ought to be able to act upon impulse and to set aside temporarily the demands of reality-testing and rationality. The items overlap those Ås classified as willingness to relinquish ego control and tolerance for regressive experiences. Representative ques-tion: "Do you often do things on the spur of the moment which you wouldn't do if considered carefully?" (Yes).

V. *Concentration and absorption.* The belief that hypnosis repre-sents a capacity to concentrate attention and to resist distractions is an old one, and this category provides a test of it. The three questions carried over from Ås come from his categories of dissociation and altered state, while the new ones deal rather directly with attention and engrossed activity. Example: "Are you frequently late for meals because you are engrossed in something?" (Yes).

Lee sorted her items into these categories on the basis of substantial agreement among a group of 10 judges, and on the basis of significant positive biserial correlations of responses to each item with the total for the category. Thus a degree of "purification" of the subscales is involved over the earlier scales.

Several points may be made about the Shor PEQ, the Ås EI, and the Lee HCI, all of which have much in common. For one thing, they call attention to the broad ranges of experiences that can be sampled in questionnaires. The assumption that the item pools of such long tests as the Strong Vocational Interest Blank, the MMPI, or the CPI, actually sample all aspects of experience is incorrect. Although a question or two can be found in the subcategories of the hypnotic-experiences inventories, there are not enough questions in these standard inventories to give anything like an adequate sample of the experiences probed for in the hypnotic-experiences questionnaires. A second point is that attempts at categorization of items are none too successful, so that items classified one way by one investigator are classified in another way by the next investigator. Actual items are in this sense "impure" or perhaps "overdetermined." What this means is that a good role-playing item may at once represent absorption, peak experience, and regression; it may be "correctly" categorized in more than one way.

With these descriptions of the inventories and their respective rationales we are ready to see what has been found when responses to them are related to tested hypnotic susceptibility.

CORRELATIONS BETWEEN INVENTORY RESULTS AND HYPNOTIC SUSCEPTIBILITY

Although others have also done some work along these lines (Barber and Glass, 1962; Evans and Thorn, 1964), we turn only to the results of the three inventories just described.

Shor's Personal Experiences Questionnaire (PEQ). The use of Shor's inventory in relation to hypnotic susceptibility was reported by Shor, Orne, and O'Connell (1962).

The PEQ was extended to 149 items, arranged to be scored for both frequency and intensity of the experience. That is, in reply to each question the subject was asked to indicate whether the experience had occurred never, very rarely, rarely, occasionally, often, very often, always. He was also asked to check whether the experience (if it occurred at all) had been intense, and to give two checks if at its most intense it had been extremely profound. These authors recognized that categories overlap, but their "search pattern" in choice of items included items that would reflect the following kinds of activities, characteristics, or abilities: sleeping or preparing for sleep; dreams and dreaming; concentration and quieting of mental activities; naturally occurring trance experiences; amnesias, absent-mindedness, or unusual forgetting in everyday life; suggestibility in everyday life situations; freedom in emotional expression; loss of awareness of reality while absorbed or preoccupied; control of attentional processes; naturally occurring illusions and hallucinations; lack of distinction between imaged or pseudoreality and actual reality; artistic, mystical, transcendental, and profound religious experiences; detachment, depersonalization, and estrangement from self or reality.

Their first test was to compare the results of the PEQ with scores on SHSS, Form A, for 29 college students. The frequency measure proved to yield nothing, although their report is unclear as to how they dichotomized their scores for the chi square tests. The intensity measure (simply the total number of checks for intense and profound experiences) proved to correlate with hypnotic susceptibility. Although the correlation was not reported as such, 95 percent of the items yielded positive phi coefficients with the Form A hypnotic scores (median $= +.22$), and 45 met a predetermined cutoff standard of phi $= +.31$ or higher. These 45 items were then used in a cross-validation study.

The cross-validation study was done on a somewhat artificial sample of 25 college students whose hypnotic performances were well known. The sample has the advantage that the sorting of the subjects into hypnotic susceptibility groups was done after thorough experience with them, so that they were all near their asymptotes of hypnotic performance. There were 7 classified as less than light, 6 as light, 4 as medium, and 8 as deep. Such a sample has a higher than usual standard deviation because of the inclusion of the 8 cases showing deep hypnosis in a sample of but 25 cases; this of course will tend to raise all correlations. At the same time, such a sample does not *create* the correlations unless they are there in fact. After careful sorting of the subjects into these groups on the basis of clinical judgments by two experienced hypnotists judging independently it was found that they agreed almost perfectly ($r = .96$); when these judgments were correlated with SHSS, Form A, scores, the correlation was found to be $r = .83$. These high agreements are in part a function of the dispersion within the sample, but they are in any case reassuring.

The correlation between the 45 best items of the PEQ, based on the earlier sample, and the SHSS, Form A, scores for this cross-validation sample turned out to be $r = .46$. The corresponding correlation with rated hypnotic depth was $r = .44$. These correlations are satisfactorily significant, but not high in view of the nature of the sample.[1] These authors went on to an interesting suggestion that the PEQ might be particularly useful in relation to the highly suggestible subjects. If they took the 8 subjects who scored at least 10 on the SHSS, Form A (rated by them clinically as deep), and divided them into three groups, deep, very deep, and extremely deep, they found on their intensity measure a correlation of .84 for these 8 subjects, based on the scatterplot of Figure 19.

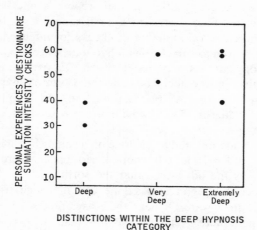

FIGURE 19. POSSIBILITY THAT HYPNOTICLIKE EXPERIENCES DISCRIMI-NATE AMONG SUBJECTS CAPABLE OF DEEP TO EXTREMELY DEEP HYP-NOSIS. From Shor, Orne, and O'Connell, 1962, p. 70.

The value of this observation, should it be confirmed, is analytical, not predictive, because the *deep* subjects in this analysis score in the same range as the *less than light* ones, and it is the low scores among the *deep* that determine the correlation because the *very deep* and *extremely deep* subjects score essentially alike.

We have attempted to examine the generality of these conclusions by making the assumption that Ås's EI and Lee's HCI measure the same thing as the PEQ intensity scale. This is not entirely accurate,

---

[1] It is to be regretted that we do not have the correlation with the full PEQ for these subjects. As we shall see later, there is no assurance that having selected the best 45 items really gained anything for the cross-validation.

but, as we shall see, the correlations with hypnotic susceptibility are essentially similar. We make a further assumption that the high scores on the SPS, Forms I and II, permit a differentiation similar to that between *deep, very deep,* and *extremely deep* as made by Shor, Orne, and O'Connell (1962).

In order to find a group that might be compared with the Shor, Orne, and O'Connell eight highest subjects, all of whom scored at least 10 on the SHSS, Form A, we selected from our records on the profile scales those subjects who had scored 10 or more on Form A, and came up with 24 subjects. We then divided these 24 subjects into two groups of 12 each on the basis of their extended profile scores, yielding a group of 12 high-high subjects and a group of 12 low-high subjects. The conjecture is that the high-high subjects ought to score much higher on the experience inventory than the low-high ones. Although there is a slight mean difference favoring the high-highs, it does not turn out to be statistically significant (Table 55). Ex-

TABLE 55. RELATIONSHIP BETWEEN SPS EXTENDED PROFILE SCALE AND EXPERIENCE INVENTORY FOR HIGH SUBJECTS ($N = 24$)

	Mean score on experience inventory	
SPS extended profile scale[a]		
High-high (SPS 40+)	35.4	
($N = 12$)		$t = 1.34$ n.s.
Low-high (SPS below 40)	30.9	
($N = 12$)		

[a] This score includes total SPS score plus motor pool and amnesia score from SHSS, Form A, a total possible score of 65.

pressed as a product-moment correlation, the relation between the experience inventory and the profile scale scores is but $r = .10$, nothing like the .84 reported by Shor, Orne, and O'Connell for their 8 cases.

Although we are therefore unable to support the special findings of an unusually high relationship for highly susceptible subjects, this does not detract from the more general finding that there is a positive relationship between the PEQ and measured hypnotic susceptibility across the whole range of subjects.

Ås's Experience Inventory (EI). In his first test of the EI with two samples of women students ($N = 50$, $N = 52$), Ås found total score correlations with SHSS, Form C, of $+.36$ and $+.31$, both significant at the .01 level (Ås, 1963). In a later replication with male students ($N = 50$) he found a correlation of $+.35$ with SHSS, Form A and $+.47$ with SHSS, Form C (Ås, 1962a).[2] Thus the generally satisfactory correlation with total scores agrees with the findings of Shor and his collaborators on their intensity measure. Ås's measure is based on a simple count of reporting the experiences as having ever occurred, thus stressing neither frequency nor intensity, although the subject may have to decide for himself whether or not the experience was sufficiently intense to be worth acknowledging, and he thus may give some intensity rating to it indirectly.

A peculiar and instructive finding came from Ås's effort to purify his scale by selecting the most discriminating items from one sample and then trying them on the next. With his two female samples he was able to do this in both directions, that is, to choose the best items from the first sample and try them on the second, and correspondingly to choose the best items from the second sample and try them on the first. As a check on this, he also chose the very poor items from each sample to see if they remained poor on replication. His results are summarized in Table 56.

The results are clear and unexpected: no matter whether successful or unsuccessful items are selected, the results with the next sample are so much alike as to be virtually identical for previously "good" and previously "poor" items. Within the two samples, for example, there were only five items in common reaching the .10 level of significance in correlation with hypnotizability in both samples, although each sample had 16 to 17 such items. Further check with the later sample showed no better correlation between items selected as "best" from the sample of 102 females than the correlation with the total scale. While these results are disappointing as far as the attempt to achieve higher correlations between the EI and hypnotizability is concerned, they are informative with respect to what may be happening. There are two major possibilities:

[2] The exigencies of publication have given the later study an earlier date.

1. It may be that there are multiple paths into hypnosis, so that a few relevant experiences are enough to provide a background for it; to some extent the more of these the better, *which ones* being unimportant. If the EI has been well constructed to include only relevant experiences, then a total score can be predictive of hypnosis, even though one kind of experience is no more prepotent than another. This interpretation assumes *content relevance* without any hierarchical structure within that content.

2. It may be that the content is largely irrelevant, and we are dealing with response styles that are related to hypnosis, particularly an acquiescence tendency. Because most replies are keyed "yes," such an acquiescence tendency would lead to higher scores among the more susceptible. This interpretation that the tests are equally content-irrelevant, permitting response styles to operate, is really opposite to the first interpretation that items are equally content-relevant.

Either of these interpretations would fit the results of Table 56, so more evidence is needed, some of which has been provided by Lee (1965), to whose work we shall return presently.

In order to get at content factors more specifically, Ås and Lauer

TABLE 56. RESULTS OF EFFORT TO PURIFY THE EXPERIENCE INVENTORY THROUGH EMPIRICAL ITEM SELECTION (Ås, 1963)

	Correlation with SHSS, Form C	
	Items selected from first sample	Items selected from second sample
Selected "good" items[a]		
In sample from which selected	.68 ($N = 50$)	.59 ($N = 52$)
In replicated sample	.29 ($N = 52$)	.27 ($N = 50$)
Residual "poor" items[b]		
In sample from which selected	.08 ($N = 50$)	.08 ($N = 52$)
In replicated sample	.26 ($N = 52$)	.34 ($N = 50$)

[a] The best 16 items in the first sample and the best 17 in the second.

[b] The 44 residual items from the first sample and 43 from the second.

(1962) conducted a factor analysis in which they included in their correlation matrix the 23 most significant items of the EI as determined from the female sample ($N = 102$) and 19 items from SHSS, Forms A and C. These 19 items were chosen so as to avoid the duplicating of hypnotic items from the two scales. When the principal components factor analysis was completed and rotated, the main finding was that there were two clusters of items falling in the same quadrant of the factor space, meaning that the two item clusters were correlated (a fact guaranteed by selecting EI items that correlated with hypnotic ones). Even so, it was quite clear that most of the hypnotic items fell together, and most of the questionnaire items fell together. There was a slight amount of intermingling, but in view of the uncertainties of factor analysis, little more can be made of the results than that the actual hypnotic behaviors clustered together in a group of correlations distinguishable from the cluster of correlations produced by the verbally reported hypnoticlike experiences.

Lee's Hypnotic Characteristics Inventory. Because she had her items grouped into scales, Lee (1965) was able to use product-moment correlations and get away from some of the uncertainties introduced by the use of fourfold correlations. She first performed a factor analysis with orthogonal rotation similar to that of Ås and Lauer (1962) but with some technical improvements. She also included a Sum–True Score on an abbreviated MMPI as a marker for the acquiescence tendency and included a set of independent interviewer predictions as a check against the differences between interviewer estimates and questionnaire findings. Her results, like those of Ås and Lauer, showed all scores falling in one quadrant, with the hypnotic scores by themselves and the inventory scores by themselves, and the interview ratings more closely related to hypnosis than to the inventories. Because the Sum–True Score on the MMPI proved most representative of the cluster of inventory items, she preferred to interpret the inventory factor as representing acquiescence, thus favoring the second of the interpretations of Ås's results given on p. 233. The results of her factor analysis are plotted in Figure 20.

Because of the evident oblique relationship between the clusters, Lee decided to use another type of factor solution that permitted oblique factors. She chose the solution toward hypothesized factors as proposed by Horst (1956).[3] By this method she found three fairly

---

[3] This is the method used later by Lauer (1965).

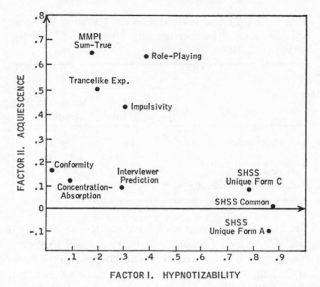

FIGURE 20. LOADINGS ON ACQUIESCENCE AND HYPNOTIZABILITY OF VAR-
IOUS SCORES RELATED TO HYPNOTIC SUSCEPTIBILITY. The hypnotizability
factor is determined by the scores on Form A and Form C; the axes have
been rotated so that the one axis runs through the median of these scores.
Then the MMPI Sum–True Scores have the highest loading on the other
factor, and three of the subscales of the Hypnotic Characteristics Inventory (HCI) (role-playing, trancelike experiences, impulsivity) all load
high on the second factor also (Lee, 1965).

defined factors, the hypnotic factor of the earlier analysis now breaking into two correlated subfactors. The three factors she named
induction-susceptibility, represented by the hypnosis items and also
by concentration and absorption on the HCI, *trance-susceptibility*
with loadings on both the hypnosis items and the inventory items, and
acquiescence-tendency, with heavy representation from the inventory
items. Because these are correlated factors, their intercorrelations turn
out to be most illuminating (Table 57).

It is most striking that trance-susceptibility correlates both with
induction-susceptibility and with acquiescence-tendency, indicating
that the inventory may be predictive for both its trancelike content
and its stylistic features; the failure of the acquiescence tendency to
correlate with induction-susceptibility ($r = -.02$) may show why the
inventory is limited in its power to predict hypnotic behavior.

TABLE 57. INTERCORRELATIONS OF FACTORS WITHIN AN EXPERIENCE INVENTORY AND HYPNOTIC SUSCEPTIBILITY (LEE, 1965)

	Correlations	
Factor	Trance-susceptibility	Acquiescence-tendency
Induction-susceptibility	.54	−.02
Trance-susceptibility		.70
Acquiescence-tendency		

All of the experience inventories have tended to have many items coded in the affirmative, because it is more natural to record experiences in that way. It is easier to ask: "Did you ever have an imaginary companion?" than to ask: "Did you never have an imaginary companion?" The latter question gets into the confusions of the double negative. While Lee was aware of this problem, she assigned the direction of the answer to the consistencies found within the subscales of her inventory *prior to* relating it to hypnosis, and some scales turned out to have more items keyed for "no" answers than others. It turned out that the scales with more items keyed "yes" correlated higher with hypnosis than those keyed "no."

In order to test the influence of the acquiescence tendency, we ignored the item contents and rescored Lee's inventories for the sum of "yes" answers and correlated these new subscale scores with hypnotic susceptibility.[4] The rationale is this. If the main point is that susceptible hypnotic subjects have a higher tendency to acknowledge hypnoticlike experiences than the less susceptible, so that in dubious cases they tend to answer "yes," then keying an answer for the response of "no" will reduce its correlation with susceptibility. By leaving the questions as they were, but counting only the "yes" answers, we have a score similar to the Sum–True Score on the MMPI, which also ignores the original intent of the question. The results are shown in Table 58. For all scales in which there were some items keyed for "no" answers, correlations with hypnosis rose when they were keyed in the direction

4 Thanks are due Janet Melei Cuca for carrying out these computations.

TABLE 58. CORRELATION WITH HYPNOTIC SUSCEPTIBILITY OF SUBSCALES OF LEE INVENTORY AS SUM–"YES" SCORES, WITH RESULTS ON AN ADDITIONAL SAMPLE

| | Correlations with SHSS, Form C | | | |
| | Lee sample (1962–63) | | New sample (1963–64) | Total (1962–64) |
Subscales	Original scores ($N = 103$)	Sum– "yes" scores ($N = 103$)	Sum– "yes" scores ($N = 82$)	Sum– "yes" scores ($N = 185$)
I. Conformity	.04	.25	.14	.21
II. Trancelike experiences[a]	.19	.19	.33	.25
III. Role-playing[a]	.38	.38	.31	.35
IV. Impulsivity	.26	.37	.23	.31
V. Concentration and absorption	.12	.15	.29	.22
Total inventory	.33	.38	.37	.38

[a] These subscales had all items keyed "yes" to begin with.

of "yes" answers regardless of content. All the correlations in the final column are significant at the .01 level. When done in this way the content differences between the subscales are lessened.

The consistent findings of relationship between hypnoticlike experiences outside and inside hypnosis, repeatedly confirmed in the Harvard and Stanford laboratories, has failed of replication in the hands of Barber and Calverley. Their study differed from the others chiefly in using the Barber Suggestibility Scale (BSS) as the indicator of hypnosis; it is not clear from the preliminary report (Barber, 1964) whether or not the questionnaires were given before or after hypnosis. Some of the subjects were tested without prior induction of hypnosis, others with prior induction. Possibly too many questions were asked at once for the subjects to take them seriously, for they were apparently given the questionnaire devised by Barber and Glass (1962) along with those of Shor, Orne, and O'Connell (1962) and that of As

(1962). In any case, their negative results deserve mention, and the differences between their studies and the others reported should ultimately receive some kind of explanation.

CONCLUSIONS REGARDING THE CONTINUITY BETWEEN WAKING EXPERIENCES AND THE ABILITY TO BE HYPNOTIZED

The results of hypnoticlike experience inventories are quite clear. Such inventories tend to correlate with a scale such as SHSS, Form C, consistently within the range of .30 to .50 with college populations; efforts to improve these correlations by finding better items, if we judge by past experience, are likely to prove futile. It is possible that the correlations would be somewhat higher for a noncollege population, in which irrationality might perhaps be less frowned upon; at the present time we do not have the evidence.

There is a certain amount of ambiguity about content-relevance in view of the prominence of the acquiescence tendency in making inventory scores predictive of hypnotizability. We shall return to a consideration of this question when we examine the results with standard personality inventories (Chap. 14).

There is little doubt, however, regardless of the pencil-and-paper results, that there are many continuities between experiences outside hypnosis and those inside. These give plausibility to the notion that the contents of the experience inventories cannot be ignored in favor of a purely response-style interpretation.

CHAPTER 13

Attitudes Toward Hypnosis
and Self-Predictions of Hypnotizability

Investigators of hypnosis commonly assert that hypnotic susceptibility has both an *ability* and an *attitude* component (for example, Shor, Orne, and O'Connell, 1962; White, 1937). That is to say, there must be present some kind of ability to become hypnotized or, no matter how favorable the attitude or how cooperative the subject, no hypnosis will result. The presence of such an ability is no guarantee, however, that the subject will become hypnotized. We know that a susceptible subject can resist becoming hypnotized if he wishes to, and there may be deep-lying (unconscious?) blocks to becoming hypnotized even if his open attitudes are favorable.[1] The experience inventories of the preceding chapter attempt to assess the ability to have the experiences called for in hypnosis, on the basis of evidence of their natural or spontaneous occurrence; in this chapter we examine the corresponding attitudinal components in relation to susceptibility.

[1] The situation is not unlike that of the human male who wishes very much to have sexual relations but is impotent with a given sexual partner, even though he has all the basic sexual abilities which find expression on other occasions. The parallel is not intended to stress anything sexual in the hypnotic relationship but merely to point out how unconscious attitudes can prevent the occurrence of types of behavior not fully under volitional control.

ATTITUDES AND SUSCEPTIBILITY [2]

Empirical studies that relate attitude to susceptibility have not been carried out as fully as the studies with the experience inventories. London (1961) studied a number of attitudes toward hypnosis in a student population, and he and his collaborators (London, Cooper, and Johnson, 1962) went on to compare some of the attitudes with hypnotic scores. They found prior experience with hypnosis and interest in being a subject to be a favorable factor for later susceptibility, correlating +.30 with scores on SHSS, Form A ($N = 86$ female subjects). Some 16 attitude and opinion items correlated +.40 with SHSS, Form A, for the same sample.

Over several years 1326 students in elementary psychology at Stanford were given a questionnaire covering attitudes toward hypnosis, previous experience with hypnosis, and their expectations (self-predictions) with regard to their own hypnotizability should they later submit to hypnosis. The questionnaire was filled out in an early session of the course, before any opportunities to volunteeer for hypnotic experiments were offered. Later 340 of these students were hypnotized, using SHSS, Form A; 281 of them were again hypnotized with SHSS, Form C, the form, as noted earlier, that on several occasions was found to correlate higher with personality measures than Form A. The predictive significance of the replies to the questionnaire could therefore be assessed. The resulting findings were reported by Melei and Hilgard (1964).

The three questions bearing on attitude toward hypnosis were in the form of declarative statements with which the student could agree or disagree:

I would be willing to serve as a subject in hypnosis experiments.

Yes   ?   No

I would like to find out how hypnotizable I am.

Yes   ?   No

I think I would find the experience of being hypnotized (check the appropriate adjectives, as many as you think apply):

---

[2] A good deal of what follows is based on the discussion in Melei and Hilgard (1964).

a. satisfying	e. exciting	i. degrading
b. annoying	f. interesting	j. pleasurable
c. confusing	g. silly	k. indifferent
d. relaxing	h. illuminating	l. frightening

A weighting was adopted on the basis of a pretest, so that these three questions led to a total possible score from −8 (extremely unfavorable to hypnosis) to +4 (favorable).

How attitudes affect the willingness to serve in hypnotic experiments. By comparing the attitude scores of those subjects who later participated as volunteers with those who did not, we can detect the sample distortion that comes about through volunteering when there is considerable pressure to volunteer because of the fulfillment of course obligations. We have occasionally referred to this group as "coerced volunteers" because they differ in their hypnotic susceptibility from the "true" volunteers who seek out the hypnotic experiences on their own (Boucher and Hilgard, 1962). The mean attitude scores of the 340 who reported for hypnosis was +.31, a favorable attitude, while for the 986 who failed to report the corresponding mean was −.18, unfavorable. With samples of this size these differences are significant at the .01 level by the Kolmogorov–Smirnov test. Although there are many favorable and unfavorable subjects who both report for experimentation and fail to report, this group difference is in the expected direction.

The relationship between attitude and susceptibility to hypnosis. For the purposes of this analysis, we treated separately those with some prior experience of hypnosis and those without such experience on the presumption that experience with hypnosis might have done something to shape attitudes. Results are presented in Table 59. The most interesting results are those obtained for subjects without prior experience of hypnosis. Here one finds significant correlations for females but not for males. The groups with prior experience are small and the correlations unstable; the only correlation that reaches the .05 level of significance is that between attitude and Form C scores for males. However, the attitudes of these same subjects fail to correlate with Form A scores and little confidence can be placed in the one marginally significant coefficient. Other correlations with Forms A and C are essentially alike, in this respect differing from

TABLE 59. CORRELATION BETWEEN ATTITUDE AND HYPNOTIC SUSCEPTIBILITY (MELEI AND HILGARD, 1964)

	Correlation with hypnotic susceptibility			
	SHSS, Form A		SHSS, Form C	
No previous hypnotic experience				
Males	.07	$(N = 161)$	.06	$(N = 119)$
Females	.37†	$(N = 125)$	.34†	$(N = 125)$
Previous experience of hypnosis				
Males	.01	$(N = 32)$	.40*	$(N = 20)$
Females	.29	$(N = 22)$	.22	$(N = 22)$

*$p \leq .05$ †$p \leq .01$

the experience inventory results, which almost always correlated higher with Form C. It is possible that the acquiescence-tendency is less prevalent in the very short attitude questionnaire on which these results are based than in the multiple-item inventory in which there is more ambiguity. If this is indeed the case, it would suggest further that the acquiescence tendency is more closely related to Form C than to Form A, but direct evidence is lacking (see Chap. 14).

We learn something more from looking at the mean attitude ratings, for correlations do not tell the whole story. When the total means are examined (combining male and female subjects), the group with prior experience of hypnosis has a mean attitude of $+.85$, which is more favorable than the mean of $+.20$ for the group without prior experience ($t = 2.83$, $p = .01$). This result conforms to the finding of London, Cooper, and Johnson (1962) that exposure to hypnosis tends to increase favorable attitudes toward it.

Here then is our first sex difference: a significant correlation between a favorable attitude and susceptibility on the part of female subjects, but not on the part of males. Quite independently of our investigation, other workers performed a related study and came to the same conclusions (Rosenhan and Tomkins, 1964). They, too, found a predictive relationship between attitude and susceptibility, but again only on the part of female subjects, not on the part of males. Their subjects completed a form in which they ranked their preference for participating in the following seven experiments: (a) communication of feeling, (b) conditioning, (c) hypnosis, (d) tests of psychoanalytic hypotheses, (e) cognitive dissonance, (f) hierarchies of motives, and (g) construction of personality tests. Those who ranked hypnosis experiments as either "1" or "2" were considered to have a high preference for hypnosis; those ranking hypnosis "6" or "7" were viewed as having a low preference. It turned out that there were 20 high preference and 14 low preference subjects among the 44 males, and 14 high preference subjects and 19 low preference subjects among the 44 females. Although the sample is too small for the sex differences to be significant, the larger proportion of female subjects negative to hypnosis is consistent with the findings of Melei and Hilgard (1964).

The high-preference female subjects were significantly more hypnotizable than the low-preference ones (Mean, high, 7.29; low, 4.37; $t = 2.86$, $p < .01$). Expressed as a correlation, the relationship between stated preference for hypnosis and score on the Harvard Group Scale (HGS) was $r = .41$ ($p < .01$). No corresponding difference between high and low subjects was found for the males. Rosenhan and Tomkins (1964) attempt to explain the sex difference by assuming that the prospect of hypnosis places males in greater conflict than it does for female subjects: "being hypnotized may be more consistent with the female sex role than with the male, and thus the correlation between preference and hypnotizability would be more substantial for females." In view of the greater frequency with which females express aversion to hypnosis, the female sex role does not appear to tell the whole story; it might be that because of the female fears of hypnosis those who are unafraid are likely to be the more susceptible ones. Such fears and lack of them would lead to higher correlations among women than among men, if such fears were less prevalent among men.

We may thus conclude on the basis of two independent studies that attitudes toward hypnosis, as measured by rather simple tests, correlate with hypnotic susceptibility for female college subjects but not for male ones. Why this sex difference should be found is an intriguing question to which we do not have conclusive answers.

ATTITUDE CHANGES AFTER EXPERIENCED HYPNOSIS

That highly susceptible subjects tend to view hypnosis more favorably than less susceptible ones has been established not only by studies such as those earlier reported, in which hypnotic susceptibility could be predicted from initial attitude, but also by a direct study of evaluative feelings toward hypnosis of those who have already had an opportunity to experience it. Brightbill and Zamansky (1963) used a form of the semantic differential (Osgood, Suci, and Tannenbaum, 1957) for this purpose. Selecting 12 of the most highly susceptible and 14 of the least susceptible among a group of 100 undergraduates screened for further experiments on hypnosis, they asked these subjects to rate eight concepts concerning hypnosis on 20 adjectival scales. The concepts were *hypnosis, sleep, trance, suggestion, science, experiment, professor,* and *magic.* The first four of these reflect the hypnotic experience more directly, while the others provide reference points for locating those four in "semantic space." Except for the concept *magic,* which was given a similar negative evaluation by both groups, all other concepts were viewed more favorably by the hypnotic than by the nonhypnotic subjects. Whether or not this represents a kind of agreeableness (acquiescence tendency) is of course uncertain, but *professor, science,* and *experiment* share in this positive evaluation along with *hypnosis, suggestion, trance,* and *sleep.* A more detailed analysis, in terms of D-scores (distance scores, in the parlance of the semantic differential), shows the nonsusceptible subjects to find the concept of *magic* closer in semantic space to *hypnosis* and the related concepts than is the case for the susceptible subjects. The authors indicate that the differences, while interesting, are not of sufficient magnitude to make it possible to predict susceptibility from the semantic differential.

Those who have experienced hypnosis tend to have more favorable attitudes toward hypnosis than those who have not, but these favorable attitudes may have led them to hypnosis in the first place, and may not have been the consequence of hypnosis at all.

SELF-PREDICTIONS OF HYPNOTIZABILITY

One of the statements we repeatedly asked our subjects to check before they volunteered for hypnosis was the following:

My guess is that if I participated I would be as hypnotizable as follows:

a. Probably not at all hypnotizable
b. Slightly hypnotizable

c. About average
d. A little above average
e. Very hypnotizable

The distribution of answers is plotted in Figure 21 for 315 subjects.

It is evident from inspection of Figure 21 that most subjects do not know what to expect of themselves, hence list themselves as

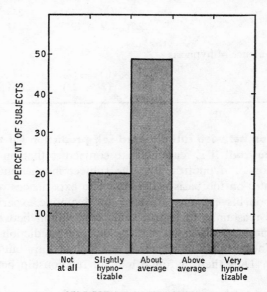

FIGURE 21. DISTRIBUTION OF SELF-PREDICTIONS OF HYNOTIZABILITY. The frequency distribution, expressed in percentages, is based on the predictions of subjects made prior to any opportunity to volunteer for hypnosis experiments.

"about average" although a few are "sure" that they will be non-hypnotizable and a few are "sure" that they will be very hypnotizable. Not only are most of them uncertain; they are also quite inaccurate in their predictions. Even so, small positive correlations result, which (with these large samples) reach conventional standards of significance (Table 60). Again the female subjects appear to be somewhat more successful than the males. There is little consistent difference between the correlations with Form A and with Form C.

TABLE 60. CORRELATION BETWEEN SELF-PREDICTIONS AND HYPNOTIC SUSCEPTIBILITY (MELEI AND HILGARD, 1964)

	Correlation with hypnotic susceptibility	
	SHSS, Form A	SHSS, Form C
No previous hypnotic experience		
Males	.16* $(N = 161)$	.24† $(N = 119)$
Females	.26† $(N = 125)$	.29† $(N = 121)$
Previous experience of hypnosis		
Males	.32 $(N = 32)$	.17 $(N = 20)$
Females	.65† $(N = 22)$	.56† $(N = 22)$

*$p < .05$ †$p < .01$

Correlation between attitude and self-prediction for those eventually hypnotized. It is reasonable to conjecture that, in making his self-prediction of hypnotizability, the subject inexperienced in hypnosis estimates on the basis of hypnoticlike experiences outside hypnosis, or upon his eagerness to have the hypnotic experience. Thus it would be reasonable to expect some correlation between attitude toward hypnosis, as discussed earlier, and self-predictions of hypnotizability. The correlations obtained are in fact low but all positive (Table 61). Thus there is found a slight relationship between a fa-

TABLE 61. CORRELATION BETWEEN ATTITUDE AND SELF-PREDICTION FOR THOSE EVENTUALLY HYPNOTIZED (MELEI AND HILGARD, 1964)

	Correlation
No previous hypnotic experience	
Males	.30* $(N = 161)$
Females	.35* $(N = 125)$
Previous hypnotic experience.	
Males	.22 $(N = 32)$
Females	.28 $(N = 22)$

*$p < .01$

vorable attitude toward hypnosis and the self-prediction that the subject will be susceptible.

It is of course possible to combine the attitude score and the self-prediction through multiple correlation. For 161 males without hypnotic experience the result is a barely significant correlation of $+.16$ with SHSS, Form A, and, because of the smaller sample, a nonsignificant correlation of the same size (.16) with Form C; for the 125 females without prior experience of hypnosis the multiple correlations are significant, .40 with Form A and .39 with Form C. Because these are as high as the correlations obtained with the longer experience inventories, they are not to be ignored even though they account for so little of the variance.

CONCLUSIONS REGARDING ATTITUDES AND SELF-PREDICTIONS

Because of the generally poor results in predicting hypnotizability from any measures other than those of primary suggestibility (such as postural sway, or other hypnoticlike waking suggestions), any consistent correlations even though small are viewed with respect, in the hope that some way may be found of building upon them. The consistent finding, especially for female subjects, that attitudes toward hypnosis and self-predictions are correlated with hypnosis means that any other measures that correlate no higher than these have to be scrutinized for their attitudinal and self-predictive components. We want to be sure that any measure upon which we rely tells us more than the direct answer to the question of how hypnotizable a subject expects to be.

CHAPTER 14

Personality Inventories, Projective Tests, and Behavioral Tests

Two purposes, one practical, one theoretical, lead investigators to use pencil-and-paper tests to try to predict hypnotizability. The practical purpose rests upon the possibility of selecting subjects for hypnotic experimentation by means of group tests that do not in themselves require participation in hypnosis. Were such tests to be sufficiently predictive, those subjects who scored high could be invited to come for experimentation; if the tests were not too obviously related to hypnosis, some other purposes could be served by permitting preliminary experimentation with subjects who did not know that they were chosen because of their hypnotic susceptibility. Experience with these tests to date suggests that this practical hope is a vain one; at best, no test that has been designed up to the present is nearly as satisfactory a predictive instrument as a simple test of hypnoticlike behavior, such as waking suggestions of postural sway, arm movements, or finger lock. In other words, *for practical purposes,* the familiar methods of selecting hypnotic subjects are far more satisfactory than any more general variety of personality test. The *theoretical purpose* can still be served by tests that are not sufficiently powerful to aid in subject selection. This purpose is to understand something of the background of those who are more or less susceptible to hypnosis. In the two previous chapters we met the experience inventories and attitude scales, which yield consistent enough results to add to the theoretical conviction that behaviors inside hypnosis and outside hypnosis have something in common. Other kinds of tests permit the testing of other hypotheses about the personality characteristics of the more hypnotizable and the less hypnotizable. For this purpose one needs merely significant relationships that bear upon the hypotheses; they need not be of sufficient magnitude to aid in subject selection. As a hypothetical case, consider the possibility that athletes are less hypnotizable as a group than nonathletes. If this could be established on a statistically significant basis it might well tell us something about personality correlates of hypnosis, even though the differences were too small to make athletic participation a criterion for rejecting subjects for hypnotic experimentation. In reviewing the results that appear at all promising, we must remember, then, that the promise lies in the direction of understanding something about hypnosis. No results to date suggest tests powerful enough to be of much aid in the practical prediction of the degree of hypnotic susceptibility.

PERSONALITY INVENTORIES

Most of the standard personality inventories, of the type in which the subject checks a large number of statements as applicable or not applicable to himself, have been tried out in relation to hypnosis. Occasional significant correlations have kept investigators hopeful that some small change might make the difference, but attempts to repeat what another investigator did have usually resulted in failure to find again his significant correlations, although some other correlation may arise to tantalize the investigator. These discouraging results have been carefully summarized by Deckert and West (1963) and by Barber (1964), and no effort will be made here to give again a complete review of the literature. Our own studies and a few others closely related to them will be mentioned, however, in order to arrive at a balanced position as to where we stand and what may be the promise of the future.

Some negative results. It is somewhat tedious to report additional negative results, but there is some obligation to report them in order to save the time of future investigators who may be tempted to plow over the same ground. As we shall see, not all of our results are negative, and in the next sections some hopeful findings are recounted.

The California Psychology Inventory (CPI) is a long scale of varied content (480 items) differing from the Minnesota Multiphasic Personality Inventory (MMPI) in its lesser pathological emphasis, both in the items themselves and in the naming of the subscales (Gough, 1957). We gave it to samples of students in advance of hypnosis during two academic years, so that we ended with correlations between its scales and SHSS, Form A, scores for 110 male and 106 female subjects (Hilgard and Lauer, 1962).[1]

The obtained correlations are given in Table 62. The correlations

TABLE 62. CORRELATION BETWEEN CPI SCALES AND SHSS, FORM A (HILGARD AND LAUER, 1962)

	Correlations	
CPI Scales	Males ($N = 110$)	Females ($N = 106$)
Dominance	−.11	.23†
Capacity for status	.07	−.02
Sociability	−.09	.12
Social presence	−.02	.09
Self-acceptance	−.13	.25†
Sense of well-being	−.20*	−.09
Responsibility	−.13	.08
Socialization	−.11	.09
Self-control	−.19*	−.12
Tolerance	−.11	.03
Good impression	.00	−.02
Communality	−.18	.26†
Achievement via conformance	−.07	.12
Achievement via independence	.01	.04
Intellectual efficiency	−.10	−.05
Psychological-mindedness	−.15	−.03
Flexibility	−.03	−.03
Femininity	.09	.15

*$p < .05$ †$p < .01$

that are significant have opposite signs for the two sexes, with the exception of the barely significant negative correlation with self-control for males, which is also negative (though nonsignificant) for females. One might interpret this as meaning that the more highly hyp-

[1] Were we to repeat the study we would use SHSS, Form C, which usually correlates somewhat higher than Form A with verbal test scores but was not available when the study was done. Forms A and C correlate sufficiently high, however, that any substantial relationships should hold for both forms.

notizable subjects are willing to relinquish control to others, but the correlations are very low indeed (−.19 and −.12), yielding an average of −.15 over the sample of 216 cases.

Although little can be made of these results, there is a hint of a correlation between disturbed personality in males (the negative correlation with sense of well-being in Table 62), and of correlation with more favorable aspects in females (positive correlation with dominance, self-acceptance, and communality in Table 62). It is better, however, to assume that these correlations show nothing until some way is found to raise them or to combine them sensibly.

The Maudsley Personality Inventory (MPI), while a very short test, has the advantage of a close relationship to a personality theory worked out over the years by Eysenck and his associates (Eysenck, 1959, 1961). Furneaux and Gibson (1961) published a study in which they related the MPI to hypnotizability. Each of their subjects, 55 university students and 44 readers of a radical journal, was hypnotized while lying on a couch by a technique that involved eye closure and repeated tests of eye catalepsy. The subject was classified as hypnotizable if eye catalepsy was successfully achieved within seven minutes, so that by that time his eyes were closed and he was unable to open them when challenged to do so. Under these circumstances 44 percent of the subjects proved to be hypnotizable. Three personality scores were derived from the replies to the MPI: a Neuroticism score (N), an Extraversion score (E), and a Lie score (L), based on a new set of 18 questions not in the original MPI Manual. Furneaux and Gibson first removed the 22 "liars" from the sample, a "liar" being defined as one who scored 10 or higher on the L-scale. These liars proved only 23 percent hypnotizable. The other subjects were classified into four "types" according to the familiar Maudsley practice by combining highs and lows on each of the scales into Stable Extraverts (SE's), Stable Introverts (SI's), Neurotic Extraverts (NE's), and Neurotic Introverts (NI's). They found that the SE and NI groups were significantly more hypnotizable than the NE and L groups, while the SI group was about average.

This result appeared to be interesting enough to deserve an attempt at replication. We therefore gave the MPI to 142 subjects of known susceptibility to hypnosis as measured by SHSS, Form A, judged to yield results most similar to the eye catalepsy criterion of hypnosis used by Furneaux and Gibson (Hilgard and Bentler, 1963).

The MPI within the Stanford sample yielded a distribution of scores, and of subjects classified by "type" (SE, NI, etc.) very similar to that of the Maudsley sample, a "goodness of fit" between the two samples showing a nonsignificant chi square. The resulting relationship to hypnosis, unfortunately, was not the same; in fact, when arranged in the form of a fourfold table, in which the London results had shown the SE and NI groups significantly superior in hypnotizability to the NE and L groups ($p < .001$), our subjects showed a significant difference in the *opposite* direction, the NE and L groups being superior to the SE and NI groups ($p < .01$).

Several other investigators have attempted to relate the MPI to hypnotizability with little success. Thorn (1961) at Sydney and Lang and Lazovik (1962) at Pittsburgh failed to replicate the Maudsley results, while the trends within their studies, particularly toward a positive correlation between extraversion and hypnotic susceptibility, agree more nearly with the Stanford results. A later attempt by Evans (1963c) to produce some concordance between the results of Furneaux and Gibson and of Thorn is rather unsuccessful, resting as it does on the acceptance of very insecure tests of significance ($p = .20$). He did not have available to him the data we had collected in our laboratory, which would have further weakened the case he was making.

The Myers-Briggs Inventory (Myers, 1962) is based on the typology of Jung; because of the phenomenology involved, with classifications as follows: extraversion (E)-introversion (I); sensing (S)-intuition (N); thinking (T)-feeling (F); and judging (J)-perception (P). The possibility seemed worth exploring that responses on this test might reflect some of the "subjective" quality of hypnosis better than more conventional scales that deal so much more concretely with behavior and symptoms.[2] It turns out that the 16 "types" that emerge are too many to provide a fair number of cases of each "type" without exceedingly large samples because some of the "types," as determined from the responses on the inventory, are quite rare in our college population. With 158 subjects, not one of the "sensing" types has as many as 10 subjects assigned to it, while six of the intuitive types have. With cells as small as this only extreme differences in susceptibility could yield significant results; the only cell that showed anything like an extreme split was that for ENFP (extravert-

[2] The data here reported were gathered in our laboratory by Mary R. Roberts. I wish to acknowledge her kindness in permitting this use of her unpublished data.

intuitive-feeling-perceptive) in which 13 proved hypnotizable and 5 not (if scores of 5 to 12 on SHSS, Form C, were used as evidence of hypnotizability, yielding 54 percent susceptible in the whole sample). This is of some interest because all 5 males falling in this cell were in the hypnotizable group, and 8 of 13 females were hypnotizable. This does not, of course, count as firm evidence, in view of the lack of differences throughout the table; it would take a sample of at least double the present size to yield anything significant, if the present direction of difference were to be sustained. The continuous measures also yielded nothing, as Table 63 shows.

TABLE 63. CORRELATION BETWEEN MYERS-BRIGGS TYPE INDICATOR CONTINUOUS MEASURES AND HYPNOTIC SUSCEPTIBILITY (SHSS, FORM C) (COURTESY MARY R. ROBERTS)

	Correlations (r)		
Myers-Briggs Scales	Males ($N = 75$)	Females ($N = 83$)	Total ($N = 158$)
Extraversion-introversion	$-.04$	.04	.00
Sensing-intuiting	.02	.18	.11
Thinking-feeling	.11	.13	.12
Judging-perceiving	.16	$-.07$	.04

To complete this negative story, mention may be made of various other inventories that have been tried out unsuccessfully. The Guilford-Zimmerman Temperament Survey and the Cattell 16 PF Questionnaire failed to discriminate the more susceptible from the less susceptible in a sample of 200 students at the University of Michigan (Weitzenhoffer and Weitzenhoffer, 1958b), although some success has been reported for Cattell's IPAT anxiety scale, two of the Guilford-Zimmerman scales, and some scales of the Edwards Personal Preference Schedule in discriminating between two small groups of subjects selected as hypnotizable and as refractory by Levitt, Persky, and Brady (1964, p. 30). Bentler (1963), using our Stanford student samples, found some correlations between the Leary Interpersonal Check List (Leary, 1957; LaForge and Suczek, 1955) and both SHSS, Forms A and C. One of the more prominent correlations was that of .34 with Form A and .29 with Form C for 84 female subjects with the LM octant (Cooperative-Overconventional). Barber and Calverley (1964a) replicated this finding, in that their only significant correlation (after induction) was one of .24 with 78 female subjects between the Barber Suggestibility Scale (BSS) after hypnotic induction and the LM octant. Despite the hope engendered by these repeated results, we have not been able to replicate the findings on a new sample in our laboratory.

Barber and Calverley (1964c) have also tried out a number of other inventories: the Edwards Personal Preference Schedule, the Jourard Self-Disclosure Scale, and the Marlowe-Crowne Social Desirability Scale, all with negative results.

Some positive findings: The Motoric-Ideational Activity Preference Scale (MIAPS).

A newly developed scale appealed to us because of its bearing on the question whether hypnotic compliance is largely a cognitive function or largely a sensorimotor one, and the distinction between motoric interests and ideational interests appeared relevant. The Motoric-Ideational Activity Preference Scale (MIAPS), developed by Stein and Craik (1962, 1965) and used by their permission, did in fact prove useful. The scale has two parts, part *a* consisting of a number of questions permitting ratings of interests on a 0–4 scale from none to extra much, while part *b* is a forced-choice arrangement in which some motor interests are pitted against some ideational ones. We found nothing of significance within part *b,* so this discussion will be concerned with the answers to part *a.*

Because of some hypotheses arising out of our interviews (see Chap. 15) we thought it of interest to study the correlations with motor interests further subdivided into 8 items reflecting work-recreation (craft hobbies, detailed planning of a vacation, etc.), 10 of competitive recreation (such as tennis), and 7 items of noncompetitive recreation (such as hiking). These short scales turn out to be satisfactorily reliable on a retest, the reliability coefficients running from .78 to .93. The results for these scales, as correlated with SHSS, Form C, are given in Table 64. It may be noted that there is a negative relationship to hypnotic susceptibility throughout, particularly marked for competitive recreational interests, such as competitive sports. This implies that there ought to be a positive relationship with ideational interests. This is, in fact, not established by correlations between the ideational items of the MIAPS and SHSS, Form C, but holds for the profile scales (Table 65). The subjects whose

TABLE 64. CORRELATION OF MOTORIC INTERESTS ON THE STEIN-CRAIK MIAPS WITH HYPNOTIC SUSCEPTIBILITY (SHSS, FORM C)[a]

	Correlations		
	Male (N = 78)	Female (N = 56)	Total (N = 134)
Work recreation (8 items)	−.02	−.25	−.11
Competitive recreation (10 items)	−.34†	−.31*	−.33†
Noncompetitive recreation (7 items)	−.20	−.13	−.19*
Total motoric interests (25 items)	−.33†	−.16	−.25†

[a] The assistance of Carol Hilgeman, H. Thomas Mudd, Jr., and Janet Melei Cuca is gratefully acknowledged.

*$p < .05$ †$p < .01$

TABLE 65. CORRELATION OF IDEATIONAL AND MOTORIC INTERESTS ON THE STEIN-CRAIK MIAPS WITH SHSS, FORM C, AND SPS, FORMS I AND II (N = 64; 29 MALES, 35 FEMALES)

	Correlations		
	SHSS, Form C	SPS, Form I	SPS, Form II
Ideational interests (25 items)	−.01	.16	.17
Motoric interests (25 items)	−.28*	−.20	−.28*
Excess of ideational interests over motoric interests	.08	.32*	.39†

*$p < .05$ †$p < .01$

results are reported in Table 65 are from the same samples as in Table 64, except that only those subjects are listed for whom profile scale scores were available. The MIAPS was given following hypnosis, but there is little reason to expect this to have made much difference; in fact, in the reliability study, scores before and after hypnosis were correlated for a fraction of the subjects, and the reliabilities were indistinguishable from those of a control group taking the test twice without intervening hypnosis. Here then is a positive finding, and one quite uncontaminated by an acquiescence tendency, for the form of the interest inventory questions for the ideational items was just the same as that for the motoric items.[3]

It is apparent that there are always just enough tantalizing positive findings to keep up the search for some new way of asking questions that may prove to be predictable of hypnotic susceptibility. The positive findings with respect to favorable attitudes toward hypnosis, self-predictions of hypnosis, experience inventories, and now a motoric scale, show that it is not impossible to find something within pencil-and-paper tests informative in relation to hypnotic susceptibility.

Some positive findings: the MMPI. The MMPI is probably the most widely used of the personality inventories; it is long and varied (566 items) and has had abundant normative data published upon it (for example, Dahlstrom and Welsh, 1960). A promising beginning was made when Sarbin (1950) reported a chi square significant at the .01 level between hypnosis and the hysteria scale (Hy) for 34 subjects retained as moderately susceptible from a sample of 70 tested. Faw and Wilcox (1958) reported some significant differences on various MMPI scales between those observed to be more or less susceptible, but Sector (1961) found no significant differences on any of the scales. Schulman and London (1963b), after obtaining more negative results with female subjects than with male, decided that this had all gone far enough, and we had better give up on ordinary personality inventories in relation to hypnosis.

Our studies of the relationship between the MMPI and hypnotic

---

[3] It is not possible to rule out entirely stylistic or social desirability factors, for it might be supposed around a university that ideational interests are more conforming to the environment than active ones. Still the forced-choice questions did not lead to any significant relation to hypnosis, and these would presumably be equally subject to value preferences for ideas over motor activity.

susceptibility were begun several years ago (autumn, 1960), but the results have only recently been prepared for publication (Hilgard, Lauer, and Melei, 1965).[4] We gave the full MMPI to a sample of 50 female students in the autumn of 1960. When we correlated the results with SHSS, Form C, we found four scales that reached conventional standards of significance for r; but when we repeated the full scale with a sample of males, the three scales that reached significance were not the same as those for the females. Two of the "significant" scales in the female sample (Pd and Pt) fell in the opposite directions from the same "significant" scales in the study by Schulman and London (1963b). Such considerations led us to interpret these differences to be more likely a matter of sampling errors than of sex differences; when both sexes were combined, the now larger number of cases ($N = 100$) permitted smaller correlations to reach a level of significance, nine scales reached the .05 level of significance (interpreting each r as though it were independent): F, K (a negative correlation), Hs (hypochondriasis), Pd (psychopathic deviate), Pt (psychasthenia), Sc (schizophrenia), Ma (hypomania), Welsh A (anxiety), and Sum-True score (number of agreeing responses). The pathological names of the MMPI scales is somewhat unfortunate and misleading when the scales are used with subjects who fall well within the normal range. It will be recalled that our interviewer estimates led to an opposite interpretation: that the more normal and outgoing subjects were generally the more hypnotizable (Chap. 11); the same interpretation is offered of the findings of Levitt, Persky, and Brady (1964). The positive correlations with the pathologically named MMPI scales suggest the misleading conclusion that the more morbid subjects were the more hypnotizable.

In the interests of saving time we used an abbreviated form of the MMPI on later samples, adopting some of the scales that other investigators had shown positively related to hypnosis: L, K, Hs, Pa, Ma, and Si. This led to a 235-item form, from which, without adding items, we also computed a Sum-True score, based on the total number of positive answers, regardless of content. The results, from several samples, are given in Table 66. While there are several scales that reach significance for the males, sufficient to yield significance for the total sample, the only scale that yields a significant relationship for both sexes separately is the Sum-True score. Because this

[4] The data are published as a brief report. Some of the material here is taken from the unpublished extended report.

TABLE 66. CORRELATIONS BETWEEN SELECTED MMPI SCALES AND HYPNOTIC SUSCEPTIBILITY (SHSS, FORM C)[a]

| | Correlations | | | | | |
| | Females | | Males | | Total | |
MMPI Scale	N	r	N	r	N	r
L (lie scale)	103	−.05	149	−.19	252	−.14*
K	152	−.05	149	−.18	301	−.12*
Hs (hypochondriasis)	152	.15	149	.22†	301	.18†
Pa (psychasthenia)	103	.05	149	.14	252	.10
Ma (hypomania)	152	.10	149	.34†	252	.25†
Si (social introversion)	152	−.02	149	−.04	301	−.03
Sum–True (235 items)	152	.17*	149	.26†	301	.22†

[a] From an extended report, available from the American Documentation Institute, as reported in Hilgard, Lauer, and Melei (1965).

*$p < .05$ †$p < .01$

correlation is as high as that for any of the individual scales, it appears that an acquiescence tendency may be producing the scores for the individual scales as well. We shall return to a discussion of the acquiescence tendency. For the present it may be noted that a number of MMPI scales have yielded low but significant correlations for males but not for females except in the first sample of 50 cases: this result is *opposite* to that found in studies of attitude in relation to susceptibility when the correlations were found for females and not males. The one stable correlation is with responsiveness on the Sum-True measure, holding for both sexes. Because such a measure is relatively content-free, it would be unwise to make much of the names of the MMPI subscales in explaining their relationship to hypnotizability.

The acquiescence tendency in relation to hypnotic susceptibility.
The one MMPI subscale that held up consistently for both male and female Subjects was the Sum-True scale. This is merely a count of the number of statements with which the subject agreed, regardless of how the statement may have been keyed in any individual scale. It does not follow that such responses are actually "content-free," that is, purely stylistic, as though the questions were not even read

by the subject. This is an area of controversial discussion in the personality measurement field as this is being written, with many writers seeing the MMPI heavily loaded with stylistic response tendencies (for example, Jackson and Messick, 1962; Wiggins, 1962), while others are now coming to the defense of personality tests and insisting that these stylistic tendencies have been overestimated (for example, Eysenck and Eysenck, 1964; Rorer and Goldberg, 1964).

Perhaps the question must always be asked in terms of what the test is being used for. With low correlations many different aspects of a test may turn out to be responsible for the correlations. It appears quite clear that in relation to hypnotic susceptibility there is indeed an acquiescence tendency. Some of the evidence will now be presented:

1. It was earlier shown by Lee (1965) that the predictive power of the subscales of the Hypnotic Characteristics Inventory (HCI) was in proportion to the number of items keyed "yes," even though the keying had been determined empirically from a larger nonhypnotic sample. This led to the conjecture that acquiescence was important. When we rescored her data, counting only the number of "yes" answers, thus emphasizing acquiescence, all subscales which had had responses keyed "no" correlated higher with hypnosis than they had before (Table 58).

2. The factor analysis showed that the HCI subscales that correlated highest with hypnotic susceptibility fell in factor space close to the Sum-True responses on the MMPI, the responses that most clearly defined the acquiescence factor (Figure 20).

3. The subscales of the MMPI have various proportions of their items keyed "true." It is thus possible to compare the correlations of these subscales with hypnotic susceptibility to see whether or not, in fact, there is a relationship to the proportion of questions calling for an agreeing answer. The hypothesis being tested is this: If the basis for correlation between the MMPI subscale and hypnotic susceptibility is the number of items keyed "true," then there ought to be a significant correlation between scales ranked according to the percentage of items keyed "true" and the ranks of the correlations with hypnosis susceptibility. That the facts are in agreement with this hypothesis is indicated by Table 91, in which the predicted positive rank correlation turns out to be .75 ($p < .001$). What this means is simply that if you know how large a proportion of items are keyed

TABLE 67. RELATIONSHIP BETWEEN PROPORTION OF ITEMS KEYED "TRUE" AND CORRELATIONS BETWEEN MMPI SCALES AND HYPNOTIC SUSCEPTIBILITY, SHSS, FORM C (HILGARD, LAUER, AND MELEI, 1965) [a]

MMPI scales in decreasing order of items keyed "true"	Percent of items keyed "true"	Rank: Percent keyed "true"	Correlation with SHSS, Form C ($N = 100$)	Rank: Size of correlation
Sum–true	100	1	.21	7
Welsh A	97	2	.20	8
Pt	79	3	.28	2
Ma	76	4.5	.27	3
Sc	76	4.5	.29	1
F	69	6	.24	5.5
Pa	62	7	.19	9
Si	49	8	.11	10
Pd	48	9	.24	5.5
Mf Male 47 Female 42		10	.08	11
Hs	33	11.5	.26	4
D	33	11.5	−.02	12
Hy	22	13	−.05	13
K	3	14	−.21	16
L	0	15.5	−.15	15
Welsh R	0	15.5	−.09	14

$rho = .75$, $t = 4.25$, $df = 14$, $p < .001$

[a] Table from unpublished extended report.

"true" you have a reasonable chance of estimating the correlation with hypnosis, estimating a higher correlation with more items keyed "true." The negative correlations are all with scales requiring a large proportion of "not true" replies.

Regardless of the controversy over the acquiescence tendency in other connections, there appears to be little doubt that it plays a part in determining the small correlation with hypnosis.

There are some things to be said on the other side. The acquiescence tendency holds only when the general domain of the questions is relevant, as it is in experience inventories, and in the more symptom-oriented type of personality inventory, such as the MMPI. If it were purely stylistic, one would expect the correlation to go up as the length of test increases (owing to increased reliability); actually the correlation with the full MMPI is no higher than with the shorter version, with subscales selected because of relevance to hypnosis. It appears that the *content* of these subscales may therefore have something to do with the agreeing tendency.

The correlation with Sum–True Scores holds only with SHSS, Form C, and not with SHSS, Form A. This is not a matter of sample differences, because the same 301 subjects were given both hypnotic tests and the correlation with Form A was .08 compared with .22 for Form C. This may be due to the more "cognitive" nature of the items in Form C as compared with Form A, so that a willingness to give a positive interpretation to cognitive ambiguity (reporting a taste not there, or having a dream under hypnosis) is more related to the acquiescence tendency than responding to sensorimotor items.

Conclusions from personality inventories. The chief positive residues from our studies of pencil-and-paper responses are as follows:

1. A self-prediction correlation of susceptibility to hypnosis by both males and females (males, $r = .24$, $N = 119$; females, $r = .29$, $N = 121$).

2. A prediction of susceptibility based on attitudes prior to hypnosis holding for females, but not for males (males, $r = .06$, $N = 119$; females, $r = .34$, $N = 125$).

3. A negative correlation of motoric interests with susceptibility, particularly competitive recreational interests (males, $r = -.33$, $N = 78$; females, $r = -.34$, $N = 56$), positive with ideational interests on the SPS, Forms I and II.

4. Experience inventory correlations with hypnotic susceptibility, both Ås's and Lee's, of the order of $+.30$ to $+.47$, both males and females.

5. The MMPI Sum–True Score on a 235-item version, correlating for males $r = +.26$ ($N = 149$) and for females $r = +.17$ ($N = 152$).

These five results have been sufficiently replicated that we have confidence that they would hold up for subjects selected as ours are; we have no way of knowing how generally they would apply to other samples, but our supposition is that many of the correlations would rise with more diverse samples.

This is a very modest yield, considering the amount of effort that has been spent on the testing program, but even so the results do not justify a nihilistic attitude toward the relationship between personality variables and hypnotic susceptibility.

PROJECTIVE TESTS

Efforts to use the Rorschach test in discriminating between the hypnotically susceptible and the nonsusceptible have led to contradictory results; some hopeful indicators noted by Sarbin and Madow (1942) and different indicators by Brenman and Reichard (1943) were contradicted by Schafer (1947), working under Brenman; Schafer's very limited results were but partially reproduced when tried on another small sample. Steisel (1952) fared no better.

Results with the Thematic Apperception Test (TAT), particularly Card 12M, which can be interpreted as a hypnotic interaction, appear to measure a favorable attitude to hypnosis, correlated with susceptibility (White, 1937; Rosenzweig and Sarason, 1942). Because, as previously noted, a verbal report of attitude also correlates with susceptibility, this does not appear to be a very profound finding. More recent experiments with Card 12M of the TAT, including a revised card, have yielded nothing (Levitt, Lubin, and Brady, 1962; Levitt and Lubin, 1963).

We have made no formal use of projective tests in our efforts to predict susceptibility, but we have occasionally used them in helping us assess "what was going on" in a hypnotic session. For example, with one subject who was participating in an experiment investigating the improvement of susceptibility with practice, the subject was asked, in the final session, to respond to some TAT-like cards that strongly suggested hypnosis. What was most striking in her case was the avoidance (whether conscious or unconscious) of any reference to hypnosis. Yet something of her attitudes could be determined by the good identifications assigned the one acting like a "hypnotist" in the pictures, and the one acting like a "subject." The "hypnotist" was identified as a priest in a wedding rehearsal, a dramatic coach, a director of a firm who was answering questions, an understanding husband, a dance partner. The subject was identified as a bride, a wife who is worried but has an understanding husband, a dance partner, and a refugee taking the oath of allegiance. There appear to be veiled references to hypnosis here, mostly implying a comfortable or at least hopeful outcome (Ås, Hilgard, and Weitzenhoffer, 1963). It is quite possible that such a "clinical" use of projective materials may turn out more satisfactory than their formal "test" use.

BEHAVIORAL TESTS OF SUGGESTION, ATTENTION, AND COGNITIVE STYLE

A certain gap always exists between the representation of behavior in words and its fulfillment in action. Therefore some investigators have hoped to find kinds of laboratory-produced behavior that would tell more about hypnosis than a verbal test. The *direct* behavioral tests of hypnosis are successful—too successful, in fact, because they raise all the controversy over whether or not induction does anything at all. So we are not here talking about tests of waking suggestibility that are very hypnoticlike, nor about actual work-samples of hypnosis. The point is to find behaviors that no one would call hypnotic, in the hope that they might correlate with behaviors called hypnotic.

Suggestion tests. We know that many suggestion tests (tests of primary suggestibility) are so directly related to hypnosis that we think of them as sampling the same order of behavior. It turns out, however, that there are *other kinds* of suggestibility tests that have little relation to hypnosis. Perhaps if all suggestibility tests were very highly intercorrelated we would lose interest in them, as representing merely other forms that hypnoticlike suggestibility can take. The fact that they are so little correlated turns out in this case to make them all the more fascinating, and to require explanation.

The study of Stukát (1958), previously referred to in relation to the susceptibility of children, is a very thorough study of both children and adults. He found, in general, that primary suggestibility (hypnoticlike) is a consistent factor, but there are other factors, which may be loosely grouped together as secondary suggestibility. In his theoretical interpretation he finds secondary suggestibility to be related to a need for conformity, on the one hand, and to the fulfillment of expectations, on the other; neurotics are somewhat more suggestible than normals in secondary suggestibility, but not in primary suggestibility. Duke (1964), in reviewing the literature on primary and secondary suggestibility, as noted earlier concludes that secondary suggestibility is so miscellaneous that the term had better be dropped.

Rosemarie K. Moore (1964) studied the relationship between hypnotic susceptibility, personality tests, and some tests of social influence. When she factor-analyzed her results she found the pencil-and-paper personality inventory results to define a bipolar factor, and hypnosis (primary suggestibility) a factor orthogonal to it. The social influence tests, in which she was primarily interested, were not significantly related to either of these factors, with the exception of the influencibility test of Schachter, which fell in factor space close to postural sway (Figure 22). While her study agrees with earlier ones in finding a primary suggestibility factor, the lack of interrelationship among the measures that might be thought of as representing secondary suggestibility leads to agreement with Duke's verdict that secondary suggestibility is not one thing.

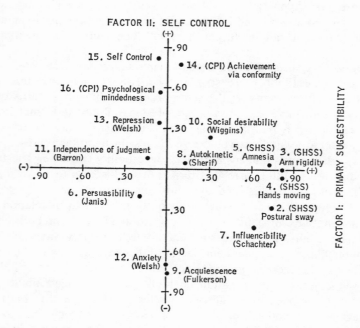

FIGURE 22. LOADINGS ON TWO FACTORS OF VARIOUS PENCIL-AND-PAPER TESTS, LABORATORY TESTS OF SOCIAL SUGGESTIBILITY, AND HYPNOTIC SUSCEPTIBILITY SCORES. Most of the nonhypnotic scores fall along a dimension that is orthogonal to hypnotic susceptibility. The influencibility measure (Schachter) falls near to the waking suggestion item (postural sway). From Moore, 1964, p. 289.

Attention and cognitive style. The notion that concentration of attention is essential to hypnosis, and hence tests of attention outside hypnosis ought to predict hypnotizability, is implied in the remarks of Barber (1960) and Leuba (1960), but the evidence is scant. Das (1964) used two behavioral tests that might be considered related to attention. One was verbal satiation, in which, with repetition a word gradually loses its meaning; the other was vigilance, the capacity to keep on responding to the third odd number in a protracted series of numbers in which these sequences are rare. Das's results are not exactly what one would expect. He found *enrichment* of meaning among the more susceptible subjects in the satiation test ($r = .67$, $N = 62$), but more *errors* in vigilance among the more hypnotizable ($r = .15$, $N = 62$). In view of some difficulties in the study, including the bilingualism of his subjects, the study ought to be repeated on other populations.

Mary R. Roberts (1964), working in our laboratory, employed various laboratory tests of attention, based on a previous study by Süllwold (1954). She found little relationship between attention so defined and hypnotic susceptibility. She also had various tests of cognitive style, including the Witkin rod-and-frame test (Witkin and others, 1962). Her one positive finding was a correlation of $-.30$ with some scores on this test for female subjects. The correlation suggests that, for females, the more field dependent are *less* hypnotizable than those who are field independent.

The behavioral tests are no more successful than the personality inventories in arriving at clear correlates of hypnosis, other than primary suggestibility which the hypnotic scales themselves represent. These results are not unimportant because they refute the glib interpretation of hypnosis as "just suggestibility" or "just a phenomenon of concentrated attention." If it were just anything as simple as this, we would find it correlated with other measures of suggestion and other measures of attention.

TESTED PERSONALITY CHARACTERISTICS IN RELATION TO HYPNOTIC SUSCEPTIBILITY

Many conjectures about hypnosis are highly plausible, so that it is something of a shock to put them to the test only to find that practically none of the plausible conjectures can be proven to be true. There "ought" to be relationships to anxiety, to social desirability, to conforming tendencies, to social influencibility, to attention, and so on, but such relationships as we find are all very low and unstable, except the criterion of hypnotic susceptibility itself, which is remarkably stable.

Enough thoughtful people have tried one thing after another with such paucity of results that some new approach appears to be desirable. Let me repeat some conjectures offered earlier (Hilgard and Lauer, 1962):

1. Because hypnotic susceptibility is so stable, it may be a highly specialized ability and hence not generalizable enough to correlate with any global tests of personality. If that were the case, hypnotic ability could be studied only by sampling it; this is what we do when we use tests of "primary suggestibility." Accepting this stable specialized ability as something that may be genetically determined, we perhaps ought to study it in identical twins. We have made some starts in this direction, but our studies have not gone far enough to be at all decisive, in view of the many complexities of the nature–nurture problem.

While this position is a defensible one, it is an easy way out and should rest on positive evidence rather than on the failure of our present testing methods to find correlates. Its refutation can come in two ways: (1) by a failure of genetic studies to find the expected twin similarities, and (2) by developmental studies showing clear steps toward the psychogenesis of hypnotic ability. At present the issue is open for lack of evidence.

2. Perhaps hypnotic susceptibility rests on "deeper" or more "unconscious" aspects of the personality than our tests tap. This, too, is hard to disprove, unless through psychotherapeutic or other clinical exploration these deeper layers can be exposed and found clearly related to susceptibility.

3. Perhaps there are domains of experience related to hypnosis that we do not tap in our ordinary inventories. This is, of course, a matter that can be explored empirically. The successes of the experience inventories and the success of the motoric-ideational interest scale indicate that there are many areas of experience that our conventional personality inventories do not cover, or do not cover in sufficient variety.

4. Another possibility is that more subtle ways of sorting subjects and of scoring tests are needed. This is, of course, the logic that

Eysenck (1959) has all along been advocating in using a double-sort of extraversion–introversion and normalcy–neuroticism. This fourfold scheme is not rich enough; the sixteen-cell scheme of the Myers-Briggs inventory is a more complex one along the same lines, but it rests on the Jungian theory that has never been well expressed in operational form. In general the use of *moderators* is likely to prove useful. Consider, for example, the negative correlation found between competitive recreational interests and hypnotizability. Because college athletes are likely to score quite "normal" on inventories, a sample that includes many of these competing athletes is likely to come up with a correlation between neuroticism and hypnosis, because the super-normal athletes will fall very low on hypnotizability and the normal hypnotizables will be less normal (more neurotic) than they. It takes only a few cases to convert an indifferent correlation into a significant one, if the cases fall together in an odd corner. It might be better, in such a sample, to remove the athletes and then see what the correlations are like for the rest of the sample. Such sample-stratification has to be done with extreme caution because of the statistical hazards involved, but it may be necessary. When relations are as tricky as they have been proven to be in hypnosis, only ingenious data handling will exhibit the underlying lawfulness.

We may remind ourselves again that there have been significant correlations:

1. Significant self-predictions of hypnotizability.

2. Significant correlations between attitudes and hypnotizability (for females).

3. Significant positive correlations between responses on experience inventories and hypnotizability, particularly those reflecting role-involvement, trancelike experiences, and impulsivity.

4. Significant negative correlations with the number of motoric interests, particularly with competitive recreational (athletic) interests.

5. Significant positive correlations with the excess of ideational over motoric interests.

6. Significant positive correlations with the acquiescence tendency as reflected in the Sum–True score on the MMPI.

7. A significant correlation (for females) between scores on the rod-and-frame test and hypnotizability, indicating that the field independent are more hypnotizable. (These are the subjects guided more from within.)

The results do not yet bring into sharp focus the personality characteristics of the hypnotizable person, but they provide a start. From the above statements a kind of personality description emerges of the hypnotizable person as one who has rich subjective experiences in which he can become deeply involved; one who reaches out for new experiences and is thus friendly to hypnosis; one who is interested in the life of the mind, and not a competitive activist; one who accepts impulses from within and is not afraid to relinquish reality testing for a time. Because these free, irrational, reality-distorting characteristics may be found in flexible combination with realistic academic and social adjustment, there are probably a great many variations on the common theme, thus attenuating the correlations between personality inventories and hypnotic susceptibility.

CHAPTER 15

Personality and Hypnotizability:
Inferences from Case Studies

by JOSEPHINE R. HILGARD, M.D.

The search for the personality qualities that make a person hypnotizable is, as we have seen, one that has not reached its goal, for the qualities that predict hypnotic susceptibility are elusive. Both the normal and the neurotic may be hypnotizable, both the withdrawn and the outgoing, the mature and the immature, the timid and the self-reliant. While this has led investigators to be pessimistic about finding personality characteristics related to hypnosis, and has led them to seek for other variables such as momentary attitudes, task motivation, or the demands of the specific experimental situation, another alternative is open, and that is to combine a clinical and a measurement approach. Clinical case studies can seek to make differentiations that are not ordinarily made in personality inventories and hopefully can relate the contemporary personality to its longitudinal history, that is, to its development within the family in early childhood and beyond.

In this context when we speak of case studies we are referring to evaluations gained in the course of a one- or two-hour interview in advance of hypnosis. All evaluations used in ratings for predictive purposes were based on these interviews prior to hypnosis. On many occasions, however, additional interviews followed hypnotic induction in order to obtain further data in regard to promising leads. Of necessity we could seldom probe beyond the surface, and our clinical studies, when compared with some long-term ones, are superficial. Nevertheless, it has been useful to probe many areas in order to untangle and follow up the more promising ones. The method of before-and-after interviews sharpened clinical judgment inasmuch as few situations have existed in which an evaluation of factors leading to an initial clinical judgment could be proved right or wrong within the course of two days, that is, the length of time it took the hypnotic scores to arrive. Through further interviewing we then could begin to reassess the cases where clearly we had been in error as well as those where we had been correct in our general prediction. One can be right for the wrong reasons.

We are attempting to achieve an understanding of hypnosis through a compromise of two traditional methods of investigation, that of the clinician and that of the psychometrician. Neither is apt to be satisfied with our data. In comparison with clinical studies of depth, our data obviously move over surfaces. When compared with an inventory check-list approach, the subject's responses have been sifted through an intermediary, the interviewer, who has interpreted and rated them. Nevertheless, clinical studies alone have not succeeded, and the inventory approach alone has produced a very limited picture of the individual. It is suggested that at this juncture in our knowledge (or lack of it) about personality in relation to hypnotizability, an amalgamation of these two approaches is needed. After this first phase of the broad search for sensitive areas, the next step may well involve more penetrating case studies as well as the construction of more exact personality inventories.

From our work thus far, we anticipate the possibility of contributing to the psychology of personality through the recognition of differentiations within role-involvements, of partial identifications with aspects of the personalities of both parents, of aspects of the play and work egos such as fantasy, feeling, achievement, and competition. The capacity for hypnotizability is interrelated with long-term trends in personality development, and as such its implications are broad.

THE INTERVIEWING PROGRAM

The interviewing program in our laboratory began several years ago with a very free exploratory interview after subjects had completed a session of attempted hypnotic induction. It soon became evident that there were lines of inquiry that would prove promising, but that within these areas careful distinctions would have to be made or the generalizations would be meaningless; in other words, while many normal outgoing subjects are readily hypnotized, an interview devoted to assessing outgoingness would not prove predictive of hypnosis because many outgoing people are not hypnotizable and many withdrawn people are (Hilgard and Hilgard, 1962).

With this start, a general plan of interviewing was developed for use in advance of hypnosis, consisting of relatively free answers but following a schedule permitting interviewer ratings of significant topics and subsequent coding for quantitative purposes. The interviews were usually of one-hour duration, although at one stage two one-hour interviews preceded hypnosis. A staff of experienced social workers ably assisted in the interviewing, which covered a span of five years.[1] I conducted many of the interviews myself, some in advance of hypnosis and most of those after hypnosis where the purpose was for reassessment. It should be emphasized again that only the interviews in advance of hypnosis were used for the ratings that will be reported in this chapter, while the interviews following hypnosis were designed to contribute to our knowledge of particular problems in special areas and enriched our case illustrations. Frequent staff conferences and case discussion tended to keep our methods and ratings as similar as they could be, consistent with the nature of the material.

In this chapter stress will be placed upon some of the insights into the personality correlates of hypnosis that have come from this case material, with only occasional reference to the quantitative findings. A monograph reporting the interview study in detail is in the course of preparation. It will describe the exact interview procedures and present material based on the coded interviews, with reliabilities of the ratings scales, intercorrelations, plus additional material of the type included in this chapter. A sufficient idea of the range of information covered in the interviews can be obtained from the following headings used in the interview forms for 1962–63:

[1] To Mrs. Martha Newman, who participated throughout this five-year period of learning and relearning, I wish to express exceptional appreciation. Mrs. Ursula Moore, who assisted for three years, and Mrs. Nancy Kautz, who assisted for two years, contributed valuable service and insight.

First Hour

1. Present status (age, year in college, major, vocational plans).
2. Prior experiences of and attitudes toward hypnosis.
3. Composition of the family.
4. Health history of subject and family.
5. Developmental or family crises.
6. Participation in activities: Special interests and hobbies.
7. Attitudes toward play activities (absorption, adventuresomeness, curiosity, etc.).
8. Religion as an interest or activity.
9. Peer relationships.
10. Leadership–followership.
11. Personal characteristics (assets and liabilities, humor, ease of relinquishing control, etc.).

Second Hour

1. Parent with whom the subject has most in common.
2. Relationship to father.
3. Relationship to mother.
4. Identification.
5. Personal problems.
6. Childhood discipline and duties.

It will be noted that the first hour centered on the subject himself, the second hour on relationships to parents as they affected the subject's development.

Following the interview, in which verbatim replies were recorded to the extent that they could be, the interviewer filled out a rating form with essentially two kinds of ratings. The first considered the topic itself, such as absorption in reading, independent of hypnosis. The second kind consisted in the interviewer's estimate of hypnotizability based on the impression given in discussion of a particular topic. To make this somewhat clearer, let us consider the approach to an estimate of absorption in reading.

The entering question was general:

Now we are especially interested in the things that interest you.
What are your special interests and hobbies? (Note duration; note source of intense interests.)

Following this open-ended discussion, if answers did not come up spontaneously, the "probes" on reading were called for as follows:

Reading (adventure, fiction, science fiction, mysteries, biography, history; absorption through high school; and now).

The interviewer did not terminate this part of the discussion until satisfied that ratings could be arrived at. Later the rating form was filled in, with the relevant rating scales here being:

Participation in reading (various kinds) Little 1–2–3–4–5–6–7–x Much
Absorption in reading through
    high school   Little 1–2–3–4–5–6–7–x Much
Absorption in reading now   Little 1–2–3–4–5–6–7–x Much

Every effort was made to get ratings on the numerical scale, but the "x" was allowed for those cases where rating seemed impossible because the evidence was lacking or self-contradictory. A general rating of hypnotic susceptibility was also recorded by the interviewer preceding the subject's hypnotic session:

Hypnotic susceptibility as estimated from activities and interests:

$$0–1–2–3–4–5–6–7–8–9–10–11–12$$

Comments on rating:

The susceptibility ratings were placed on the 12-point scale because the predicted scores of SHSS, Form C, were on that same scale. These ratings were made on the basis of portions of the interview, and finally a general hypnotic susceptibility rating was arrived at in a group conference of the interviewers.

This, then, is the kind of material available for analysis. The interviews following hypnosis tended to be less routine than those preceding because they were often held in order to answer specific questions related to the responsiveness of the individual subject within the hypnotic session.

ALTERNATIVE PATHS INTO HYPNOSIS

The interviews in advance of hypnosis began in the fall of 1960 and continued in the autumn and winter quarters of 1960–61, 1961–62, and 1962–63, and were resumed in the winter quarter of 1963–64, with some changes in detail as the program progressed. It was natural at first to look for positive and negative indicators of hypnosis and to expect susceptibility to be a kind of algebraic resultant of positive and negative factors. Basing global predictions on this general conception of hypnotizability led to rather indifferent correlations, similar to those obtained with the various inventories. While results were positive, they were not encouraging, as we see from Table 68. The corre-

TABLE 68. HYPNOTIC SUSCEPTIBILITY PREDICTED FROM INTERVIEWS AS COMPARED WITH PREDICTIONS FROM AN EXPERIENCE INVENTORY

	Correlations with SHSS, Form C	
Sample	Interviewer ratings	Experience inventory
1960–61: N = 99 females	.30†	.34†
1961–62: N = 98 males	.35†	.38†
1962–63: N = 103 (50 males; 53 females)	.23*	.33†

$*p < .05$ $†p < .01$

lations are positive and significant, but they are small, and the inferences made from the interviews are about on a par with those from the 60-item experience inventories of Ås and of Lee.

Review of these results, plus the other low correlations such as those reported in Chapters 12, 13, and 14, led us to the conjecture that we were in error in trying to assess positive and negative factors as though they were in such a relationship that a negative one would cancel out a positive one. The alternative presented itself that a *single* highly favorable predictor might lead to high susceptibility in the *absence* of other favorable predictors. This leads to the conception of *multiple paths* into hypnosis, *any one* of which can lead to a high score.

If such is the situation, as we believe it may be, then the ordinary additive kind of personality test (including additive ratings from an interview) will yield only low correlations with hypnosis because several moderate scores on predictive items will not equal the effect of a single strong one.

An implication of reliance on single predictors is that they have to be assessed very carefully. This raises great practical problems. Suppose, for example, that there are a dozen paths into hypnosis, each of which may alone carry the whole weight. Then every one of these has to be assessed accurately, for an error in underestimating the crucial or overestimating a noncrucial one may destroy whatever predictive significance there is in the available information. This inherent difficulty will be clearer as we proceed; it doubtless plays a role in the issues between clinical and statistical prediction (Meehl, 1954; Gough, 1962).

Among the multiple paths that we hypothesize may lead into hypnosis as single dominant determiners are compelling interests such as:

1. *Reading.* The hypnotic susceptible are found among those who can become deeply involved in novels, adventure, mystery stories. We shall deal with some illustrations of these later on.

2. *Dramatic arts.* The hypnotic susceptible include certain actors and viewers who respond with deep involvement; those who have had imaginary companions in childhood may also be following this same path into hypnosis.

3. *Esthetic involvement.* Those who derive keen pleasure from sights or sounds, such as nature lovers or music lovers, tend to be hypnotically susceptible.

4. *Religious dedication.* As in all of these paths, differentiations have to be made between the mere churchgoer and the one with a sense of devotion and discipleship. When the involvement is profound, it is a favorable sign for hypnotizability.

5. *Adventure.* Those with a spirit of adventure, who are willing to tolerate danger or disapproval in order to explore the unknown, who have a rich curiosity about the ranges of human experience, tend to be hypnotically susceptible. We have found it useful to classify some of these as physical and mental space travelers, as they will be described later in this chapter.

While these five paths are not to be considered exhaustive, they are representative of the kinds of interests that characterize our subjects and differentiate subgroups of hypnotizable subjects. In the pure case, in which a subject has only one of these interests, but has it at a very high level, we shall refer to his personality characteristics related to this kind of interest and involvement as providing a *"one-path model"* within the multiple-path theory of hypnotic susceptibility. It is a "model" in that the single-path approach, while perhaps theoretically defensible, is not often to be found; more commonly the hypnotically susceptible subject will have several paths that can lead him into hypnosis, but the theory says that he will not be *more* susceptible than he would be if he followed the one-path model of the highest one of these interests.

What general evidence can we gather for the theory of multiple paths? In an earlier report by E. R. Hilgard (Hilgard, 1964), two such paths were considered: adventuresomeness and childhood fantasy. It was there pointed out that if one of these determiners was high the other was largely irrelevant. Thus for subjects high in fantasy there was a nonsignificant correlation with adventuresomeness, and for subjects high in adventuresomeness there was a nonsignficant correlation with fantasy. The obverse conditions led to significant correlations, that is, between adventure and hypnosis when fantasy was low, and between fantasy and hypnosis when adventure was low. The relationships are shown in Table 69.

TABLE 69. ADVENTURESOMENESS AND CHILDHOOD FANTASY IN RELATION TO HYPNOTIC SUSCEPTIBILITY AS MEASURED BY THE STANFORD HYPNOTIC SUSCEPTIBILITY SCALE, FORM C (E. R. HILGARD, 1964)

Items correlated	Correlations with SHSS, Form C	
	N	r
Adventuresomeness vs. hypnotic susceptibility		
Low fantasy subjects	67	.32*
High fantasy subjects	37	.03 n.s.
Childhood fantasy vs. hypnotic susceptibility		
Low adventure subjects	49	.34†
High adventure subjects	55	.11 n.s.

*$p < .01$ †$p < .05$

These results are coherent with the notion that *either* high adventure or high fantasy can lead to hypnotic susceptibility, thus conforming to the theory of alternative or multiple paths.

A somewhat more direct test can be made in a sample in which a larger number of alternative paths were carefully rated prior to hypnosis. The seven paths rated were the five already discussed, with the further subdivision of two of them: dramatic arts into the distinction between acting and viewing, and esthetic involvement into music listening involvement and esthetic interest in nature. Thus the

seven were reading, dramatic acting, dramatic watching, music listening, nature interest, religion, and adventure. Now we may ask the
questions: Are those who are rated high in more than one of these
areas any more hypnotizable than those rated high in a single one,
and are both of these groups higher in hypnotic susceptibility than
those who do not score high in any one of these areas? Results within
a sample of 45 cases studied in the winter of 1964 are given in Table
70. Interests were rated on a 7-point scale with ratings of 6 or 7
unusually high.

TABLE 70. HYPNOTIC SUSCEPTIBILITY OF SUBJECTS CLASSIFIED ACCORDING
TO HIGH RATINGS IN MORE THAN ONE INTEREST AREA, IN ONE ONLY, AND
IN NONE OF SEVEN AREAS CONSIDERED TO BE PATHS INTO HYPNOSIS

| Ratings | Hypnotic susceptibility (Form C′) | | |
	N	Mean	SD
A. Ratings of 6 or 7 in more than one area	14	5.36	1.38
B. Rating of 6 or 7 in one area only	12	5.50	2.38
C. No rating of 6 or 7	19	2.76	1.86
Total	45	4.30	2.30

Significances:
Between groups, F–ratio $= 10.16$, $df = 2, 42$, $p < .001$
Groups A and B vs. Group C, $t = 6.25$, $df = 43$, $p < .001$

The hypothesis of multiple paths is supported by the lack of difference between those high in one path and high in more than one,
and by the difference between those high in one or more paths from
those not high in any. A little reflection will show that this situation
can at best result in low correlations on an additive basis. Within this
sample of 45 cases if the ratings on the seven areas are all added to
yield a predictive score of the ordinary kind, the result is a correlation
of but $r = .39$. If, as an alternative, the *highest* rating in *any* area
is used, the correlation becomes $r = .42$.

Let me repeat that a major reason for studying these interest paths in detail resides in what we can learn about the *personality character-istics* of the subject at the time he is participating. It should be noted that the single-path theory, while a useful corrective to a theory that assumes purely additive contributors to hypnotic susceptibility, is itself incomplete. The subjects who receive the top ratings on any one of these paths are not by any means at the maximum of hypnotic susceptibility, and there must be some inhibiting processes derived from other characteristics of their personalities. Some of these char-acteristics inhibiting susceptibility probably lie outside the investigated paths. The interactions are doubtless subtle ones; if, for example, the pertinent path is relatively conflict-free, hypnotic susceptibility can reach high levels despite other features (such as achievement orienta-tion) that might be expected to interfere with hypnosis; at the same time, there could be *degrees* of conflict (or, stated another way, de-grees of dissociation) that make for differences in hypnotic perform-ance which we are not yet able to predict from our interview data.

The quantitative results given in Tables 69 and 70 are sufficient justification for looking more closely at the case material to see what is involved in the various one-path models. In another report all of the interest paths mentioned here (and some others) will be explored along with related aspects of personality. As an introduction to this kind of thinking about hypnosis, however, two areas have been selected for discussion now to illustrate the path-model approach: reading and adventure. Because of the limitations of space in condensing mate-rial for this chapter, emphasis will be placed on these two path models only, and not on the individual as a whole. It is regrettable that it is not possible on this occasion to provide a description of the whole individual, for this is the essence of the clinical approach and everyone accustomed to reading case material will wish for more.

READING AND HYPNOTIC SUSCEPTIBILITY

The reader who becomes absorbed in novels, adventure stories, mysteries, science fiction, and related types of literature is likely to have his imagination stirred and his emotions aroused. The reader of books of a more specifically factual kind, stressing analytic or scientific thinking, may also be absorbed and involved in his reading, but with quite a different attitude and outcome. We are here con-cerned with reading of the first kind only, with those who become absorbed in tales of romance and adventure; it is they who tend to be highly hypnotizable. The following brief case summaries illustrate some of the remarks that subjects make about their absorption in reading.

Case 12. Kathy, who follows the author closely. Kathy scored high in hypnosis (7.5 on a 10-point scale) and in the interview before hypnosis was rated at the 6 level in reading absorption, in curiosity, and in adventuresomeness. When asked the direct question in an interview following hypnosis as to whether there was any similarity between reading involvement and hypnotic involvement, she replied:

"In general, yes. When reading, you suspend yourself, your background; you don't have a personality of your own, you're not using your judgments of right or wrong or standards of value, you're dealing with the author on his home ground. I become more involved with the author than with the characters. The author has something to put across and in order to get it you have to be as much like him as you can."

She further explained that she is always following the author during the course of the book and agreeing until the end. She is experiencing the feelings, not identifying with anyone. After she has finished the book and laid it aside a critical process ensues, and she will review and think about it. In *Walden II* she thought the characters were not put across strongly, but "I lived the whole fantasy with the author."

It became so apparent that she became deeply immersed in books that I asked her whether she ever had a prolonged after-experience from a book. She said: "I'll carry around a feeling of a book for several days. After reading *Walden II* I was watching for the colony going up. You don't read and forget." She can still be in the book for 15 or 20 minutes after she has finished the book while she sits where she was reading.

Case 13. Tom, who identifies with the characters. This subject also scored high in hypnosis (7 of 10) and prior to hypnosis was rated high in both reading and adventurousness, the latter represented by skiing and car racing. In the interview following hypnosis we discussed reading along with other topics, but the material here will be confined to reading.

He cited his reactions to books such as *Nineteen Eighty-Four* and *Brave New World*. "I identify myself with the character in *Nineteen Eighty-Four*, with Winston Smith, who was tortured at the end, fearing rats. His head was in a cage and he felt he would have to submit. I *felt* the fear that he felt as it came closer, closer. Walking back from the Union after finishing the book I had a problem relating myself to my present environment, to the stuff around me, for I was so entangled in the story that I had become exhausted."

In *The Death of a Salesman* he identified with Willy, and said that he had cried at the end. "I identified him with my father and myself, afterwards felt the same way." He said that he was sitting somewhere, watching the rain out of the window for quite a while after finishing the book, not really thinking of anything, but somehow in a depression relating not so much to what had happened as to what might happen to him.

The intense absorption of these two subjects, although one of them thinks about the author and the other about the characters, shows the temporary transformation of the self that relates these experiences to hypnosis. After interviewing numbers of readers who were hypnotizable, the following characteristics appeared prominently with this group.

1. *A high level of fantasy.* There is a tolerance for, acceptance of, and pleasure in the fantasy world represented by books. The words of the author can lead to a "matched fantasy" on the part of the reader. This is accompanied by a willingness to suspend reality testing.

2. *Appropriate "feeling" accompaniment.* The reader's fantasy is a fantasy-with-feeling; he may reflect the whole gamut of emotional responses intended by the author, or, if he responds in a more circumscribed way, he responds with appropriate feeling in identification with one particular character.

3. *Sensitivity to the power of words.* The author's words can evoke experience. Through the use of words the author can exercise a powerful manipulation of another person's ideas and emotions.

4. *Capacity to live in and for the present.* An individual may be reading about a romance dealing with past historical events or about space travel of the future but his pleasure is felt as though the events were occurring at the moment. He does not postpone much of his gratification until the project is finished, for example, when the "scores" come in later, as in athletics or grade-making.

5. *A prompt, almost immediate engagement of interest and attention.*

6. *Time-limited experiencing.* Reading is a time-limited experience, beginning when the book is opened and ceasing very soon after it has been set aside. The subject who has read a great deal comes to hyp-

nosis with much of this time-limited experience; he is not in danger of being swept away by an experience which departs *temporarily* from reality. This is of course something of what is meant by temporary "regression in the service of the ego."

7. *An active receptivity.* It is a mistake to think of the receptivity we are describing as passive, although it may occasionally be so. The involved reader is active, "putting his mind to the task," a feature that is common to hypnosis also.

It is probable, then, that absorption in reading and hypnotizability are related. There are some difficulties in estimating reading absorption appropriately, however, because of the lack of relationship between certain kinds of reading absorption and hypnosis. One kind of absorption makes of reading a kind of *addiction,* so that its meaning is very different to the subject than in the cases just described. The following case illustrates this kind of absorption, which is unrelated to hypnotic susceptibility.

Case 14. Ruth, for whom reading addiction is not a sign of hypnotizability. This subject scored near the bottom of the group in hypnotizability (a score of 2 on one day and of 1 on another day). Yet in the interview in advance of hypnosis she was rated at the 7 level in absorption in reading. Does this mean that reading absorption is not a predictor of hypnotic susceptibility? Actually, it means that some additional differentiations in regard to kinds of reading need to be made.

Ruth learned to read early, and she read every available minute. By the age of 8 she was reading the Nancy Drew books; she read while she was supposed to be napping at boarding school and with a flashlight after lights had to be turned out. This tendency continued so that in her late teens, while spending summer vacations at a lake with her parents, she would go to parties until 1 or 2 A.M., then read from 2 A.M. to 7 A.M. before being ready to sleep. If she had an interesting book, she would continue to read that; if not, she rummaged through the family library to find another one. Her first year at the university was a fiasco because she would read for days at a time, neglecting classes.

Despite this constant reading, it was difficult to get the subject to describe what reading meant to her. On being pressed for an answer she said: "It's an interest. I must definitely be interested. It is not exactly pleasure." She denied that she could use such terms as "satisfaction" or "gratification" as applicable to her reading. She simply wanted more and more of it; this is evidence for its addictive quality.

"I never imagined myself as one of the characters. I just located the central characters and read very quickly." "I don't read discerningly; I read quickly." "I'll have a general impression afterwards rather than vivid recall." "I couldn't talk about a book with anyone, for I can't recall it that well."

There is no role involvement. "The closest I've ever come is to *try* to imagine what it would be like to be someone else." There is no savoring of the experience while it is going on, no deep feeling, and no residue after it is finished. Her reading has a voracious quality in the sense that she devours a book instead of enjoying it. Thus her reading differs enormously from Cases 12 and 13, and its lack of relationship to hypnotizability is understandable.

We may amplify what was said about the nature of the persons who become absorbed in reading by some inferences about what the reading situation is like for these hypnotizable people.

1. An almost immediate response, with involvement and appropriate feeling, has taken over as a reader follows an author closely along paths to which the latter has directed him via the medium of words.

2. A suspension of some of the reality testing processes of the ego has occurred. Subjects describe what we would term a disengagement by the ego in regard to certain of its functions, such as independent initiative, thinking, judgment, decision-making, and the like.

3. The reality testing or observing ego continues to be present though it has been relegated to a subsidiary role for the duration of the story. Somewhere within himself the reader actually knows what is real and what is unreal, he is aware that the book is only fantasy, but he is engrossed for the time in "make-believe logic" with the author. The individual feels he could give up the book anytime he wanted to, but he doesn't want to.

4. A dissociation with the cooperation of the ego or in the service of the ego has resulted. Whether this should be termed "regression in the service of the ego," will depend on further, more precise formulations in regard to the meaning of regression. The idea of regression has been used to cover a great deal of territory. Dissociation as the broader concept can include regression.

Such a dissociation or regression is not threatening because the boundaries in time and place and person have been tested many times. Fantasy and feeling without boundaries belong to the world of the psychotic, to the schizophrenic. Substantial, long-tested boundaries surround the world of the reader.

ADVENTURE: MENTAL- AND PHYSICAL-SPACE TRAVELERS

There are two broad categories of athletics or physical sports that we have found it necessary to distinguish: the competitive sports, in which the goal is to win and to score points, and the noncompetitive sports in which there is an enjoyment of the out-of-doors and of vigorous muscular exertion. This second kind of athlete is an adventurer interested in skiing, skin-diving, or mountain-climbing, in which he enjoys the immediate experience and does not have to win against an adversary. We shall have something further to say about competitive athletics later on, but now we are interested in the adventurers among the athletes. Related activities include airplane flying, cave exploring ("spelunking"), boating. Because so many of these activities defy gravity or take place in unusual spatial contexts (of either location or speed) we have tended to refer to these cases as *physical-space travelers,* a term we adopted to distinguish between them and some other adventurers, whom we have called *mental-space travelers.*

This other group of adventurers, the mental-space travelers, seek adventures through the mind. They can have their adventures sitting in a chair or lying down. They may carry out expeditions through science fiction, or expand their consciousness in experiments with LSD-25, marijuana, mescaline, or ether (by sniffing glue); they may test the edges of their belief through reading about or toying with ESP, the Ouija board, or fortune tellers. Such people wish to probe the limits of mental space. They may suggest that the usual reality testing measures available to us now are insufficient to explore the vastness of our mental universe. All of them—and they are admittedly diverse—have one thing in common: a desire for a new and different experience beyond the accepted realm of ordinary experience, a wish to embark on adventure without sallying forth into the outside world. It is their curiosity that is high; their adventuresomeness does not have within it the requirement of physical stamina or the desire to take physical risks that characterize the physical-space traveler. It is easy to see that hypnosis fits easily into this type of interest.

Our most extensive information about space travelers occurred when we interviewed the first group of volunteer subjects in our laboratory. In response to an advertisement in the college newspaper asking for volunteers for hypnosis (with no recompense provided) volunteers were lined up before the doors when the office opened the next morning. On the whole, their hypnotic susceptibility proved higher than that of the more-or-less "coerced" volunteers from the introductory psychology course, the ones who made up our usual samples (Boucher and Hilgard, 1962). Included in their numbers was an impressive collection of both physical- and mental-space travelers. Their characteristics led us to look for cases in our regular samples where they were not as prominent, but always a few were to be found. Some illustrative cases will now be presented.

Case 15. Frank, a physical-space traveler. He scored moderately high (6.5 of 10) following hypnotic induction, but scored at 0 when suggestions were given under waking-imagination instructions. The high rating in adventuresomeness was his only high rating, so he is a nearly "pure case" of the path model of adventure as a way into hypnosis.

In describing his adventurous streak he said: "I call it adventurous. My parents would say foolhardy." Skin-diving he described thus: "It's *free* competition, like an adventure. It's exhilarating." Of motorcycling: "The *power* appeals to me; I like to feel the wind whistling by. The freedom is like flying." Because he had mentioned flying he was asked about this: "I've always wanted to fly and snow ski but I've had no opportunity. I would like to learn to do stunts in flying. My father was a fine pilot."

The main points to be noted in these descriptions of his experiences are such terms as "exciting," "exhilarating," "wind whistling by," "freedom." Although he once used the word competition, it was *free* competition, like an adventure; there is no emphasis on the goals of achievement and winning over someone else.

Case 16. A mental-space traveler, Edward. This young man scored at 6 of 10, somewhat above the mean in hypnosis. The adventuresomeness of "mental space" was his only high rating, so that he, too, belongs to that rare group that follows a single path into hypnosis and hence helps to define more clearly the path model.

He started to read science fiction early in grammar school and read a book about every two days until this type of reading tapered off. However, he was still reading some of it last year. He imagined *himself* out in space. He recalls identifying with one character, John Carter, in vicarious pleasures. "I enjoyed thinking and imagining myself as him, but I never thought I could be."

The science fiction interest has led to a curiosity about what is "really so," and he is now majoring in electronics. A rather inarticulate and somewhat withdrawn person, he contrasts markedly with the outgoingness and easy conversation of Case 15. It is easy to see why global personality tests fail to yield high predictions of hypnotizability.

Case 17. John, with physical- and mental-space interests combined. John scored 6.5 of 10 in hypnosis.

He likes the physical-space interests of flying and skiing. In skiing the appeal is "the flying, the speed." "Down the slope you have complete control, you go fast and you can feel the wind going by on all sides, it feels like you take off." (Take off?) "It feels like you're jumping loose—the faster you go the more you feel you're coming apart from the ground." He has been skiing since the age of 10.

But he is a mental-space traveler, too. He has read science fiction since age 11; after age 13 he read all the science fiction he could find. In high school, reading of science fiction became more intermittent, but he still reads it occasionally. "It is uninhibited. For a while you're completely free to let your logic be swept away. You're free and uninhibited. You don't have to think it through. . . . For a while you're illogical." "The author thought of the ridiculous, the free. . . . It's the sweep of the imagination. . . . It's thinking about the infinite, to the limits of the imagination. . . . It feels like you're moving." (Your body?) "No . . . your mind. Things are opening wider and wider. You feel like you're drawn into it."

After the study of many such cases, it becomes clear that these adventurers share characteristics in common, despite the personality differences among them:

1. *Enjoyment of feelings of the moment.* In flying and skiing, subjects describe feelings of excitement, of exhilaration, of power, and of thrilling sensation as they feel the wind blow upon their faces. It will be recalled that the subject above said that in skiing he had a sense of jumping loose, of coming apart from the ground, of taking off into the air. This is freedom from the usual bounds of everyday experience, from restraints that more and more surround the adult as he leaves childhood.

The same enjoyment of feelings and sensations of the moment

mark the individual who has embarked on a mental space flight via science fiction, ESP, or LSD.

2. *Escape from the world of reality and entrance into a world of unreality.* The physical-space travelers escape the everyday world of reality by exploring the skies, the mountain-tops, or the fantastic world inside a cave> The mental-space adventurers speak of escaping from the real world and entering into the limitless space of an imaginary world. Instead of probing and testing the physical limits of space, they have embarked on a more extended journey into mental space.

The escape from ordinary reality and entrance into the world of excitement requires a certain amount of discipline on the part of the physical-space travelers. Most of them stress the care they take in making preparations, being sure their equipment is in order, carrying maps, and watching the weather reports. They are adventurers but few are dare-devils. They express this in various ways, and some are of course more reckless than others. Some say: "I want to stay alive!" One put it: "I enjoy walking on the thin edge of danger." The mental-space travelers are on the whole somewhat less disciplined than the physical-space travelers; while they must show some caution, particularly in the use of drugs, many of their other "adventures" are quite carefree and unbounded. Members of this group are apt to be less impeded by the demands of reality through actual restraints imposed by the world around them.

3. *Time-limited experiences.* The adventures of both the physical- and mental-space travelers are usually "excursions" away from everyday reality, with return within a fairly short time, thus sharing both with reading and with hypnosis this time-limited aspect.

4. *Active involvement.* Although the degree of active involvement is more evident in the physical-space traveler, it is present also in the mental-space traveler. Even the one who gains his experiences through drugs usually has prepared himself in some manner for what he expects to experience, and this active preparation no doubt influences what he does actually experience.

5. *Zest for excitement and new experience.* The characterization of these people as adventurers implies that they have curiosity and seek novelty, and they enjoy so doing.

6. *Enjoyment of feelings of omnipotence and freedom from restraint.* These motifs run prominently through the case material; because these characteristics are prominent in childhood they contribute

to the "regressive" interpretation of these experiences, and probably to the corresponding "regressive" interpretation of hypnosis.

When summarized in this way, and with clear illustrations before us, the generalizations appear somewhat firmer than they are. Perhaps the generalizations are indeed sound, and we hope they are, but their practical applications (as in predicting hypnotizability) present difficulties.

For example, a particular problem arises over the relationship between *impulsivity* and hypnosis. These adventurers appear to be impulsive people; their "primary process" approach to life is in terms of feeling, enjoyment, and thus, to some extent, impulse. But there is a distinction to be made between disciplined impulse and capricious impulse. Many subjects who describe themselves as impulsively adventuresome are not hypnotizable.

Case 18. Impulsivity in Paul, a nonhypnotizable subject. Paul, who scored 2 of 12 points on SHSS, Form C, was rated 6 in adventurousness in advance of hypnosis because of descriptions such as the following. He said that he liked to climb to the tops of trees or walk around third floor gutters. This could be dangerous at times but he would take off whenever the spirit moved him, especially if he thought he had an appreciative audience. When on a hike with a group he might decide on a shortcut over a wobbly log bridge, rather than taking the safe, longer route. As a boy he liked the same sort of excitement, for instance, jumping from the roof of his house to the garage roof several feet away. This required a running start and a fast stop at the other side because of the distance between the buildings and the slope of the roof.

When questioned about participation in the kinds of activities characteristic of our physical-space travelers, we found no orderly or sustained ones. His adventures were pranks or stunts done for the momentary attention of an audience rather than for an experience in which he was deeply involved. While there was a certain reckless impulsiveness about what he did, it reflected more bravado than feeling.

This case was studied early in our interviewing experience and would no longer be given a high rating for involvement in adventurous activities.

When impulse is not channeled it appears unrelated to hypnotizability. Thus the impulsiveness to perform a stunt like climbing to the roof, or throwing water-filled balloons into a girls' dormitory, or setting off firecrackers, is not the kind conducive to hypnosis. Both science fiction and hypnosis provide structure and guidelines for exercising the imagination. Skiing and flying demand structure also in their emphasis upon the development of skills before an individual can participate successfully in the experience.

INVOLVEMENTS UNRELATED TO HYPNOTIZABILITY

Because intense involvement is so characteristic of the hypnotic experience and because the interests reflecting involvement tend to be correlated with hypnosis, it is easy to make the mistake of thinking that *all* involvements are related to hypnosis. We have found three groups of interests that are often fully absorbing, but that *when found alone* are associated with insusceptibility to hypnosis: competitive athletics, scientific curiosity, and recreation that takes the form of work. Where interest in athletic competition is found to be high, in the absence of other kinds of involvement, hypnotic susceptibility tends to be minimal. Correspondingly, in the absence of the interests known to be positively related to hypnosis, an intellectual involvement in logically verified and rationally related truths, characteristic of the physical scientist *per se* (though by no means characteristic of all physical scientists) tends to negate susceptibility. While the capacity to enjoy play is favorable to hypnosis, when that play takes the form of involvement in activities that are achievement-oriented, with high standards of excellence (a form of play here called work-recreation), the prognosis for hypnotizability is poor. Such people build boats, rebuild cars, repair or build rooms on houses, work hard at gardening, knitting, or serving others. For these people leisure time provides an opportunity for recreation through useful work projects. Such people, generally nonhypnotizable, provide an illustration of capacity for deep involvement, but of a kind unrelated to the involvement within hypnosis.

The competitive athlete. We shall use the competitive athlete to illustrate involvement not leading to hypnosis, leaving the scientific-rational and the work-recreation interests for the report in preparation.

We are talking about the competitive athlete who has no other interests that will lead him into hypnosis; in that case he is likely to prove quite unsusceptible. The situation, from the quantitative standpoint, is summarized in Table 71, in which athletes and non-athletes are compared.

TABLE 71. ATHLETIC INTERESTS AND HYPNOTIC SUSCEPTIBILITY

	Hypnotic susceptibility scores (Form C′)					
	Those high in athletic interests (6–7)			Those not high in athletic interests (0–5)		
	N	Mean	SD	N	Mean	SD
Those high in one or more interests related to hypnotic susceptibility	13	5.38	1.78	13	5.46	2.06
Those not high in any interest related to hypnotic susceptibility	12	2.42	1.64	7	3.36	2.04
Total	25	3.96	2.26	20	4.72	2.29

Significance test:
Those high in athletic interests vs. those not high in athletic interests, $t = 1.12$, $df = 42$, not significant.

The main point of Table 71 is that athletic interest is almost irrelevant to hypnosis; at least being very high in athletic interest does not constitute one of the model paths into hypnosis, for with that alone, without any other interest, the average hypnotic scores are very low indeed. Neither does adding high athletic interest to other interests improve the hypnotic scores.

The reason for treating those with athletic interests alone is to see why an area that commands the tremendous involvement which athletes describe should be so unrelated to susceptibility. Involvement is one of our key concepts in hypnotizability. Again, some cases will prove informative.

Case 19. Dave, a baseball and basketball player who scores low in hypnotic susceptibility. Prior to hypnosis Dave's high involvement in athletics was rated 7, at the top of the rating scale, and no other area was above 3. He scored very low in hypnotizability (2 of 10).

When interviewed after the attempted hypnotic induction he helped to explain why his intense involvement in basketball and baseball (at the varsity level) was unrelated to hypnotizability. "It's a lot more real and takes less imagination." He went on to elaborate: *"You have complete control of yourself* in almost all situations. Ever since I was very young, I've played ball. My brothers taught me, and I got a lot of training. There's a pressure on you to perform, and you can't let emotion in any way impede your physical abilities or response. In a game, you can't let yourself be bothered by any emotion. You control your physical responses and don't let emotion control you at all."

(You lose yourself in a game; why can't you lose yourself in hypnosis?) "You do lose yourself in the game, but the game has an object, to put the ball in the basket. You are completely concentrated on something in the real world."

"I *wanted* to be hypnotized but I doubted it because I've always had control over myself."

Case 20. Helen, a competitive woman swimmer. She was rated at 6 in athletic involvement before hypnosis, with no other interest area rated high. Helen scored at the bottom of the scale on hypnotic susceptibility (0 of 10).

"I was extremely interested in being hypnotized. I'm not a skeptic. . . . Hypnosis was too much like what you see in the movies. I tried to do it, but it seemed corny."

She began to talk about her athletic interests. She had been swimming competitively since the age of 8, and had won trophies in badminton. "People who are competitive," she said, "are far from being imaginative. You realize what you are fighting. It's the reality of the struggle. Imagination and competition are mutually exclusive. In competing, the whole world around you is more real. My imagination is extremely limited.

"In competitive sports you're taught never to take your opponent for granted. You keep a critical eye on everything. Even though your opponent looks scrawny and not apt to do anything, you don't trust that situation. . . . I can never say die. I've got to win. I've always got to try to beat the person; I never give up. Even if I run myself too hard and get ill, I'll keep trying to win."

Some of the characteristics of athletes, derived from interviews with this group of highly successful and involved athletes, lacking in other interests, follow:

1. *Sensitivity to exact information from the environment.* For these athletes the demands of reality are constantly in the forefront. Environmental stimuli are used for exact information about that reality and therefore are interpreted according to their precise meanings. Information that is to be used for accomplishment in a particular task must be evaluated according to its relevance to that task.

2. *Focus on those aspects that lead to decision and control.* The goals of the athlete include a desire for greater skill and for better performance against an adversary. Bodily responses are keyed to coordination and automaticity in the service of that decision and control. Athletes, long trained to know exactly what body movements they are making, speak of their difficulty within attempted hypnosis when the hypnotist tells them the body is doing something that they know immediately it is not doing. They have well-learned decision signals connected with the body in space.

3. *Stress on activity.* Achievement and competition require constant activity, vigilance, and striving. Mental alertness to precise meanings of incoming stimuli or signals has become heightened, and the "metered" appropriate response is ready and well learned. Both areas (detection and response) require an active alertness.

These characteristics tend to be found in the absence of some other ones that would be relevant for hypnosis. These particular athletes are not able to range widely through imagination and feeling, they tend to find less enjoyment of the moment than in anticipation of the final victory, and they are uneasy with passive or receptive experiences in view of their activity orientation. They are not given to contemplation and relaxation.

Their involvements thus contrast sharply with those we have described for the hypnotizable readers and the hypnotizable adventurers.

The requirements of alertness, of planned responsiveness, and of activity apply also to those of our competitive athletes who score high on hypnosis by virtue of other kinds of interests. Why, then, do not these other interests (fantasy, free imagination, and so forth) interfere with their athletic prowess? This is an interesting question, and shows how careful one has to be about making plausible generalizations without examining the exceptions that occur.

There are, in fact, three answers to be given:

1. Some competitive athletes are able to dissociate the athletic activity from other kinds of absorbed activities, so that the two spheres are kept entirely distinct. Hence the hypnotic ability, evident in these other activities, does not interfere with the reality-orientation of competition.

2. Other competitive athletes find ways of making use of their hypnotic abilities in competition, through the kinds of athletic roles they play. A case of a baseball pitcher will be described presently, but presumably track events (such as long distance running) would permit the same sort of use of hypnotic ability within the sport itself, even though it counts as competitive because there are adversaries to be met.

3. Many of the athletes in our sample are not primarily competitors at all. Their athletic interests merge with the interests of those we have called physical-space travelers.

The first two of these solutions to the problem of the hypnotizability of athletes will be illustrated by cases, the third by further discussion.

Case 21. George, an athlete whose athletics is kept separate from his reading. Prior to hypnosis, George was rated high in reading, especially science fiction, theater, and sports. He scored slightly above average in hypnosis (5.5 of 10 points).

He is a doer; he loves activity. This is reflected in his athletic interest. He said it was easy to concentrate on athletics because he was directly involved, and there was action. It was not easy for him to sit down and concentrate. Playing golf and participating in athletics in general was for accomplishment and not for relaxation. Thus far he sounds very much like the other athletes (Cases 19 and 20).

There is, however, another side to him. This is illustrated in his reading. "I don't read. I *live* the character. I *become* that character; I put myself in his place rather than putting him in my place."

Thus he is able to combine in one person the realism of the athlete and the reality-distortion of his reading without conflict.

Case 22. Vance, a baseball pitcher who is able to use his hypnotic ability in competition. Not all athletic roles are alike. A baseball shortstop has to be ready for what happens, while a pitcher can exercise more initiative. This subject, a baseball pitcher, by contrast with many of our athletes, was at the top of the hypnotic scale, scoring 10 of 10 possible points. What follows is based on a second interview, this one after hypnosis.

It turns out that he has had many experiences that might be described as essentially self-hypnotic. When faced with a personal problem he often went into a kind of mental trance, he said. When he came out of it he would not remember what he had been thinking about, but he knew only that the problem was on the way to a solution. This had been true for many years.

When I asked him whether or not the baseball player had to be alert and on his toes all of the time, he answered: "I am different from other people. Before a ball game, I set myself emotionally in a particular mood through concentration on making my senses more keen, and my mind more alert. It's a state of mind that's carried me through the ball game. It supports itself, once I set myself." He may spend 10 minutes or so creating this mood, not concentrating on anything in particular, but rather on nothingness as in a completely dark room. He is able to relax completely, and this "state of suspended animation" may take from 3 to 5 minutes while he gets everything out of his system, such as the problems of the day. The first step is complete relaxation; the second step is used to build up emotional tension. This is done without words, but his mind is on baseball. "It's a feeling of complete confidence that I'm going to do well, that I'm going to play to the peak of my ability." When asked about the relation of this to hypnosis he said simply and confidently: "I can assume many roles, depending upon the necessity."

Whether or not his use of a kind of self-hypnosis would serve for other positions than pitcher is an open question; at least for him hypnosis and athletic prowess do not conflict.

The third solution to the relationship between the athletic ability and hypnosis may be that those who have athletic ability alone tend to be more competitive than those whose athletic ability is combined with other interests of the kind associated with susceptibility. This has led to a reexamination of the data entering into Table 96. Actually the rating of athletic involvement that was made prior to hypnosis was not differentiated as to the degree of competition involved. It is therefore of interest to know whether there is some difference in kinds of athletic participation of those who have athletic interests alone and those with athletic interests in combination with other interests.

Of 16 athletes who have only athletic interests, 12 clearly place their interest in competition above the intrinsic interest in the enjoyment of the sport; of 9 with high athletic interest combined with other interests, only three are in more strictly competitive sports—tennis, basketball, and football, respectively; the football player says less about wanting to win than that the sport provides an outlet for aggression. The other six find enjoyment in the activity itself. While these exact numerical values are unimportant, the impression is clear that there is some difference in the modal hypnotizability of those who have only athletic interests (usually an interest in competition) and those who combine athletic interests with other interests (usually more enjoyment in becoming involved in the activity itself).

DEVELOPMENTAL ASPECTS OF PERSONALITY IN RELATION TO HYPNOSIS

The effort to untangle the personality differences leading to hypnotizability has been an interesting one. We began our investigations by assuming that the concept of *transference* in hypnosis was similar to, or parallel to, that of transference in therapeutic situations (Macalpine, 1950; Gill and Brenman, 1959). Hence we studied parent-child interactions, passive gratifications, identification patterns, the development of trust in interpersonal situations, types of childhood discipline. While these variables are proving useful now, in conjunction with areas of interest, the kernel of the answer to our question eluded us. Gradually our emphasis shifted to the importance of specific interests, some partially related to susceptibility, and some that proved to be unrelated.

The study of various groupings of interests permitted us to postulate a multiple-path theory, with a number of specific-path models on which a capacity for hypnosis might rest.

In studying a variety of paths, such as reading, religion, the dramatic arts, the adventuresome physical- and mental-space travelers, we were able to describe personality attributes shared by individuals at times when they were involved in such pursuits. Although only reading and adventure have been discussed in detail here, the study of other paths involves a number of attributes that are similar as well as some that are different.

Our second goal involved a study of the life history of such interests. Were they of long duration or of recent origin? Were they continuous or discontinuous? If they had existed earlier but were not now present, were they still significant? The answer appears to be that such interests are long-term, continuous ones such as would be represented by reading. Reading that begins early and continues with unabated enthusiasm represents a typical picture favorable for hypnosis. Perhaps the individual has less time for reading novels now but when he does, he reports that he becomes quickly involved in the way he used to do. On the other hand, if he tells us that for many years he became greatly involved but for the last two years he has not been able to generate the same interest in novels, and further that his reading has changed entirely to a scientific type, the subject may no longer be hypnotizable. This assumes that reading was the specific path model and that there were no others. If reading interests began late, were delayed, for example, until the teens, such reading, though it may be described as intense, lacks some essential element. We suspect that there is a period during childhood when the *potential for involvement* is at its height. If reading or other interests catch hold during this developmental phase, it appears that a continuing capacity for an almost involuntary interest in these areas can result. Involved reading, for example, may represent one of the most frequent partial dissociative processes in the normal individual.

One exception to the foregoing remarks illustrates the extent to which care in making general assertions must be exercised. Reading that is really involved *may* begin late. In this situation, however, we believe that it is building on an already developed involvement in a related area, for example, that of involved movie viewing. Thus reading involvement here probably parallels hypnotic involvement, inasmuch as *both* may be building on an already well-developed pathway via involvement in movies.

It looks as though there is a developmental period for interest in mental-space pursuits such as science fiction, mental telepathy, and hypnosis. In the usual situation, these reach a natural peak around the ages of 11 to 14, then gradually recede. Among avid mental-space travelers, however, involvement has never been lost, though reading of such literature may or may not have diminished.

After first describing the contemporary situation, second, its substantial history in the life span of the individual, we move to our third and very important question. How were such interests fostered? For most of the paths we have studied, though not all, their origins were closely related to the parental figures, thus the significance of the concept of contagion in interpersonal relations. Interest, enthusiasm, and dedication shown by parents can be reflected in interested, enthusiastic, and dedicated children. This is probably the easiest way of learning and the most free of conflict.

The adventurous physical-space travelers represent this par excellence. One of our high-scoring subjects who loved to fly told us that his father had been a pilot in World War I, and that though both father and mother enjoyed flying, his maternal grandfather was the "red hot" of the bunch. When the bi-wing planes made their first appearance, he went barnstorming, did loop-the-loops and wing-walking. Grandfather lived with the family, owned his own plane, and piloted it until a year or so before. Subject, who had flown for years with grandfather and father, described what he liked about flying: the feeling of speed, of the wind going by on all sides, and of taking off. Father also taught the subject how to ski. When asked what he thought the appeal of skiing was for father, the subject replied, "I think he likes to be in the tree tops and the white snow."

Thus this subject and members of his family have developed great skill in piloting a plane or in skiing, but their goals in pursuit of such recreation are primarily adventurous and emphasize feeling. We suggest that the subject identified with the contagious enthusiasm of his grandfather and father in this type of activity, which would possess *intrinsic interest* for a growing boy. The latter is an important consideration in the development of interests that serve as paths into hypnosis.

Another highly hypnotic subject who was rated at the 7 level of adventuresome interests was identifying with an earlier, younger version of his father, that is, the way father had been until the subject was 12 or 13 years old. Father had been a pilot in World War II with a record marked by extraordinary initiative and courage. After the war for a number of years he became an instructor of student pilots, occasionally demonstrating hair-raising maneuvers. For the last few years, having settled into a civilian job, he had been content to forget such exploits and admonished his son not to be so foolhardy. The long period of support for adventuresome activities, however, meant that our subject was traveling the path that his father had traversed at a similar age. The identification was marked.

When we turn to reading, we find that two major but alternative sources account for the development of involved reading interests in our subjects: (a) loneliness that has led the subject during childhood to seek the companionship to be found in books, and (b) enthusiastic parental support that has existed in the home.

Among the lonely, books can fill a need and a wish for friends. The child may be an only child, or an oldest child with much younger siblings, or a youngest child with much older siblings, or there may be some other family situation that promotes separation from other children. In addition the family may live in an isolated area, as on a farm, a mountain top, or a large estate where neighboring children are few and far between.

Seeking pleasure through companionship in books has carried the tacit support of the parents even though the latter may not themselves have been oriented toward books. This matter of parental support appears to be important because it means that the subject is free to pursue his interest in books without conflict. What we are implying here is that wholehearted involvement may be difficult to achieve or retain if it conflicts with parental wishes.

The following cases illustrate the motif of partial isolation as one factor in the development of involved reading interests.

Case 23. Craig, a high-scoring hypnotic subject who came from a farm family in which two older sisters operated in coalition so that he felt on the outside. The nearest neighbor had four girls with whom he had little in common. Thus his closest playmates were at school. Of his situation at home, he said, "I was sitting on the outside. Stories offered more variety of playmates. I saw the variety of life through books. If I read about an island, I could see it, I could see the sandy beach there. If they wrote about a race track, I could see the race track in my mind."

Case 24. James, a subject scoring above average in susceptibility, who attributed the strong development of his reading interest to the fact that he was an only child and the family lived on an estate. The parents were socially active and not at all bookish people. Whenever he wanted to play with other children, they had to be brought to him or he had to be transported to them. This restricted easy communication, so instead he found playmates and adventure through the medium of books, which were close at hand.

Where enthusiasm for books has been contagious, the parents have read many stories to the child before he was able to read for himself, and they enjoyed doing it. This had been no mere exercise in parental duty. One or both parents enjoyed reading novels, mysteries, adventure tales, amusing and whimsical stories, whether they were reading to the child or to themselves. Many subjects raised in this type of environment report that they started to read quite early. Books had been made accessible to them through a home library, a community library, or at school.

Case 25. *Henry, who scored at the highest level in hypnotic susceptibility and who loved reading.* Henry said that both of his parents enjoyed romantic literature; he added that father read poetry and he doubted whether mother had ever read a nonfiction story in her life. He aligned himself with his parents' interest in romantic literature and said further that he did not become interested in reading anything that was very practical.

The subject matter in this chapter has been concerned primarily with the subjects' recreational or play ego, and we hypothesize that enthusiasm of interest on the part of a parent of either sex generates an identification pattern through contagion.

We have been touching on the subject of identification with parents, particularly identification in these recreational interests. Identification as we have perceived it in our subjects can best be described as a plural entity. Occasionally an identification may be global with one parent, but for the most part subjects at this age show a very mixed picture. As an initial effort toward differentiation, we divided identification into three general areas: identification in work, identification in play (that is, recreational activities that included reading), and identification in personality characteristics. Further divisions within each of these categories were frequently necessary in a final description of the subject. E. R. Hilgard (1964) has presented an analysis of 1962–63 data comparing identification patterns in relation to hypnotizability. He found, for example, that those subjects who resembled one parent in work and the other parent in play tended to have predominantly hypnotizable parents as models for their play egos.[2] It may be noted that play interests are not highly sex-typed in our culture, so that a boy who is masculine and a girl who is feminine are violating few established mores in identifying with the recreational interest of the opposite-sex parent.

[2] Interviewers estimated probable hypnotizability of parents on the same type of evidence as was used to predict hypnotic scores of the subjects in advance of hypnosis. Naturally the secondhand nature of the information about the parents presented a troublesome problem. The fact that there was never a follow-up hypnotic session of the parents prevented any answers or closure to our predictions.

In this discourse we have mentioned the subject of conflict. We have observed that the subjects were able to give themselves wholeheartedly to reading or to adventure. Is this wholehearted quality attenuated by the presence of conflict? Is there apt to be some hesitation, some holding back, some lack of confidence if conflict is present? We believe that this is probably the case. Conflict is apt to be minimal when interests were developed early in life, either in association with parents or with their tacit support.

CONCLUDING REMARKS

Throughout the discussion comparisons have been made between the involvement of subjects as they reported their participation in such single-path models as reading or adventure and their involvement as they have reported their participation in hypnosis. The inferences, though tentative, offer exciting possibilities for further study. One of the most puzzling aspects of hypnosis, for example, has been the immediate readiness of the susceptible subject to be hypnotized within a few minutes, regardless of many variations in the hypnotist's qualifications or practices. It is possible that the initial attitude of the subject, that is, the "initial transference," is similar to that of opening a special book or embarking on a new adventure among those who are attuned to these interests through long experience. In hypnosis, the subject responds to the power of words, uses "trance logic," and shows a more or less active receptivity. Does an author operate as a hypnotist, leading the subject by the power of his words into the "make-believe logic" of a matching fantasy? In both, there exist role-enactment, role-involvement, and partial dissociation. In both areas, the degree of involvement may vary; in some subjects it is always deep, in others it is present but far less pervasive. If interests such as reading provide models for hypnosis it is easy to see why hypnosis is not sleep and that the EEG in hypnosis does not follow the pattern of sleep at all. In both hypnosis and in involved reading, certain processes of the ego concerned with reality, such as individual initiative, judgment, and decision, appear to be set aside on a temporary basis.

While this setting aside of reality checks seems to imply a dependence upon inner experience, fantasy, and imagination, this is true only to a limited extent. Actually, the environment plays a very important role for the hypnotized subject, as it does for the reader or the space traveler. The retained contact with the environment, however, stresses receptivity rather than rational thought; the sensory emphasis differs somewhat in the reader, the mental-space traveler, and the physical-space traveler.

It is easy to see how many of the characteristics that we have enumerated in the pathway models are part and parcel of childhood: the blurring of fantasy and reality, the involvement in "pretend games," the implicit following of adult words, the enjoyment of sensation, the feelings of excitement and of omnipotence. They form an attractive arena for the interpretation of regressive phenomena.

In the course of our investigations we recognized that the single-path models appeared to be relatively conflict-free spheres of ego activity, supported for the most part by parental participation or approval; by inference, we suppose that hypnosis, too, may be more successful where conflict is minimal. We are not saying that the individual, as a whole, is free of conflict. Not at all. We conjecture, however, that the processes or paths connected with hypnosis may be little involved in the basic areas of discord or dissension within the personality. This observation may have important ramifications in therapy that utilizes hypnosis.

The variety of experiences represented by the multiple paths suggests one of the reasons why subjects may be successful in some areas of hypnosis and unsuccessful in others. These well-traveled paths that serve as background models may also provide reasons why practice in hypnosis seldom succeeds in broadening the pattern of successes.

Although we have considerable confidence in the promise that lies ahead in the directions we have been taking, it is important to emphasize the tentative nature of our present conclusions. Hypnotic responsiveness bears a complex relationship to personality development; as we come to know more about involvement and about dissociation we should be able to state with greater assurance what makes one person hypnotizable and what prevents another from becoming hypnotized.

Part IV

Theory of Hypnosis

In this final chapter we take stock of where we have arrived regarding the hypnotic experience. Some proposals will be made by way of summarizing what we believe has been found out, proposals that have to do with the childhood background out of which hypnotizability develops and the present interaction with the hypnotist as this personal background is used and transformed into the hypnotic experience. There are some concluding comments about the relation to hypnosis of role-theory, dissociation, and learning.

CHAPTER 16

A Developmental-Interactive Theory
of Hypnotic Susceptibility

Some of the prevalent theories of hypnosis were considered in the first chapter of this book. A theory can serve various purposes and may be stated at various levels of generality: a descriptive theory tries to state what is going on by reducing the unfamiliar to the familiar, while explanatory or reductive theories usually try to find the explanation of one level of phenomena through events at a lower level. Thus a theory that states that hypnosis is merely heightened attention or heightened suggestibility describes it as something supposedly more familiar and hence less in need of explanation, while a theory that explains hypnosis in terms of the spread of cortical inhibition is an effort to be reductive and to explain the psychological facts on a neurophysiological basis. A third kind of theory, sometimes called hypothetico-deductive, tries to work from postulates and theorems, or from a model, resulting in a network of lawful relationships, this whole network constituting the theory.

Most of the theories of hypnosis have attempted to account for the common features of hypnotic performance, that is, what happens during induction, how the trance is established, what it is like, and what the behavior of a hypnotized person is in comparison with familiar behavior outside hypnosis. Such theories at this stage may be more or less eclectic, as in the proposals of White (1941), and Shor (1959, 1962c), which attempt to give as sensible an account as possible of what is observed without developing a highly articulated theory. Their theories thus stress motivational characteristics of the trance state, archaic involvement, reality-orientation, and hypnotic role-taking involvement, the exclusive preoccupation of Sarbin (Sarbin, 1950; Sarbin and Andersen, 1967). Or hypnosis may be assimilated to an established theory, as in Gill and Brenman's (1959) relating of hypnosis to psychoanalytic theory, thus stressing regression, transference, and ego structure as these are understood in contemporary psychoanalysis. The model-building type of theory is best represented in the work of Blum (1961, 1963), in which hypnosis is not only fitted into a general model, but is the favorite laboratory technique by which the model is tested. In the context of this model the essential ingredients of hypnosis are: "an optimal stage of low arousal with sufficient nonspecific sensory input to maintain amplification throughout the Mental System, and (2) controlled restriction of sensory inputs to those repeatedly emanating from the experimenter" (Blum, 1963, p. 141).

These are all legitimate concerns, and each of the accounts is thoughtful and helpful in understanding hypnosis. For present purposes, however, with our interest focused on individual differences, we approach the problem with somewhat more specific questions in view and, in some sense, questions that ought to be easier to answer. Our questions have to do (at this point) not with how a trance is possible or what its essential nature is (although these matters also interest us), but rather with the questions: Why is one person more hypnotizable than another? How do different profiles of hypnotic susceptibility come about? We may first examine the kinds of answers that the theorists have given to these questions.

HYPNOTIC SUSCEPTIBILITY IN CURRENT THEORIES OF HYPNOSIS

While most of the theorists have not phrased their theories to account specifically for individual differences, such differences are so pervasive that nearly all writers on theory have had something to say about susceptibility and insusceptibility.

1. The problem denied. The known facts of differences in test scores on hypnotic susceptibility tests cannot be denied, but the existence of a fundamental problem of persisting individual differences in hypnotic susceptibility may be seen as unreal. Thus Blum (1963, p. 137) implies that by taking enough time, almost any subject can be trained to become more highly susceptible, and Dorcus (1963) believes that a skilled hypnotist can adapt methods to personality and thus change hypnotic susceptibility scores. Barber (1964) believes that motivational and situational factors are so much more important than personality ones that the problem of personality differences in susceptibility has probably been wrongly stated.

2. The waking-hypnotic parallelism. If it can be shown that individual differences in behavior and experience outside hypnosis are similar to those inside hypnosis (after hypnotic induction), then one step is taken toward the understanding of individual differences in susceptibility. This is the approach of Sarbin, when, for example, he shows that role-playing in the waking state, as judged by a dramatic coach, correlates with hypnotizability (Sarbin and Lim, 1963). It is the approach of those who have used the various forms of experience inventory to square behavior outside hypnosis with that within hypnosis, such as the work of Shor (PEQ), As (EI), and Lee (HCI), previously discussed. This may be considered also the emphasis of Barber and his collaborators, whose many studies have shown for various hypnotic phenomena that the ability is there outside hypnosis as well as inside.

From the point of view of theory, however, the waking-hypnotic parallelism is only a first step, because the demonstration of the consistency of the individual differences inside and outside hypnosis does not account for the differences in the first place. Consider the parallel case of a correlation between a scholastic aptitude test and grades in college. Such a correlation does indeed tell us that they have something in common, but further steps are needed to explain scholastic aptitude. Similarly, further steps of theory are needed to explain the individual differences in the kinds of ordinary experience that are found to correlate with hypnotic susceptibility.

3. The psychoanalytic explanation of individual differences. While psychoanalysis as a therapeutic process is concerned intimately with the details of individual development, psychoanalysts in their theoretical writings often gloss over these differences through stressing the universals in development. Gill and Brenman (1959, pp. 76–85) devote a few pages to the personality structure of the hypnotic subject, as revealed by psychological tests and by clinical interviews, but their reported material at this point, or in their later case studies, gives very little evidence as to how the limited individual differences that they found came about. Schafer (1958) has attempted to account for individual differences in the ability to make use of regression in the service of the ego; because the capacity for such regression is essential within the Gill and Brenman theory one might take Schafer's account as a source of suggestions on what makes a person hypnotizable. Unfortunately his criteria of ability to use regression in this way are merely the criteria for good mental health; it is doubtful that they can really serve to make operational the differences between the susceptible and the nonsusceptible.

4. An eclectic position regarding the nature of hypnotic depth. Shor (1959, 1962c) ably summarized the positions taken by earlier writers, and added observations of his own with reference to the depth of the trance state. While individual differences in susceptibility were not his primary concern, the dimensions of depth, as he describes them, at the same time give hints as to the kind of person who can travel along these dimensions. His point of departure is some proposals by White (1941), but he has also found a favorable place for some of the psychoanalytic propositions of Schilder and Kauders (Schilder, 1956) and of Gill and Brenman (1959). He ends up with three main dimensions of hypnotic depth: (1) depth of role-taking involvement, (2) depth of trance, and (3) depth of archaic involvement.

The first of these, which is reminiscent of Sarbin, specifies, however, that the complex of motivational and cognitive structures has "sunk below the level of purely conscious compliance and volition, and has become nonconsciously directive" (Shor, 1962c, p. 28). Thus role-taking does not signify hypnotic depth for him until it has become involuntary and in some respects nonconscious.

Trance depth, the second dimension, is defined for him by the fading of a generalized reality-orientation into what he calls nonfunctional awareness. A special new orientation becomes the only possible reality for the hypnotized person at the time.

The third dimension, depth of archaic involvement, is added in recognition of the regressive nature of hypnosis and its regressive-transference possibilities.

While I believe we have in Shor's propositions a fair summary of where we are in describing the phenomenology of hypnosis, particularly for the extremely susceptible subject, the statements are not sufficiently quantifiable to help in describing the moderately hypnotizable subject, or in treating more specific individual differences. Thus, while individual differences are implied, they are not delineated, except in the sense that a subject may achieve depth in any combination of the three dimensions.

Anyone familiar with hypnotic phenomena will recognize that the different investigators have sharpened the description of various aspects of hypnosis. The problem is left in an unsatisfactory state not because the theorists are deficient, but because the data necessary to precise theorizing are lacking.

A DEVELOPMENTAL-INTERACTIVE THEORY OF SUSCEPTIBILITY

In order to supply the need for a theory to explain individual differences in susceptibility to hypnosis, we evolved a framework for such a theory early in our experimentation and called it a developmental-interactive theory (Hilgard, 1962; Hilgard and Hilgard, 1962).

The theory as it has evolved can be stated in the form of three sets of propositions.[1] The first of these are *developmental* propositions (D–propositions), which have to do with the lifelong experiences that produce the kind of person who can or cannot enter the hypnotic state, and who can yield some hypnotic phenomena and not others. What we are looking for is the *explanation* for the ability to relinquish reality-orientation, to become involved in a role, to accept archaic regressions. Many psychological explanations take this *historical* form, as in the old adage that the child is father to the man. The second set of propositions is called *interactive* (I–propositions), having to do with what happens within the induction of hypnosis and within the established hypnotic state. It is evident that some important interaction is taking place between the subject and the hypnotist, and the character of this interaction depends upon the kinds of persons they are, the roles they assume, and the particular manipulations the hypnotist employs. These propositions are *contemporary* or *ahistorical,* and as such correspond to many of the propositions of psychology that stress interaction with the environment, or between people, or reaction in the face of conflicting demands in the present. The developmental and interactive propositions are of course

---

[1] The propositional structure of Shor's work (Shor, 1959, 1962c) has appealed to us in this respect, although our concerns are slightly different from his.

related, in that the interaction capitalizes upon the readiness produced through development.

A third set of propositions is comprised of propositions relating to the hypnotic state, which we call *state* propositions (S–propositions) Such problems as the physiological correlates of hypnotic behavior fall within this third set of propositions, having no necessary critical relationship either to development or to the interactions between subject and hypnotist. Thus if a blister can be raised when a burn has been suggested, we need some theory as to how this somatic effect is brought about, granted that the subject believes himself to have been burned by the eraser of a pencil.

This then is the framework for the theory. Some of the propositions stated earlier (Hilgard, 1962) have been replaced, so that the current statement can be considered a new version of a theory that will continue to be revised; it is also a limited version, because the propositions presented here are those concerned only with individual differences in susceptibility and how they come about.

DEVELOPMENTAL PROPOSITIONS (D–PROPOSITIONS)

The following seven developmental propositions, suggested by available data, can serve as guides for more precise formulations later on. They occasionally go a little beyond the data, but venturesomeness is needed in theory construction; at this stage a theory is to be entertained as plausible, and need not command commitment.

Proposition D–1. All normal infants are born with the potential to develop the ability for profound hypnotic experiences.

The proposition assumes that hypnotic ability does not have to be learned, but rather that it can be lost. This suggestion was made earlier by Shor, who put it this way: "The mystery is not why some people can achieve deep trance states. Rather, it is why most people are *not* able to do so" (Shor, 1959, p. 601). He went on to ask the question as to the kind of learning that interferes with the natural capacity to relinquish voluntarily our usual functional orientations.

The alternative that is here being denied is that susceptibility is an inherited capacity in which people differ. While there is no crucial evidence to deny such inheritance, neither is there positive evidence for it from family similarities, twin studies, and so on. Rather, the position is being taken here that hypnosis is as natural as, say, sleep;

if some people later become insomniacs it is not that they were born that way. So (without implying any special relationship between hypnosis and sleep) the insusceptible person probably *became* that way.

Proposition D–2. The ability of a child to disengage himself from reality-orientation and to become deeply involved in fantasy or adventure may be preserved if sufficient experiences of this kind are encouraged by example and tolerated or rewarded in childhood. There has recently come a new interest in imitation as a source of behavior (for example, Bandura and Walters, 1963), so that we may look to *contagion* as an important source of the child's attitudes and values. If parental figures can play comfortably with reality-distortion, if, for example, they enjoy telling fairy tales as if they were true, or if they have enthusiasm and fun when they play, these attitudes become instilled in the child. To the extent that these are illustrations of dissociation, the child becomes comfortable with such partial dissociations, for the adult models who engage in this behavior also act like sensible adults at other times; in other words, they depart from reality only temporarily.

Proposition D–3. There is probably a critical period during which these behaviors will either be sustained or lost, the period lying between the acquisition of language and the onset of adolescence. We have some evidence from our interview material that changes in a positive direction after the onset of adolescence with respect to the background conditions of susceptibility do not promote susceptibility unless there have been favorable earlier experiences. The course of decline of hypnotic ability in childhood, which begins somewhere between the eighth and tenth years, suggests that the decline is a preadolescent phenomenon, so that it is inferred that these years are critical ones for sustaining the experience for those in whom it is not going to decline.

Proposition D–4. Once a favorable background has been created for sustaining the natural capacity for involvement, new experiences can be grafted upon this background, thus reinforcing the appropriate abilities. The presumption is that the child who is comfortable in flexible role-taking, in fantasy, in adventure, in creating without intense self-criticism, can later learn to become absorbed in new interests, such as reading, or music, or skin-diving, and will derive satisfactions from these new experiences which keep alive in adolescence and adulthood the ability to become hypnotized that others have already lost.

Proposition D–5. Parental influences and identifications are very important in preserving and extending or reducing and destroying hypnotic susceptibility. Some data reported elsewhere have shown complex relationships to parental identification, summarized as follows:

1. Temperamental resemblance to the parent of the *opposite* sex is favorable to hypnotic susceptibility in both male and female subjects, whether or not that parent is judged to be hypnotizable.

2. Temperamental resemblance to the parent of the *same* sex is favorable to susceptibility, provided that parent is judged to be hypnotizable; however, it is a very unfavorable sign for hypnotic susceptibility to resemble temperamentally a like-sexed parent judged to be nonhypnotizable.

3. Highly hypnotizable subjects tend to be identified with their hypnotically susceptible parents in *play ego* rather than *work ego*. This helps account for the cross-sexed identification, for, as pointed out earlier, there are no taboos against being like the opposite-sexed parent in recreational interests.

4. If a subject is not recognizably identified with *either* parent in some important respect, whether in work ego or play ego, he is little likely to be susceptible to hypnosis (Hilgard, 1964).

These results are consistent with our proposition in showing the importance of parental influences. They assume that important aspects of personality structure are formed relatively early in life, when parental influences are great. The identifications that are important go beyond sex-role identification with the parent of the same sex; both parents contribute through identification to the formation of the child's personality. The opposite-sexed parent may be important in hypnosis because it is playful behavior that can be copied without contradicting sex-typed roles, and this playful behavior is relevant for hypnosis.

Proposition D–6. Not all "favorable" parental attitudes from a mental hygiene standpoint are conducive to susceptibility; contrariwise, not all "unfavorable" ones inhibit it. One has to be careful to avoid value judgments that make hypnotic susceptibility either "good" or "bad." In general, it is easy to make a case for susceptibility being "good," because people capable of flexible role-behavior, intense involvements, and nonthreatening regressions are commonly interesting and creative people. At the same time, there are many interesting, productive, and intensively involved people who are not hypnotically susceptible. Their involvements are likely, however, to be in competitive enterprises, in which they pride themselves on their skill, on their alertness, on their stick-to-it-iveness against odds. Such vigilant, reality-bound, striving people do not make successful hypnotic subjects unless some part of them fits other characteristics. Successful college athletes in such alert skill sports as basketball or tennis, as we saw in Chapter 15, are not usually hypnotizable.

On the other hand, there are some susceptible subjects whose backgrounds from a mental health standpoint are less favorable, with lonely childhoods, perhaps accompanied by parental neglect; possibly from broken homes where there was never adequate replacement of the parent lost by death or separation. The question here is how the difficulty was resolved; it may be that imaginary companions, or absorption in reading helped to cover the lonesomeness and kept active the reality-distortions essential to hypnosis. Perhaps an open seeking for an adult on whom to depend, rather than a withdrawal from people, makes the transference relationship to the hypnotist an easy one.

It sounds paradoxical that backgrounds both favorable and unfavorable to mental health can lead to hypnotic susceptibility, but the fact is that they can. We have seen this in the reported successful hypnotizing of neurotic and psychotic patients. A theory must comprehend this, not in an after-the-fact rationalization of what is found to be the case, but in the kind of differentiation that ultimately will make it possible to predict which subject with what background will be hypnotizable.

Proposition D–7. Individualizing experiences of various kinds may produce selective responsiveness within hypnotic susceptibility. We know from the results of testing with our profile scales (SPS, Forms I and II) that subjects at the same general level of susceptibility to hypnosis may have quite different "profiles," that is, they may be successful on a different pattern of hypnotic tests.

It is a fascinating problem to try to predict, beyond hypnotic susceptibility in general, just what performances are likely to succeed. Will the girl who is involved in ballet dancing find it easier than others to do the muscular things asked for in hypnosis because she is accustomed to automatic motor response to her ballet master? Will the person who gets absorbed in music do better than others with sensory hallucinations? Will the drama student carry out posthypnotic tasks more readily than others? We shall have more evidence to report on these matters at another time, but, in principle, the proposition is a sound one.

These, then, are the developmental propositions. They go behind the relationships between behavior outside hypnosis and behavior inside hypnosis to detect the early experiences, identifications, imitative patterns, contagious attitudes, and learned behaviors that produce the differences that we find among our young-adult subjects.

INTERACTIVE PROPOSITIONS (I–PROPOSITIONS)

The developmental propositions give us a natural history of hypnotic susceptibility, telling us why some people are more hypnotizable than others and why their hypnotizability may take individual forms. They do not tell us, however, how the hypnotist–subject relationship alters the state of awareness in order to capitalize on susceptibility and to produce the specific phenomena of hypnosis. Concepts such as transference, dissociation, and regression provide natural bridges between the present interactions and the residues from earlier development.

Gill and Brenman (1959) solve the problem theoretically, as we noted earlier, by positing a difference between the induction phase and the established trance. The induction phase is disruptive, but as the trance is established the ego performs an act of synthesis by which a substructure is set up. The over-all ego maintains its nonhypnotic reality-oriented relationship to the hypnotist; only the partially regressed subsystem is under the control of the hypnotist. Bellak (1955) in an earlier but related discussion, refers to the self-excluding function of the ego, found in one form in entering sleep, in another form in entering hypnosis. Thus something has to go on in the present before the hypnotic phenomena will show themselves. To say something sensible about what this is that is going on is the role of the interactive propositions: for our purposes, the problem is not what goes on *in general,* but what goes on specifically in relationship to the varying developmental histories of our subjects.

Proposition I–1. Providing that the setting for hypnosis is one that evokes confidence, initial responsiveness to attempted hypnotic induction depends very little upon the personal characteristics of the hypnotist. There are subjects who have told us that they gladly volunteered for our experiments but would not volunteer for a stage hypnotist, and an occasional one told us that he volunteered but resisted a stage hypnotist, while participating freely and successfully for us. These extremes aside, we have found it very difficult to demonstrate any hypnotist differences, although we have characteristically changed hypnotist from session to session when the reliabilities of our scales were under study. In theoretical terms the subject brings with him his readiness for the hypnotic experience, and he can be hypnotized by any responsible person; if one wishes to think of transference at all in this connection, it would reflect what Macalpine (1950) called "transference-readiness."

Proposition I–2. In the first few sessions, a susceptible subject learns to enter the trance much more promptly than he did initially, but this does not mean that the depth of the trance is also increased. Apparently entering the trance has features of learning within it and can be studied as such (Hull, 1933). It is a mistake to suppose that therefore the subject also learns to go into a deeper trance with practice. Our experience (Ås, Hilgard, and Weitzenhoffer, 1963), and that of many others (for instance, Gill and Brenman, 1959; Shor, Orne, and O'Connell, 1962) is that some adjustment of level may take place, but a plateau or asymptote is soon reached that is broken with only the greatest of difficulty, if at all.

Proposition I–3. With repeated inductions by the same hypnotist, a differentiated transference results, and the individual characteristics of the hypnotist and subject in their interaction become more important than they were initially. The rapport of the initial induction, which is highly generalized and quite impersonal, is likely to become much more personal with repeated inductions, and hence bring out both positive and negative "transference" reactions. The specific qualities of the hypnotist's voice and manner will activate specific patterns from the subject's past to the extent that the hypnotist reminds him of significant persons in his early experience. Such reminding can be largely unconscious ("I do not like thee, Dr. Fell, the reason why I cannot tell. . . ."), but it need not be wholly so.

Most studies of transference have grown out of a patient–therapist relationship, in which it is difficult to tell what belongs to the therapy and what belongs to the hypnosis. Careful experimentation on non-patient populations, perhaps using their dreams or projective productions, will be needed to see just what role this plays in hypnosis *per se.*

Proposition I–4. The hypnotic interaction goes on most smoothly in conflict-free áreas; if a conflict area is tapped in the hypnotic interaction, defenses are aroused that may interfere with the hypnosis.

One reason that depth of involvement is possible is that this kind of involvement has received the support and encouragement of parents in childhood, and can go on with very little conflict. We have noted the importance of this kind of support and encouragement in such fields as reading, religion, play, and adventure. This does not imply that the individual is without conflicts, but only that there is a relevant and relatively conflict-free path open into hypnosis. We have seen subjects with conflicts manifested in disturbing tics, or near-psychotic behavior, who were comfortable in reading or religious commitment and entered hypnosis smoothly.

The defenses that are aroused in hypnosis are those in the subject's repertoire in the waking state. Thus there may be denial, and in hypnotherapy probing of conflict areas under hypnosis may in some cases hit the same blank wall that it does in the waking state. Vigilant reactions may be aroused, and when the subject is put on guard his trance is likely to be weakened. Occasionally sleep intervenes as an escape. This was seen prominently in one patient in a mental hospital being studied by two of our staff members. Hypnosis readily put the patient to sleep, but he was then out of contact and totally inaccessible to questioning. Psychosomatic reactions occur, such as speeded up heartbeat, heavy breathing, coughing, or headache; when intense, these may rouse the subject from hypnosis.

It may be that there will be some shifts in defense preference within hypnosis. For example, Meares (1957) has noted that compulsives behave in more hysteroid fashion when they become hypnotized, and possibly other subjects shift their defensive patterns in the direction of hysteria. The prevalence of amnesia within hypnosis may be one manifestation of the tendency to turn to repression as a defense—and amnesia is a defense that since Freud has been thought of as characteristic of hysteria (for example, Freud, 1926).

A fuller understanding of these considerations will eventually be important in proposing a strategy for psychotherapy with the aid of hypnosis.

Proposition 1–5. The various dissociative experiences activated by hypnotic induction and by suggestions within hypnosis are correlated with specific developmental experiences. Some of the most puzzling problems of hypnosis lie at this point. Our work with the profile scales shows that among even quite susceptible subjects there are great differences in their profiles of susceptibility, some with quite specific gaps in an otherwise uniformly high level of hypnotizability. We need to ask, then, why some subjects can give positive hallucinations and not negative ones, why some can react with muscular contractures, but not with posthypnotic amnesia, and so on. The conjecture is that, were we astute enough, we could find the developmental experiences to account for these individual differences.

Some of the hints that we have with respect to the development of the hypnotically relevant dissociative experiences are the following:

1. Parental "magic" in childhood may have produced effects similar to those requested under hypnosis. Thus when a mother says: "Come here; I'll rub your head and the bump won't hurt anymore" she is providing a background for the control of pain through suggestion.

2. Time-limited experiences of immersion in a make-believe world make the prospect of such experiences inviting and little threatening. Parents shift from telling fairy tales to saying, "Now it's time to brush your teeth and go to bed." Thus reality is restored after vivid fantasy has been supported by the wise adult. Parental figures must have this same role-flexibility if they are to communicate it to their children. They must be able to work hard when they are working, and to then play freely in a world not burdened with vigilant reality-testing.

3. Amnesia has the qualities of both active repression and of mere inattention ("absentmindedness"). Because amnesia is so prevalent in early childhood, the inattention theory deserves consideration. The hypnotic subject is not making his own plans, but is doing what the hypnotist directs; hence episodes are not tied together as they are in intentional study or memorizing, but more as they are in passive incidental learning. Such loosely joined material must in any case be more subject to inhibition than systematically ordered material; we know this from studies of the role of meaningful organization in retention. The difficulty is that recall following hypnosis is quite good once the amnesia has been lifted, so that everything cannot be blamed on poor registration. If the inhibition is merely one of recall, an inattention theory is still applicable. For instance, the reader of a book may follow the lead of the author in having episodes in the life story of the hero out of order (the "flashback" technique); the absorbed reader may follow the childhood of the character, forgetting temporarily that he knows anything about the adult to whom he was earlier introduced. Later, when the thread of the story is again

picked up, he remembers everything. This temporary forgetting under the leadership of the author may not be too different from the temporary forgetting under the leadership of the hypnotist. The lack of a need to control the continuity of memories is common to both experiences.

4. Defensive and coping styles are developed in childhood, so that one child rationalizes, another projects, another represses. One is intropunitive, another extrapunitive, and so on. Although, as stated in Proposition I–4, these defense preferences may shift somewhat under hypnosis, the regressive types of defense must not be overlooked. They include various appeals for aid (dependency responses) appropriate to younger ages, hence regressive.

Proposition I–6. There are multiple paths into hypnosis that can be activated through induction; if any one of these exists in sufficient strength as a substructure (or habit system) within the personality, induction may communicate with it and thus lead to the hypnotic state. In a previous account the two distinct paths into hypnosis of fantasy and adventure were contrasted (Hilgard, 1964). It was shown that for those high in fantasy, the degree of hypnotizability was uncorrelated with rated adventuresomeness and, similarly, for those high in adventuresomeness it was a matter of indifference how much fantasy life they had. Thus the two paths were alternative and did not interact; having both of them was no more indicative of susceptibility than being high in one of them. Somewhat similar considerations have been explained in Chapter 15, as, for example, in entering hypnosis by way of appropriate intense involvement in reading. Gill and Brenman (1959) made a related point, in a somewhat different way, in proposing that two types of induction, one by way of monotony and sensory deprivation, the other by way of transference, led to similar hypnotic states. Thus the activation of quite different habit patterns may lead to hypnosis, with its usual phenomena, though with subtle enough instruments of measurement we would expect some differences in hypnotic behavior on the part of those who come to hypnosis by way of separate paths; many of the behaviors will, however, overlap, for the general factor running through hypnotic behavior is always high.

This matter of multiple paths into hypnosis makes the problem of predicting hypnotic susceptibility a very difficult one. If paths are really alternative, then the usual type of additive scoring of predictive indicators will fail; at the same time the quantitative estimate of the possible path into hypnosis has to be made very precisely indeed to determine whether or not it is sufficiently strong to produce hypnosis. Thus one cannot count on church attendance as an indicator of religious commitment, or attendance at concerts as musical involvement, or the number ,of books read as a measure of genuine self-losing absorption in reading.

What happens within hypnosis will capitalize upon what has gone into the development of the individual. Yet something is added by the relationship to the hypnotist, for susceptible people do not go around in a trance all the while; many of them can enter the initial trance very quickly, but they are often amazed by it.

HYPNOTIC STATE PROPOSITIONS (S–PROPOSITIONS)

These propositions are intended to round out the theory of hypnosis by indicating something of the nature of the hypnotic state.

Proposition S–1. The trance is itself a product of suggestion and can be considered separately from the responsiveness to suggestions given within this state. This proposition refutes the definition of hypnosis as a state of hypersuggestibility. It may very well be such a state, but it need not be; one can be hypnotized and not at all responsive to ordinary suggestions. If this proposition is accepted, then different kinds of trances can be recognized. Orne (1959) believes that the kinds of trances we see today are more or less historical accidents according to what we have been led to expect and hence lead our subject to expect; Shor (1959) quotes a communication from Maslow expressing his belief that we have been misled by emphasizing a "striving-hypnosis" (role-playing) rather than a "being-hypnosis" (inner experiencing).

In our experiments comparing responsiveness to suggestion within the waking state and within the trance state we found that there was a *correlation* between the subjective state reports and the amount of suggestibility, but the regression lines were different in the two states; that is, subjects highly suggestible in the waking state did not feel as "entranced" as those who, following hypnotic induction, yielded the same objective suggestibility scores (Chap. 2, Fig. 2).

What this means is that suggestible people can be hypnotized, but they do not have to be hypnotized to reveal their suggestibility; they have to be hypnotized to show the effects of trance, however, because *the induction is a trance-producing set of suggestions,* and the hypnotist subtly and repeatedly reminds the subject of what kind of trance he expects.

Proposition S–2. Although there is some increase in suggestibility following trance induction, it is relatively slight and not sufficient to define susceptibility. One may then well ask, why are susceptibility tests useful when they rely on tests of suggestion after induction? The answer is twofold: first, there is a slight increase in suggestibility, which may as well be capitalized on, and second, people capable of giving responses to suggestion, such as the susceptibility scales measure objectively, *are the same people who are responsive to the suggestion that they will enter a trance,* and they tend to have the subjective experiences corresponding to it.

Proposition S–3. Hypnosis is not to be identified with suggestibility in general. There are various subvarieties of suggestibility of which the kind of suggestibility that is exhibited by the hypnotically susceptible person represents a limited set. We have met a good deal of evidence along the way that there is a "primary suggestibility" that runs throughout hypnotic performances, but there are other kinds of suggestibility (secondary suggestibility, although this is not one thing) that are unrelated to hypnosis.

This proposition bears upon the matter of individual differences, for some individual differences in suggestibility (gullibility, perseverative responses to impersonal suggestions) will not be predictive of hypnosis.

Proposition S–4. The hypnotic state is characterized by various partial dissociations. When dissociation is dismissed as a concept appropriate to hypnosis, it is commonly assumed that dissociation can be disproved if there is any interaction between hypnotic behavior and normal (nonhypnotic) behavior. Thus Rosenberg (1959) believed that he had disconfirmed dissociation by showing that attitudes implanted within hypnosis, for which the subject was amnesic, modified his attitudes in the waking state. Consider Rosenberg's statement that "the regressive state attained in hypnosis involves an activation of primitive impulses which the subject, upon emergence from trance, and for purposes of anxiety-control, is motivated to hold beyond conscious acknowledgment" (Rosenberg, 1959, p. 202). It seems appropriate to me to say that something "held beyond conscious acknowledgment" may be considered partially dissociated, even though it interacts with waking behavior or experience. Automatic writing is a classical illustration of an activity going on at one level of integration while the "normal" attention is directed elsewhere. Such automatic writing can be thought of as partially dissociated, even though the interaction can be demonstrated with other concurrent behavior.

It may be that the capacity for dissociation is based in part upon split identifications with parental figures, as when a male subject is identified with a father's work ego and a mother's play ego. The relaxed attitude of hypnosis may then permit the mother-identification to have freer play than it normally does. This line of interpreting the mixed identification material has been discussed elsewhere (Hilgard, 1964).

Probably a set of propositions stating the physiological correlates of hypnosis will appear in time. Published evidence to date is too contradictory, and our own work along these lines is in its very early stages. What we are able to say now must be put in negative form: hypnosis is *not* sleep, it is *not* functional decortication, it is *not* irradiated inhibition. One difficulty in explaining hypnosis is that the physiological correlates of verbally controlled behavior are particularly obscure. The verbal controls within hypnosis, all calling for explanation, extend not only to striate muscles but to smooth muscles and glandular processes as well.

The scaffolding for a theory of individual differences in hypnotic susceptibility has been presented in the form of seven developmental propositions, six interactive propositions, and four state propositions. The developmental propositions are historical, based on the conception that hypnotic susceptibility in the young adult is the result of the preservation into later life of a tendency shared by all children, and built upon through later experiences when the ability has not been destroyed in early childhood. The interactive propositions are contemporary and ahistorical, and they are concerned with the manner in which the social interaction with the hypnotist capitalizes upon the present readinesses to produce hypnotic behavior. Finally, the hypnotic-state propositions have to do with the hypnotic state in relation to other psychological phenomena, with the distinction between the state itself and the manifestations of hypnosis in heightened suggestibility.

SOME PROBLEMS WITHIN THE THEORY OF HYPNOSIS

The developmental-interactive theory that we have proposed is in unfinished form because the data of hypnosis have proved so puzzling. It is easy to say plausible things about hypnosis but very difficult to account for the concrete behavior of the individual hypnotic subject. Although we have found the current theories of hypnosis appropriate at many points, no one of them handles the material that we have uncovered in our susceptibility studies, and in the tests and interviews that have accompanied them. A few remarks on the limitations of the more hopeful concepts seem to be in order.

The role-enactment theory. We have a great deal of evidence that is coherent with a role-enactment theory, such as the prominence of role-playing items in the experience interviews that are correlated with hypnotic susceptibility. But we find areas of deep involvement in a role, as in the case of successful competitive athletes, that do not lead to hypnotizability. The strong emphasis upon the drama in the writings of Sarbin overlooks the more important area of involvement in reading, an area which we have found preeminent in its relationship to hypnotizability. The behavior of the absorbed reader is not one thing, either; some identify with and practically become characters. Sometimes a character is transformed into the likeness of the reader. But for many hypnotized subjects identification is not the significant feature at all; what is important is the magic of words and the capacity to be guided by the author to observe the experiences he wishes the reader to observe and to become emotionally involved in them. In other words, we have not found the concept of role-taking sufficient to make the differentiations that we found necessary to make. There is nothing wrong with the role-enactment theory as such, but it is a little too easy a solution to a difficult set of problems.

The empirical evidence for the role-enactment hypothesis rests on positive correlations between measures of role playing and hypnotic susceptibility, but these correlations are not universally high, and do not justify a theory based exclusively on role enactment. In a recent study, Madsen and London (1966) tested the role-playing ability of children by means of two standardized tests, one testing dramatic acting, the other the ability to simulate hypnosis. While the ability to simulate hypnosis correlated significantly with hypnotic susceptibility measures ($r = .60$ with total scores), the dramatic acting test did not ($r = .13$ with total scores).

Dissociation and regression. Gill and Brenman (1959) are so convinced of the essentially regressive nature of hypnosis that they subtitle their book on hypnosis *Psychoanalytic studies in regression*. As in the case of role-enactment theory, we find much that is congenial in a regressive interpretation of hypnosis. We believe, however, that the use of the term *regression* to cover all of the experiences is misleading, and for this reason we prefer *dissociation* as the general term, with regressive behavior often representing one form of dissociation.

The difficulty with the term *regression* lies in part within psychoanalytic theory. Within psychoanalytic theory regression covers various kinds of functioning at a more primitive level. Thus it may mean the revival of an actual experience from early life, or it may mean merely a more primitive mode of functioning ("primary process" thinking) as in dreams and hallucinations. Transference phenomena tend to be called regressive because they involve acting in the present to the therapist with action patterns appropriate to a person reacted to in earlier life. If all departures from a reality-orientation and all reactivation of earlier experiences are called regressive, that is a permissible practice but not very clarifying. If one were to push this to an extreme, any activation of an earlier habit would be regressive. Because *all* habits have been acquired in the past, little would be left but regressive behavior.

The notion of a partial regression, as in the concept of regression in the service of the ego, has a natural appeal about it, but upon examination it is also an unclear concept. Actually little was made of it by its originator (Kris, 1952), but it has gradually become more important in the writings of the ego-theorists among the psychoanalysts. As noted earlier, the most careful delineation of what is meant by it (Schafer, 1958) turns out to make its conditions those of positive mental health. If those are indeed its conditions, then this concept cannot account for the hypnotizability of neurotics and psychotics.

We believe the concept of partial dissociation to cover the same ground, leaving open the interpretation of the varieties of dissociative behavior that are possible for a given individual. If the individual has alternative modes of expressing his personality, they may both have a continuous history, and one not be any more "regressive" than the other, in terms of his own life history. Note that our discussion here is not in substantive disagreement with those who extend the term regression, but rather in theoretical disagreement over the undue extension of the term. It would be better to use regression to refer to a return to some previous experience that was actually lived and outgrown, rather than to cover by it so much that is continuous and contemporary.

Learning theory. Little has been said about those theories that base hypnotic phenomena upon learning and habit formation (Hull, 1933; Weitzenhoffer, 1953). Our developmental propositions are unspecific about the mechanisms according to which the modes of personality functioning are acquired in childhood and then preserved as the paths into hypnosis.

It is evident enough that a great deal of learning is involved, whether that learning is a result of associative repetition, the influences of rewards and reinforcements, or by some subtle process of imitation and contagion little represented in contemporary learning theories. Our developmental theory says, in essence, that much habit formation, of the kind leading to achievement-orientation and vigilant reality testing, is antithetical to hypnotic susceptibility, but that other kinds of habit formation, leading to absorption in reading or in adventure, can keep these abilities alive. Then the hypnotic interaction is a situation in which what has been learned is generalized to a new setting. Such generalization of prior learning may be called regressive if that prior learning took place very early in life, but there is no reason why the generalization should not be from something active at present, as from contemporary interest in reading, music, or religion.

Generalization from previous learning rather than the process of verbal conditioning that takes place in hypnotic induction seems to be the relevant concept. While some learning goes on there, evidenced by the more rapid entrance into the hypnotic state with repeated inductions, we are dealing more with "performance" than with "learning," that is, more with the activation of old patterns than with the acquiring of new ones. Some learning takes place within hypnosis, leading to novelty in behavior, so that there are surprises in what the subject can do. This may well turn out to be a form of verbal conditioning, although present evidence is not confirmatory (Clarke and Long, 1964). But the new learning, according to our theory, is grafted upon a base with a long developmental history.

In conclusion, then, we are not ready to go along with any one approach to understanding hypnosis but will favor an eclectic position until the difficulties of explanation have been faced more concretely. While much of this book has been devoted to the ways in which individual differences are expressed within the hypnotic state, the susceptibility scales and their results are not ends in themselves. They provide essential instruments and background knowledge through which eventually, by appropriate further studies, the propositions of the kind sketched in this chapter will become tightened into a body of theory that will make hypnosis understandable.

APPENDIX

Sources of Published Materials
on Hypnotic Susceptibility Scales

The scales of Davis and Husband (1931), Friedlander and Sarbin (1938), Weitzenhoffer and Sjoberg (1961), and Barber (Barber and Glass, 1962) can be found described in detail in the publications mentioned, but are not separately published. The following scales, with supplementary materials, are all published by Consulting Psychologists Press, Inc., 577 College Avenue, Palo Alto, California, 94306:

Children's Hypnotic Susceptibility Scale (CHSS)
   London, P. The Children's Hypnotic Susceptibility Scale (1962).
Harvard Group Scale of Hypnotic Susceptibility (HGS)
   Shor, R. E., and Orne, Emily C. Harvard Group Scale of Hypnotic Susceptibility (1962). The authors also have available a tape to provide a standardized administration of the test. Those interested should communicate with them at Unit for Experimental Psychiatry, Institute of the Pennsylvania Hospital, 111 N. 49th Street, Philadelphia, Pa., 19139.
Stanford Hypnotic Susceptibility Scale, Forms A and B (SHSS: A,B)
   Weitzenhoffer, A. M., and Hilgard, E. R. Stanford Hypnotic Susceptibility Scale, Forms A and B (1959), with accompanying Interrogatory and Scoring Forms.
Stanford Hypnotic Susceptibility Scale, Form C (SHSS: C)
   Weitzenhoffer, A. M., and Hilgard, E. R. Stanford Hypnotic Susceptibility Scale, Form C (1962), with accompanying Scoring Booklet.
Revised Stanford Profile Scales of Hypnotic Susceptibility, Forms I and II (RSPS: I, II)
   Weitzenhoffer, A. M., and Hilgard, E. R. Revised Stanford Profile Scales of Hypnotic Susceptibility, Forms I and II (1967). With revised standardization data prepared by E. R. Hilgard, L. M. Cooper, Lillian W. Lauer, and Arlene H. Morgan. Scoring Booklets and separate Profile Sheets are also available.

Bibliographical Index

The numbers in boldface following each reference give the text pages on which the book or paper is cited. Citations in the text are made by author and date of publication.

Abrams, S. (1963) Short-term hypnotherapy of a schizophrenic patient. *Amer. J. clin. Hyp.*, 5:237–47. — **219**

Abrams, S. (1964) The use of hypnotic techniques with psychotics. *Am. J. Psychother.*, 18:79–94. — **219**

Amadeo, M., and Shagass, C. (1963) Eye movements, attention, and hypnosis. *J. nerv. ment. Dis.*: 136, 139–45. — **7**

Andersen, M. L., *see* Sarbin and Andersen (1965).

Ås, A. (1962a) Non-hypnotic experiences related to hypnotizability in male and female college students. *Scand. J. Psychol.*, 3:112–21. — **232, 238**

Ås, A. (1962b) The recovery of forgotten language knowledge through hypnotic age regression: A case report. *Amer. J. clin. Hyp.*, 5:24–29. — **174**

Ås, A. (1963) Hypnotizability as a function ·of nonhypnotic experiences. *J. abnorm. soc. Psychol.*, 66:142–50. — **232, 233**

Ås, A., Hilgard, E. R., and Weitzenhoffer, A. M. (1963) An attempt at experimental modification of hypnotizability through repeated individualized hypnotic experience. *Scand. J. Psychol.*, 4:81–89. — **71, 171, 263, 313**

Ås, A., and Lauer, Lillian W. (1962) A factor-analytic study of hypnotizability and related personal experiences. *Int. J. clin. exp. Hyp.*, 10:169–81. — **233, 234**

Ås, A., O'Hara, J. W., and Munger, M. P. (1962) The measurement of subjective experiences presumably related to hypnotic susceptibility. *Scand. J. Psychol.*, 3:47–64. — **223**

Austin, M., Perry, C., Sutcliffe, J. P., and Yeomans, N. (1963) Can somnambulists successfully simulate hypnotic behavior without becoming entranced? *Int. J. clin. exp. Hyp.*, 11:175–86. — **18**

Balint, M. (1959) *Thrills and regressions*. New York: Int. Univ. Press. — **225**

Bandura, A., and Walters, R. H. (1963) *Social learning and personality development*. New York: Holt, Rinehart and Winston. — **309**

Barber, T. X. (1960) The necessary and sufficient conditions for hypnotic behavior. *Amer. J. clin. Hyp.*, 3:31–42. — **7, 224, 265**

Barber, T. X. (1961) Antisocial and criminal acts induced by hypnosis: A review of experimental and clinical findings. *Arch. gen. Psychiat.*, 5:301–12. — **189**

327

Barber, T. X. (1962a) Toward a theory of "hypnotic" behavior: The "hypnotically induced dream." *J. nerv. ment. Dis.*, 135:206–21. — **163**

Barber, T. X. (1962b) Hypnotic age regression: A critical review. *Psychosom. Med.*, 24:286–99. — **172**

Barber, T. X. (1962c) Toward a theory of hypnosis: Posthypnotic behavior. *Arch. gen. Psychiat.*, 7:321–42. — **185**

Barber, T. X. (1963) The effects of "hypnosis" on pain: A critical review of experimental and clinical findings. *Psychosom. Med.*, 24:303–33. — **20**

Barber, T. X. (1964) Hypnotizability, suggestibility, and personality: V. A critical review of research findings. *Psychol. Rep.*, 14:299–320. — **237, 249, 305**

Barber, T. X. (1967) "Hypnotic" phenomena: A critique of experimental methods. In Gordon, J. E. (Ed.), *Handbook of hypnosis*. New York: Macmillan, 444–80. — **34**

Barber, T. X., and Calverley, D. S. (1962) "Hypnotic behavior" as a function of task motivation. *J. Psychol.*, 54:363–89. — **32, 34, 35, 37, 38, 186**

Barber, T. X., and Calverley, D. S. (1963a) Toward a theory of hypnotic behavior: Effects on suggestibility of task motivating instructions and attitudes toward hypnosis. *J. abnorm. soc. Psychol.*, 67:557–65. — **32, 34, 35, 38**

Barber, T. X., and Calverley, D. S. (1963b) "Hypnotic-like" suggestibility in children and adults. *J. abnorm. soc. Psychol.*, 66:589–97. — **91, 92, 214, 215, 216**

Barber, T. X., and Calverley, D. S. (1964a) Hypnotizability, suggestibility, and personality: IV. A study with the Leary Interpersonal Check List. *Brit. J. soc. clin. Psychol.*, 3:40–41. — **254**

Barber, T. X., and Calverley, D. S. (1964b) Effects of E's tone of voice on "hypnotic-like" suggestibility. *Psychol. Rep.*, 15:139–44. — **39n.**

Barber, T. X., and Calverley, D. S. (1964c) Hypnotizability, suggestibility, and personality: I. Two studies with the Edwards Personal Preference Schedule, the Jourard Self-Disclosure Scale, and the Marlowe-Crowne Social Desirability Scale. *J. Psychol.*, 58:215–22. — **254**

Barber, T. X., and Calverley, D. S. (1964d) Toward a theory of hypnotic behavior: Effects on suggestibility of defining the situation as hypnosis and defining response to suggestions as easy. *J. abnorm. soc. Psychol.*, 68:585–92. — **116**

Barber, T. X., and Calverley, D. S. (1964e) An experimental study of "hypnotic" (auditory and visual) hallucinations. *J. abnorm. soc. Psychol.*, 68:13–20. — **143**

Barber, T. X., and Glass, L. B. (1962) Significant factors in hypnotic behavior. *J. abnorm. soc. Psychol.*, 64:222–28. — **30, 34, 36, 37, 90, 91, 92, 228, 311, 325**

Barber, T. X., and Hahn, K. W., Jr. (1962) Physiological and subjective responses to pain-producing stimulation under hypnotically suggested and waking-imagined "analgesia." *J. abnorm. soc. Psychol.*, 65:411–18. — **32, 34, 127**

Barber, T. X., Karacan, I., and Calverley, D. S. (1964) Hypnotizability and suggestibility in chronic schizophrenics. *Arch. gen. Psychiat.*, 11:439–51. — **219**

Barron, F. (1963) *Creativity and psychological health*. Princeton, N.J.: Van Nostrand. — **161**

Barron, J. N., *see* Kelsey and Barron (1958).

Barry, H., MacKinnon, D. W., and Murray, H. A., Jr. (1931) Studies on personality: A. Hypnotizability as a personality trait and its typological relations. *Hum. Biol.*, 13:1–36. — **75, 79**

Bartemeier, L. H., *see* Rosen and Bartemeier (1961).

Beaunis, H. (1887) *Le somnambulisme provoqué*. Paris: Bailière. — **213**

Bellak, L. (1955) An ego-psychological theory of hypnosis. *Int. J. Psychoanal.*, 36:375–78. — **312**

Bentler, P. M. (1963) Interpersonal orientation in relation to hypnotic susceptibility. *J. consult. Psychol.*, 27:426–31. — **253**

Bentler, P. M., and Hilgard, E. R. (1963) A comparison of group and individual
induction of hypnosis with self-scoring and observer-scoring. *Int. J. clin. exp.
Hyp.*, 11:49–54. — **83, 85, 88**

Bentler, P. M., and Roberts, M. R. (1963) Hypnotic susceptibility assessed in
large groups, *Int. J. clin. exp. Hyp.*, 11:93–97. — **83, 85**

Bentler, P. M., *see also* Hilgard and Bentler (1963).

Bernheim, H. (1888) *Hypnosis and suggestion in psychotherapy.* Reprinted, New
Hyde Park, N.Y.: University Books, 1964. — **73, 115n., 218**

Bernstein, C., Jr., *see* Saul and Bernstein (1941).

Berreman, J. V., and Hilgard, E. R. (1936) The effects of personal hetero-sugges-
tion and two forms of autosuggestion upon postural movement. *J. soc.
Psychol.*, 7:289–300. — **101**

Blum, G. S. (1961) *A model of the mind: Explored by hypnotically controlled
experiments and examined for its psychodynamic implications.* New York:
Wiley. — **207, 304**

Blum, G. S. (1963) Programming people to simulate machines. In Tomkins, S. S.,
and Messick, S. (Eds.), *Computer simulation of personality.* New York:
Wiley. Pp. 127–57. — **70, 207, 304**

Bordeaux, J., *see* LeCron and Bordeaux (1947).

Boucher, R. G., and Hilgard, E. R. (1962) Volunteer bias in hypnotic experiments. *Amer. J. clin. Hyp.*, 5:49–51. — **215, 242, 284**

Bowers, Margaretta K., and Brecher, Sylvia. (1955) The emergence of multiple
personalities in the course of hypnotic investigation. *J. clin. exp. Hyp.*,
3:188–99. — **207**

Brady, J. P., and Levitt, E. E. (1964) Hypnotically-induced "anosmia" to ammonia. *Int. J. clin. exp. Hyp.*, 12:18–20. — **122**

Brady, J. P., *see* Levitt and Brady (1964); Levitt, Lubin, and Brady (1962);
Levitt, Persky, and Brady (1964).

Braid, J. (1843) *Neurypnology: Or the rationale of nervous sleep considered in
relation to animal magnetism.* London: Churchill. — **72**

Bramwell, J. M. (1903) *Hypnotism* (Rev. ed.). New York: Julian, 1956. — **74, 75**

Brecher, Sylvia, *see* Bowers and Brecher (1955).

Brenman, Margaret, Gill, M. M., and Knight, R. P. (1952) Spontaneous fluctuations in depth of hypnosis and their implications for ego function. *Int. J.
Psycho-anal.*, 33:22–33. — **11**

Brenman, Margaret, and Gill, M. M. (1947) *Hypnotherapy: A survey of the
literature.* New York: Int. Univ. Press. — **51, 52**

Brenman, Margaret, and Reichard, Suzanne. (1943) Use of the Rorschach test
in the prediction of hypnotizability. *Bull. Menninger Clin.*, 7:183–87. — **262**

Brenman, Margaret, *see also* Gill and Brenman (1959).

Brennan, E. P., *see* Kramer and Brennan (1964).

Breuer, J., and Freud, S. (1895) *Studies on hysteria.* New York: Basic Books,
1957. — **4**

Brickner, R. M., and Kubie, L. S. (1936) A miniature psychotic storm produced
by a superego conflict over simple posthypnotic suggestion. *Psychoanal.
Quart.*, 5:467-87. — **64**

Brightbill, R., and Zamansky, H. S. (1963) The conceptual space of good and
poor hypnotic subjects: A preliminary exploration. *Int. J. clin. exp. Hyp.*,
11:112–21. — **244**

Brightbill, R., *see also* Zamansky, Scharf, and Brightbill (1964).

Bunney, W. E., see Schiff, Bunney, and Freedman (1961).

Calverley, D. S., see Barber and Calverley (1962, 1963a, 1963b, 1964a, 1964b, 1964c, 1964d, 1964e); Barber, Karacan, and Calverley (1964).

Charcot, J. M. (1882) Physiologie pathologique: Sur les divers états nerveux déterminés par l'hypnotization chez les hystériques. CR Acad. Sci., Paris, 94:403–05. — 72

Clarke, J. R., and Long, T. E. (1964) On the lack of relationship between hypnotizability and response to verbal conditioning. Psychol. Rep., 14:103–05. — 322

Clemes, S. R. (1964) Repression and hypnotic amnesia. J. abnorm. soc. Psychol., 69:62–69. — 184

Cole, A. A., see Wilson, Cormen, and Cole (1949).

Cooper, L. M., see London, Cooper, and Johnson (1962).

Cormen, H. H., see Wilson, Cormen, and Cole (1949).

Craik, K. H., see Stein and Craik (1962, 1965).

Dahlstrom, W. G., and Welsh, G. S. (1960) An MMPI Handbook: A guide to use in clinical practice and research. Minneapolis, Minn.: Univ. of Minn. Press. — 256

Damaser, E. C., Shor, R. E., and Orne, M. T. (1963) Physiological effects during hypnotically requested emotions. Psychosom. Med., 25:334–43. — 202

Das, J. P. (1964) Hypnosis, verbal satiation, vigilance, and personality factors: A correlational study. J. abnorm. soc. Psychol., 68:72–78. — 7, 265

Davis, L. W., and Husband, R. W. (1931) A study of hypnotic susceptibility in relation to personality traits. J. abnorm. soc. Psychol., 26:175–82. — 76, 77, 80, 325

Deckert, G. H. (1964) Pursuit eye movements in the absence of a moving visual stimulus. Science, 143:1192–93. — 145

Deckert, G. H., and West, L. J. (1963) The problem of hypnotizability: A review. Int. J. clin. exp. Hyp., 11:205–35. — 249

Dorcus, R. M. (1960) Recall under hypnosis of amnestic events. Int. J. clin. exp. Hyp., 7:57–61. — 167

Dorcus, R. M. (1963) Fallacies in predictions of susceptibility to hypnosis based on personality characteristics. Amer. J. clin. Hyp., 5:163–70. — 70, 167, 305

Dorcus, R. M., see also Kirkner, Dorcus, and Seacat (1953).

Duke, J. D. (1964) Intercorrelational status of suggestibility tests and hypnotizability. Psychol. Rec., 14:71–80. — 263

Dyk, R. B., see Witkin, Dyk, Faterson, Goodenough, and Karp (1962).

Edmonston, W. E., Jr. (1962) Hypnotic age-regression: An evaluation of role-taking theory. Amer. J. clin. Hyp., 5:3–7. — 172

Edwards, G. (1963) Duration of post-hypnotic effect. Brit. J. Psychiat., 109:259–66. — 189

Ehrenreich, G. A. (1949) The relationship of certain descriptive factors to hypnotizability. Trans. Kansas Acad. Sci., 52:24–27. — 218, 220

Erickson, M. H. (1937) Development of apparent unconsciousness during hypnotic reliving of a traumatic experience. Arch. neurol. Psychiat., 38:1282–88. — 15

Erickson, M. H. (1938) A study of clinical and experimental findings on hypnotic deafness: I. Clinical findings and experimentation. J. gen. Psychol., 19:127–50. — 15

Erickson, M. H. (1943) Hypnotic investigation of psychosomatic phenomena: I. Psychosomatic interrelationships studied by experimental hypnosis. Psychosom. Med., 5:51–58. — 201

Hilgard, E. R., and Hommel, L. S. (1961) Selective amnesia for events within hypnosis in relation to repression. *J. Pers.*, 29:205–16. — **183, 184**

Hilgard, E. R., and Lauer, Lillian W. (1962) Lack of correlation between the CPI and hypnotic susceptibility. *J. consult Psychol.*, 26:331–35. — **250, 266**

Hilgard, E. R., Lauer, Lillian W., and Melei, Janet P. (1965) Acquiescence, hypnotic susceptibility, and the MMPI. *J. consult. Psychol.* (To appear) — **257, 258, 260**

Hilgard, E. R., Lauer, Lillian W., and Morgan, Arlene H. (1963) *Manual for Stanford Profile Scales of Hypnotic Susceptibility, Forms I and II.* Palo Alto, Calif.: Consulting Psychologists Press. — **12, 84, 125, 132, 196**

Hilgard, E. R., and Marquis, E. G. (1940) *Conditioning and learning.* New York: Appleton-Century-Crofts. — **120n.**

Hilgard, E. R., and Tart, C. T. (1966) Responsiveness to suggestions following waking and imagination instructions and following induction of hypnosis. *J. abnorm. Psychol.*, 71:196–208. — **36, 38, 41, 42, 44, 45, 46, 107, 123, 143, 144, 153**

Hilgard, E. R., Weitzenhoffer, A. M., and Gough, P. (1958) Individual differences in susceptibility to hypnosis. *Proc. Nat. Acad. Sci.*, 44:1255–59. — **80, 217**

Hilgard, E. R., Weitzenhoffer, A. M., Landes, J., and Moore, Rosemarie K. (1961) The distribution of susceptibility to hypnosis in a student population: A study using the Stanford Hypnotic Susceptibility Scale. *Psychol. Monogr.*, 75 (8, Whole No. 512). — **33, 71n., 72, 73, 75, 79, 179, 213**

Hilgard, E. R., *see also* As, Hilgard, and Weitzenhoffer (1963); Bentler and Hilgard (1963); Berreman and Hilgard (1936); Boucher and Hilgard (1962); Hilgard and Hilgard (1962); Hilgard, Hilgard, and Newman (1961); Liebert, Rubin, and Hilgard (1965); Melei and Hilgard (1964); Slotnick, Liebert, and Hilgard (1964); Tart and Hilgard (1965); Weitzenhoffer and Hilgard (1959, 1962, 1963).

Hilgard, Josephine R., Hilgard, E. R., and Newman, Martha F. (1961) Sequelae to hypnotic induction with special reference to earlier chemical anesthesia. *J. nerv. ment. Dis.*, 133:461–78. — **27, 50, 53, 55, 60, 132n.**

Hilgard, Josephine R., and Hilgard, E. R. (1962) Developmental-interactive aspects of hypnosis: Some illustrative cases. *Genet. Psychol. Monogr.*, 66:143–78. — **271, 307**

Hoaken, P. C. S., *see* Heath, Hoaken, and Sainz (1960).

Hoffer, A., *see* Fogel and Hoffer (1962).

Hommel, L. S., *see* Hilgard and Hommel (1961).

Horst, P. (1956) A simple method of rotating a centroid factor matrix to a simple structure hypothesis. *J. exp. Ed.*, 24:251–58. — **234**

Hull, C. L. (1933) *Hypnosis and suggestibility: An experimental approach.* New York: Appleton-Century. — **4, 10, 23n., 28, 34, 76, 101, 166, 313, 322**

Husband, R. W., *see* Davis and Husband (1931).

Imm, C. (1965) Repression in hypnotic dreams of situations suggested during regression. Doctoral dissertation, Stanford Univ. — **161**

Jackson, D. N., and Messick, S. (1962) Response styles on the MMPI: Comparison of clinical and normal samples. *J. abnorm. soc. Psychol.*, 65:285–99. — **259**

James W. (1890) *Principles of psychology.* New York: Holt, 2 vols. — **4, 8, 31, 97**

Janet, P. (1920) *Major symptoms of hysteria.* New York: Macmillan. — **207**

Johnson, H. J., *see* London, Cooper, and Johnson (1962); Williamsen, Johnson, and Eriksen (1964).

Johnson,, W. R., and Kramer, G. F. (1961) Effects of stereotyped nonhypnotic, hypnotic, and posthypnotic suggestions upon strength, power, and endurance. *Amer. Ass. Hlth Phys. Educ. Recr.*, 32:522–29. — 114

Johnson, W. R., Massey, B. H., and Kramer, G. F. (1960) Effect of posthypnotic suggestions on all-out effort of short duration. *Res. Quart. Amer. Ass. Hlth Phys. Educ. Recr.*, 31:142–46. — 114

Joseph, E. D., Peck, S. M., and Kaufman, R. (1949) A psychological study of neurodermatitis with a case report. *J. Mount Sinai Hosp.*, New York, 15:360–66. — 53

Karacan, I., *see* Barber, Karacan, and Calverley (1964).

Karp, S. A., *see* Witkin, Dyk, Faterson, Goodenough, and Karp (1962).

Katz, J., *see* Newman, Katz, and Rubenstein (1960); Rubenstein, Katz, and Newman (1957).

Kaufman, R., *see* Joseph, Peck, and Kaufman (1949).

Kelsey, D., and Barron, J. N. (1958) Maintenance of posture by hypnotic suggestion in patient undergoing plastic surgery. *Brit. Med. J.*, 5073:756–57. — 114

Kent, G. H., and Rosanoff, A. J. (1910) A study of association in insanity. *Amer. J. Insan.*, 67:37–96. — 184

Kirkner, F. J., Dorcus, R. M., and Seacat, Gloria. (1953) Hypnotic motivation of vocalization in an organic motor aphasic case. *J. clin. exp. Hyp.*, 1:47–49. — 201

Knight, R. P., *see* Brenman, Gill, and Knight (1952).

Kramer, E., and Brennan, E. P. (1964) Hypnotic susceptibility of schizophrenic patients. *J. abnorm. soc. Psychol.*, 69:657–59. — 219, 220

Kramer, E., *see also* Vingoe and Kramer (1964).

Kramer, G. F., *see* Johnson and Kramer (1961); Johnson, Massey, and Kramer (1960).

Kris, E. (1952) *Psychoanalytic explorations in art.* New York: Int. Univ. Press.— 26, 224, 321

Kroger, W. S. (1963) *Clinical and experimental hypnosis.* Philadelphia: Lippincott. — 201

Krueger, R. G. (1931) The influence of repetition and disuse upon rate of hypnotization. *J. exp. Psychol.*, 14:260–69. — 23n.

Kubie, L. S., and Margolin, S. (1944) The process of hypnotism and the nature of the hypnotic state. *Amer. J. Psychiat.*, 100:611–22. — 24, 25

Kubie, L. S., *see also* Brickner and Kubie (1936); Erickson and Kubie (1941).

LaForge, R., and Suczek, R. (1955) The interpersonal dimension of personality: III. An interpersonal check list. *J. Pers.*, 24:91–112. — 253

Landes, J., *see* Hilgard, Weitzenhoffer, Landes, and Moore (1961); Weitzenhoffer, Gough, and Landes (1959).

Lang, P. J., and Lazovik, A. D. (1962) Personality and hypnotic susceptibility. *J. consult. Psychol.*, 26:317–22. — 252

Lauer, Lillian W. (1965) Factorial components of hypnotic susceptibility. Doctoral dissertation, Stanford Univ. — 234n.

Lauer, Lillian W., *see* Ås and Lauer (1962); Hilgard and Lauer (1962); Hilgard, Lauer, and Melei (1964); Hilgard, Lauer, and Morgan (1963); Moore and Lauer (1963).

Lazovik, A. D., *see* Lang and Lazovik (1962).

Leary, T. (1957) *Interpersonal diagnosis of personality.* New York: Ronald Press. — 253

Leavitt, H. C. (1947) A case of hypnotically produced secondary and tertiary personalities. *Psychoanal. Rev.*, 34:274–95. — 207

LeCron, L., and Bordeaux, J. (1947) *Hypnotism today.* New York: Grune and Stratton. — 75

Lee-Teng, Evelyn (1965) Trance-susceptibility, induction-susceptibility, and acquiescence as factors in hypnotic performance. *J. abnorm. Psychol.,* 70:383–89. — 226, 233-36, 259

Leuba, C. (1940) Images as conditioned sensations. *J. exp. Psychol.,* 26:345–57. — 146

Leuba, C. (1942) The experimental induction of a multiple personality. *Psychiatry,* 5:179–86. — 207

Leuba, C. (1960) Theories of hypnosis: A critique and a proposal. *Amer. J. clin. Hyp.,* 3:43–48. — 7, 224, 265

Levitt, E. E., and Brady, J. P. (1964) Muscular endurance under hypnosis and in the motivated waking state. *Int. J. clin. exp. Hyp.,* 12:21–27. — 114

Levitt, E. E., Lubin, B., and Brady, J. P. (1962) On the use of TAT Card 12M as an indicator of attitude toward hypnosis. *Int. J. clin. exp. Hyp.,* 10:145–50. — 262

Levitt, E. E., and Lubin, B. (1963) TAT card "12 MF" and hypnosis themes in females. *Int. J. clin. exp. Hyp.,* 11:241–44. — 262

Levitt, E. E., Persky, H., and Brady, J. P. (1964) *Hypnotic induction of anxiety.* Springfield, Ill.: Charles C. Thomas. — 207, 253, 257

Levitt, E. E., *see also* Brady and Levitt (1964).

Liébeault, A. A. (1889) *Le sommeil provoqué et les états analogues.* Paris: Doin. — 72, 73

Liebert, R. M., Rubin, Norma, and Hilgard, E. R. (1965) The effects of active and passive hypnosis on attention, acquisition, and retention during paired associate learning. *J. Pers.,* 33:605–12. — 114

Liebert, R. M., *see also* Slotnick, Liebert, and Hilgard (1964).

Lim, D. T., *see* Sarbin and Lim (1963).

Loewenfeld, L. (1901) *Der hypnotismus.* Wiesbaden: Bergmann. — 74, 75

London, Perry. (1961) Subject characteristics in hypnosis research: Part I. A survey of experience, interest, and opinion. *Int. J. clin. exp. Hyp.,* 9:151–61. — 240

London, P. (1962a) *The Children's Hypnotic Susceptibility Scale.* Palo Alto, Calif.: Consulting Psychologists Press. — 86, 88, 325

London, Perry. (1962b) Hypnosis in children: An experimental approach. *Int. J. clin. exp. Hyp.,* 10:79–91. — 89, 214, 215, 217

London, P. (1965a) Developmental experiments in hypnosis. *J. proj. Tech. pers. Assess.* (To appear) — 214

London, P. (1965b) Hypnosis in children. (Manuscript in preparation) — 88n.

London, P., Cooper, L. M., and Johnson, H. J. (1962) Subject characteristics in hypnosis research. *Int. J. clin. exp. Hyp.,* 10:13–21. — 240, 242

London, P., and Fuhrer, M. (1961) Hypnosis, motivation, and performance. *J. Pers.,* 29:321–33. — 114, 115, 116

London, P., *see also* Madsen and London (1964); Rosenhan and London (1963a, 1963b); Schulman and London (1963a, 1963b); Slotnick and London (1964).

Long, T. E., *see* Clarke and Long (1964).

Lubin, B., *see* Levitt and Lubin (1963); Levitt, Lubin, and Brady (1962).

McCay, A. R. (1963) Dental extraction under self-hypnosis. *Med. J. Australia,* June 1, 820–22. — 126

McNemar, Q. (1962) *Psychological statistics* (3rd ed.). New York: Wiley. — 180

Macalpine, I. (1950) The development of the transference. *Psychoanal. Quart.,* 19:501–39. — **294, 313**

MacKinnon, D. W., *see* Barry, MacKinnon, and Murray (1931).

Madow, L. W., *see* Sarbin and Madow (1942).

Madsen, C. H., and London, P. (1966) Role-playing and hypnotic susceptibility in children. *J. Pers. soc. Psychol.,* 3:13–19. — **320**

Marcuse, F. L. (Ed.). (1964) *Hypnosis throughout the world.* Springfield, Ill.: Charles C. Thomas. — **4**

Margolin, S., *see* Kubie and Margolin (1944).

Marquis, D. G., *see* Hilgard and Marquis (1940).

Maslow, A. H. (1959) Cognition of being in the peak experiences. *J. genet. Psychol.,* 94:43–66. — **225**

Massey, B. H., *see* Johnson, Massey, and Kramer (1960).

Mazer, Milton. (1951) An experimental study of the hypnotic dream. *Psychiatry,* 14:265–77. — **160**

Meares, A. (1957) A working hypothesis as to the nature of hypnosis. *A.M.A. Arch. Neurol. Psychiat.,* 77:549–55. — **314**

Meehl, P. E. (1954) *Clinical vs. statistical prediction.* Minneapolis, Minn.: Univ. of Minn. Press. — **275**

Meldman, M. J. (1960) Personality decompensation after hypnotic symptom suppression. *J. Amer. Med. Assn.,* 173:359–61. — **53**

Melei, Janet P., and Hilgard, E. R. (1964) Attitudes toward hypnosis, self-predictions, and hypnotic susceptibility. *Int. J. clin. exp. Hyp.,* 12:99–108. — **240, 242, 243, 246**

Melei, Janet P., *see* Hilgard, Lauer, and Melei (1964).

Menninger, K. (1948) Changing concepts of disease. *Ann. Intern. Med.,* 29:318–25. — **54**

Messerschmidt, R. (1927) A quantitative investigation of the alleged independent operation of conscious and subconscious processes. *J. abnorm. soc. Psychol.,* 22:325–40. — **207**

Messerschmidt, R. (1933a) Response of boys between the ages of 5 and 16 years to Hull's postural suggestion test. *J. genet. Psychol.,* 43:405–21. — **213**

Messerschmidt, R. (1933b) The suggestibility of boys and girls between the ages of six and sixteen years. *J. genet. Psychol.,* 43:422–37. — **213**

Messick, S., *see* Jackson and Messick (1962).

Miller, G. A., Galanter, E., and Pribram, K. H. (1960) *Plans and the structure of behavior.* New York: Holt. — **24n., 200**

Moore, Rosemarie K. (1964) Susceptibility to hypnosis and susceptibility to social influence. *J. abnorm. soc. Psychol.,* 68:282–94.— **264**

Moore, Rosemarie K., and Lauer, Lillian W. (1963) Hypnotic susceptibility in middle childhood. *Int. J. clin. exp. Hyp.,* 11:167–74. — **214, 215, 216, 217**

Moore, Rosemarie K., *see also* Hilgard, Weitzenhoffer, Landes, and Moore (1961).

Morgan, Arlene H., *see* Hilgard, Lauer, and Morgan (1963).

Moss, C. S. (1961) Experimental paradigms for the hypnotic investigation of dream symbolism. *Int. J. clin. exp. Hyp.,* 9:105–17. — **160**

Munger, M. P., *see* Ås, O'Hara, and Munger (1962).

Murray, H. A., Jr., *see* Barry, MacKinnon, and Murray (1931).

Myers, Isabel B. (1962) *The Myers-Briggs Type Indicator.* Princeton, N.J.: Educational Testing Service. — **252**

Nachmansohn, M. (1925) Ueber experimentell erzeugte Träume nebst kritischen Bemerkungen über die psychoanalytische Methodik. *Z. Neurol. Psychiat.,* 98:556–86. — **160**

Reyher, J. (1962) A paradigm for determining the clinical relevance of hypnotically induced psychopathology. *Psychol. Bull.*, 59:344–52. — **162**

Reyher, J., *see also* Wiseman and Reyher (1962).

Richer, P. (1885) *Etudes cliniques sur la grande hystérie ou hystéro-épilepsie.* Paris: Delahaye & Lecrosnier. — **72**

Richet, C. (1884) *L'homme et l'intelligence.* Paris: Alcan. — **73**

Riddle, E. E., *see* Stalnaker and Riddle (1932).

Roberts, Mary R. (1964) Attention and related abilities as affecting hypnotic susceptibility. Doctoral dissertation, Stanford University. — **7, 265**

Roberts, Mary R., *see also* Bentler and Roberts (1963).

Roffenstein, G. (1924) Experimentelle Symbolträume: ein Beitrag zur Diskussion über Psychoanalyse. *Z. Neurol. Psychiat.*, 87:362–72. — **160**

Rorer, L. G., and Goldberg, L. R. (1964) On the negligibility of acquiescence response variance. *Amer. Psychologist*, 19:493-94. (Abstract) — **259**

Rosanoff, A. J., *see* Kent and Rosanoff (1910).

Rosen, H. (1953) *Hypnotherapy in clinical psychiatry.* New York: Julian. — **53**

Rosen, H. (1959) Hypnosis in medical practice: Uses and abuses. *Chicago Med. Soc. Bull.*, 62:428–36. — **53**

Rosen, H. (1960) Hypnosis: Applications and misapplications. *J. Amer. Med. Assn.*, 172:683–87. — **53**

Rosen, H., and Bartemeier, L. H. (1961) Hypnosis in medical practice. *J. Amer. Med. Assn.*, 175:976–79. — **53**

Rosenberg, M. J. (1959) A disconfirmation of the descriptions of hypnosis as a dissociated state. *Int. J. clin. exp. Hyp.*, 7:187–204. — **208, 318**

Rosenhan, D., and London, P. (1963a) Hypnosis: Expectation, susceptibility, and performance. *J. abnorm. soc. Psychol.*, 66:77–81. — **118**

Rosenhan, D., and London, P. (1963b) Hypnosis in the unhypnotizable: A study in rote learning. *J. exp. Psychol.*, 65:30–34. — **115**

Rosenhan, D., and Tomkins, S. S. (1964) On preference for hypnosis and hypnotizability. *Int. J. clin. exp. Hyp.*, 12:109–14. — **242, 243**

Rosenzweig, S., and Sarason, S. (1942) An experimental study of the triadic hypothesis: Reaction to frustration, ego-defense, and hypnotizability: I. Correlational approach. *J. Pers.*, 11:1–19. — **262**

Rubenstein, R., Katz, J., and Newman, R. (1957) On the sources and determinants of hypnotic dreams. *Canad. Psychiat. Ass. J.*, 2:154–61. — **160**

Rubenstein, R., *see also* Newman, Katz, and Rubenstein (1960).

Rubin, Norma, *see* Liebert, Rubin, and Hilgard (1965).

Sainz, A. A., *see* Heath, Hoaken, and Sainz (1960).

Saito, T., *see* Umemoto, Saito, and Osawa (1964).

Sarason, S., *see* Rosenzweig and Sarason (1942).

Sarbin, T. R. (1950) Contributions to role-taking theory: I. Hypnotic behavior. *Psychol. Rev.*, 57:255–70. — **10, 19, 224, 256, 304**

Sarbin, T. R. (1956) Physiological effects of hypnotic stimulation. In Dorcus, R. M. (Ed.), *Hypnosis and its therapeutic applications.* New York: McGraw-Hill. — **10, 19**

Sarbin, T. R., and Andersen, M. L. (1967) Role-theoretical analysis of hypnotic behavior. In Gordon, J. (Ed.), *Handbook of clinical and experimental hypnosis.* New York: Macmillan, 319, 43. — **10, 19, 304**

Sarbin, T. R., and Lim, D. T. (1963) Some evidence in support of the role-taking hypothesis in hypnosis. *Int. J. clin. exp. Hyp.*, 11:98–103. — **305**

Sarbin, T. R., and Madow, L. W. (1942) Predicting the depth of hypnosis by means of the Rorschach test. *Amer. J. Orthopsychiat.*, 12:268–71. — **262**

Sarbin, T. R., *see also* Friedlander and Sarbin (1938).

Saul, L. J., and Bernstein, C., Jr. (1941) The emotional settings of some attacks of urticaria. *Psychosom. Med.*, 3:349–69. — 52

Schafer, R. (1947) A study of personality characteristics related to hypnotizability. Master's thesis, Univ. of Kansas. — 262

Schafer, R. (1958) Regression in the service of the ego: The relevance of a psychoanalytic concept for personality assessment. In Lindzey, G. (Ed.), *Assessment of human motives.* New York: Rinehart. Pp. 119–48. — 306, 321

Scharf, B., and Zamansky, H. S. (1963) Reduction of word-recognition threshold under hypnosis. *Percept. mot. Skills,* 17:499–510. — 115, 148

Scharf, B., *see also* Zamansky, Scharf, and Brightbill (1964).

Scheerer, M., *see* Reiff and Scheerer (1960).

Schiff, S. K., Bunney, W. E., and Freedman, D. X. (1961) A study of ocular movements in hypnotically induced dreams. *J. nerv. ment. Dis.*, 133:59–68. — 150

Schilder, P. (1956) *The nature of hypnosis.* New York: Int. Univ. Press. — 306

Schmidkunz, H. (1894) Zur statistik des hypnotismus. *Wien. med. Wschr.*, 23:1022–24. — 74, 75

Schulman, R. E., and London, P. (1963a) Hypnosis and verbal learning. *J. abnorm. soc. Psychol.*, 67:363–70. — 7, 114

Schulman, R. E., and London, P. (1963b) Hypnotic susceptibility and MMPI profiles. *J. consult. Psychol.*, 27:157–60. — 256, 257

Schultz, J. H. (1922) *Gesundheitsschädigungen nach Hypnose. Ergebnisse einer Sammelforschung.* (2nd unaltered edition, 1954). Berlin: Carl Marhold Verlagsbuchhandlung. — 51

Seacat, Gloria, *see* Kirkner, Dorcus, and Seacat (1953).

Secter, I. I. (1961) Personality factors of the MMPI and hypnotizability. *Amer. J. clin. Hyp.*, 3:185–88. — 256

Seitz, P. F. D. (1951) Symbolism and organ choice in conversion reactions: An experimental approach. *Psychosom. Med.*, 13:254–59. — 53

Seitz, P. F. D. (1953) Experiments in the substitution of symptoms by hypnosis: II. *Psychosom. Med.*, 5:405–24. — 53

Shagass, C., *see* Amadeo and Shagass (1963).

Shor, R. E. (1959) Hypnosis and the concept of the generalized reality-orientation. *Amer. J. Psychother.*, 13:582–602. — 9, 224, 303, 306, 307, 308, 317

Shor, R. E. (1960) The frequency of naturally occurring "hypnotic-like" experiences in the normal college population. *Int. J. clin. exp. Hyp.*, 8:151–63. — 223, 225

Shor, R. E. (1962a) On the physiological effects of painful stimulation during hypnotic analgesia: Basic issues for further research. In Estabrooks, G. H. (Ed.), *Hypnosis: Current problems.* New York: Harper & Row. Pp. 54–75. — 127

Shor, R. E. (1962b) Physiological effects of painful stimulation during hypnotic analgesia under conditions designed to minimize anxiety. *Int. J. clin. exp. Hyp.*, 10:183–202. — 127

Shor, R. E. (1962c) Three dimensions of hypnotic depth. *Int. J. clin. exp. Hyp.*, 10:23–38. — 9, 303, 306, 307

Shor, R. E., and Orne, Emily C. (1962) *Harvard Group Scale of Hypnotic Susceptibility.* Palo Alto, Calif.: Consulting Psychologists Press. — 83, 325

Shor, R. E., and Orne, Emily C. (1963) Norms on the Harvard Group Scale of Hypnotic Susceptibility, Form A. *Int. J. clin. exp. Hyp.*, 11:39–48. — 83, 85, 215

Shor, R. E., Orne, M. T., and O'Connell, D. N. (1962) Validation and cross-validation of a scale of self-reported personal experiences which predicts hypnotizability. *J. Psychol.*, 53:55–75. — 70, 228, 230, 231, 237, 239, 313

Shor, R. E., *see also* Damaser, Shor, and Orne (1963).

Sirna, A. A. (1945) An electroencephalographic study of the hypnotic dream. *J. Psychol.*, 20:109–13. — **150**

Sjoberg, B. M., Jr. (1965) The effect of drugs upon suggestibility and susceptibility to hypnosis. Doctoral dissertation, Stanford University. — **145**

Sjoberg, B. M., *see* Weitzenhoffer and Sjoberg (1961).

Slotnick, R. S., Liebert, R. M., and Hilgard, E. R. (1965) The enhancement of muscular performance in hypnosis through exhortation and involving instructions. *J. Pers.*, 33:37–45. — **116, 118**

Slotnick, R. S., and London, P. (1965) Influence of instructions on hypnotic and non-hypnotic performance. *J. abnorm. Psychol.*, 70:38–46. — **114, 115, 116**

Stalnaker, J. M., and Riddle, E. E. (1932) The effect of hypnosis on long delayed recall. *J. gen. Psychol.*, 6:429–40. — **166**

Stein, K. B., and Craik, K. H. (1962) A motoric-ideational typology. Presented at a meeting of the California State Psychological Association, Los Angeles, December 14–15. — **254**

Stein, K. B., and Craik, K. H. (1965) Relationship between motoric and ideational activity preference and time perspective in neurotics and schizophrenics. *J. consult. Psychol.*, 29:460–67. — **254**

Steisel, I. M. (1952) The Rorschach test and suggestibility. *J. abnorm. soc. Psychol.*, 47:607–14. — **262**

Sternlicht, M., and Wanderer, Z. W. (1963) Hypnotic susceptibility and mental deficiency. *Int. J. clin. exp. Hyp.*, 11:104–11. — **218**

Stoyva, J. M. (1965) Posthypnotically suggested dreams and the sleep cycle. *Arch. gen. Psychiat.*, 12:287–91. — **160**

Stukát, K.-G. (1958) *Suggestibility: A factorial and experimental analysis.* Stockholm: Almqvist and Wiksell. — **213, 214, 263**

Suci, G. J., *see* Osgood, Suci, and Tannenbaum (1957).

Suczek, R., *see* LaForge and Suczek (1955).

Süllwold, F. (1954) Ein Beitrag zur Analyse der Aufmerksamkeit. *Z. exp. angewand. Psychol.*, 2:495–513. — **7, 265**

Sutcliffe, J. P. (1960) "Credulous" and "skeptical" views of hypnotic phenomena: A review of certain evidence and methodology. *Int. J. clin. exp. Hyp.*, 8:73–101. — **14, 16**

Sutcliffe, J. P. (1961) "Credulous" and "skeptical" views of hypnotic phenomena: Experiments on esthesia, hallucination, and delusion. *J. abnorm. soc. Psychol.*, 62:189–200.— **14, 15, 16**

Sutcliffe, J. P., *see also* Austin, Perry, Sutcliffe, and Yeomans (1963).

Sweetland, A., and Quay, H. (1952) An experimental investigation of the hypnotic dream. *J. abnorm. soc. Psychol.*, 47:678–82. — **160**

Tannenbaum, P. H., *see* Osgood, Suci, and Tannenbaum (1957).

Tart, C. T. (1964) A comparison of suggested dreams occurring in hypnosis and sleep. *Int. J. clin. exp. Hyp.*, 12:263–289. — **150, 160**

Tart, C. T. (1965) The hypnotic dream: Methodological problems and a review of the literature. *Psychol. Bull.*, 63:87–99. — **150n.**

Tart, C. T. (1966) Some effects of posthypnotic suggestions on the process of dreaming. *Int. J. clin. exp. Hyp.* 14:30–46. — **160**

Tart, C. T., *see also* Hilgard and Tart (1965); Troffer and Tart (1964).

Teitel, B. (1961) Post-hypnotic psychosis and the law. In *Scientific Papers of the One Hundred and Seventeenth Annual Meeting of the American Psychiatric Association in Summary Form,* pp. 108–10. Washington, D. C.: American Psychiatric Association. — **53**

Thorn, Wendy A. F. (1961) The correlates of dissociation. Paper read at British Psychological Society (Australian Overseas Branch), Sydney, Australia, August. — **252**

Thorn, Wendy A. F., *see also* Evans and Thorn (1963, 1964)

Tomkins, S. S., *see* Rosenhan and Tomkins (1964).

Troffer, Suzanne H. (1965) The effect of role-support on age-appropriate be‹ havior under hypnosis and simulated hypnotic regression. Doctoral dis‹ sertation, Stanford University. — **173**

Troffer, Suzanne H., and Tart, C. T. (1964) Experimenter bias in hynotist performance. *Science*, 145:1330–31. — **39**

Turner, J. A. (1960) Hypnosis in medical practice and research. *Bull. Men‹ ninger Clin.*, 24:18–25. — **64**

Vingoe, F. J., and Kramer, E. (1966) Hypnotic susceptibility of hospitalized psychotic patients: A pilot study. *Int. J. clin. exp. Hyp.*, 14:47–54. — **219n**.

Walters, R. H., *see* Bandura and Walters (1963).

Wanderer, Z. W., *see* Sternlicht and Wanderer (1963).

Watkins, J. G. (1949) *Hypnotherapy of war neurosis: A clinical psychologist's handbook.* New York: Ronald Press. — **75**

Webb, R. A., and Nesmith, C. C. (1964) A normative study of suggestibility in a mental patient population. *Int. J. clin. exp. Hyp.*, 12:181–83. — **220**

Weitzenhoffer, A. M. (1953) *Hypnotism: An objective study in suggestibility.* New York: Wiley. — **10, 148, 172, 217, 322**

Weitzenhoffer, A. M. (1956) Hypnotic susceptibility as related to masculinity-femininity. Doctoral dissertation, University of Michigan. — **79**

Weitzenhoffer, A. M. (1957) *General techniques of hypnotism.* New York: Grune and Stratton. — **22, 56**

Weitzenhoffer, A. M., Gough, P. B., and Landes, J. (1959) A study of the Braid effect: Hypnosis by visual fixation. *J. Psychol.*, 47:67–80. — **31**

Weitzenhoffer, A. M., and Hilgard, E. R. (1959) *Stanford Hypnotic Susceptibility Scale, Forms A and B.* Palo Alto, Calif.: Consulting Psychologists Press. — **81, 325**

Weitzenhoffer, A. M., and Hilgard, E. R. (1962) *Stanford Hypnotic Susceptibility Scale, Form C.* Palo Alto, Calif.: Consulting Psychologists Press. — **37, 82, 168, 325**

Weitzenhoffer, A. M., and Hilgard, E. R. (1963) *Stanford Profile Scales of Hypnotic Susceptibility, Forms I and II.* Palo Alto, Calif.: Consulting Psychologists Press. — **82, 154, 194, 197**

Weitzenhoffer, A. M., and Hilgard, E. R. (1967) *Revised Stanford Profile Scales of Hypnotic Susceptibility, Forms I and II.* Palo Alto, Calif.: Consulting Psychologists Press. — **325**

Weitzenhoffer, A. M., and Sjoberg, B. M. (1961) Suggestibility with and without "induction of hypnosis." *J. nerv. ment. Dis.*, 132:204–20. — **28, 29, 34, 82n., 88n., 145, 325**

Weitzenhoffer, A. M., and Weitzenhoffer, Geneva B. (1958a) Sex, transference, and susceptibility to hypnosis. *Amer. J. clin. Hyp.*, 1:15–24. — **217**

Weitzenhoffer, A. M., and Weitzenhoffer, Geneva B. (1958b) Personality and hypnotic susceptibility. *Amer. J. clin. Hyp.*, 1:79–82. — **253**

Weitzenhoffer, A. M., *see also* Ås, Hilgard, and Weitzenhoffer (1963); Hilgard, Weitzenhoffer, and Gough (1958); Hilgard, Weitzenhoffer, Landes, and Moore (1961).

Weitzenhoffer, Geneva B., *see* A. M. Weitzenhoffer and Geneva B. Weitzenhoffer (1958a, 1958b).

Wells, W. R. (1940) Ability to resist artificially induced dissociation. *J. abnorm. soc. Psychol.,* 35:261–72. — **109**

Welsh, G. S., *see* Dahlstrom and Welsh (1960).

West, L. J., *see* Deckert and West (1963).

White, M. M. (1930) The physical and mental traits of individuals susceptible to hypnosis. *J. abnorm. soc. Psychol.,* 25:293–98. — **76**

White, R. W. (1937) Two types of hypnotic trance and their personality correlates. *J. Psychol.,* 3:265–77. — **108, 239, 262**

White, R. W. (1941) A preface to the theory of hypnotism. *J. abnorm. soc. Psychol.,* 36:477–505. — **225, 303, 306**

Wiggins, J. S. (1962) Strategic, method, and stylistic variance in the MMPI. *Psychol. Bull.,* 59:224–42. — **259**

Wilcox, W. W., *see* Faw and Wilcox (1958).

Willey, R. R. (1951) An experimental investigation of the attributes of hypnotizability. Doctoral dissertation, Univ. of Chicago. — **108**

Williams, G. W. (1953) Difficulty in dehypnotizing. *J. clin. exp. Hyp.,* 1:3–12. — **56**

Williamsen, J. A., Johnson, H. J., and Eriksen, C. W. (1965) Some characteristics of posthypnotic amnesia. *J. abnorm. Psychol.,* 70:123–31. — **185**

Wilson, C. P., Cormen, H. H., and Cole, A. A. (1949) A preliminary study of the hypnotizability of psychotic patients. *Psychiat. Quart.,* 23:657–66. — **219**

Wiseman, R. J., and Reyher, J. (1962) A procedure utilizing dreams for deepening the hypnotic trance. *Amer. J. clin. Hyp.,* 5:105–10. — **70**

Witkin, H. A., Dyk, R. B., Faterson, H. F., Goodenough, D. R., and Karp, S. A. (1962) *Psychological differentiation.* New York: Wiley. — **265**

Yates, A. J. (1961) Hypnotic age regression. *Psychol. Bull.,* 58:429–40. — **172**

Yeomans, N., *see* Austin, Perry, Sutcliffe, and Yeomans (1963).

Young, P. C. (1927) Is *rapport* an essential characteristic of hypnosis? *J. abnorm. soc. Psychol.,* 22:130–39. — **109**

Zamansky, H. S., Scharf, B., and Brightbill, R. (1964) The effect of expectancy for hypnosis on prehypnotic performance. *J. Pers.,* 32:236–48. — **115, 148**

Zamansky, H. S., *see also* Brightbill and Zamansky (1963); Scharf and Zamansky (1963).

Subject Index

DATE DUE

		DEC	

Demco, Inc. 38-293